D1597522

Financial Reporting of Environmental Liabilities and Risks after Sarbanes-Oxley

Advance Praise for *Financial Reporting of Environmental Liabilities and Risks after Sarbanes-Oxley*

"Greg Rogers has done a masterful job of compiling and explaining everything of relevance to environmental disclosure obligations after Sarbanes. Lawyers advising public companies on disclosure obligations will find much of interest, and some surprising conclusions, in this work. It is certain to become a staple of every securities law library."

Jim Showen
Partner
Hogan & Hartson L.L.P.

"A ground-breaking book that has implications well beyond determining the appropriate environmental accounting treatments. The inconsistencies in financial reporting of environmental liabilities frequently create unnecessary uncertainties that can delay or kill financial transactions. The guidance in this book offers more than the "defensible position" many directors and officers are currently seeking. It offers the opportunity to eliminate environmental "surprises" from the financial transaction process thereby improving the flow of capital."

Steve Courcier
CFO
GaiaTech, Inc.

"Following the great stock market scandals of the early 2000s, Congress and the American people are demanding that accountants and auditors assume more responsibility for preventing fraud and making more honest disclosures about liabilities and potential liabilities of publicly traded companies. Environmental liabilities are a prime concern because of the potential for huge unrecorded obligations and because this is a largely misunderstood area by accountants. Greg Rogers has produced a unique and comprehensive discussion in his book, marrying a plain English discussion of the legal issues with current accounting and reporting practice and obligations. This book is must reading for any professional engaged in environmental liability determination and disclosure."

John C. Malone, JD, CPA
Managing Partner
Malone & Bailey, PC
www.malone-bailey.com
Houston, Texas

"The book provides a useful guide for the environmental management professional, who seeks a better understanding of the interrelationships among emerging accounting standards, environmental law, and environmental management practice. From the perspective of the Environmental Manager or consultant, the book provides an overview of these related fields of expertise as well as a roadmap to specific, current financial reporting and legal requirements. I expect that the reader will take this book off the shelf repeatedly, to guide day-to-day environmental management practice."

Robert C. Weber, P.E.
President & Chief Executive Officer
ENSR International, Inc.

"New standards for environmental transparency are rapidly reshaping how corporations and shareholders perceive environmental risks and liabilities. Familiarity with the background materials and insights in this book is a must for insurance and risk management professionals serving companies with significant environmental loss exposures."

Donna H. Sandidge
Managing Director
Marsh, Inc.
Environmental Practice Leader

Financial Reporting of Environmental Liabilities and Risks after Sarbanes-Oxley

C. Gregory Rogers

John Wiley & Sons, Inc.

This book is printed on acid-free paper. ♾

Published by John Wiley & Sons, Inc., Hoboken, New Jersey.

Published simultaneously in Canada.

For general information on our other products and services, or technical support, please contact our Customer Care Department within the United States at 800-762-2974, outside the United States at 317-572-3993 or fax 317-572-4002.

Wiley also publishes its books in a variety of electronic formats. Some content that appears in print may not be available in electronic books.

For more information about Wiley products, visit our Web site at *http://www.wiley.com.*

Library of Congress Cataloging-in-Publication Data:

Rogers, Gregory C., 1962-

Financial reporting of environmental liabilities and risks after Sarbanes-Oxley / Gregory C. Rogers.

p. cm.

Includes bibliographical references and index.

ISBN-13: 978-0-471-71743-0 (cloth : alk. paper)

ISBN-10: 0-471-71743-6 (cloth : alk. paper)

1. Environmental auditing--United States. 2. Liability for environmental damages--United States--Accounting. I. Title.

TD194.7.R64 2006

657'.3--dc22

2005007459

Printed in the United States of America

10 9 8 7 6 5 4 3 2 1

Contents

About the Author

C. Gregory Rogers, J.D., CPA, is a practicing environmental lawyer and management consultant in Dallas, Texas. He is "of counsel" with Guida, Slavich & Flores, a law firm focusing on environmental legal matters, where he advises public and non-public companies on the purchase, sale, financing, and redevelopment of contaminated real estate. He is also President of C.G. Rogers & Co, LLC, a management consulting firm specializing in environmental financial reporting and related business strategies.

Mr. Rogers is a non-practicing CPA and former financial auditor with Arthur Andersen & Co. He began his legal career with two national law firms in Washington, D.C. and Dallas as a corporate securities lawyer, where he became versed in the U.S. federal securities laws and SEC regulations. After gaining experience in environmental law, he left legal practice for several years to work with General Motors Corp. and other clients on the reengineering of various environmental and financial business processes.

Following the enactment of the Sarbanes-Oxley Act of 2002, Mr. Rogers drew upon his background in accounting, law, and consulting to analyze the environmental-related accounting, legal, and management implications of that far-reaching legislation. He has since written numerous articles on various aspects of environmental financial reporting that have appeared in publications sponsored by the National Association of Corporate Directors, the American Bar Association, Financial Executives International, the Risk and Insurance Management Society, and the National Brownfields Association. Mr. Rogers is an active member of the American Bar Association's Special Committee on Environmental Disclosures and was one of 30 national experts who participated in the U.S. Government Accountability Office (GAO) investigation and report to Congress on Environmental Disclosures (July 2004).

Mr. Rogers earned his law degree from the Southern Methodist University School of Law where he was a Hatton W. Sumners Scholar and law review editor. He received his B.B.A. from the University of Oklahoma.

Preface

This book serves three primary objectives. First, and most important, it describes the complex (and sometimes obscure) interrelationships among U.S. securities laws, financial reporting standards, and environmental law. The term *environmental law* is here used to embody the broad interaction of environmental public policy, legislation, common law, science, and engineering. These important interrelationships often go unrecognized by professionals working within their respective specialized fields. As a result, the accuracy, completeness, and overall reliability of reported financial information can suffer, and reporting entities and their directors, officers, employees, and professional advisors can be put at risk for failing to meet internal and external financial reporting objectives. Readers seeking to gain a more in-depth understanding of environmental financial reporting are advised to read the book from start to finish at least once.

Second, this book provides a primer for designing and implementing an environmental financial reporting system sufficient to satisfy the requirements of sections 302 and 404 of Sarbanes-Oxley. Although a comprehensive guide to environmental financial reporting systems is beyond the scope of this book, the fundamental elements of an effective system—objectives, standards, policies, and procedures—are addressed at relevant points throughout each of the book's four parts. With a firm grasp on these core elements, reporting entities should have little difficulty in completing the design and implementation of environmental financial reporting systems capable of providing reasonable assurance that reported environmental financial information is indeed reliable.

Finally, this book provides a single reference source for the numerous legal and accounting standards governing environmental financial information presented in U.S. corporate financial statements and reports filed with the Securities and Exchange Commission (SEC). Anyone who has attempted to identify and assemble the various FASs, FINs, EITFs, SOPs, APBs, CFRs, and SABs applicable or relevant to environmental financial reporting will appreciate that a single source for this information is long overdue. This book brings the relevant content of many hard-to-find source documents within easy reach in a single volume. In particular, Part Three ("Financial Reporting Standards") and Part Four ("Audit Standards and Practices") of this book, which intentionally contain some repetitive information, are structured to serve as a convenient desk reference for practitioners.

SCOPE

This book serves as a guide to financial reporting requirements under generally accepted accounting principles (GAAP) in the United States and the U.S. federal securities laws. It does not address voluntary environmental reporting of nonfinancial information outside of financial statements and SEC filings. Accordingly, this book does not examine the various voluntary environmental reporting standards and initiatives such as the Global Reporting Initiative. This book does cover two standards issued by ASTM International that address measurement and disclosure of environmental costs and liabilities. Although these standards do not officially represent GAAP and are not mandated under U.S. securities laws, I have included them because they were designed to supplement and be consistent with existing authoritative standards and they are being advocated in the courts and before the SEC as evidence of best practice.

Due to the relative amount of available authoritative guidance, this book devotes significantly more attention to accounting for historical transactions, conditions, and events than to disclosure of forward-looking assessments of trends, uncertainties, and risks. The financial reporting framework applicable to disclosure of environmental risks, such as global warming, is covered in Chapter 24. However, readers will not find a comprehensive policy discussion regarding the arguments for and against increased compulsory or voluntary reporting of forward-looking information on environmental risks.

RELEVANCE

In the wake of the Sarbanes-Oxley Act of 2002 (Sarbanes-Oxley or the Act), the recent issuance of important new financial accounting standards, and growing interest among institutional investors and politicians, environmental financial reporting is becoming a matter of increasing importance for both public and nonpublic companies operating in the United States as well as foreign companies whose securities are traded on U.S. stock exchanges. Environmental liabilities and risks can have a significant adverse impact on the current and anticipated future financial condition of companies in a wide range of industries, including (but not limited to) oil and gas, chemicals, mining, energy, pharmaceuticals, forestry and wood products, manufacturing, transportation, and real estate.

New financial reporting standards now require companies to report environmental financial information that previously has not been subject to disclosure under GAAP or SEC regulations. These new reporting standards will have a far-reaching impact on long-standing corporate environmental practices. Sarbanes-Oxley has greatly increased the level of scrutiny to be applied to environmental financial information and the financial reporting systems used to generate that information. The Act has also raised the stakes for boards, CEOs, CFOs, attorneys, financial auditors, and environmental managers and consultants. Environmental financial reporting practices once accepted without scrutiny may now be grounds for shareholder litigation, civil penalties, or even imprisonment.

The level of interest in environmental financial reporting among politicians, institutional investors, securities analysts, lenders, insurance carriers, and environmental advocacy groups is significant and continues to grow at a steady pace. Most recently, in 2004 the U.S. Government Accountability Office (GAO) completed an exhaustive study into congressional concerns that corporate environmental liabilities and risks are significantly understated in filings with the SEC. The GAO's findings highlighted the ambiguity and lack of assurance that characterize environmental financial reporting in the United States today.

New standards, increased regulatory scrutiny, and heightened interest on the part of public- and private-sector policy makers are just three reasons why environmental financial reporting warrants greater attention and increased rigor. The accuracy, comprehensiveness, and timeliness of reported environmental financial information is more important now than ever before.

APPLICABILITY

This book focuses on environmental financial reporting requirements applicable to public and nonpublic business entities. It does not address reporting requirements applicable to governmental and nonprofit entities, although such entities may be subject to similar or identical environmental financial reporting requirements.

Not every business entity need be concerned about environmental financial reporting. Many companies and some entire industry sectors have little or no exposure to environmental losses from their ongoing operations. Environmental financial reporting is an important consideration, however, for companies that face significant environmental loss exposures, especially public companies subject to increased scrutiny under Sarbanes-Oxley.

Because environmental losses in the tens or even hundreds of millions of dollars can result from a single pollution condition, few companies are self-evidently immune from environmental financial reporting considerations. Moreover, a company that might appear to be environmentally benign may upon closer scrutiny be found to face significant environmental loss exposures associated with a legacy of acquisitions and divestitures. When determining whether a business entity potentially faces significant undisclosed environmental liabilities, a reasonable question to ask is: Would a prudent person agree to purchase the entity without first conducting some amount of environmental due diligence?

AUDIENCE

This book is intended primarily for accountants, managers, and lawyers responsible for (1) preparing, reviewing, certifying, or auditing environmental financial information in audited financial statements and SEC reports, and (2) designing, implementing, certifying, or auditing environmental financial reporting systems. For these individuals, this book will serve as a conceptual bridge across the many distinct but interrelated disciplines that bear on environmental financial reporting.

Environmental financial reporting is a multidisciplinary exercise. It requires the effective collaboration of accounting, legal, financial, scientific, engineering, and management professionals. Achieving effective collaboration among experts in so many fields is a central challenge facing reporting entities. The gaps in understanding between these disciplines are wide. Few accountants, for example, are experienced in environmental law and engineering, even though most environmental financial reporting decisions are based on underlying environmental legal and engineering determinations. Similarly, lawyers specializing in environmental law are generally unfamiliar with financial accounting standards and financial reporting systems.

It is tempting for specialists in one field to shift the burden to specialists in another field for matter that they do not well understand or wish to learn. Thus, accountants and attorneys sometimes rely blindly on the other, with neither taking full responsibility for the ultimate reliability of the financial reports or the financial reporting system. Such behavior carries significant risk in the post-Sarbanes-Oxley era.

Other audiences that may be interested in certain aspects of this book include:

- *Certifying officers under sections 302 and 906 of Sarbanes-Oxley.* Certifying officers of public companies faced with potentially material environmental loss exposures may be interested in Part One (especially Chapter 5) and Part Two of the book.
- *Audit committees (especially audit committee financial experts).* In addition to the sections noted above, these individuals may be interested in reviewing Part Three of the book to update their financial literacy with regard to environmental financial reporting. Such persons may also wish to read Part Four of the book to gain a more in-depth understanding of the role of the independent auditor in auditing environmental financial information and environmental financial reporting systems.
- *Directors serving on environmental committees of the board of directors.* Because of their functional responsibility for pollution risk oversight, these individuals may be interested in reviewing Parts One and Two of the book.
- *Corporate compliance and ethics officers.* Because of the inherent legal and social aspects of corporate environmental performance, corporate compliance and ethics officers may be interested in Chapter 5 (objectives of environmental financial reporting) and Chapter 8 (internal control).
- *Corporate real estate managers.* Because they may unwittingly be harboring undisclosed environmental liabilities, corporate real estate managers should consider reviewing Chapter 22 (asset retirement obligations) and Chapter 23 (asset impairments).
- *Corporate M&A specialists.* The requirements of sections 302 and 404 of Sarbanes-Oxley (see Chapters 7 and 8) are driving greater emphasis on internal control over financial reporting, including environmental financial reporting, during preclosing due diligence for business mergers, acquisitions, and financing transactions.
- *Environmental consultants.* Current developments in environmental financial reporting present new business opportunities (see e.g., Chapter 22) and new legal risks (see Chapter 9) for environmental consultants. Envi-

ronmental consultants may be particularly interested in learning more about the environmental financial reporting process (Chapter 1).

- *Insurance professionals.* Most undisclosed environmental liabilities are also uninsured environmental liabilities. As new financial reporting requirements drive companies to identify, assess, measure, and report environmental liabilities and risks, the use of environmental insurance can be expected to increase also. Evidence of effective internal control over environmental financial reporting on the part of an insured may also be a consideration for insurers in offering pollution coverage in director and officer liability policies.
- *Lenders.* Financial institutions routinely require borrowers to perform environmental assessments of collateralized real estate prior to closing a loan. Lenders may wish to consider if and to what extent evidence of effective internal control over financial reporting on the part of a borrower (Chapter 8) should influence the lender's environmental risk management practices.
- *Institutional investors and fiduciaries.* Long-term institutional investors need reasonable assurance that environmental financial information reported by public companies is accurate, complete, and timely. Accordingly, these investors should be concerned when public companies report material weaknesses in internal control (Chapters 8 and 27) over environmental financial reporting. Institutional investors calling for increased environmental transparency by public companies also may wish to "walk the talk" with respect to their direct investments in nonpublic entities by taking reasonable steps to ensure that such entities meet the same financial reporting standards demanded of public companies.
- *Securities analysts.* Securities analysts looking for benchmarks of environmental-related investment risk may be interested in learning more about internal control over financial reporting of environmental financial information (see Chapters 1, 8, and 27).

ORGANIZATION OF BOOK

This book is organized into four parts. Part One provides background information that serves as a foundation for the remaining sections of the book. Part Two gives an overview of Sarbanes-Oxley and describes how the Act has forever changed the landscape of environmental financial reporting. Part Three describes and analyzes the various financial reporting standards applicable to environmental financial information under GAAP and SEC regulations. Finally, Part Four examines the application of financial auditing standards to environmental financial reporting.

Acknowledgments

With the exception of any inaccuracies or misstatements, for which I am solely responsible, I can take credit for very little of the information and ideas contained in this book. Instead, the credit belongs to the countless men and women who have gone before me and to those who joined with me in my search for understanding. My mental wanderings included countless insightful conversations with Steve Courcier, Howard Gilberg, Pete Gilbertson, Joe Guida, Jeffrey Hubbard, Robert Lipscomb, Jason Minalga, Norm Radford, Jim Redwine, Donna Sandidge, John Slavich, and David Whitten, to name just a few.

The scope of this book required me to research several areas in which I lacked prior experience. As such, I am deeply grateful to Jim Showen, Gayle Koch, John Slavich, and Kenneth Tramm for assessing the technical accuracy of selected portions of the manuscript. I am particularly indebted to Jeffrey Smith, John Malone, Bob Weber, Michelle Chan-Fishel, William Thomas, Robert Lipscomb, and Steve Probst for undertaking a thorough review of the entire manuscript and providing invaluable comments and suggestions. The final product is far better for their efforts. Finally, Bill Kleist created the graphics used throughout the book.

Financial Reporting of Environmental Liabilities and Risks after Sarbanes-Oxley

PART ONE

Introduction to Environmental Financial Reporting

CHAPTER ONE

Financial Reports and the Financial Reporting Process

1.1 INTRODUCTION

Environmental financial reporting deals with accounting for and reporting on environmental transactions, conditions, and events that affect, or are reasonably likely to affect, the financial position of an enterprise. Although there are circumstances in which an entity may hold an environmental asset, for the most part, environmental financial reporting is concerned with environmental liabilities and risks, as these are the factors of greatest concern to investors and other stakeholders. Typically, when environmental-related assets are reported, they are reported as offsets to corresponding environmental liabilities.

For purposes of this book, environmental financial reporting encompasses only those environmental matters covered by the existing financial reporting framework in the United States. Accordingly, this book addresses only those environmental transactions, conditions, and events that affect, or are reasonably likely to affect, the financial position of an enterprise. It does not address the recognition and measurement of costs that are external to the entity, such as the impact of air pollution and water pollution on the environment and society as a whole, and that are not currently absorbed by the entity (often referred to as *external costs* or *externalities*).

The boundaries between internal costs and external costs can and do shift over time. Environmental legislation, for example, may convert an external cost into an internal cost by imposing an obligation on an entity to undertake specific action for which there was previously no such obligation. For example, U.S. companies historically have not been required to internalize the costs associated with emission of carbon dioxide and other greenhouse gases into the atmosphere. Future legislation arising from concerns about global warming, however, may force companies to incur significant costs to reduce the level of greenhouse gas (GHG) emissions. Laws curtailing GHG emissions might also have an adverse effect on other industries, such as the automotive industry, which produce products that are sources of such emissions. The foreseeable transition from external costs to internal costs can be a primary element of environmental risk to the enterprise. Although generally accepted accounting principles (GAAP) are not designed to account for environmental risks of this type, the federal securities laws do require disclosure of known trends, events, or uncertainties that are reasonably likely to affect the entity's future financial condition.

Environmental accounting includes both financial accounting and management accounting. *Financial accounting* is a standardized means for compiling and communicating financial information, including environmental financial information, to external audiences. By contrast, *management accounting* is internally focused. Management accounting supplies information that helps managers achieve business objectives and evaluate performance of the enterprise, including financial performance and environmental performance. Environmental management accounting involves the identification and evaluation of environmental impacts, and the integration of those impacts into corporate decisions on product costing, product pricing, capital budgeting, product design, and performance evaluation. The focus of this book is environmental financial reporting to external audiences. This includes both the display of quantitative information in the financial statements and the disclosure of quantitative and nonquantitative information outside of the financial statements, as necessary to fairly present the financial condition and results of operations of the reporting entity.

The owners of the enterprise are the principal audience for environmental financial information. Stockholders rely on financial reporting to assess the current financial condition of the enterprise, the financial performance of the enterprise over time, and the future prospects of the enterprise. Current and prospective stockholders therefore have an interest in the relative transparency of an entity's material environmental costs, liabilities, and risks (including reputation risks) that could adversely affect the future financial condition and performance of the enterprise. An expanded list of secondary audiences for environmental financial information includes the entity's management and board of directors, employees, suppliers, consumers, competitors, financial institutions, insurers, government, interest groups, media, the scientific community, and the general public. This extended audience has a wide range of interests in environmental reporting of enterprise activities.

For example, creditors have a vested interest in complete and timely disclosure of environmental liabilities to assess credit risks and potential joint liability for loans secured by contaminated properties. Employees prefer to work for companies with reputations for environmental responsibility, and they expect safe and healthy working conditions. The general public may simply be interested in how environmental performance affects the quality of the environment or the country's economic growth.

The leaders of an enterprise can use information about current and potential future environmental obligations to:

- Encourage defensive and prudent operations and waste reduction.
- Improve manufacturing, waste disposal, and shipping practices.
- Negotiate and settle disputes with insurance carriers.
- Influence regulators and public policy makers.
- Determine suitable levels of financial resources.
- Reassess corporate strategy and management practices.
- Articulate a comprehensive risk management program.
- Improve public citizenship.
- Assess hidden risks in takeovers and acquisitions.

1.2 FINANCIAL REPORTS

Financial statements, the notes to the financial statements, and nonfinancial statement disclosures (collectively, *financial reports*) (see §§ 4.2, 4.3, and 4.4, are the primary focus of financial reporting. The financial reports are the final output of a financial reporting process that involves identification, assessment, measurement, and reporting (financial statement display and financial statement and nonfinancial statement disclosures).

The dissemination of reliable environmental information within the financial reports is the purpose of environmental financial reporting. To be reliable, environmental financial information must be prepared and presented in accordance with widely accepted financial reporting standards. Standards provide a consistent and uniform basis on which to record and analyze the financial condition and performance of the enterprise and to compare the financial condition and performance of different companies within or across industries. Standards are intended to reduce the ambiguity of analysis and provide a separation of fact from opinion and unverified facts. It is a notable weakness of the environmental financial reporting framework in the United States that existing standards have largely failed to achieve these objectives.

Financial reporting standards have developed over long periods and have responded to changes in the nature of business enterprises, technology, legal standards, and stakeholder expectations. The expansion of environmental regulation (beginning in the late 1960s), increasing concerns about global environmental impacts on national economies and international trade, and heightened expectations for environmental transparency and sound environmental risk management by institutional investors now pose new challenges to the framework of environmental financial reporting standards.

Recently, stakeholders—including environmental protection groups, investors and analysts with an interest in the social responsibility of corporate enterprises, researchers, and others—have complained that existing environmental financial reporting standards allow too much flexibility and are too narrowly scoped to provide adequate disclosure of relevant information. These stakeholders maintain that the existing regulations give companies too much leeway in determining what environmental information to disclose and limit the extent of disclosure by defining environmental information narrowly. As a result, they believe, companies' disclosure of environmental information is inadequate, hindering investors' ability to assess companies' overall financial condition and the risks they face.

Identified areas of concern regarding perceived gaps in the financial reporting framework for environmental information in the U.S. and internationally include:

- *Expansion of reportable corporate obligations beyond purely legal obligations to include equitable obligations.* The expansion of corporate obligations beyond purely legal ones is particularly important to developing countries. Transnational corporations often account for, and report on, environmental liabilities arising from legal obligations in developed countries, but are silent regarding similar conditions in developing countries that do not have well developed environmental laws. The concept of equitable obligation has been put forth as a means of closing a perceived gap where companies are reporting only when they have no discretion not to report, such as in the case of a legal obligation.
- *Disclosure to shareholders of contamination on one's own property even though the company has no immediate legal obligation for cleanup.* Most U.S. environmental remediation laws, although they are stringent once contamination is discovered, do not require companies to search for historical pollution conditions on their own property. At issue is whether existing financial reporting standards require companies to disclose unasserted claims for conditional legal obligations associated with company-owned properties and facilities.
- *Gradual or immediate recognition of environmental retirement obligations for long-lived assets.* Environmental exit costs associated with the retirement of long-lived assets, such as nuclear power plants and hazardous waste landfills, can have a material effect on the future financial condition of an enterprise. The appropriate manner in which to account for such costs has been a subject of ongoing controversy and disagreement.
- *Measurement of environmental liabilities.* The inherent difficulty in measuring environmental liabilities means that estimates of environmental liabilities rarely represent a single predicted outcome. Various accounting approaches have been developed to address measurement of contingent liabilities in situations in which a single most-likely amount is not available. Controversy exists as to which of these methodologies best achieves the objectives of environmental financial reporting.
- *Assessment of materiality of environmental liabilities on an individual or aggregate basis.* Financial reporting standards do not explicitly require companies to aggregate the estimated costs of similar potential liabilities, such as multiple hazardous waste sites, when assessing materiality.

Consequently, some entities assess the materiality of each environmental liability on an individual basis. Many stakeholders believe that disclosure should be made when an entity believes its environmental liability for an individual circumstance or its environmental liability in the aggregate is material. Also, U.S. Securities and Exchange Commission (SEC) regulations do not require companies to disclose quantitative information on the total number of environmental remediation sites, related claims, or the associated liabilities. As a result, some investors contend that they cannot determine whether companies have enough reserves to cover current and future liabilities.

- *Reporting of environmental assets and nonfinancial environmental performance data.* Existing financial reporting standards do not require companies to disclose information about their environmental assets or environmental performance. A growing body of socially responsible investors believes that such information could be material to many investors or indicative of effective corporate management.

1.3 THE FINANCIAL REPORTING PROCESS

As discussed in Chapter 5, the entity's environmental financial reporting objectives relate principally to the accuracy, completeness, and relevance of the environmental financial information contained in its financial reports. Ultimately, if the entity's financial reports fail to conform with GAAP or fail to fairly present the financial condition of the company, the entity's financial reporting objectives will not be met.

To have any assurance that the entity's financial reporting objectives will be achieved, management must design, implement, and maintain an appropriate financial reporting process. Of course, the establishment of environmental financial reporting objectives and an associated financial reporting process is not warranted for all companies, given the nature of their assets and operations. The threshold criteria for determining whether circumstances warrant the development of objectives and the design and implementation of an environmental financial reporting process are discussed in Chapter 8.

GAAP and SEC disclosure rules assume that the entity has identified those aspects of its business that are subject to financial reporting and collected the information necessary to prepare the financial statements and related disclosures. For example, FASB Statement of Financial Accounting Standards No. 5, "Accounting for Contingencies" (FAS 5) (see Chapter 19) requires the accrual of a liability for environmental loss contingencies meeting certain criteria, but does not require the reporting entity to identify its environmental loss contingencies in the first place. Nor does FAS 5 specify how the entity is to collect the information needed to determine whether the criteria for accrual are met. Rather, FAS 5 assumes that the entity has already identified and assessed the environmental loss contingencies that might be reportable.

As depicted in Exhibit 1.1, the environmental financial reporting process comprises four major sets of activities: identification, assessment, measurement,

EXHIBIT 1.1

Environmental Financial Reporting Process

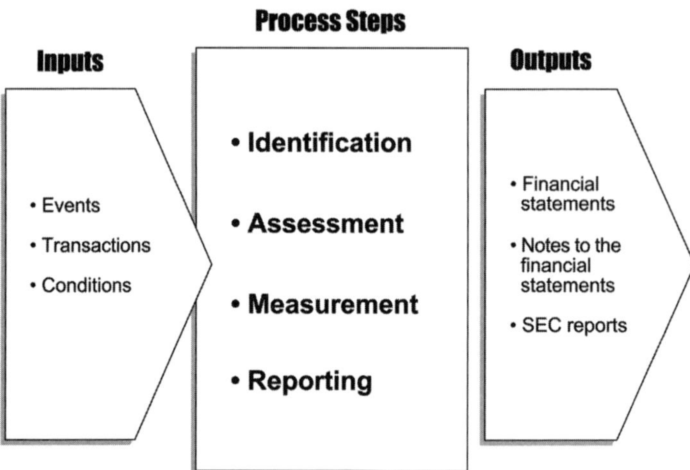

and reporting (financial statement display and financial statement and nonfinancial statement disclosures).

(a) IDENTIFICATION

Identification involves activities designed to discover and monitor transactions, events, and conditions that have caused or could give rise to material environmental costs, liabilities, or risks. The process of identifying environmental costs, liabilities, and risks in the context of corporate mergers, asset acquisitions, and financing transactions is commonly called *environmental due diligence*. The process of identifying environmental costs, liabilities, and risks affecting one's own company, often focused primarily on assessment of compliance with environmental laws, is commonly called *environmental auditing*. The identification phase of the environmental financial reporting process involves both environmental due diligence and environmental auditing (in the broader sense of identifying all significant environmental costs, liabilities, and risks).

An in-depth examination of environmental due diligence and environmental auditing is beyond the scope of this book. Depending on the type of environmental conditions of concern, there are several well-established standards that companies can employ to provide reasonable assurance that environmental liabilities and risks are identified in a timely manner. These standards include, but are not limited to:

- *ASTM E 2107, "Standard Practice for Environmental Regulatory Compliance Audits."* This standard, issued by ASTM International, identifies the minimum requirements for environmental regulatory compliance audits. It also provides information on the terms and procedures associated with audits as practiced in the United States and serves as a source to which interested parties may refer for definitions and descriptions of accepted audit terms and procedures.

- *ASTM E 1528, "Standard Practice for Environmental Site Assessments: Transaction Screen Process (Transaction Screen)."* The transaction screen is a preliminary inquiry as to the environmental condition of a parcel of commercial real estate; it is intended to provide a reasonable basis to determine whether further inquiry is warranted. ASTM E 1528 is often used with respect to commercial properties that are initially considered to be uncontaminated. If the entity finds that further inquiry is necessary, ASTM E 1527 may be used.
- *ASTM E 1527, "Standard Practice for Environmental Site Assessments: Phase I Environmental Site Assessment Process."* The purpose of this standard is to define good commercial and customary practice in the United States for conducting an environmental site assessment of a parcel of real estate with respect to petroleum products and the range of contaminants within the scope of the Comprehensive Environmental Response, Compensation, and Liability Act (CERCLA) (see § 3.2(a)(i)). ASTM E 1527 is commonly used in connection with environmental due diligence for sales and financing transactions involving commercial or industrial real estate. Information gathered during these preclosing assessments sometimes forms the basis for postclosing disclosure of environmental financial information by the acquiring company. The standard is less often used to identify environmental conditions affecting company-owned real estate for purposes of financial reporting. Items that are considered outside the scope of this standard and which may require additional investigation procedures include asbestos-containing materials, radon, lead-based paint, lead in drinking water, wetlands, regulatory compliance, cultural and historic resources, industrial hygiene, health and safety, ecological resources, endangered species, indoor air quality, and high-voltage power lines.
- *ASTM E 2247, "Standard Practice for Environmental Site Assessments: Phase I Environmental Site Assessment Process for Forestland and Rural Property."* This standard is intended for environmental site assessments conducted on 120 acres or more of forestland or rural property or with a developed use of only managed forestland or agriculture. The standard includes an optional checklist for threatened and endangered species consideration and nonpoint source pollution evaluations.
- *ASTM E 2356, "Standard Practice for Comprehensive Building Asbestos Surveys."* This standard describes procedures for conducting comprehensive surveys of buildings and facilities for the purpose of locating, identifying, quantifying, and assessing asbestos-containing materials.
- *ISO 14015, "Environmental Assessments of Sites and Organizations."* The purpose of the ISO 14000 series of environmental management system standards, issued by the International Standards Organization (ISO), is to provide organizations with the bases of an effective system of

environmental management for reaching their environmental and economic objectives. A central component of an ISO 14000 environmental management system is the requirement to establish and maintain a procedure to identify the environmental aspects of the organization's activities, products, or services that it can control and over which it can be expected to have an influence, in order to determine those that have or can have significant impacts on the environment.

(b) ASSESSMENT

Assessment involves activities designed to enable the measurement and reporting of environmental-related transactions, events, and conditions. Evaluation of pollution conditions often involves highly specialized environmental science and engineering services. Evaluation of pollution conditions for financial reporting purposes may involve many of the same activities required to develop appropriate corrective action plans to remove or control environmental contamination.

Entities may be obligated under environmental laws to assess identified pollution conditions. The Superfund law (see § 3.2(a)) and the remediation provisions in RCRA (see § 3.2(b)), for example, contain specific requirements for assessment of identified pollution conditions. In addition, there are various nongovernmental standards pertaining to assessment of pollution conditions, including:

- *ASTM E 1903, "Standard Guide for Environmental Site Assessments: Phase II Environmental Site Assessment Process."* A Phase II environmental site assessment typically follows a Phase I environmental site assessment that identified known or suspected pollution conditions. A Phase II environmental site assessment is a more detailed investigation requiring sampling and analysis of environmental media (e.g., soil, groundwater, surface water, and sediment). The purpose of the Phase II investigation is to estimate the nature and extent of contamination and to provide the basis for a preliminary assessment of the cost for corrective or preventive action.
- *ASTM Phase II Environmental Site Assessment Implementation Standards.* ASTM has issued more than 20 guides, practices, and test methods addressing various elements of the Phase II environmental site assessment process, including conceptualizing subsurface and contaminant conditions to adequately focus subsurface investigations, selecting and using drilling and soil sampling techniques, classifying and describing soils, designing and installing groundwater monitoring wells, sampling and monitoring groundwater, and soil gas monitoring.

(c) MEASUREMENT

Measurement involves activities designed to quantify the financial impact of environmental-related transactions, events, and conditions. Measurement of environmental liabilities, in particular, is a complex undertaking and involves many subjective judgments. Also, the techniques used to measure these items vary depending on the nature of the underlying circumstances. The primary methodologies and related standards for measurement of environmental liabilities include:

- *Fair value measurement.* Fair value measurement is required by several financial accounting pronouncements applicable to environmental obligations associated with environmental guarantees (see § 21.3), asset retirement obligations (see § 22.3), and asset impairments (see § 23.3). The fair value of a liability is the amount at which the liability could be settled in a current transaction between willing parties (other than in a forced or liquidation transaction). Guidance from the Financial Accounting Standards Board (FASB) states that market prices quoted in active markets are the best evidence of fair value and should be used, if available. If quoted market prices are not available, fair value should be estimated based on the best information available in the circumstances, including prices for similar liabilities and the results of expected present value (or other valuation) techniques. The fair value of an environmental liability will typically be measured by estimating the price that the entity would have to pay a third party (e.g., an insurance company) having a comparable credit rating to assume the liability.
- *Expected present value.* Statement of Financial Accounting Concepts No. 7, "Using Cash Flow Information and Present Value in Accounting Measurements" (SFAC 7) provides guidance on the application of expected present value measurement. This robust measurement approach is also favored by ASTM E 2137, "Standard Guide for Estimating Monetary Costs and Liabilities for Environmental Matters." ASTM E 2137 is a voluntary guide for estimating costs and liabilities for environmental matters in the United States (see § 25.2). In summary, the measurement approach involves calculation of the net present value of estimated future cash flows that reflect, to the extent possible, a marketplace assessment of the cost and timing of performing the activities required to settle an obligation.

  The expected present value approach allows use of present value (discounting) techniques when the timing of cash flows is uncertain, by developing a probabilistic weighted average of various possible future scenarios. Like any accounting measurement, however, the application of an expected present value approach is subject to a cost-benefit constraint. In some cases, an entity may have access to considerable data and may be able to develop many cash-flow scenarios. In other cases, the entity may not be able to develop more than general statements about the variability of cash flows without incurring considerable cost. The accounting challenge is to balance the cost of obtaining additional information against the additional reliability that information will bring to the measurement.
- *Best estimate.* Under FAS 5, recognized liabilities for environmental loss contingencies should be measured based on the reporting entity's best estimate of the liability (see §§ 19.3 and 20.3). FAS 5 does not prescribe the use of a specific measurement methodology.

- *Most likely value.* The most likely value is the estimated cost of the scenario believed to be most likely to occur (e.g., a stated preferred remedy).
- *Known minimum value.* With respect to measurement of recognized contingent liabilities under FAS 5, FASB guidance states that when no amount within a range of possible outcomes is a better estimate than any other amount, the minimum amount in the range should be used.
- *ASTM framework.* ASTM E 2137, "Standard Guide for Estimating Monetary Costs and Liabilities for Environmental Matters," is a guide for estimating costs and liabilities for environmental matters (see § 25.2). The central component of ASTM E 2137 is a decision framework for estimating environmental costs and liabilities that guides an entity in choosing among various alternative measurement techniques.

(d) REPORTING

Reporting involves activities designed to ensure that the quantitative and nonquantitative information required to be disclosed in an entity's financial statements and SEC reports is recorded, processed, summarized, and reported within the appropriate time periods. Such activities include procedures designed to ensure that the information required to be disclosed is accumulated and communicated to the entity's senior management, to allow timely decisions regarding required disclosure. The final stage of the reporting process is the presentation of environmental financial information in the entity's financial statements and SEC reports. The standards governing environmental financial reporting are set forth in Part Three of this book.

Display of quantitative environmental information in the financial statements is prescribed by GAAP and requires limited subjective judgment. By contrast, disclosure of financial and nonfinancial information in the notes to the financial statements and in SEC reports often requires significant judgment and careful drafting to properly apply highly subjective criteria. Reporting also involves activities designed to update reported environmental financial information to reflect changes in circumstances and assumptions. Environmental financial reporting typically concerns inchoate transactions, events, or conditions as to which the ultimate financial impact to the enterprise will not be known for many years into the future. As circumstances and assumptions change over time, previously reported information must be updated.

(e) SPECIAL CONSIDERATIONS

These four phases of the environmental financial reporting process—identification, assessment, measurement, and reporting—are generically applicable to a broad range of accounting estimates. However, their application to environmental matters requires special consideration due to the unique characteristics of environmental liabilities and risks. In general, the financial impact on the enterprise of environmental transactions, events, and conditions is not obvious and apparent. Environmental problems are often difficult to identify, evaluate, and measure. There are often long delays between the occurrence of the underlying obligating event and the ultimate financial impact on the organization. Moreover, as noted in Chapter 5, reporting entities are often faced with competing objectives that may motivate management to seek something less than full environmental transparency.

For these reasons, limited aspects of environmental financial reporting (e.g., environmental information reported in the company's financial statements) cannot be evaluated in isolation from the overall environmental financial reporting process. Familiarity with financial reporting standards alone is insufficient. Although these standards dictate procedures for measuring and reporting environmental liabilities and risks, they provide little or no instruction on the procedures for identifying and assessing the underlying environmental-related transactions, events, and conditions in the first place.

(f) RELATION TO OTHER ENVIRONMENTAL BUSINESS PROCESSES

The environmental financial reporting process has certain elements—identification and assessment—in common with environmental business processes more familiar to environmental managers, lawyers, and consultants (e.g., environmental compliance management and environmental risk management). However, as shown in Exhibit 1.2, there are also significant differences.

Environmental compliance management comprises an entity's efforts to ensure compliance with applicable environmental laws. Environmental compliance management generally focuses primarily on pollution control laws, as these laws typically affect day-to-day business operations. By contrast, pollution remediation laws do not affect routine operations and tend to impose fewer compliance obligations. Environmental compliance management typically involves the following process activities:

- Identification of instances of possible noncompliance with environmental laws.

EXHIBIT 1.2

Environmental Management Processes

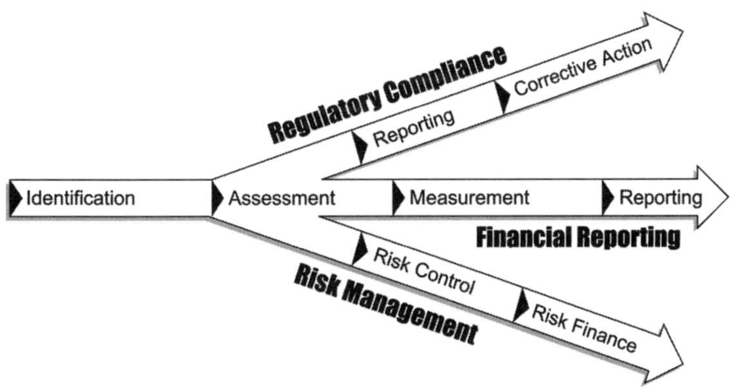

- Assessment of relevant factual and legal circumstances to confirm that a violation has occurred and, if so, to determine the consequences of the violation.
- Reporting of violations to environmental regulatory authorities (if required by law or voluntarily elected by management).
- Selection and implementation of corrective action measures to achieve and maintain compliance.

Environmental risk management comprises an entity's efforts to cost-effectively manage its environmental loss exposures. As used in this book, *environmental risk* concerns the potential for adverse financial impacts to the organization arising from environmental losses, as opposed to the degree of actual or potential risk to human health and the environment (although the latter may have an influence on the former). Environmental risk management typically involves the following process activities:

- Identification of environmental loss exposures.
- Assessment of the probability of occurrence and the magnitude of the potential loss to the enterprise.
- Selection and implementation of measures to control identified risks.
- Selection and implementation of mechanisms to finance risks that cannot be avoided or eliminated (e.g., insurance, reserves, indemnification agreements, and so forth).

Environmental managers, lawyers, and consultants generally are experienced in the areas of identification and assessment, but have only limited experience and background with respect to measurement and reporting. Conversely, financial statement preparers and independent auditors generally are experienced in the areas of measurement and reporting, but have little, if any, expertise in the areas of identification and assessment. This lack of expertise presents a significant challenge to financial statement preparers and independent auditors in assuring the reliability of reported environmental financial information.

1.4 PROCESS CONTROL

GAAP and SEC disclosure rules, by themselves, do nothing to prevent the entity from:

- Failing to identify transactions, conditions, or events that have caused or could give rise to material environmental liabilities or risks.
- Failing to evaluate the nature and extent of known or reasonably suspected environmental conditions or events to determine whether such matters are reportable.
- Failing to collect the information and perform the procedures necessary to properly estimate the liability associated with reportable environmental conditions or events.

- Failing to properly and consistently apply appropriate accounting policies to reportable environmental transactions, events, or conditions.
- Failing to periodically reevaluate and update previously reported environmental financial information.

Such failures may occur as the result of intentional or unintentional errors and omissions at various levels within the organization. Given the inherent complexity of environmental financial reporting, to have any assurance that such failures will not occur, management first must develop clearly understood financial reporting objectives, and thereafter implement and maintain a financial reporting process designed to achieve those objectives. Environmental financial reporting is a goal-driven exercise. In the absence of clearly understood objectives and a well-defined financial reporting process, organizations stand little chance of achieving acceptable standards of performance.

U.S. companies, even in the same industry, vary significantly in what they choose to report in their SEC filings and how they report it. This undesirable result led members of Congress to request a U.S. Governmental Accountability Office (GAO) study of perceived problems with environmental reporting. The GAO study concluded in 2004, with a report to Congress entitled *Environmental Disclosure: SEC Should Explore Ways to Improve Tracking and Transparency of Information*. One of the GAO's most significant findings was that "one cannot determine whether a low level of disclosure means that a company does not have existing or potential environmental liabilities, has determined that such liabilities are not material, or is not adequately complying with disclosure requirements." Though this is undoubtedly due in part to the flexibility in applicable financial reporting standards, the GAO's finding also highlights a larger problem: a general lack of confidence in the environmental reporting objectives of U.S. companies and the integrity of the financial reporting processes maintained to achieve these objectives.

Even with clearly understood objectives and a well-defined financial reporting process, there are many risks that may prevent the organization from achieving its objectives. For these reasons, the financial reporting process must: (1) operate within an organizational environment that is dedicated to ethical behavior and compliance with legal requirements and financial reporting standards, and (2) incorporate appropriate controls to effectively prevent and detect intentional and unintentional process deviations. These elements form the foundation of an effective internal control system intended to provide stakeholders with reasonable assurance that the entity's financial reporting objectives will be achieved.

Generally accepted accounting principles and SEC disclosure regulations set forth specifications and guidelines for the output of the financial reporting process—the financial statements, notes to the financial statements, and nonfinancial statement disclosures. These financial reporting standards provide little guidance for designing and implementing an effective environmental reporting process.

Guidance on process control is provided in the internal control provisions of generally accepted auditing standards (GAAS) and the federal securities laws and related SEC and Public Company Accounting Oversight Board (PCAOB) rules. In addition, several nongovernmental standards for internal control—most notably, the COSO Internal Control: Integrated Framework (see § 8.2)—set forth specifications and guidelines for establishing appropriate controls over the financial reporting process. These guidelines, however, do not specifically address environmental reporting. Each organization, therefore, must apply the general principles of internal control to the specific objectives and risks associated with environmental financial reporting.

1.5 ADDITIONAL CONSIDERATIONS FOR PUBLIC COMPANIES

A centerpiece of the Sarbanes-Oxley Act of 2002[1] (Sarbanes-Oxley or the Act) covered in Part Two is the heightened focus on *process* versus *output*. It is often stated that Sarbanes-Oxley does nothing to change the financial reporting standards applicable to environmental costs, liabilities, and risks. With only limited exceptions, this is an accurate characterization of the law. Sarbanes-Oxley, however, has dramatically increased management's accountability for the integrity of the financial reporting process. Sarbanes-Oxley can be expected to greatly increase the rigor applied by public companies to the design and implementation of effective environmental financial reporting processes. This in turn is likely to improve the accuracy and completeness of environmental financial reporting and thereby increase investor confidence in the environmental financial information reported by U.S. public companies.

The SEC and the PCAOB, established by Sarbanes-Oxley, have issued guidance relevant to the scope of internal control as it pertains to environmental financial reporting. This guidance, which is further discussed in § 8.3, expands the scope of the internal control requirements under the federal securities laws to encompass the full breadth of the financial reporting process described in § 1.3. According to PCAOB guidance, *internal control over financial reporting encompasses controls over the identification, measurement, and reporting of all material actual loss events which have occurred, including controls over the monitoring and risk assessment of areas in which, given the nature of the company's operations, such actual loss events are reasonably possible.*[2]

As illustrated in Exhibit 1.3, the implications of the PCAOB's guidance are significant. The PCAOB has in effect determined that environmental operations that are not directly related to financial reporting (e.g., activities to identify and assess environmental transactions, conditions, and events for purposes of maintaining compliance with environmental laws or controlling environmental risks) may be subject to the federal securities laws, if such operations are relevant to fair presentation of the company's financial position. Public companies with more than a remote exposure to material environmental liabilities now must pay special attention to the design and effective operation of environmental financial

---

1 H.R. 3763, Pub. L. No.107-204, 116 Stat. 745 (2002).

2 *See* PCAOB, *Staff Questions and Answers: Auditing Internal Control over Financial Reporting*, Question 27 (Oct. 6, 2004) (emphasis added).

EXHIBIT 1.3

Scope of Internal Control over the Financial Reporting Process

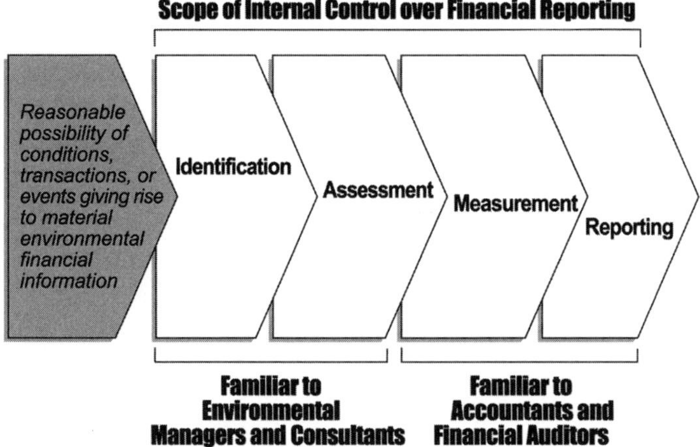

reporting processes and controls capable of achieving the rigorous standards imposed by Sarbanes-Oxley. Significant challenges lie ahead for the accounting and environmental professionals who together will be responsible for designing, implementing, and auditing these systems.

CHAPTER TWO

The Law and Accounting Sandwich

2.1 INTRODUCTION

Environmental financial reporting is particularly challenging because it involves a complex and sometimes bewildering interaction of corporate, securities, and bankruptcy law, financial accounting standards, and environmental law. (*Environmental law* is used here to represent the broad interaction of environmental public policy, legislation, common law, science, and engineering.) As shown in Exhibit 2.1, the interrelationship of these three elements can be depicted as a sandwich.

EXHIBIT 2.1

The Law and Accounting Sandwich

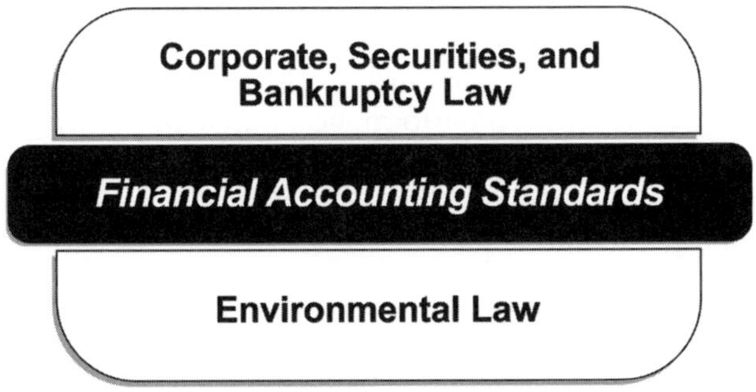

The top slice of bread represents a combination of corporate, securities, and bankruptcy law. Public corporations in the United States are subject to financial reporting requirements under the federal securities laws and regulations promulgated by the SEC. The federal securities laws, including Sarbanes-Oxley, impose potential liability for issuers that fail to accurately report material environmental financial information. This liability also extends to the issuer's directors and officers.

Both public and private entities are further subject to various financial reporting considerations arising under state and federal corporation laws and bankruptcy laws. These laws contain provisions intended to protect creditors at a time when the corporation is at or near insolvency. To ensure compliance with these laws, it is imperative that corporate decision makers know the true financial condition of the enterprise, taking into account environmental liabilities and loss contingencies. Failure to be reasonably informed of the entity's true financial condition potentially can result in personal liability of corporate directors. Although corporate and bankruptcy laws do not impose financial reporting obligations, they nonetheless belong in the top slice of bread along with the securities laws because they provide a strong motivation for corporate boards to demand an accurate assessment of the corporation's current and anticipated future financial condition, including a thorough accounting of environmental financial information.

The filling in the sandwich represents the financial accounting standards, commonly known as generally accepted accounting principles, that set forth rules and principles for fairly presenting environmental financial information in the financial statements. Entities subject to U.S. federal securities laws are required to report their financial condition and results of operations in accordance with GAAP. Although private entities are not legally required to follow GAAP, stockholders and lenders often insist that they do so. Environmental financial reporting is unusual because the most important accounting principles applicable to environmental matters expressly rely on determinations of environmental law.

The bottom slice of bread represents the complex interaction of the various elements of environmental protection. These elements include:

- *Public policy regarding protection of the environment and conservation of natural resources.* Public policy is dynamic. For example, since the adoption of the major U.S. environmental statutes, environmental public policy has evolved from a government command-and-control orientation toward a model of self-regulation combined with increased disclosure and transparency of environmental performance. Public policy may be reflected in various forms, including environmental laws, government enforcement policies, and investor expectations of corporate environmental responsibility and stewardship.

- *Federal, state, and local environmental laws.* These laws form the basis for most environmental legal obligations and loss exposures that give rise to environmental liabilities reported in the financial statements under GAAP.

Legal determinations made by the entity's environmental lawyers bear directly on whether environmental matters must be presented in the financial statements. Similarly, environmental legal judgments often determine whether information on environmental matters must be disclosed in an issuer's SEC reports. In this regard, environmental law is inextricably intertwined with both financial accounting standards and the federal securities laws.

- *Environmental science and engineering*. The disciplines of environmental science and engineering are required to assess the actual or potential risk to human health and the environment posed by pollution conditions and society's use of natural resources. Environmental law precipitates the need for most environmental financial information, but the identification, evaluation, and measurement of environmental transactions, events, and conditions typically involve an interdisciplinary team of professionals with skills in environmental law, science, and engineering.

Environmental financial reporting unquestionably is a complex subject. Bridging the gap in understanding horizontally across the various environmental disciplines can be a significant challenge in itself. Bridging the gap vertically across the layers of the law and accounting sandwich is an even greater undertaking.

The scope of the challenge was acknowledged by an environmental issues roundtable sponsored by the American Institute of Certified Public Accountants (AICPA) in 1993. More than 30 individuals representing public accounting firms, industry, the Financial Accounting Standards Board, the Securities and Exchange Commission, and the AICPA participated in the roundtable. Referencing a 1992 survey conducted by Price Waterhouse, *Accounting for Environmental Compliance: Crossroad of GAAP, Engineering and Government—Second Survey of Corporate America's Accounting for Environmental Costs*, the participants found that:

> Financial statement preparers and independent auditors should be more knowledgeable about the significant federal laws on environmental remediation and the concepts of strict liability, and joint and several liability applicable to remediation costs. Participants expressed concern that too many preparers and auditors of financial statements are unaware that the nationally recognized issue of environmental cleanup costs affects them directly.

Many years later, these same conditions persist. If anything, environmental financial reporting has become even more complex and multidisciplinary. This presents the accounting profession with a dilemma. Corporate accountants and independent auditors are primarily responsible for assuring stakeholders that environmental financial reporting processes are effective and that environmental financial information is fairly presented. Yet, based on their training and experience, accountants generally lack expertise in important aspects of the environmental financial reporting process. Accordingly, accountants often are ill-prepared to attest to the accuracy and completeness of reported environmental financial information. For example, how can a corporate accountant or

EXHIBIT 2.2

Outputs and Processes

	OUTPUT	PROCESS
Securities Law	• Periodic SEC reports (§ 4.4) • Sarbanes-Oxley §§ 302 and 906 financial statement certifications (see § 7.2)	• Disclosure controls and procedures (see § 8.4) • Sarbanes-Oxley § 302 process certification (§ 7.3(a))
Financial Accounting	• Financial statements (§ 4.2) • Notes to the financial statements (§ 4.3) • Auditor's opinion on the financial statements (Ch. 26)	• Measurement • Reporting (display and disclosure) • Internal control (§ 8.3) • Sarbanes-Oxley § 404 attestation (Ch. 27) • Sarbanes-Oxley § 404 internal control report (§ 7.3(b))
Environmental Law	• Environmental costs • Environmental assets • Environmental liabilities • Environmental guarantees • Environmental asset retirement obligations • Environmental impairments • Environmental risks	• Identification • Assessment • Environmental compliance management • Environmental risk management

independent auditor reasonably be expected to give implied or express assurances that all transactions, conditions, and events that could potentially give rise to reportable environmental financial information have been identified and adequately assessed? Overcoming this challenge will likely require accountants to make extensive use of environmental specialists (see § 26.3(g)).

Exhibit 2.2 shows how the environmental financial reporting outputs and processes align with the law and accounting sandwich.

2.2 SECURITIES, CORPORATE, AND BANKRUPTCY LAWS

(a) SECURITIES LAWS

The federal securities laws consist of two principal statutes and the rules promulgated thereunder by the SEC. The Securities Act of 1933 (Securities Act) requires companies to register their securities with the SEC before offering them to the public. The Securities Act is aimed at protecting the initial buyers of securities.

The Securities Exchange Act of 1934 (Exchange Act) requires publicly traded companies to file periodic reports with the SEC. These reports include annual reports (Form 10-K), quarterly reports (Form 10-Q), and episodic reports (Form 8-K). The Exchange Act is primarily oriented toward protecting investors engaged in buying and selling securities on the U.S. exchanges.

With regard to environmental financial reporting, the federal securities laws require public companies to perform the following:

- Present material environmental financial information in accordance with GAAP (see § 4.7(b)).
- Present certain narrative and quantitative environmental information in the nonfinancial statement portions of the issuer's SEC filings (see § 4.8).
- Provide additional environmental information, either within the financial statements or outside the financial statements, as necessary to enable reasonable investors to make informed investment decisions (see § 4.9).
- Implement and maintain a financial reporting system capable of providing reasonable assurance that the foregoing requirements will be satisfied (see Chapter 8).

The antifraud provisions of the federal securities laws (i.e., sections 12 and 13(a)(2) of the Securities Act, section 10(b) of the Exchange Act, and SEC Rule 10b-5) prohibit the making of false or misleading statements or omissions in connection with the purchase or sale of securities. Failure to present financial information in conformance with GAAP is deemed to be a material misstatement. In such event, the issuer could be required to restate its prior years' financial statements.

Registrants and issuers who fail to make the required disclosures or make untrue or misleading disclosures can be subject to civil or criminal enforcement actions. Moreover, shareholders and investors may bring private actions against registrants and issuers for losses caused by misleading statements or omissions of material information. For U.S. corporations regulated by the SEC, timely and accurate financial reporting in accordance with GAAP and other applicable rules and regulations is a legal requirement under the federal securities laws.

As discussed in Part Two, Sarbanes-Oxley made significant changes to the Securities Act and the Exchange Act. Changes of particular importance with respect to environmental financial reporting include:

- *CEO/CFO reimbursement to issuer*. Pursuant to section 304 of the Act, if a public company is required to restate its financial statements due to noncompliance with the federal securities laws, the CEO and CFO must reimburse the company for any bonus or incentive or equity-based compensation received during the 12-month period following the filing of the financial statements subsequently restated and any profits realized from the sale of issuer securities during that same period.
- *CEO/CFO certifications*. Sections 302 and 906 of the Act require the CEO and CFO of public companies to sign and certify the company's SEC reports and accompanying financial statements. False statements can subject certifying officers to civil and criminal penalties.
- *Internal control*. Sections 302 and 404 of the Act require the certifying officers to assume personal accountability for, and certify the effectiveness of, the financial reporting process used to develop the issuer's periodic

reports filed with the SEC. The Act further requires the issuer's independent auditor to attest to the effectiveness of the issuer's internal control over financial reporting.

(b) CORPORATE AND BANKRUPTCY LAWS

Directors of financially troubled corporations are vulnerable to personal liability arising from claims by stockholders, creditors, and the corporation itself. State corporation statutes and related case law present several financial reporting concerns for corporate directors and officers relating to the entity's state of solvency:

- Failure to exercise reasonable oversight over the financial reporting process.
- Fiduciary duties of directors in the zone of insolvency.
- Illegal dividends in the event of dissolution or insolvency.
- Fraudulent conveyances.

(i) FAILURE TO EXERCISE REASONABLE OVERSIGHT

As reported by the National Association of Corporate Directors' Blue Ribbon Commission on Risk Oversight, the benchmark for directors' risk oversight obligations was established in *In re Caremark International, Inc.*,[1] a 1996 landmark Delaware decision. The derivative suit before the court involved claims that members of Caremark's board of directors had breached their fiduciary duty of care to Caremark in connection with alleged violations by Caremark employees of federal and state laws and regulations.

The court noted that director liability for a breach of the duty to exercise appropriate attention may arise in two distinct contexts. First, such liability may follow from a board decision that results in a loss because that decision was ill-advised or negligent. In such cases, liability is typically subject to the director-protective business judgment rule, assuming that the decision made was the product of a process that was either deliberately considered in good faith or was otherwise rational.

Second, liability to the corporation for a loss may arise from an unconsidered failure of the board to act in circumstances in which due attention would, arguably, have prevented the loss. In such cases, corporate boards must satisfy their duty of care to be reasonably informed by:

> assuring themselves that information and reporting systems exist in the organization that are reasonably designed to provide to senior management and to the board itself timely, accurate information sufficient to allow management and the board, each within its scope, to reach informed judgments concerning both the corporation's compliance with law and its business performance.[2]

---

1 698 A.2d 959 (Del. Ch. 1996).
2 *Id.* at 970.

The court in Caremark did not elaborate on the elements and characteristics of a "reasonable information and reporting system," stating only that the level of detail appropriate for such systems is a question of business judgment. In the context of financial reporting, however, reasonable information and reporting systems may be interpreted to mean effective internal control over financial reporting (see Chapter 8).

(ii) FIDUCIARY DUTIES OF DIRECTORS IN THE ZONE OF INSOLVENCY

Off-balance-sheet liabilities, including hidden, understated, or even unknown loss contingencies, may render a company insolvent retroactively. With respect to environmental financial reporting, such matters may include environmental liabilities and asset impairments associated with historical pollution conditions, pending or anticipated litigation, environmental indemnity agreements, and risks that the corporation could be held accountable for the liabilities of a related entity under veil-piercing or alter-ego theories. This point is illustrated by a federal bankruptcy decision discussed in § 2.2(b)(v).

State corporation statutes typically provide that the business and affairs of a corporation shall be managed by or under the direction of its board of directors. Courts have long recognized the fiduciary nature of the relationship between the board of directors and the corporation.

Directors of a solvent corporation owe their primary (if not sole) responsibility to the corporation's owners—the stockholders. Directors of a solvent corporation generally do not owe fiduciary duties to the creditors of the corporation. By contrast, when a corporation becomes insolvent, the fiduciary duties of corporate directors change. Directors of an insolvent corporation must act in the best interests of the corporation's creditors, rather than the corporation's shareholders. Directors must act cautiously when a corporation begins to approach insolvency—a situation sometimes referred to as entering the *zone of insolvency*—as decisions made during this period may be subject to heightened scrutiny if the entity ultimately becomes insolvent.

(iii) ILLEGAL DIVIDENDS IN THE EVENT OF DISSOLUTION OR INSOLVENCY

Under most state corporation laws, directors are personally liable to the corporation, or to the corporation's creditors in the event of dissolution or insolvency, for any willful, and possibly even merely negligent, payment of an unlawful dividend. Generally, a dividend is unlawful if it is made at a time when the corporation is insolvent, or if there are reasonable grounds to believe that the corporation would be rendered insolvent by payment of the dividend. In most states, directors are protected from personal liability for illegal dividends if they relied in good faith on reports prepared by officers of the corporation or outside advisors indicating that the dividend is appropriate.

A case from 2003, *Pereira v. Cogan*,[3] illustrates how corporate directors of private corporations as well as public corporations can incur personal liability for

---

[3] 2003 WL 21039976 (S.D.N.Y. 2003).

improper actions taken when the corporation is insolvent or operating in the zone of insolvency. Trace International Holdings, Inc., was a private corporation controlled by Marshall S. Cogan, a well-known businessman and investor in New York City. Trace went bankrupt in 1999, and the trustee in bankruptcy brought an action against the directors of Trace, alleging that they had violated their fiduciary duties with respect to numerous acts of self-dealing by Cogan during a period when Trace was in the zone of insolvency. The challenged acts included inappropriate and allegedly illegal dividends.

The court found that Trace had been insolvent or in the zone of insolvency from 1995 (except for a short period in 1996) until it filed for bankruptcy protection in 1999. Payment of stock dividends while the corporation is insolvent, or a payment that renders a company insolvent, is illegal under applicable Delaware law, as are any dividends not declared by the board of directors. Despite the fact that they knew or should have known of dividends proposed by Cogan, the directors took no action to ensure that such dividends were approved by the board, and engaged in no calculations to verify that the entity was solvent even though they were aware of the corporation's precarious financial position. In so doing, the directors failed to satisfy their fiduciary duty owed to creditors during the period from 1995 to 1999 when Trace was insolvent. Accordingly, the court found that the directors were personally liable for illegal dividends in the amount of $4,309,823.[4]

(iv) FRAUDULENT CONVEYANCES

Creditors of a financially distressed corporation, or the corporation itself, may be able to set aside or undo certain transactions made while the corporation was insolvent or in the zone of insolvency. For example, a court may set aside transfers or obligations made or incurred for which the corporation did not receive reasonably equivalent value if the corporation was insolvent or rendered insolvent by the transfer or retained unreasonably small capital to conduct its business following the transfer. Transfers of this type are referred to as *constructive fraudulent transfers* and are prohibited, to prevent the dissipation of assets otherwise available to creditors.

If a corporation or its creditors have the ability to recover fraudulent or preferential transfers, the corporation's directors may be liable for these improper transfers if they breached their fiduciary duties in approving the relevant transfer.

(v) DETERMINATION OF SOLVENCY

Because the insolvency of the corporation alters their duties and risks, directors have reason to want to be continuously aware of whether the corporation is insolvent or within the zone of insolvency. Generally, a corporation is considered *insolvent* when either (1) it is unable to pay its obligations as they become

---

4 For more information on the liability exposure of directors of financially distressed corporations, *see* Cieri, Richard M. & Riela, Michael J., *Protecting Directors and Officers of Corporations That Are Insolvent or in the Zone or Vicinity of Insolvency: Important Considerations, Practical Solutions,* 2 DePaul Bus. & Com. L.J. 295 (2004).

due (i.e., the equity measure of insolvency) or (2) its liabilities exceed its assets (i.e., the balance-sheet measure of insolvency). A corporation may be insolvent under these tests even if it has not commenced a bankruptcy case.

In assessing balance-sheet solvency, directors must evaluate off-balance-sheet liabilities and loss contingencies. With respect to environmental financial reporting, such matters may include environmental liabilities and asset impairments associated with historical pollution conditions, pending or anticipated litigation, environmental indemnity agreements, and risks that the corporation could be held accountable for the liabilities of a related entity under veil-piercing or alter-ego theories.

The value of loss contingencies for purposes of a solvency analysis under corporate and bankruptcy law is typically measured by determining the potential amount of the liability and adjusting this amount to account for the likelihood that the contingency will materialize. The measurement techniques applied by a court in this context may or may not conform to GAAP used in financial accounting. GAAP may be relevant to the court's determination of solvency, but courts are not bound to consider or apply GAAP in the corporate and bankruptcy context.

Directors must be cognizant that even apparently remote loss contingencies, as well as loss contingencies that cannot reasonably be estimated, ultimately may be realized. Despite a director's prior reasonable assessment that such contingencies were unlikely to affect the entity's solvency, a court using 20-20 hindsight in the future may determine nevertheless that the corporation was in fact insolvent.

This point is illustrated by the federal bankruptcy decision in *Official Committee of Asbestos Personal Injury Claimants v. Sealed Air Corp.*[5] W. R. Grace (Grace) sold a division of the company to Sealed Air Corporation in March 1998, at a time when Grace was facing pending and anticipated future asbestos-related liability claims. Grace thereafter did in fact experience a substantial increase in asbestos claims that eventually drove the company into bankruptcy.

Asbestos claimants filed suit against Grace seeking to set aside the sale under the Uniform Fraudulent Conveyances Act, arguing that Grace was insolvent at the time of the conveyance (or became insolvent as a result thereof) based on unasserted asbestos injury claims that were filed after the date of transfer. By 1998, the harmful nature of asbestos in general and Grace's asbestos liability in particular were nationally known and had been so for decades. Grace averaged about 31,500 asbestos claims per year from 1995 through 1998. In 2000, Grace received about 48,700 claims. Grace filed bankruptcy in April 2001 due to asbestos-related liabilities.

Grace argued that the liabilities that should be considered to determine its solvency on the transaction date were those that were known on that date or those that the debtor reasonably should have known about at that time. The plaintiffs argued that Grace's insolvency should instead be determined by Grace's actual liabilities on the transaction date, net of assets, and that what Grace may have known about those liabilities, reasonably or otherwise, was

---

5 281 B.R. 852 (Bankr. D. Del. 2002).

irrelevant. The court sided with the plaintiffs in holding that the determination of Grace's solvency must be based on objective reality of whether Grace was in fact insolvent at the time of the transfer, and not on what Grace might reasonably have estimated its liabilities to be.

The statute in question defined *debt,* for purposes of determining solvency under the balance-sheet measure of insolvency, as a *liability on a claim*. The court reasoned that of the tens of thousands of persons making claims for asbestos personal injury against Grace after the 1998 transfer date, substantial numbers of them had viable claims against the company prior to that time. Asbestos had not been manufactured or employed in industry for many years before 1998, so any person with a post-1998 claim must have been exposed long before the transfer date. Moreover, the fact that such exposure could lead to long-term, serious health effects with long latency periods had been common knowledge for 20 to perhaps 30 years. Consequently, the court found that the post-1998 claimants possessed a right to payment (in other words, a *claim*) for solvency purposes, on the transaction date even though they did not assert their claims until later.

The court rejected Grace's contention that the post-1998 claims were contingent and thus subject to discounting by the reasonable probability that the contingency would not arise. The court stated that "a contingent claim is one in which the debtor will be called upon to pay only upon the occurrence or happening of an extrinsic event. To say that the act of making the [formal legal] claim was the extrinsic event stretches the meaning of that phrase too far; the formal claim is not extrinsic to the underlying liability, nor is it an event creating liability where none existed before."[6] Because the unasserted asbestos claims against Grace were not contingent, the court found that it was inappropriate, in assessing Grace's solvency, to discount the value of such claims based on the probability that such claims would be filed.

In conclusion, the court in *Sealed Air* determined that, notwithstanding a contrary Louisiana bankruptcy court decision from just five months earlier,[7] it was entitled to consider in hindsight information regarding Grace's post-1998 asbestos injury claims experience in order to conduct a fair and accurate assessment of Grace's solvency as of the 1998 transfer date. By contrast, the *Babcock* court refused to apply hindsight, instead finding that the transferor's efforts to estimate its asbestos liability were reasonable, notwithstanding posttransaction events confirming errors in the calculations.[8]

The important point for corporate boards and management is that off-balance-sheet environmental liabilities, including hidden, understated, or even incurred but not reported (IBNR) loss contingencies, can render a company insolvent and can potentially result in personal liability for corporate decision makers.

---

6 *Id.* at 863.

7 Official Asbestos Claimants' Comm. v. Babcock & Wilcox Co., 274 B.R. 230 (Bankr. E.D. La. 2002).

8 For more information on judicial determinations of the solvency of financially distressed businesses, *see* Aczel, Alisa H., *The Solvency of Mass Tort Defendants: A "Reasonable" Approach to Valuing Future Claims,* 20 Emory Bankr. Dev. J. 531 (2004).

2.3 FINANCIAL REPORTING STANDARDS

Financial accounting standards guide public issuers and private entities in presenting environmental financial information in a manner that fairly presents the financial condition and results of operations of the enterprise. For public issuers, adherence to GAAP is mandatory. Similarly, adherence to GAAP is necessary for a broad range of nonpublic entities that are required to have audited financial statements.

Chapter 4 provides an overview of environmental financial reporting and identifies the aspects of GAAP that pertain to environmental financial information. Part Two of this book provides a detailed discussion of applicable financial accounting standards.

Although the federal securities laws compel public issuers to adhere to GAAP, such adherence for purposes of environmental financial reporting relies largely on interpretations of environmental laws. As set forth in Exhibit 2.3, whether an environmental matter is subject to presentation in the financial statements under GAAP or applicable SEC disclosure rules often rests an interpretation of applicable environmental laws and extrapolation from the scientific inquiries and data that may have been created as a result of such laws.

Exhibit 2.3

Relationship of Environmental Law to Financial Reporting Standards

Reporting Standard	Environmental Legal Issues
FASB Statement of Financial Accounting Standards No. 5, *"Accounting for Contingencies"*	Probability that a liability has been incurred because of pollution conditions
	Estimation of monetary award in pending environmental legal proceedings
FASB Statement of Financial Accounting Standards No. 143, *"Accounting for Asset Retirement Obligations"*	Determination of legal obligations under environmental laws associated with the retirement of long-lived assets
	Probability and timing of settlement of legal obligations
FASB Statement of Financial Accounting Standards No. 144, *"Accounting for the Impairment or Disposal of Long-Lived Assets"*	Determination of events or conditions indicating a potential environmental impairment
FASB Interpretation No. 39, *"Offsetting of Amounts Related to Certain Contracts"*	Determination of whether a right of recovery applicable to an environmental liability constitutes a right of setoff
Regulation S-K, Item 101 "Description of Business"	Determination of the applicability and impact of new environmental regulations
Regulation S-K, 103 "Legal Proceedings"	Determination of "proceeding" and "sanctions" under environmental law
Regulation S-K, Item 303 "Management Discussion & Analysis"	Assessment of potential impact of known environmental legal trends, events, and uncertainties

In practice, the interrelationship of financial reporting standards, environmental legal determinations, and environmental technical information often reveals the need for a clear delineation of roles and responsibilities among an entity's independent auditors, legal counsel, and environmental specialists. For example, the determination of if and how to report a contingent environmental liability often requires the effective collaboration of all three groups:

1. Legal counsel must determine the likelihood that an asserted claim will result in an unsuccessful outcome;
2. Environmental scientists, engineers, and financial experts must work with legal counsel to estimate the amount of a probable loss; and
3. The entity's accountants and independent auditor must determine whether the amount of the loss, either individually or when combined with the entity's other environmental liabilities, is material (see § 12.2).

The failure of any one of these parties to adequately fulfill its respective role puts the other parties and the reporting entity at risk of failing to meet the entity's financial reporting objectives. This simple example highlights the critical need for effective interdisciplinary coordination. The general lack of such coordination represents one of the primary risks to achieving corporate and public policy objectives for accurate and complete financial reporting of environmental liabilities and risks.

Because of the close interrelationship of the financial accounting standards applicable to environmental financial reporting and environmental laws, reporting entities and their financial auditors must have a basic understanding of U.S. environmental law, a topic addressed in the next chapter.

CHAPTER THREE

Environmental Laws

3.1 INTRODUCTION

For purposes of environmental financial reporting, environmental laws can be divided into two principal categories: (1) laws governing the ongoing or future release of pollutants to the environment (pollution control laws), and (2) laws governing the cleanup of historical pollution conditions (pollution remediation laws). The federal Clean Water Act and Clean Air Act, the operational components of the Resource Conservation and Recovery Act (RCRA), and the Toxic Substances Control Act (TSCA) are examples of pollution control laws. The federal Comprehensive Environmental Response, Compensation, and Liability Act

(CERCLA or Superfund) and the remedial components of RCRA, along with their state counterparts, are the primary pollution remediation laws.

Environmental laws can give rise to significant monetary costs in several different ways, including:

- Capital expenditures and operating expenses required to achieve and maintain compliance with pollution control laws.
- Fines and penalties for violations of pollution control laws.
- Cleanup costs imposed under pollution remediation laws.
- Increased raw material and energy costs.
- Restrictions on product mix and operating throughput.

Such costs can have a significant adverse effect on an entity's financial condition and results of operations. In addition, many federal and state environmental laws permit government agencies to issue orders requiring violators to comply with a statutory or regulatory obligation or cease and desist the illegal activity.

Exhibit 3.1 lists various penalties and assessments that may be imposed under the major U.S. environmental laws.

The original statutory penalty amounts shown in Exhibit 3.1 have been subsequently adjusted upwards for inflation pursuant to the EPA's Civil Monetary Penalty Inflation Adjustment Rule, as mandated by the Debt Collection

EXHIBIT 3.1

Penalties for Noncompliance with Environmental Laws

Statute	Civil Penalties and Assessments	Criminal Penalties and Other Remedies
CERCLA	$25,000 per day per violation for specified provisions Natural resource damages up to $50 million	Remediation orders Contribution for cleanup costs $250,000 and/or imprisonment up to five years
Clean Air Act	$25,000 per day per violation	$25,000 per day per violation and/or imprisonment up to two years
Clean Water Act	$25,000 per day of noncompliance Cost of restoring or replacing damaged natural resources	$50,000 per day per violation and/or imprisonment up to six years $250,000 and/or imprisonment up to 15 years for knowing endangerment
RCRA	$25,000 per day per violation	$50,000 per day per violation and/or imprisonment up to two years $250,000 and/or imprisonment up to 15 years for knowing endangerment
TSCA	$25,000 per day per violation	$25,000 per day per violation and/or imprisonment up to one year

Improvement Act of 1996. 40 CFR 1 19.4 Table 1 (Civil Monetary Penalty Inflation Adjustments) provides a list of all of the applicable statutory penalty provisions and current maximum civil penalties.

3.2 POLLUTION REMEDIATION LAWS

The primary federal environmental remediation provisions are contained in CERCLA and the corrective action provisions of the RCRA. The remediation provisions in CERCLA apply to historical pollution conditions at operating facilities and facilities that are abandoned or inactive, and sudden and accidental pollution conditions (e.g., spills) at operating facilities or along transportation routes. A typical Superfund site is an abandoned hazardous waste landfill that accepted wastes from hundreds or thousands of companies over a period of many years.

(a) SUPERFUND

Congress enacted CERCLA in 1980 to facilitate remediation at facilities where certain hazardous substances were known or suspected to be located by establishing a program to:

- Identify contaminated sites;
- Ensure the cleanup of contaminated sites by responsible parties or the government;
- Create a procedure for parties that have cleaned up sites or spent money to restore natural resources to recover costs from other responsible parties;
- Compensate the United States, states, municipalities, and tribes for damages to natural resources; and
- Using a $1.6 billion trust fund (the Superfund), cover the costs associated with orphan sites and costs incurred while the Environmental Protection Agency (EPA) seeks reimbursement from responsible parties.

Costs imposed under CERCLA include cleanup costs and natural resource damages (see § 3.2(a)(viii)). CERCLA imposes liability for cleanup costs and natural resource damages on the following four classes of potentially responsible parties (PRPs):

1. Current owners or operators of sites at which hazardous substances have been disposed of or abandoned.
2. Previous owners or operators of sites at the time of disposal of hazardous substances.
3. Parties that arranged for disposal of hazardous substances found at the sites.
4. Parties that transported hazardous substances to a site, having selected the site for treatment or disposal.

(i) CERCLA LIABILITY

The liability scheme under CERCLA is dramatically different from traditional common law and statutory liability schemes. CERCLA is characterized by the way in which it imposes strict, retroactive, and joint and several liability on persons deemed to be responsible for environmental contamination.

(A) Strict Liability

Generally, a plaintiff in a bodily injury or property damage suit must prove that the defendant was *at fault* (e.g., that the defendant was negligent or acted in bad faith) before a court will award damages. This would be difficult in many Superfund cases because wastes may have been deposited decades ago, and the records and memories of witnesses are often unreliable. Under CERCLA, the plaintiff need only prove that the defendant falls within one (or more) of the four categories of responsible parties defined by the statute. CERCLA liability is imposed regardless of whether a party was negligent, whether the site was in compliance with environmental laws at the time of the disposal, or whether the party participated in or benefited from the deposit of the hazardous substances. Liability for cleanup costs and natural resource damages under CERCLA is unrelated to regulatory compliance.

(B) Retroactive Liability

In the case of the first federal Superfund site, Love Canal, all the waste was dumped long before CERCLA was passed in 1980. Nevertheless, the *release* of that waste into the environment was ongoing and caused harm after the statute was enacted. *Retroactive liability* means that parties found responsible for causing a release are liable even if their actions occurred prior to the enactment of CERCLA. Congress intended that the parties responsible for creating the problem should pay for cleaning it up, whether or not those actions occurred before CERCLA.

(C) Joint and Several Liability

Under the doctrine of joint and several liability, each PRP is potentially liable for the entire cost of cleanup, and it is the responsibility of the PRPs to allocate shares of liability among themselves. This doctrine is intended to assure that the PRPs, not the public, will bear the risk of any uncertainty over who was responsible for which part of the harm. Notwithstanding the general applicability of the doctrine of joint and several liability, there are various circumstances in which the Superfund liability of a PRP may be limited to a fraction of the total response costs or avoided altogether.

Statutory defenses to CERCLA liability are limited. They include acts of God, acts of war (which might or might not include an act of environmental terrorism, but not a response to an act of war, such as the manufacturing of munitions), and, in limited circumstances, acts or omissions of a third party. CERCLA also has long contained a defense available to innocent landowners who acquired contaminated properties without knowing or having had reason to know about the existence of the contamination.

In 2002, President Bush signed into law the Small Business Liability Relief and Brownfields Revitalization Act (Brownfields Amendments), which amends various provisions of CERCLA. The Brownfields Amendments modify the existing innocent landowner defense and create two new exemptions from CERCLA liability, the contiguous property exemption and the bona fide prospective purchaser exemption. It also imposes limitations on the EPA's ability to pursue enforcement actions on sites remediated under a state brownfields cleanup program (see § 3.2(f)). The liability relief provided by the Brownfields Amendments applies only to CERCLA liability and does not protect a developer against liability arising from other sources, such as RCRA (e.g., leaking petroleum underground storage tanks), TSCA (e.g., PCB contamination), state Superfund laws, and common law tort actions for bodily injury and property damage.

The Brownfields Amendments modify the existing innocent landowner defense to prescribe more detailed and prescriptive eligibility requirements that include both preacquisition threshold criteria and continuing postacquisition obligations. These common elements apply equally to the innocent landowner, contiguous property, and bona fide prospective purchaser liability exemptions. The common elements are described in § 3.2(a)(ii).

The innocent landowner defense applies in situations in which the party "did not know or had no reason to know" of contamination.[1] This defense applies to the landowner who appropriately investigated the site prior to acquisition, failed to find contamination, and then later discovered contamination from a latent source.

Before enactment of the Brownfields Amendments, no liability exemption was available to developers who investigated a site, found contamination, and nonetheless elected to purchase the property. The Brownfields Amendments added a new liability exemption to CERCLA to address this class of bona fide prospective purchasers. To qualify as a bona fide prospective purchaser, the party must demonstrate that it satisfied certain preacquisition threshold criteria as well as certain postacquisition continuing obligations.

If a party qualifies as a bona fide prospective purchaser, mere ownership of the property is insufficient to establish CERCLA liability. However, there is a twist designed to prevent a prospective purchaser from reaping a financial benefit as a result of buying property below market value, satisfying the elements of the defense, taking advantage of an EPA cleanup at the property, and realizing a profit on resale of the property. This windfall lien provision provides that when the United States incurs response costs at a facility for which an owner is not liable because of the bona fide prospective purchaser exemption, the United States will have a lien on such property for its unrecovered response costs. The lien arises at the time the EPA first incurs the response costs and continues until the response costs are paid or the lien is satisfied by sale or other means. The amount of the lien cannot exceed the increase in fair market value of the property attributable to the response action at the facility.

The Brownfields Amendments also created a new contiguous property exemption, which codifies EPA's preexisting contaminated aquifer policy. The

---

[1] 42 U.S.C. § 9601(35(A)(i).

new liability exemption provides that a party with property contiguous to or otherwise similarly situated with respect to a contaminated property will not be liable for contamination that migrates onto the party's property if the party can demonstrate that it satisfied the threshold criteria and continuing obligations.

Although the Brownfields Amendments provided significant liability relief under CERCLA, the new liability exemptions do not entirely eliminate the strict, joint and several, and retroactive liability scheme for owners and operators of contaminated properties, for the following reasons:

- The new CERCLA defenses are not a defense to liability under the remediation provisions of RCRA or other federal environmental laws.
- The Brownfields Amendments provide no relief from liability under state Superfund laws, many of which also impose strict, joint and several, and retroactive liability.
- The defenses under CERCLA never relieve the actual polluter from liability.
- Qualification for the various defenses under CERCLA requires adherence to the common elements requirements described in the next section. The continuing nature of these obligations is in effect a form of continuing liability.

(ii) *COMMON ELEMENTS*

(A) Threshold Criteria

To qualify as a bona fide prospective purchaser, contiguous property owner, or innocent landowner, a person must perform *all appropriate inquiry* before acquiring the property. Bona fide prospective purchasers and contiguous property owners must, in addition, demonstrate that they are not potentially liable or affiliated with any other person that is potentially liable for response costs at the property. Bona fide prospective purchasers may acquire property with knowledge of contamination, after performing all appropriate inquiry, and maintain their protection from liability. In contrast, knowledge, or reason to know, of contamination prior to purchase defeats the contiguous property owner liability protection and the innocent landowner liability defense.

The Brownfields Amendments specify the inquiry standard to be applied. Purchasers of property before May 31, 1997, must take into account such things as commonly known information about the property, the value of the property if clean, the defendant's ability to detect contamination, and other similar criteria. For property purchased on or after May 31, 1997, the procedures set forth in ASTM Standard E 1527, "Standard Practice for Environmental Site Assessments: Phase 1 Environmental Site Assessment Process," are to be used. The Brownfields Amendments require the EPA to promulgate a regulation containing standards and practices for all appropriate inquiry and to set out criteria that must be addressed in EPA regulation.

(B) Continuing Obligations

The bona fide prospective purchaser, contiguous property owner, and innocent landowner defenses to CERCLA liability are conditional on compliance with continuing postacquisition obligations. Those continuing obligations require the party claiming the defense to demonstrate that it has:

- Complied with land use restrictions and institutional controls;
- Undertaken reasonable steps with respect to hazardous substance releases (i.e., stop continuing releases; prevent threatened future releases; and prevent or limit human, environmental, or natural resource exposure to hazardous substances);
- Provided full cooperation, assistance, and access to persons that are authorized to conduct response actions or natural resource restoration;
- Complied with information requests and administrative subpoenas; and
- Provided all legally required notices.

Failure to demonstrate compliance with any one of these requirements could make the party ineligible for the bona fide prospective purchaser, contiguous property owner, or innocent landowner defenses.

(iii) ENFORCEMENT

CERCLA provides the EPA with several powerful enforcement tools. Most significant is the EPA's power to issue a unilateral administrative order to PRPs requiring them to take a response action at a site where there is an imminent and substantial endangerment to the public health or welfare or the environment because of an actual or threatened release of hazardous substances.

Whereas the existence of historical pollution conditions is not, in and of itself, a violation of CERCLA, failure to respond to an EPA order is a legal violation. A respondent that fails to perform the response action or fails to report as required under CERCLA is potentially subject to penalties of $25,000 per day. In addition, if the EPA performs the action, it may recover treble damages. Judicial review of an EPA administrative order is not available until after the remedy is implemented, money is spent, and the EPA commences an enforcement action for cost recovery. Thus, even a party with a reasonably good defense to liability takes great risk in not complying with an EPA cleanup order.

(iv) HAZARDOUS SUBSTANCES

Hazardous substances include a much broader scope of materials than hazardous wastes under RCRA (see § 3.3(a)). Hazardous substances are not necessarily wastes; in fact, they are often integral components of materials widely used in nonindustrial applications. For example, perchloroethylene (PERC), a substance commonly used in dry cleaning, is a hazardous substance and a pervasive source of groundwater contamination in urban and suburban areas. Hazardous substances include substances identified in EPA regulations promulgated pursuant to a number of federal statutes, including the Clean Water Act and the Clean Air Act. EPA regulations list more than 1,000 chemicals and chemical compounds that are considered hazardous substances under CERCLA.

Petroleum and any derivative or fraction thereof that is not specifically listed or designated as a hazardous substance are specifically excluded from the definition of *hazardous substance* under CERCLA. Also excluded are natural gas, natural gas liquids, liquefied natural gas, and synthetic gas of pipeline quality. Discharges of petroleum substances into the surface waters or shorelines of the United States are covered under several other federal laws, but are exempt from CERCLA. This *petroleum exclusion* does not extend to nonindigenous materials added to petroleum products. For example, lead (a hazardous substance) that is added to gasoline would not be covered by the petroleum exclusion because it is not an indigenous constituent of petroleum.

(v) SUPERFUND SITES AND BROWNFIELDS

The effects of CERCLA's strict, retroactive, and joint and several liability extend far beyond the most seriously contaminated sites listed on the National Priorities List (NPL). CERCLA, and corresponding state Superfund laws, effectively cast a cloud of liability across any property impacted by historical pollution conditions—including multiparty waste disposal sites, abandoned and operating industrial facilities, and commercial/retail properties, such as strip shopping centers affected by a release of dry cleaning solvents.

Fear of CERCLA liability has discouraged the investigation, sale, financing, and redevelopment of brownfields by the private sector. In the real estate context, *brownfields* are previously developed sites (as opposed to undeveloped *greenfield* sites). In the environmental context, *brownfields* are sites with low-level contamination that are not listed on the NPL. *Brownfields* are defined under CERCLA as abandoned, idled, or underused industrial and commercial sites where expansion or redevelopment is complicated by real or perceived historical pollution conditions that might add cost, time, or uncertainty to a redevelopment project. The EPA estimates that there are more than 400,000 brownfields in the United States.

Under CERCLA, a new owner could potentially be held liable for environmental contamination that occurred long ago. With such potentially costly and ambiguous liability, businesses often choose the safety of suburban locations over inner-city brownfields. Inconsistencies between state and federal environmental laws governing brownfield redevelopment projects further discourage private investment.

Current owners of brownfield sites sometimes choose to mothball these properties as a means of avoiding transactions, conditions, or events that might trigger obligations under environmental laws to investigate known or reasonably suspected historical pollution conditions, report these conditions to federal and state regulators, and incur uncertain costs for environmental cleanup. Moreover, owners of contaminated sites may be justifiably distrustful of a buyer's promise to remediate the site following the sale; despite such promises, past owners generally remain jointly and severally liable for cleanup costs under state and federal remediation laws. As a result of the disincentives to current owners, market supply of contaminated properties has not kept pace with market demand.

Even as shortages of prime urban real estate are forcing businesses and families to move to greenfield developments in the suburbs, inner-city brownfields are remaining idle. The adverse results include urban blight and suburban sprawl. The Brownfields Amendments and EPA's Brownfields program are designed to promote the cleanup and economic redevelopment of brownfields. An important issue is whether the owners of these brownfields—often publicly traded U.S. corporations—are fully disclosing in their financial reports the environmental obligations associated with these properties. As government and societal pressure builds to address the growing brownfields problem, owners of these sites can expect to see increasing pressure for full financial disclosure.

(vi) SUPERFUND REMEDIATION PROCESS

Superfund site cleanups are conducted under the procedures contained in the National Oil and Hazardous Substances Pollution Contingency Plan,[2] typically referred to as the National Contingency Plan (NCP). The NCP is a highly structured process governing every aspect of the investigation and cleanup. Exhibit 3.2 depicts the typical stages of this process.

The detailed discussion of the Superfund cleanup process that follows is provided as background for the discussion in Chapter 20 regarding estimation of environmental remediation liabilities. The Superfund cleanup process has little or no relevance to the measurement of other types of environmental liabilities (e.g., environmental loss contingencies, asset retirement obligations, and asset impairments).

(A) Site Identification and Screening

Beginning in 1981, the EPA identified more than 30,000 sites for scrutiny based on reports, filed pursuant to section 103(c) of CERCLA, in which companies disclosed locations where they had disposed of hazardous substances. This information formed the basis for a database called the Comprehensive Environmental Response, Compensation, and Liability Information System (CERCLIS).

EXHIBIT 3.2

Superfund Remediation Process

Listing of Site on NPL
Possible Removal Action
Remedial Investigation
Risk Assessment
Feasibility Study
Selection of Remedial Action Plan
Public Comment and ROD
Remedial Design
Remedial Action
Operation/ Maintenance *(Including Postremediation Monitoring)*
PRP Identification and Allocation...
Government Oversight...

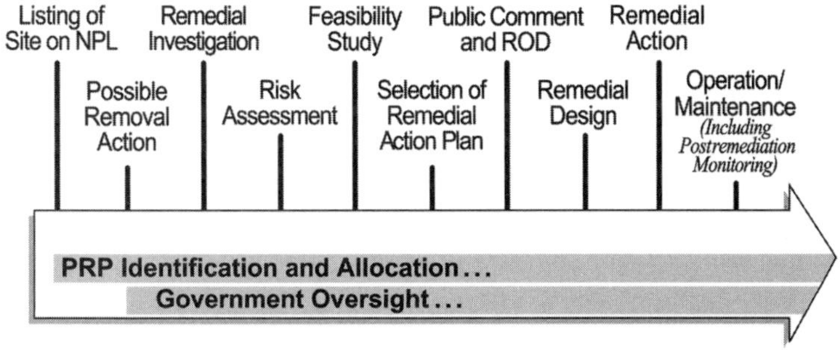

2 40 C.F.R. § 300.

Each site in the CERCLIS database has undergone or will undergo a preliminary assessment of available information as a first step in determining what, if any, response action is needed at the site. Based on this information, the EPA determines whether further investigation is warranted to rank the site according to the Hazard Ranking System.

The Hazard Ranking System is a mathematical rating scheme that considers the probability of a release to cause harm to human health or the environment and the severity or magnitude of the potential harm. Using the numerical scores from this scheme, the EPA and states prioritize sites and allocate resources for further investigation, enforcement, and remediation. Sites receiving high scores are proposed for inclusion on the NPL.

(B) Removal Action

Sites presenting an imminent and substantial endangerment to public health or the environment may require a removal action. A removal action is a relatively short term response. In such cases, the EPA may undertake, or order PRPs to undertake, appropriate action to prevent, abate, stabilize, mitigate, or eliminate a release or threatened release of hazardous substances. Sites need not be on the NPL for the EPA to undertake or order removal actions.

(C) Remedial Investigation

The remedial investigation (RI) is a comprehensive study performed by environmental scientists and engineers that is intended to delineate the nature and extent of hazardous substances at a site and to assess potential risks to human health and the environment. The RI usually involves extensive sampling of soil and groundwater.

(D) Feasibility Study

A feasibility study (FS) is generally performed simultaneously with the RI in an iterative process. The FS uses the information generated by the RI to evaluate alternative remedial actions. The FS:

- Identifies a list of potential remedial alternatives;
- Estimates the cost of each remedial alternative;
- Screens the remedial alternatives for their ability to meet technical, public health, and environmental requirements in a reasonable time frame given available technologies; and
- Completes a detailed analysis of the screened alternatives with respect to various criteria established by the EPA.

A baseline risk assessment often is performed during the RI/FS phase. A site-specific baseline risk assessment quantifies the risk posed by the site. The reduction in risk attained by each remedial system is measured and overall risk is reassessed as part of the process.

The RI/FS phase generally takes a minimum of two years to complete and, depending on factors such as the types of hazardous substances, soil formations, and number of PRPs involved, may take more than five years and cost in excess of $1 million.

(E) Remedial Action Plan

Once the RI/FS is complete, a remedial plan is selected for cleanup of the site. In selecting a remedial program, the EPA first decides what cleanup standards are to be applied to the site. The selected remedy must achieve cleanup standards derived from applicable or relevant and appropriate requirements (ARARs). The cost of achieving alternative cleanup standards is not considered. After setting the target cleanup standards, the EPA then identifies which remediation methods can achieve the standards. Finally, the EPA specifies which of the alternative remediation methods is most cost-effective.

(F) Public Comment and Record of Decision

EPA makes the proposed remedial action plan (PRAP) available to interested parties for public comment. After reviewing any public comments received, the EPA modifies the remedial plan, if necessary, and issues a record of decision (ROD), which specifies both the remedy and the time frame in which the remedy is to be implemented. The ROD is part of a written administrative record documenting the basis of the EPA's remedy selection.

(G) Remedial Design

Following issuance of the ROD, the site enters the remedial design phase. This phase includes development of a complete site remediation plan, including engineering drawings and specifications for the site remediation.

(H) Remedial Action

The remedial action phase involves actual construction and implementation of the remedial design. The remedial action phase can last years and cost millions of dollars.

(I) Operation and Maintenance

After the remedial action is completed, activities must be conducted at the site to ensure that the remedy is effective and operating properly. For example, after a system to pump and treat groundwater is constructed (remedial action), the system must be operated and maintained. In addition, the EPA may require post-remediation monitoring. These operation and maintenance activities may continue for decades.

(J) Government Oversight

CERCLA grants the President of the United States broad latitude to respond to actual or threatened releases of hazardous substances. The president in turn has delegated this authority principally to the EPA for protection of land, groundwater, and surface water. The EPA thus oversees and controls each step of the remediation process.

(vii) PRP INVOLVEMENT

The identification and allocation of costs among PRPs is an ongoing process over the course of the remediation process, and sometimes beyond. Specific stages of PRP involvement do not necessarily correspond to specific stages of the cleanup process.

(A) Notification of Involvement

A company may first learn of its potential involvement in a Superfund site through the appearance of the site on a government list such as the NPL, in the CERCLIS database, or on a state priorities list. More often, an entity learns of its involvement when it receives an information request, known as a *Section 104(e) Request*, from the EPA regarding wastes the company may have sent to a designated site. Full-scale Superfund involvement generally does not begin until a company is notified by the EPA that it is a PRP. The EPA may do this in several ways:

- Issue a Notice Letter to all PRPs indicating that Superfund-related action is to be undertaken at a site for which the recipient is considered a PRP.
- Issue a Special Notice Letter to PRPs stating that the EPA intends to initiate work at the site or issue an administrative order to force the PRPs to take response actions at the site unless the PRPs commit within a specified period (typically 60 to 120 days) to take response actions. The Special Notice Letter provides the names and addresses of other PRPs (to facilitate negotiations among the parties), and it may include a draft of a consent decree for each party to share in the costs or assume the responsibility for performing an investigation of the site. The EPA also normally includes information about the nature of the material at the waste site and any knowledge it has obtained about the amount of waste contributed by each party.
- Summon all targeted PRPs to a meeting to discuss possible actions at a given site.

Depending on the evidence it has collected to that point, the EPA may not be aware of all PRPs. In such situations, CERCLA authorizes the EPA to bring enforcement action against one or more identified PRPs, thereby shifting the burden to those parties to find and seek cost recovery from others who may also be liable. PRPs are generally prohibited under Superfund from obtaining immediate judicial review of EPA decisions identifying them as liable or requiring them to take response actions. Judicial review generally is available only after the EPA decides to bring an enforcement action for cost recovery, long after the remedy has been implemented.

(B) Negotiation

Once notified, PRPs at a multiparty site face the difficult task of organizing among themselves to negotiate with the government. If the PRPs are unable to reach an agreement to carry out the investigation or remedial work, the EPA has the power to clean up the site itself and sue for full reimbursement of cleanup costs. The 60- to 120-day period allowed by the Special Notice Letter is intended to give multiple PRPs sufficient time to organize and to make a good faith offer to the government to perform the requested response actions.

Negotiations often take place in stages. For example, PRPs may agree to share the costs of the RI/FS while continuing to negotiate how and whether to address the remediation itself. Such preliminary cost-sharing agreements often are based on the volume of waste contributed to a site by each party (without regard to the relative toxicity of the waste or associated response action costs), with an understanding that the allocation may subsequently be revised as additional information about the site becomes available.

The negotiation process ultimately results in one of three outcomes:

1. *Negotiated settlement*. The parties and the EPA can agree on who will clean up the site and how much each party will pay. One or more minor participants may negotiate a *de minimis* settlement with the EPA in which they agree to pay their shares, usually with an agreement from the EPA that they are relieved of their liability at the time of settlement. Such shares typically include some kind of premium over the settling contributor's fair share. A *de minimis* settlement saves the PRP from incurring further legal fees, and it is the closest thing available to a final cash settlement.

   For the EPA to be receptive to a *de minimis* settlement, one of the following conditions generally must be met: (1) both the amount and the toxicity or hazardous properties of substances the PRP contributed are minimal in comparison to other hazardous substances at the site; or (2) the PRP is a current or past owner of the site, did not allow generation, transportation, storage, treatment, or disposal of any hazardous substance at the site, did not contribute to the release or threat of release at the site, and did not purchase the property knowing that it had been used for generation, transportation, storage, treatment, or disposal of any hazardous substances.

   Further, *de minimis* settlements typically occur only when a participant's share of the liability is less than 1 percent. Moreover, the EPA typically is unwilling to commit time and resources to negotiate with *de minimis* contributors individually. *De minimis* settlements therefore generally must take place as part of negotiations with the larger PRP group or with a separate group of *de minimis* contributors.

   PRPs usually establish and contribute to a trust fund, from which an independent contractor is paid to do the RI/FS and remedial work. The contractor's work typically is overseen by a technical committee of the contributing PRPs and by either a finance committee of those PRPs or a management firm hired by the trust. PRPs seldom perform the RI/FS or remedial work themselves.

2. *Unilateral administrative order*. In the absence of a negotiated settlement, the EPA can issue a unilateral administrative order under section 106 of CERCLA to compel one or more PRPs to clean up a site where there may

be an imminent and substantial endangerment to human health or the environment because of actual or threatened contamination.

3. *Cost recovery*. Alternatively, the EPA can investigate and clean up the site using money from the Superfund and then seek recovery of its costs from PRPs under section 107 of CERCLA. To obtain reimbursement, the EPA issues letters to PRPs demanding payment for its response costs (costs of removal, remediation, and enforcement action). If these letters do not result in settlement, the EPA can seek reimbursement in the courts by referring the case to the Department of Justice.

(C) Cost Recovery Litigation

PRPs that participate in the remediation can, and generally do, bring legal claims to recover costs against PRPs that did not participate in the cleanup—assuming those parties can be found and are solvent. Responsible parties that pay response costs as the result of an EPA enforcement action under Superfund may sue other responsible parties to recover at least a part of such costs. In resolving such suits, courts are authorized by CERCLA to apportion liability for response costs among responsible parties using such equitable factors as the court determines are appropriate. A private party that has not been sued by the EPA under CERCLA may not be entitled to recover voluntary cleanup costs from other PRPs under CERCLA.[3]

(viii) NATURAL RESOURCE DAMAGES

Lawsuits by government agencies to impose liability for *natural resource damages* under CERCLA and corresponding state Superfund laws are becoming increasingly common. For example, in May 2004, New Jersey filed ten natural resource damage complaints under the state's Spill Compensation and Control Act, in what the state attorney general said was the first round in an unprecedented initiative to make responsible parties compensate the residents of New Jersey for damage to or loss of natural resources due to pollution. The viability of these claims remains uncertain.

Like many state Superfund laws, CERCLA authorizes the recovery of damages for injury to, destruction of, or loss of natural resources, including reasonable costs for assessing such injury resulting from a release of a hazardous substance. Under CERCLA, *natural resources* are defined as land, fish, wildlife, biota, air, water, groundwater, drinking water supplies, and other such resources belonging to, managed or held in trust by, or otherwise controlled by the United States, state or local governments, foreign governments, or Indian tribes. Natural resource damage claims against PRPs may include restoration costs, lost use values, and, in some cases, nonuse values, such as the intrinsic public value of protecting or restoring resources that may not be used but are valuable for their mere existence. Monetary awards for natural resource damage liability can run into the millions of dollars. For example, in 2003, the state of New Jersey reached a $17 million set-

[3] Cooper Indus., Inc. v. Aviall Servs., Inc., No. 02-1192 125 S.Ct. 577 (2004) (holding that a PRP conducting a voluntary cleanup cannot seek contribution under CERCLA § 113(f)(1)).

tlement with three major corporations for environmental damages caused by chromium contamination throughout two counties.

(ix) RELEASE REPORTING

The CERCLA hazardous substance release reporting regulations[4] are intended to ensure an appropriate response to sudden and accidental pollution conditions (e.g., accidental spills), thereby minimizing harm to people and the environment. CERCLA directs the person in charge of a facility to report to the National Response Center (NRC) as soon as that person has knowledge of any environmental release of a listed hazardous substance exceeding a specified threshold quantity. The hazardous substances and reportable quantities are defined and listed in 40 C.F.R. § 302.4. The report of such a release may trigger responses by one or more federal, state, and local emergency response agencies.

Although CERCLA imposes immediate reporting obligations in the event of a spill, there is no threshold quantity to create liability for cleanup costs and natural resource damages associated with historical releases. For example, discarding industrial equipment on which there is leaded paint may not trigger a reporting obligation, but if that equipment is discovered at a Superfund site, the responsible party could be required to pay some or all of the cleanup costs required to remediate the site.

(b) REMEDIATION PROVISIONS IN RCRA

In addition to its "cradle-to-grave" pollution control provisions for hazardous wastes (see § 3.3(a)), the Resource Conservation and Recovery Act also authorizes the EPA to conduct removal actions, seek affirmative injunctive relief, and maintain cost recovery actions when an imminent and substantial endangerment to the public health or welfare or to the environment is found to exist. As with CERCLA, companies that have contributed to the disposal of waste that is causing an imminent and substantial endangerment can be required to perform or pay for cleanup under section 7003 of RCRA.

The 1984 Hazardous and Solid Waste Amendments to RCRA (HSWA) expanded owner-operator responsibility for environmental cleanup liability associated with hazardous waste treatment, storage, or disposal facilities (TSDFs). As amended, RCRA requires facilities—whether they continue operating or intend to close—to remedy releases of hazardous wastes. These corrective action provisions of RCRA, which are separate from Superfund, apply only to facilities that are operating under RCRA permits (see § 3.3(a)) or that have applied for such permits. However, because the EPA generally takes the position that the TSDF includes all of the property surrounding the TSDF, from "fencepost to fencepost," permitting of a very small area can subject a much larger, unrelated part of a property to RCRA's corrective action provisions.

RCRA corrective action may be initiated either as part of the RCRA permitting process or through an interim status corrective action order. Interim status is the period during which the owner/operator of a TSDF is treated as having

4 40 CFR Part 302.

been issued a RCRA permit even though a final determination on the permit has not yet been made. Owners/operators of TSDFs in existence on November 19, 1980, or brought under RCRA regulation due to a legislative or regulatory change, may continue to operate as if they have a permit until their permit is issued or denied as long as they comply with applicable requirements. Non-permitted facilities that fail to establish and maintain compliance with interim status requirements also may be subject to corrective action under RCRA.

Corrective action for releases of hazardous waste or its constituents from waste management units, whether they are onsite or offsite, is a condition for obtaining any operating or postclosure RCRA permit. The EPA may also order corrective action while a TSDF is in interim status (before it receives its permit) based on information that there has been a release to the environment from the TSDF. The EPA does not need to demonstrate imminent and substantial endangerment to human health or the environment from a real or threatened release to issue an interim status corrective action order.

Exhibit 3.3 depicts the RCRA corrective action process, which is divided into the following five stages:

1. RCRA facility assessment
2. RCRA facility investigation
3. Interim measures
4. Corrective measures study
5. Corrective measures implementation

The detailed discussion of the RCRA cleanup process that follows is provided as background for the discussion in Chapter 20 regarding estimation of environmental remediation liabilities. The RCRA cleanup process may also be relevant to the measurement of certain types of asset retirement obligations (see Chapter 22).

(i) RCRA FACILITY ASSESSMENT

The RCRA facility assessment (RFA) identifies areas and units at the facility from which hazardous waste or hazardous waste constituents may have been

EXHIBIT 3.3

RCRA Corrective Action Process

Requirement for RCRA Permit
RCRA Facility Investigation
Corrective Measures Study
RCRA Facility Assessment
Interim Measures
Corrective Measures Implementation
Reporting Obligations
Government Oversight . . .

released, and collects all existing information regarding the releases. The RFA may be conducted by the EPA, a delegated state environmental agency, agency contractors, or the facility owner. There is no stage in the Superfund remediation process analogous to the RFA.

(ii) RCRA FACILITY INVESTIGATION

The RCRA facility investigation (RFI) is a detailed investigation to characterize releases of hazardous wastes and constituents to the environment by identifying the environmental setting, characterizing the sources of releases, identifying potential receptors, determining if remediation is necessary, and, if so, collecting data to support the evaluation of remediation alternatives. This stage is analogous to the Superfund remedial investigation stage.

(iii) INTERIM CORRECTIVE MEASURES

Interim corrective measures (ICM) are measures (typically containment) conducted at any time before selection of the final remedy by the environmental agency. This stage is analogous to a removal action under Superfund.

(iv) CORRECTIVE MEASURES STUDY

If the RFI reveals a potential need for corrective measures, the agency requires the owner to perform a corrective measures study (CMS) to identify and recommend specific measures to correct the releases. The CMS assesses possible corrective measures in terms of technical feasibility, ability to protect public health and the environment, and possible adverse environmental effects of the corrective measures. The CMS is analogous to the Superfund feasibility study, although it is usually less complicated.

(v) CORRECTIVE MEASURES IMPLEMENTATION

The corrective measures implementation (CMI) stage includes designing, constructing, operating, maintaining, and monitoring selected corrective measures that have been approved by the EPA or a delegated state environmental agency. This stage combines activities that are often segregated under Superfund as remedial design, remedial action, and operation and maintenance.

(vi) REPORTING AND OVERSIGHT

Beginning with the application for a RCRA permit, owner-operators are required to report to the EPA or a delegated state environmental agency throughout the RCRA corrective action process. The government agency oversees and controls each stage of the process.

(c) UNDERGROUND STORAGE TANKS

The 1984 amendments to RCRA created the Underground Storage Tank (UST) program to address the widespread contamination of soil and groundwater by leaking underground petroleum storage tanks. Because of the petroleum exclusion in CERCLA (see § 3.2(a)(iv)), Congress chose to address the problem under RCRA, which does not contain a similar exclusion. The UST program:

- Requires owners and operators of tank systems used for storage of petroleum and petroleum-based substances and certain other designated hazardous substances to meet technical standards specified by the EPA that are designed to prevent future releases to the environment.
- Imposes cleanup liability for UST releases.
- Establishes financial assurance requirements for closure and postclosure remediation of TSDFs and USTs.

(d) STATE LAWS

Many states have enacted pollution remediation laws that are similar to CERCLA and the remedial provisions of RCRA. Also, under RCRA, delegated states are authorized to promulgate regulations to implement and enforce the federal program, as long as the state regulations are at least as stringent as the federal standards. States are generally free to impose standards more stringent than those under federal law, and some states have done so. For example, unlike CERCLA or RCRA, New Jersey's Industrial Site Recovery Act (ISRA) imposes certain preconditions on the sale, transfer, or closure of "industrial establishments" involved in the generation, manufacture, refining, transportation, treatment, storage, handling, or disposal of hazardous substances or wastes. With certain exceptions, owners of facilities subject to ISRA must identify, investigate, and agree to remediate environmental contamination before they can close a sale or transfer of the facility. ISRA is intended to ensure that a financially responsible party remains on the hook to perform needed remediation after the closing.

(e) FOREIGN LAWS

Most developed and many developing countries have pollution remediation laws in place, some of which are more far-reaching than CERCLA and RCRA. For example, in 2004 the European Union enacted a broad—and controversial—directive aimed at preventing environmental damage by forcing industrial polluters to pay prevention and remediation costs. Levels of enforcement of environmental laws vary widely among different countries.

(f) VOLUNTARY CLEANUP PROGRAMS

Most states have passed brownfields legislation or developed voluntary cleanup programs to encourage and facilitate cleanup and redevelopment of brownfields sites. Specific elements of these programs vary, but there are some common features, including:

- *Liability relief.* Many programs release buyers and lenders from liability for cleanup costs to the state during and following cleanup.

- *Risk-based cleanup standards*. The programs generally include risk-based standards that match cleanup levels to actual exposure pathways and proposed land use (e.g., residential or commercial/industrial).
- *Financial incentives*. Some state programs facilitate use of federal, state, and local financial incentives to encourage redevelopment of brownfields sites. Available incentives include grants, low-interest loans, federal income tax incentives, and state and local property tax abatements.

3.3 POLLUTION CONTROL LAWS

Pollution control laws generally seek to assure a uniform level of environmental performance through permitting, reporting, recordkeeping, inspection, enforcement, and end-of-pipe control technology requirements. Noncompliance with pollution control laws can result in administrative, civil, and criminal enforcement. In extreme cases, noncompliance can result in the temporary or permanent shutdown of operations. Such events can have a material adverse effect on the entity's financial condition. Conversely, compliance with market-based pollution control regulations can give rise to intangible assets that may represent significant value to the enterprise (see Chapter 14).

(a) RCRA

RCRA provides comprehensive federal regulation of hazardous wastes from the point of generation to final disposal. All hazardous waste generators and transporters, as well as owners and operators of hazardous waste TSDFs, must comply with the applicable requirements of RCRA. Less stringent requirements apply to certain small-quantity generators (up to 1,000 kilograms of a waste per month).

For generators of hazardous waste, RCRA requirements include:

- Hazardous waste determination
- Manifest requirements
- Packaging and labeling
- Recordkeeping and annual reporting
- Management standards

The cradle-to-grave management of hazardous wastes under RCRA hinges on the hazardous waste determination, in which the facility determines whether the material it handles is a hazardous waste. A step-by-step identification procedure is prescribed. Initially, one must determine whether the material is a *solid waste*. If so, one must determine whether that solid waste is hazardous. Some wastes that are specified by regulation are automatically deemed hazardous. These are the so-called *listed wastes*. Other wastes must be evaluated to determine whether they exhibit the characteristics of toxicity, corrosivity, reactivity, or ignitability. If so, they too are deemed hazardous.

Exclusions from the definitions of solid and hazardous wastes are provided for wastewaters regulated under the Clean Water Act; certain types of reuse, recycling, and reclamation; and wastes associated with the exploration and production of oil and natural gas.

With some exceptions, a waste generator that accumulates hazardous waste in excess of 90 days or treats the hazardous waste will be deemed the operator of a TSDF and be subject to the comprehensive TSDF regulations. Among other things, these regulations require owners-operators to obtain a permit.

Each TSDF is also subject to specific technical requirements designed to prevent any release of hazardous waste into the environment. These regulations require, for example:

- Containers and tanks must be of sufficient integrity to contain hazardous wastes properly.
- In certain cases, waste containers must be separated or protected by dikes, berms, or walls.
- Surface impoundments, waste piles, and landfills must be equipped with liners to prevent migration of wastes into soil, groundwater, or surface water during the active life of the facility, and must be constructed to prevent runoff or breaks. Groundwater monitoring may be required to confirm the absence of leakage.
- Land treatment units that treat hazardous wastes biologically must ensure that hazardous wastes are degraded, transformed, or immobilized within the treatment zone and do not reach the underlying water table.

RCRA contains provisions for closure of TSDFs and requires financial assurance (e.g., letters of credit, insurance policies, bonds, and demonstration of financial wherewithal) for closure and postclosure obligations. RCRA also contains provisions governing the management of solid (nonhazardous) wastes (e.g., petroleum storage tanks, municipal solid waste landfills).

(b) CLEAN AIR ACT

The federal Clean Air Act comprehensively regulates mobile and stationary sources of air pollution. Under the Clean Air Act, every area of the United States is evaluated for its compliance with the National Primary and Secondary Ambient Air Quality Standards (NAAQS). The EPA has issued NAAQS for six criteria pollutants: sulfur dioxide, particulates, nitrogen dioxide, carbon monoxide, ozone, and lead. In areas where the NAAQS have not been attained, new and significantly modified stationary sources must use available pollution control equipment capable of meeting the lowest achievable emissions rate (LAER). This determination is made without regard to cost. The permittee must also provide emissions offsets, or greater than one-to-one reduction, for any nonattainment pollutant that the source would emit in significant amounts. These offsets must be sufficient to provide a net air quality benefit in the affected area.

In areas that have attained the NAAQS for particular pollutants, new or modified stationary sources that would emit these pollutants in significant amounts must obtain permits under the Prevention of Significant Deterioration (PSD) program. Under the PSD program, a facility emitting air pollutants must apply the best available control technology (BACT). BACT is determined on a case-by-case basis, taking into account energy, environmental, and economic factors and other relevant costs and benefits.

The Clean Air Act also contains new source performance standards (NSPS), which are applicable to newly constructed or modified stationary sources. The NSPS program is designed to ensure that new sources are built with state-of-the-art controls and that when existing sources are modified, new controls are installed. Each NSPS establishes design or performance criteria for a specific source. There are numerous specific industrial facilities and operations for which NSPS have been developed.

Section 107(a) of the Clean Air Act directs that each state "shall have the primary responsibility for assuring air quality within the entire geographic area of such state." To that end, the EPA has developed regulations governing state implementation plans pursuant to which a state assumes Clean Air Act regulation of all mobile and stationary sources within its borders. The Clean Air Act also contains citizen suit provisions that augment government enforcement with citizen enforcement.

In addition to the NAAQS, the Clean Air Act also regulates certain hazardous air pollutants under the National Emission Standards for Hazardous Air Pollutants (NESHAP) program. NESHAP is a set of national emission standards for listed hazardous pollutants emitted from specific classes or categories of new and existing sources.

The Clean Air Act Amendments of 1990 added several market-based incentive programs, including:

- An innovative system of tradable emission allowances for sulfur dioxide.
- Performance-based standards for hazardous pollutants.
- Incentives or credits for companies that act quickly to reduce toxic emissions or go beyond minimum compliance requirements.
- Tradable emission credits for producers of certain kinds of reformulated fuels, for manufacturers of clean-fuel vehicles, and for vehicle fleets subject to clean-fuel requirements.

As discussed in § 4.6(e), market-based programs can give rise to environmental assets.

(c) CLEAN WATER ACT

The Federal Water Pollution Control Act (Clean Water Act) comprehensively regulates all sources of water pollution. The Clean Water Act requires National Pollutant Discharge Elimination System (NPDES) permits on all facilities that discharge pollutants into the waters of the United States. The Clean Water Act utilizes ambient water quality standards to set individual permit limitations and technology-based limitations that, in varying degrees, impose the most cost-effective pollution control technology on dischargers. These include effluent limitations utilizing specified technology, compliance with performance standards, use of specified practices for facility design and operation requirements, use of specified treatment or pretreatment methods, and detailed assessments and evaluations of the impact of proposed discharges. Technology-based effluent limitations provide minimum discharge standards. More stringent water-quality-based limitations may also be imposed when needed to maintain or protect water quality in specific bodies of water.

As with the Clean Air Act, the Clean Water Act imposes more stringent standards on facilities on which construction or modification commenced after publication of applicable regulations. In the promulgation of these standards, the EPA may consider incorporating alternative production processes, operating methods, and in-plant control procedures and other factors. Industrial facilities that discharge into publicly owned treatment works (POTWs) must also meet discharge standards, called *pretreatment standards*, designed to regulate the discharge of pollutants from nonpermitted point sources. In addition, EPA has issued regulations requiring permits for stormwater discharges from industrial and municipal sources.

The Clean Water Act authorizes cleanup, injunctive, and cost-recovery actions when an imminent hazard is caused by pollution. It also prohibits the discharge of oil and other hazardous substances into the navigable waters of the United States, imposes a criminal penalty for failure to notify the appropriate entity of such discharges, and provides for citizen suits.

If a facility discharges pollutants into navigable waters pursuant to a Clean Water Act permit, it must file a discharge monitoring report (DMR) with the EPA or the appropriate state agency. The DMR gives notice to the authorities of any violations of the permit.

The citizen suit provision of the Clean Water Act permits citizens to commence a civil action against persons or entities alleged to be in violation of the statute. Numerous citizen groups have used the citizen suit provision to bring suits against companies based on violations reported in DMRs.

Most states have assumed enforcement of the Clean Water Act within their borders through state regulations that are required to be at least as stringent as the federal regulations.

(d) TOXIC SUBSTANCES CONTROL ACT

The Toxic Substances Control Act regulates the manufacture, processing, and distribution in commerce of chemical substances and mixtures capable of adversely affecting health or the environment. TSCA may require testing and impose use restrictions, along with requirements for the reporting and retention of information, on the risks of TSCA-regulated substances.

TSCA requires that any person who manufactures, processes, or distributes in commerce a chemical substance or mixture and who obtains information that reasonably supports the conclusion that such substance or mixture presents a substantial risk of injury to health or the environment shall immediately inform the EPA. The only excuse for not meeting this duty is actual knowledge that the EPA has already been adequately informed. The act also provides that any person who manufactures, processes, or distributes in commerce any chemical substance or mixture shall maintain records of actual or alleged significant adverse reactions to health or the environment. Records of any adverse health reactions of employees must also be kept. In addition, records of other problems, including those stemming from consumer complaints and reports of occupational diseases or injuries to nonemployees or harm to the environment, must be maintained. Any person who manufactures, processes, or distributes in commerce a listed chemical under this TSCA section must submit to the EPA lists of health and safety studies conducted by the person, known to the person, or reasonably ascertainable.

EPA regulations promulgated under TSCA also govern the manufacturing, processing, and distribution in commerce of polychlorinated biphenyls (PCBs) and asbestos. PCBs once were widely used as a dielectric fluid in electrical transformers and capacitors. Their manufacture in the United States and Great Britain ceased in 1977. However, a large number of installations still contain PCBs, often without being labeled as such. The PCB regulations contain stringent requirements for the labeling, storage, and disposal of PCBs.

Federal asbestos regulations require all persons who manufacture, import, or process asbestos to report quantity, use, and exposure information to the EPA. In addition, federal and corresponding state regulations applicable to asbestos-containing materials (ACM) generally require the following:

- Affected parts of a facility being renovated or demolished must be inspected for the presence of ACM prior to beginning the renovation or demolition project.
- Regulated ACM (friable ACM and nonfriable ACM that will be made friable) that would be disturbed as part of a renovation or demolition must be properly removed before beginning the project.
- Asbestos-containing waste material must be properly disposed of in an approved landfill.
- The appropriate government agency must be notified at least ten days prior to commencement of a demolition project or a renovation project that will affect regulated ACM.

Financial reporting of current and anticipated future asbestos abatement costs is covered in § 13.2(a) (cleanup costs) and Chapter 22 (asset retirement obligations).

(e) EMERGENCY PLANNING AND COMMUNITY RIGHT TO KNOW ACT

The Emergency Planning and Community Right to Know Act (EPCRA) requires facilities that have certain quantities of extremely hazardous substances to notify their state emergency response commission that they are subject to the emergency planning requirements of CERCLA. They must also report releases to the local emergency planning committee. In addition, facilities that store chemicals over specified threshold amounts must submit material safety data sheets (MSDSs), or their equivalent, to the appropriate local emergency planning committee, the state emergency response commission, and the fire department with jurisdiction over the facility.

Each facility subject to EPCRA reporting requirements must report the maximum amount of the hazardous chemical present at the facility and provide a description of the storage or use of the chemical and its location at the facility. This inventory report must be submitted to local and state emergency response officials annually.

Section 313 of EPCRA also includes requirements for annual reporting of releases of certain toxic chemicals that occur as a result of normal business operations (as distinguished from emergency releases). Facilities subject to these reporting requirements are required to complete a Toxic Chemical Release Inventory Form (Form R) for specified chemicals. This form also includes source reduction and recycling information required under the Pollution Prevention Act of 1990. All the information described here is made available to the general public (see § 3.5).

(f) OSHA

Occupational health and safety laws, such as the federal Occupational Safety and Health Act, are intended to protect workers against workplace injuries. In addition to regulating workplace safety, the U.S. Occupational Safety and Health Administration (OSHA) has adopted regulations to protect workers from pollution conditions in the workplace. OSHA sets permissible exposure limits (PELs) to protect workers against the health effects of inhalation or dermal exposure to hazardous and toxic substances. OSHA currently regulates worker exposure to approximately 400 hazardous and toxic substances, including dusts, mixtures, and common materials such as paints, fuels, and solvents. Failure to comply with OSHA regulations can result in significant fines, or worse, bodily injury to workers.

(g) STATE LAWS

Congress intended for the states to administer most federal environmental programs. In almost all cases, U.S. federal pollution control laws allow state agencies to implement their own regulations as long as the state's regulations are at least as stringent as the federal rules. Through a formal federal approval process commonly known as *delegation,* the states have become the primary environmental protection agencies across the nation.

(h) FOREIGN LAWS

Most developed and many developing countries have enacted pollution control laws. Often the environmental laws of foreign countries are more stringent than U.S. environmental laws. Levels of enforcement of environmental laws, however, vary widely among different countries.

The Kyoto Protocol is an international treaty that is intended to reduce the impact of greenhouse gases on global warming. Negotiations on the Kyoto Protocol to the United Nations Framework Convention on Climate Change (UNFCCC) were completed December 11, 1997, committing the industrialized nations to specified, legally binding reductions in emissions of six greenhouse gases: carbon dioxide (CO_2), methane (CH_4), nitrous oxide (N_2O), hydrofluorocarbons (HFCs), perfluorocarbons (PFCs), and sulphur hexafluoride (SF_6). In accordance with the Kyoto Protocol, participating developed countries must reduce their combined greenhouse gas emissions by at least 5 percent from 1990 levels by the period 2008 to 2012. The targets cover the six main GHGs, along with some activities in the land-use change and forestry sector that remove carbon dioxide from the atmosphere (*carbon sinks*).

The Kyoto Protocol also establishes three innovative mechanisms, known as *joint implementation, emissions trading,* and the *clean development mechanism*. These mechanisms are intended to help contracting parties reduce the costs of meeting their emission targets. The clean development mechanism also aims to promote sustainable development in developing countries.

More than 36 countries, including all members of the European Union, have signed the protocol. The United States, under President Bush, withdrew from the protocol in 2001, putting the treaty's future in doubt. Its adoption by Russia in 2004, however, finally allowed the sweeping environmental pact to go into effect after years of delays. Although the United States is not a signatory to the Kyoto Protocol, many U.S. companies do business in countries that now have or soon will have regulatory schemes in place to reduce GHG emissions (see Chapter 17).

3.4 COMMON LAW

In addition to state and federal environmental statutes, pollution conditions can be actionable under state common law. Persons responsible for contamination may be liable for bodily injury and property damage under common law tort theories, such as negligence, negligence per se, nuisance, and trespass. Neighboring tenants, landowners, and other third parties frequently file claims for personal injury and property damage allegedly caused by the hazardous substances released into the environment, in lieu of (or in addition to) statutory claims for corrective action and cost recovery.

3.5 DISCLOSURE OF ENVIRONMENTAL ENFORCEMENT AND COMPLIANCE HISTORY

The EPA maintains a searchable Web-based database of environmental enforcement and compliance information. The database, known as *Enforcement & Compliance History Online (ECHO)*, is found at *www.epa.gov/echo*.

ECHO provides compliance and enforcement information for hundreds of thousands of regulated facilities nationwide. The site allows users to find inspection, violation, enforcement action, informal enforcement action, and penalty information about facilities for the preceding three years. The database contains information on facilities regulated under the Clean Air Act Stationary Source Program, Clean Water Act, and RCRA. The ECHO database also contains information collected under TSCA and EPCRA.

ECHO reports provide information on key components of the enforcement process at regulated facilities, including:

- The occurrence of a compliance monitoring event, such as an inspection/evaluation or a self-report.
- The determination of a violation.
- The occurrence of a government enforcement action to address violations.
- Penalties associated with enforcement actions.

CHAPTER FOUR

Environmental Financial Reporting: Overview

4.1 INTRODUCTION

Financial reporting includes not only financial statements but also other means of communicating information that relates, directly or indirectly, to the information provided by the financial reporting system (i.e., information about an enterprise's resources, obligations, earnings, and so forth). Management may communicate information to those outside an enterprise by means of financial reporting other than formal financial statements, either because the information is required to be disclosed by authoritative pronouncement, regulatory rule, or custom or because management considers it useful to those outside the enterprise and discloses it voluntarily (e.g., corporate social responsibility reports).

Corporate annual reports, prospectuses, and annual reports filed with the SEC are common examples of reports that include financial statements, other financial information, and nonfinancial information. News releases, management's forecasts or other descriptions of its plans or expectations, and voluntary corporate social responsibility reports describing the enterprise's social responsibility and environmental impact are examples of reports giving financial information other than financial statements or giving only nonfinancial information.

As used throughout this book, *environmental financial reporting* refers to the activities associated with the presentation of financial and nonfinancial environmental information in financial statements and SEC filings in accordance with generally accepted accounting principles and SEC rules. Appendix A contains a list of authoritative pronouncements (accounting standards and SEC rules and interpretations) that are applicable or relevant to environmental financial reporting.

Voluntary reporting of nonfinancial information concerning an enterprise's social responsibility or environmental impact is an increasingly important consideration for large public companies. Standards such as the Global Reporting Initiative (GRI) now exist for voluntary use by organizations for reporting on the economic, environmental, and social aspects of their activities, products, and services. Because the audience for a reference book on voluntary reporting standards is sufficiently distinct from that for compulsory financial reporting, a detailed discussion of voluntary standards such as the GRI has been omitted from this book. For readers seeking more information on this subject Appendix B contains references on the GRI and other aspects of voluntary environmental reporting.

4.2 FINANCIAL STATEMENTS

Financial statements include the income statement, balance sheet, statement of owners' equity, and statement of cash flows. These financial reports serve two primary purposes:

1. To present the financial condition of the reporting entity; and
2. To show how the entity has performed (financially) over a particular period of time (an accounting period), typically one year divided into four calendar quarters.

For purposes of environmental financial reporting, the two key financial statements are the balance sheet and the income statement. A *balance sheet* shows at a particular point in time the resources owned by the reporting entity (*assets*) and what the entity owes to other parties (*liabilities*). It also shows how much has been invested in the enterprise and the sources of that investment. It is often helpful to think of a balance sheet as a snapshot of the business—a picture of the financial position of the enterprise as of the end of the quarterly or annual reporting period. Environmental liabilities, environmental asset impairments, and intangible environmental assets all appear on the balance sheet.

The *income statement* provides a perspective on the financial performance of the enterprise over the accounting period. The income statement shows the sources of income (*revenue*), the associated costs to generate that income (*expenses*), and the resulting profit or loss (*net income*). The income statement also includes various items of gain and loss associated with specific transactions (e.g., sale of an asset). Cleanup costs, pollution control costs, accruals for environmental liabilities, and asset impairment losses all appear on the income statement as expenses or losses. Proceeds from environmental insurance, envi-

EXHIBIT 4.1

Environmental Financial Information

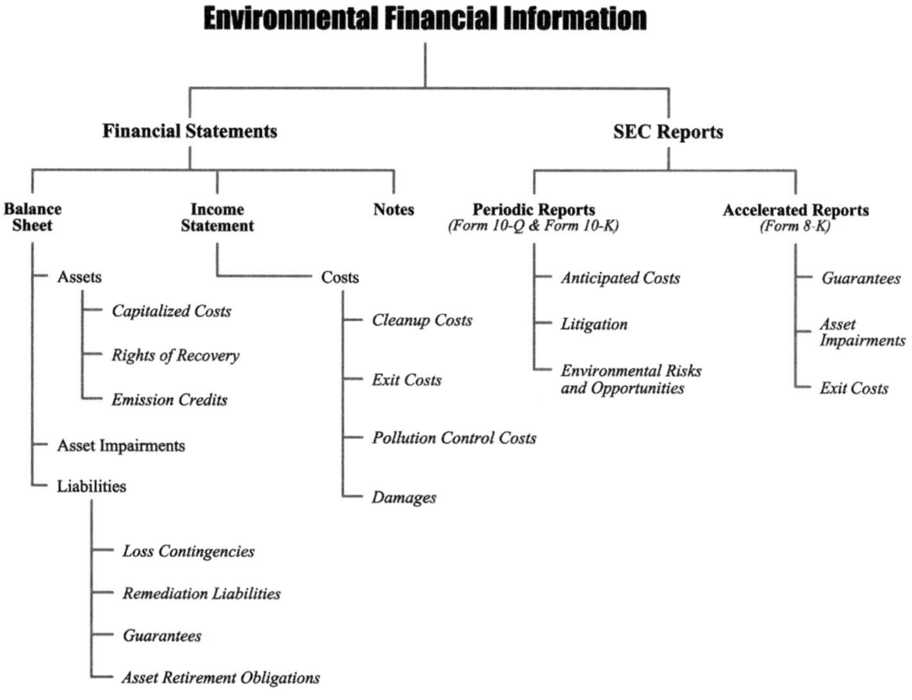

ronmental indemnity agreements, and other rights of recovery appear on the income statement as revenues offsetting associated expenses.

Audited financial statements are reviewed by an independent accounting firm and must be prepared in accordance with GAAP. The nature and scope of generally accepted accounting principles are covered in Part Three. Chapter 26 addresses issues of special concern in connection with the auditing of environmental financial information contained in financial statements.

Exhibit 4.1 shows where environmental financial information may be contained in the financial statements and SEC reports.

4.3 NOTES TO THE FINANCIAL STATEMENTS

Narrative information needed to supplement or explain the quantitative data in the balance sheet, income statement, or statement of cash flows is included in the *notes to the financial statements*. The notes to the financial statements (sometimes called *footnotes*) are also an integral part of the presentation of the entity's financial condition and results of operations.

Generally speaking, there are two types of footnotes:

1. *Accounting Methods*. This type of footnote identifies and explains the entity's major accounting policies, including those applicable to environmental

financial reporting. This is also where the entity reports changes in accounting policies.

2. *Disclosure.* The second type of footnote provides additional disclosures that simply could not be put in the financial statements. For example, the notes will contain details regarding the assumptions and calculations used by the entity in determining the fair value of its asset retirement obligations.

4.4 NONFINANCIAL STATEMENT DISCLOSURES

Although business enterprises of all types and sizes commonly prepare financial statements, only those entities that are subject to the federal securities laws submit reports to the SEC. SEC reports include registration statements (prospectuses used in the offering of securities), periodic reports (quarterly Form 10-Q and annual Form 10-K), and episodic reports (Form 8-K). Periodic reports filed on Form 10-Q and Form 10-K contain both financial (i.e., quantitative monetary values) and nonfinancial information (i.e., narrative disclosures). The Form 10-Q contains unaudited financial statements in addition to certain nonfinancial information prescribed under rules developed by the SEC. The Form 10-K contains audited financial statements and more extensive nonfinancial information.

The nonfinancial information that appears in SEC registration statements and periodic reports is prescribed under SEC Regulation S-K. Regulation S-K requires disclosure regarding a wide variety of environmental information, including:

- Anticipated future pollution control costs.
- Pending environmental legal proceedings.
- Known environmental trends, events, and uncertainties.
- Environmental risk factors affecting the entity or the industry.
- Environmental off-balance-sheet arrangements.

Regulation S-K encompasses certain aspects of environmental management that overlap with environmental financial reporting. Exhibit 4.2 illustrates how environmental financial reporting overlaps with environmental compliance management and environmental risk management.

The area of overlap between environmental financial reporting and environmental compliance management represents environmental compliance matters of sufficient importance to be included in SEC reports pursuant to Regulation S-K. Similarly, the area of overlap between environmental financial reporting and environmental risk management represents environmental risks (and the entity's actual or proposed response to such risks) of sufficient importance to be included in SEC reports pursuant to Regulation S-K. Exhibit 4.3 shows examples of environmental regulatory compliance and environmental risk management matters that could be subject to financial reporting requirements under Regulation S-K depending on their relative importance to the current or future financial performance of the enterprise.

EXHIBIT 4.2

Environmental Management Overview

4.5 REPORTING ENTITIES

Many types of organizations, including public and private corporations, non-profit and charitable organizations, public services, and governmental and quasi-governmental agencies, prepare financial statements. This book focuses exclusively on the financial reporting laws and standards applicable to public and private for-profit business enterprises.

Throughout this book, the term *issuer* is used with the meaning assigned to that term in section 2 of Sarbanes-Oxley to reference the class of companies subject to the provisions of that Act. As defined in section 2 of the Act, the term *issuer* means an issuer (as defined in section 3 of the Exchange Act), the securities of which are registered under section 12 of the Exchange Act of 1934, or that is required to file reports under section 15(d) of the Exchange Act, or that files or has filed a registration statement that has not yet become effective under the Securities

EXHIBIT 4.3

Possible Environmental Disclosures under Regulation S-K

REGULATORY COMPLIANCE	RISK MANAGEMENT
• Anticipated capital expenditures and operating costs to comply with proposed environmental regulations • Environmental permit violations that could result in an interruption of ongoing operations • Discovery and self-reporting of criminal violations of environmental laws	• Unrecognized obligations relating to historical pollution conditions at nonowned sites • Current or anticipated water shortages expected to adversely affect the entity's operations • The anticipated future impact of climate change on the entity's financial performance

Act of 1933, and that it has not withdrawn. This broad definition encompasses banks, savings associations, small-business issuers, and non-U.S. companies.

The term *registrant*, as defined by the SEC, means the issuer of securities for which a registration statement is filed under the Securities Act. In addition to being subject to the provisions of Sarbanes-Oxley, registrants are also subject to reporting requirements under the Securities Act. Foreign issuers with securities traded in the United States are subject to the requirements of Sarbanes-Oxley even though they may never have filed a registration statement with the SEC.

As used throughout this book, the term *entity* is used interchangeably with the terms *company* and *enterprise* to refer to all business organizations, public and private, that prepare audited financial statements in accordance with GAAP.

4.6 ENVIRONMENTAL FINANCIAL INFORMATION

Environmental financial information can be classified into five broad categories: (1) environmental costs, (2) environmental liabilities, (3) environmental impairments, (4) environmental risks and opportunities, and (5) environmental assets. In practice, it is often difficult to differentiate between these categories for financial reporting purposes.

(a) ENVIRONMENTAL COSTS

Environmental costs are expenditures for steps taken to manage an enterprise in an environmentally responsible manner, including compliance with environmental laws, as well as other costs driven by the environmental objectives of the enterprise. Environmental costs fall into three categories: (1) cleanup costs, (2) pollution control costs, and (3) environmental damages.

Cleanup costs are expenses, including legal expenses, incurred for the investigation, removal, remediation (including associated monitoring), or disposal of soil, surface water, groundwater, or other contamination (generally as required by environmental laws), plus costs incurred to repair, replace, or restore real or personal property damaged in the course of such activities. Cleanup costs arise under the pollution remediation laws covered in § 3.2.

Pollution control costs are expenditures other than cleanup costs incurred to achieve or maintain compliance with environmental laws. Entities with ongoing operations that result in significant environmental impacts are generally subject to a wide range of prescriptive governmental regulations designed to control and prevent pollution (see § 3.3). Examples of prescriptive regulations include construction and operating permit requirements, environmental performance standards for industrial processes, personnel training requirements, emergency planning, periodic and episodic reporting requirements, and spill response procedures. Pollution control costs may include direct costs for labor, material, and equipment, as well as indirect labor and overhead costs.

Pollution control costs are capitalized as assets when they relate, directly or indirectly, to future economic benefits that will flow to the enterprise (see § 4.6(e)). Many pollution control costs, however, do not result in a future benefit or are not sufficiently closely related to future benefit to enable them to be capitalized.

Environmental damages are costs associated with noncompliance with environmental laws or breach of a duty owed to others under principles of common law. Noncompliance with pollution control laws can result in administrative, civil, and criminal enforcement. In some cases, noncompliance can result in a government-ordered shutdown of operations. In addition, historical pollution conditions and accidents resulting in the release of hazardous substances can give rise to common law and statutory claims for cleanup costs, bodily injury, and property damage. Damages include:

- Monetary awards or settlements of compensatory damages.
- Punitive, exemplary, or multiple damages.
- Civil fines, penalties, or assessments for bodily injury or property damage.
- Costs, charges, and expenses incurred in the defense, investigation, or adjustment of claims.

Financial reporting requirements applicable to environmental costs are examined in Chapter 13.

(b) ENVIRONMENTAL LIABILITIES

Environmental liabilities represent obligations to pay environmental costs at some point in the future. Environmental liabilities are most commonly related to historical pollution conditions. Under U.S. law, certain classes of *responsible persons* are obligated to remediate environmental contamination from past industrial and commercial practices (see § 3.2(a)). Environmental liabilities may also arise in other ways, including common law tort claims for bodily injury or property damage arising from both historical pollution conditions and contemporaneous spills of hazardous materials (see § 3.4).

Financial reporting requirements applicable to environmental liabilities are examined in Chapter 18.

(c) ENVIRONMENTAL IMPAIRMENTS

Pollution conditions often have a direct adverse impact on the entity's long-lived assets, such as land or buildings, causing a reduction in their economic value. For example, the presence of soil and groundwater contamination can adversely affect the value of land. Similarly, the presence of asbestos-containing materials can adversely affect the value of a building. In effect, the pollution conditions injure or impair the associated asset. Accordingly, it is sometimes appropriate to account for such conditions as asset impairments.

Financial reporting requirements applicable to environmental-related asset impairments are examined in Chapter 23.

(d) ENVIRONMENTAL RISKS AND OPPORTUNITIES

Business enterprises often face a wide range of environmental-related risks. Environmental risks include, for example, future pollution conditions that might arise from the entity's business operations (e.g., a future onsite industrial accident) or from the actions of others beyond the entity's control (e.g., terrorism, acts of tenants, and migration of pollution from offsite locations).

Environmental-related risks may be industry-wide or specific to a particular company. An example of an industry-wide risk is the potential impact on the energy and automotive industries of future regulations to address global warming. The outcome of pending toxic tort litigation for which the entity denies liability is an example of a company-specific risk.

Public companies are required to disclose material environmental risks in their financial reports filed with the SEC. Financial reporting requirements applicable to environmental risks are examined in Chapter 24.

In addition to disclosing the risk itself, management will often characterize its ability to effectively manage the risk. Current and prospective shareholders may be concerned about the entity's ability to ensure compliance with environmental laws and effectively manage environmental risks. Knowing this, management may make representations in SEC registration statements and periodic reports regarding the entity's capabilities, in an effort to reassure investors. If inaccurate, such statements may impose liability on the entity under the antifraud provisions of the federal securities laws.

The opposite of environmental risks are environmental opportunities. An increasing amount of environmental financial reporting involves disclosure of environmental business opportunities. For example, during the implementation of the reformulated gasoline regulation under the Clean Air Act, makers of the fuel additive methyl tertiary butyl ether (MTBE) touted the Clean Air Act as driving increased demand for their products. Similarly, companies targeting environmental product and service niches (e.g., lightweight plastics that replace metals in propellers for wind farms) may have positive market-based disclosures to make.

Disclosures of environmental business opportunities may be appropriate and allowable under the federal securities laws. If made, such disclosures can give rise to liability if they are false or misleading. The decision to report environmental opportunities in the first place, however, generally rests entirely within the discretion of management. Excepting those situations involving environmental niche businesses, where pursuit of environmental opportunities represents the entity's core business strategy, disclosure of such opportunities would rarely, if ever, be mandatory under the federal securities laws. Reporting of environmental opportunities is closely related to voluntary reporting of nonfinancial information about the enterprise's social or environmental impact. Because it is generally voluntary, financial reporting of environmental business opportunities is not addressed elsewhere in this book.

(e) ENVIRONMENTAL ASSETS

Environmental assets are discussed generally in Chapter 14. For purposes of financial accounting, environmental assets fall into three categories: (1) capitalized environmental costs, (2) environmental-related rights of recovery, and (3) emission credits (allowances). In addition, if such matters are considered material to investors, an entity may elect to disclose nonfinancial information regarding positive environmental-related achievements (e.g., ISO 14001 certification or company-wide reductions in toxic air emissions or greenhouse gas emissions) that would not qualify as assets in the accounting sense.

Environmental costs are capitalized as assets when they relate, directly or indirectly, to future economic benefits that will flow to the enterprise, as evidenced by meeting one or more of the following criteria:

- The costs extend the life, increase the capacity, or improve the safety or efficiency of property owned by the entity.
- The costs mitigate or prevent future environmental contamination while also improving the property.
- The costs are incurred in preparing for sale a property that is currently held for sale.

Some environmental costs may not directly increase economic benefits to the enterprise, but may be necessary if the enterprise is to benefit from its other assets. In most instances, environmental costs that are capitalized are related to another capital asset and should be included as an integral part of that asset, and not recognized separately (e.g., the removal of asbestos from a building). It would be inappropriate to recognize asbestos removal as a separate asset, as it does not result in a separate future economic benefit. Alternatively, a piece of machinery that removes pollution from the water or the atmosphere has a separate future benefit (e.g., the equipment enables the facility to maintain compliance with environmental laws) and therefore should be recognized as a separate tangible asset. Capitalized environmental costs are discussed further in Chapter 15.

Environmental-related rights of recovery include claims against other responsible parties, environmental guarantees owed to the entity, environmental insurance, and other forms of financial assurance designed to offset existing environmental liabilities and loss contingencies. Financial reporting requirements applicable to environmental rights of recovery are covered in Chapter 16.

Emission credits arise under market-based environmental laws, such as the Clean Air Act (see § 3.3(b)) and the Kyoto Protocol (see § 3.3(h)). Financial reporting standards applicable to environmental emission credits are examined in Chapter 17.

4.7 ENVIRONMENTAL FINANCIAL ACCOUNTING

Environmental financial reporting comprises financial accounting and SEC disclosure. Environmental financial accounting consists of the activities required to present environmental financial information in the entity's financial statements and notes in accordance with GAAP. Audited financial statements of public and nonpublic companies alike are reviewed by independent public accounting firms for conformance with GAAP.

(a) GENERALLY ACCEPTED ACCOUNTING PRINCIPLES

GAAP comprises a set of rules and practices that are recognized as authoritative guidance for financial reporting purposes. These principles are *generally accepted* because an authoritative body has set them or the accounting profession widely accepts them as appropriate. The Financial Accounting Standards Board, the American Institute of Certified Public Accountants , and the SEC are the primary authoritative sources for GAAP pronouncements in the United States.

GAAP includes FASB Statements of Financial Accounting Standards (FASs), FASB Interpretations of FASs (FINs), SEC Releases and Staff Accounting Bulletins (SABs), AICPA Accounting Principles Board Opinions (APBs), and AICPA Accounting Research Bulletins (ARBs). These pronouncements are ranked in a hierarchy as follows:

- Level 1 (most authoritative)
  - FASB Standards and Interpretations
  - APB Opinions
  - Accounting Research Bulletins
- Level 2
  - FASB Technical Bulletins
  - AICPA Industry Guides
  - AICPA Statements of Position
- Level 3 (least authoritative)
  - FASB Emerging Issues Task Force (EITF)
  - AICPA Practice Bulletins
  - Other authoritative pronouncements

(b) SEC REGULATION S-X

Regulation S-X sets forth the form and content required of financial statements included in filings with the SEC. Rule 210.4-01 of Regulation S-X provides that financial statements filed with the SEC, but not prepared in accordance with GAAP, are presumed to be misleading or inaccurate, despite footnotes or other disclosures, unless the SEC has otherwise provided.

Regulation S-X rules, in general, are consistent with GAAP, but contain certain additional disclosure items not provided for by GAAP. Regulation S-X contains no requirements beyond GAAP that specifically affect environmental financial reporting.

(c) ENVIRONMENTAL GAAP

Very few GAAP pronouncements are specifically applicable to environmental financial reporting. For the most part, the treatment of environmental financial information is prescribed by a limited number of generally applicable rules and practices.

Environmental financial reporting under GAAP relies principally on the following pronouncements. Exhibit 4.4 correlates these standards to the various categories of environmental financial information described in § 4.6.

- FASB Statement of Financial Accounting Standards No. 5, "Accounting for Contingencies" (FAS 5)
- FASB Statement of Financial Accounting Standards No. 143, "Accounting for Asset Retirement Obligations" (FAS 143)
- FASB Statement of Financial Accounting Standards No. 144, "Accounting for the Impairment or Disposal of Long-Lived Assets" (FAS 144)
- FASB Statement of Financial Accounting Standards No. 146, "Accounting for Costs Associated with Exit or Disposal Activities" (FAS 146)
- FASB Statement of Financial Accounting Standards No. 154, "Accounting Changes and Error Corrections, a replacement of APB Opinion No. 20 and FASB Statement No. 3" (FAS 154)
- FASB Interpretation No. 14, "Reasonable Estimation of the Amount of a Loss—An Interpretation of FASB Statement No. 5" (FIN 14)
- FASB Interpretation No. 39, "Offsetting of Amounts Related to Certain Contracts" (FIN 39)
- FASB Interpretation No. 45, "Guarantor's Accounting and Disclosure Requirements for Guarantees, Including Indirect Guarantees of Indebtedness of Others" (FIN 45)
- FASB Interpretation No. 47, "Accounting for Conditional Asset Retirement Obligations—An Interpretation of FASB Statement No. 143" (FIN 47)
- FASB Emerging Issues Task Force 89-13, "Accounting for the Cost of Asbestos Removal" (EITF 89-13)
- FASB Emerging Issues Task Force 90-8, "Capitalization of Costs to Treat Environmental Contamination" (EITF 90-8)
- FASB Emerging Issues Task Force 96-5, "Accounting for Environmental Liabilities" (EITF 93-5) (incorporated into SOP 96-1)
- FASB Emerging Issues Task Force 95-23, "Treatment of Certain Site Restoration/Environmental Exit Costs When Testing a Long-Lived Asset for Impairment" (EITF 95-23)
- FASB Emerging Issues Task Force 03-8, "Accounting for Claims-Made Insurance and Retroactive Insurance Contracts by the Insured Entity" (EITF 03-8)
- FASB Statement of Financial Accounting Concepts No. 2, "Qualitative Characteristics of Accounting Information" (SFAC 2)
- FASB Statement of Financial Accounting Concepts No. 6, "Elements of Financial Statements" (SFAC 6)
- FASB Statement of Financial Accounting Concepts No. 7, "Using Cash Flow Information and Present Value in Accounting Measurements" (SFAC 7)
- AICPA Statement of Position 96-1, "Environmental Remediation Liabilities" (SOP 96-1)

EXHIBIT 4.4

Environmental GAAP

CATEGORY OF ENVIRONMENTAL FINANCIAL INFORMATION	APPLICABLE GAAP PRONOUNCEMENTS
All categories	SAB 99 (materiality)
Environmental costs	EITF 90-8
Environmental assets	SFAC 6, FIN 39, EITF 90-8, EITF 03-8
Environmental liabilities	FAS 5, SOP 96-1, FIN 14, FAS 143, FIN 45, FIN 47, SFAC 6, SFAC 7, SAB 103
Environmental loss contingencies	FAS 5, FIN 14
Environmental remediation liabilities	FAS 5, SOP 96-1, FIN 14
Environmental guarantees	FIN 45, SAB 103
Environmental asset retirement obligations	FAS 143, FIN 47
Environmental impairments	FAS 5, FAS 144, EITF 95-23
Environmental risks	FAS 5, SOP 96-1

- AICPA Statement of Position 94-6, "Disclosure of Certain Significant Risks and Uncertainties" (SOP 94-6)
- AICPA Statement on Auditing Standards No. 47, "Audit Risk and Materiality in Conducting an Audit" (SAS 47)
- SEC Staff Accounting Bulletin No. 92, 58 *Fed. Reg.* 32,843 (June 14, 1993) (SAB 92)
- SEC Staff Accounting Bulletin No. 103, 68 *Fed. Reg.* 26,840 (May 16, 2003) (SAB 103) (amends SAB 92)
- SEC Staff Accounting Bulletin No. 99, 64 *Fed. Reg.* 45,150, 45,151 (Aug. 19, 1999) (SAB 99)

Appendix A contains a list of authoritative pronouncements under GAAP and the U.S. securities laws that are applicable or relevant to environmental financial reporting.

4.8 ENVIRONMENTAL DISCLOSURE

Environmental disclosure consists of the activities required to present, in accordance with U.S. securities laws and applicable SEC rules, narrative and quantitative environmental information in the nonfinancial statement portions of the issuer's SEC filings. Appendix A includes a listing of federal securities laws and SEC rules and interpretations that are applicable or relevant to environmental financial reporting.

SEC Regulation S-K describes the narrative and quantitative information to be included in the nonfinancial statement portions of SEC disclosure documents, including SEC registration statements and periodic reports. The four narrative provisions of greatest relevance to environmental financial reporting are Item 101 (Description of Business), Item 103 (Legal Proceedings), Item 303 (Management's Discussion and Analysis of Financial Condition and Results of Operations, or MD&A), and Item 503(c) (Risk Factors Disclosed in a Registration Statement). These disclosure requirements are examined in Chapter 24.

4.9 ANTIFRAUD PROVISIONS

The antifraud provisions of the federal securities laws (i.e., sections 11 and 12(a)(2) of the Securities Act, section 10(b) of the Exchange Act, and SEC Rule 10b-5) are relevant to the extent that registrants or issuers are required to include environmental information in their SEC filings (beyond that specifically required by Regulation S-K) to ensure that the reports are not otherwise misleading. These provisions prohibit the making of false or misleading statements or omissions in connection with the purchase or sale of securities.

4.10 NON-GAAP REPORTING

The SEC's new Regulation G relates to conditions for use of non-GAAP financial information in SEC reports and amendments to Form 8-K under sections 401(b) and 409 of Sarbanes-Oxley. The new rules apply to all public disclosures made after March 28, 2003, and all annual or quarterly reports for periods ending after that date.

Whenever an issuer publicly discloses any material information that includes a non-GAAP financial measure, the company must provide the following information as part of the disclosure or release:

- A presentation of the most directly comparable GAAP financial measure; and
- A reconciliation of the differences between the non-GAAP financial measure and the most directly comparable GAAP financial measure (the reconciliation must be quantitative for historic measures).

A company cannot make public a non-GAAP financial measure that, taken together with the information accompanying that measure, is materially false or omits material information. *Non-GAAP financial measures* are numerical measures of historical or future financial performance, financial position, or cash flows that:

- Exclude amounts, or are subject to adjustments that have the effect of excluding amounts, that are included in the most directly comparable GAAP financial measure; or
- Include amounts, or are subject to adjustments that have the effect of including amounts, that are excluded in the most directly comparable GAAP financial measure.

Regulation G and the use of non-GAAP financial measures are unlikely to have significant relevance to environmental financial reporting.

CHAPTER FIVE

Financial Reporting Objectives

5.1 INTRODUCTION

An entity's environmental financial reporting objectives determine the policies and procedures necessary to achieve those objectives. Clarity of objectives is therefore an essential first step in the design and implementation of an effective financial reporting system.

A reporting entity may have several objectives with regard to environmental financial reporting. Some objectives are discretionary, and may vary among entities, whereas others are effectively mandatory for law-abiding organizations. Objectives may serve the needs of external stakeholders, such as investors and creditors, as well as internal stakeholders, such as the board of directors, senior management, and employees.

The following sections provide examples of discretionary and nondiscretionary environmental financial reporting objectives.

5.2 NONDISCRETIONARY OBJECTIVES

(a) CONFORM WITH GAAP

Conformance with generally accepted accounting principles is a mandatory objective for reporting entities that are subject to the federal securities laws. Failure to present financial information in accordance with GAAP is deemed to be a material misstatement under the federal securities laws.[1] In addition, nonpublic reporting entities with audited financial statements must aspire to conform with GAAP or risk the consequences of a qualified opinion from their independent financial auditor. A qualified opinion could place the entity in violation of various contractual agreements such as loan covenants.

(b) COMPLY WITH SEC DISCLOSURE REQUIREMENTS

Compliance with the general antifraud provisions (see § 4.9) of the federal securities laws and the specific environmental reporting requirements contained in SEC regulations (see § 4.8) is another mandatory objective for public companies.

(c) FAIRLY PRESENT THE ENTITY'S FINANCIAL CONDITION WITHOUT LIMITATION TO GAAP

Section 302 of Sarbanes-Oxley requires the CEO and CFO to certify, in each periodic report filed with the SEC, that the issuer's financial statements "fairly present," in all material respects, the financial condition and results of operations of the company. According to the SEC, this certification is not limited to a representation that the financial statements and other financial information have been presented in accordance with GAAP, and is not otherwise limited by reference to GAAP. Conformance with GAAP thus is no guarantee of compliance with federal securities laws.

5.3 DISCRETIONARY OBJECTIVES

(a) ACCURATELY REPORT THE ENTITY'S SOLVENCY

Directors of public and nonpublic corporations have a compelling personal interest in having a timely and accurate understanding of the entity's state of solvency when making major corporate decisions or authorizing dividends and other distributions. The state of the entity's solvency is not definitively determined according to GAAP. For example, as discussed in § 2.2(b)(iii), under corporate law in many states, directors may be held personally liable for dividends and distributions authorized at a time when the entity was insolvent without regard to GAAP. Unreported environmental liabilities and loss contingencies, although in conformance with GAAP, can distort a corporation's true financial position, leading directors who rely on the financial statements to unwittingly make unlawful decisions that expose them to personal liability.

---

[1] 17 C.F.R. § 240.4-01(a)(1).

(b) MEET EXTERNAL STAKEHOLDER DEMANDS AND EXPECTATIONS

Institutional investors, fiduciaries, creditors, rating agencies, and other stakeholders may pressure reporting entities to disclose more environmental financial information than is required by GAAP and SEC regulations (see Chapter 24 on environmental risks). Although not legally required, many U.S. corporations today voluntarily issue supplemental environmental reports to satisfy the demands and expectations of external stakeholders. The Global Reporting Initiative is an example of a supplemental environmental reporting framework that has gained broad international acceptance.

5.4 COMPETING OBJECTIVES

Establishing environmental financial reporting objectives that align with the letter and spirit of GAAP and the federal securities laws is complicated by several powerful competing objectives. FASB Statement of Financial Accounting Concepts No. 1, "Objectives of Financial Reporting by Business Enterprises" (SFAC 1), acknowledges some of these competing objectives. SFAC 1, which recognizes the basic principle that the benefits of information provided by financial reporting generally should at least equal the cost involved, points out that the costs of financial reporting not only include the resources directly expended to provide the information, but also may include adverse effects of disclosure on an enterprise or its stockholders. SFAC 1 notes, for example, that comments about a pending environmental lawsuit may jeopardize a successful defense, or comments about a future business initiative may jeopardize a competitive advantage.

Because the relative cost-benefit of financial information is usually difficult or impossible to measure objectively, reasonable persons can be expected to disagree about whether the benefits of the information justify its costs. This makes the task of balancing competing objectives a matter of considerable judgment.

(a) TRANSPARENCY VS. CONFIDENTIALITY

A primary objective of financial reporting is to provide outside stakeholders with a transparent view of the financial condition of the reporting entity. This objective may run directly counter to the entity's objective to maintain the confidentiality of certain highly sensitive information.

Entities often consider information regarding environmental matters to be highly confidential. For example, information regarding historical pollution conditions, if made public, could lead to administrative, civil, or even criminal enforcement against the entity, or give rise to third-party claims for bodily injury or property damages. Faced with these risks, reporting entities may feel significant pressure to avoid implementing the procedures necessary to collect information about known or suspected historical pollution conditions that could give rise to reporting requirements under environmental laws, GAAP, or SEC disclosure rules.

For similar reasons, entities often are reluctant to implement effective environmental compliance programs. An advisory group to the U.S. Sentencing

Commission has studied whether the effectiveness of legal compliance programs could be enhanced by addressing the exogenous pressures that temper the clear benefits of proactive structures. The advisory group found that:

> [W]eighty incentives created by forces *outside* the organization may persuade organizations to pursue less than optimal, and in some cases, ineffective compliance programs. Specifically, . . . the institution of truly effective programs, the auditing and monitoring that such programs require, and the training and internal reporting systems that such programs contemplate, all create a real risk that information generated by these admirable practices will be used by other potential litigants to harm the organization. This situation is often referred to as the "litigation dilemma," and it is recognized as one of the greatest impediments to the institution or maintenance of truly effective compliance programs. The litigation dilemma, and the related issue of waivers of attorney-client privilege and the work product protection doctrine, also have a potential negative impact on organizational incentives to self-report misconduct and cooperate in the investigation and rededication of that wrongdoing.[2]

When establishing environmental financial reporting objectives, senior management and the board of directors must carefully balance the entity's desire for confidentiality against the objective of transparency in financial reporting. Entities subject to the federal securities laws must also weigh the legal consequences of failing to collect and disclose potentially material environmental financial information.

(b) APPROPRIATE INQUIRY VS. CONSERVATION OF CORPORATE ASSETS

CERCLA has long contained a defense against liability for cleanup costs for innocent landowners who acquire ownership of property without knowing or *having had reason to know* that the property was impacted by historical pollution conditions. To establish that the property owner had no reason to know of the historical pollution conditions, the would-be innocent landowner must demonstrate that it conducted *all appropriate inquiries* into the previous ownership, uses, and environmental conditions of the property prior to acquiring title, and that notwithstanding such inquiries, the historical pollution conditions were not discovered (see § 3.2(a)(ii)(A). Accordingly, prospective buyers, tenants, and lenders routinely conduct environmental due diligence to satisfy the all-appropriate-inquiry test.

EPA standards for all appropriate inquiry offer no liability protection to property owners who either caused the pollution conditions or unwittingly acquired title to contaminated property without first conducting appropriate environmental due diligence. Such property owners may perceive little incentive, and significant disincentive, to investigate known or suspected historical pollution conditions for financial reporting purposes.

---

2 *Report of the Ad Hoc Advisory Group on the Organizational Sentencing Guidelines* 6 (Oct. 7, 2003).

Investigation of known or suspected historical pollution conditions can lead to discovery of conditions that must be reported to environmental regulatory agencies under environmental laws. Such agencies can in turn require the reporting entity to conduct further investigation and corrective action, resulting in immediate expenditures for cleanup costs (see § 3.2(a)). U.S. environmental laws, as generally interpreted and applied, do not require landowners to conduct voluntary investigations of historical pollution conditions. Without consideration of financial reporting requirements, reporting entities are faced with a choice: proactively identify and investigate historical pollution conditions, and thereby risk immediate expenditures for cleanup costs; or avoid investigation of known or suspected historical pollution conditions and thereby delay, and potentially avoid altogether, cleanup costs. Given this choice, the compelling desire to conserve corporate assets has led some companies to adopt a "don't ask, don't tell" strategy regarding historical pollution conditions.

The concern is that the intentional failure to identify and assess historical pollution conditions may be in direct conflict with the entity's obligations to comply with GAAP; for public corporations, this may constitute a violation of federal securities laws, including certain sections of Sarbanes-Oxley. Therefore, when establishing environmental financial reporting objectives, senior management and the board of directors must carefully weigh the entity's legitimate desire to conserve corporate assets against its financial reporting obligations to identify, assess, measure, and report environmental conditions, events, and transactions that could have a material adverse impact on the entity's financial condition.

(c) PROTECTION OF PROSPECTIVE INVESTORS VS. PROTECTION OF CURRENT SHAREHOLDERS

Full disclosure of previously unreported environmental financial information can have a negative impact on the valuation of a public entity's stock. Corporate directors and officers may believe that the potential harm to existing shareholders justifies continuing nondisclosure. This rationalization, however, is in conflict with the objectives of U.S. securities laws.

The Securities Act of 1933 requires securities to be registered with the SEC before they are sold to the public. The purpose of the Securities Act is to protect prospective investors from misrepresentation, manipulation, and other fraudulent practices in connection with the public offering of an entity's securities.

In contrast to the Securities Act, which is primarily concerned with the initial distribution of securities, the Securities Exchange Act of 1934 imposes periodic reporting obligations on issuers with publicly held securities. The principal objective of the Exchange Act is the dissemination of significant financial and other information relating to securities traded on the national securities exchanges. Generally, Exchange Act registration statements and reports are intended to assist a person in reaching an informed opinion as to whether to purchase, hold, or sell an entity's securities at a given price. Accurate and timely information is required to maintain the integrity of the national securities markets. As the Supreme Court stated, "an animating purpose" of the Exchange Act is "to insure honest markets, thereby promoting investor confidence."[3]

When establishing environmental financial reporting objectives, senior management and the board of directors of public corporations must bear in mind that the federal securities laws are not intended solely to protect the interests of existing shareholders. The interests of prospective investors and overall investor confidence in the securities markets demand that public corporations disclose previously unreported environmental financial information, in accordance with GAAP and the federal securities laws, even when doing so may be expected to bring harm to existing shareholders.

5.5 RISKS OF FAILING TO MEET REPORTING OBJECTIVES

Failure to achieve mandatory financial reporting objectives can have serious adverse consequences for the reporting entity and its directors and officers. The nature and severity of risk varies depending on whether the entity is a public or nonpublic company. Some risks, such as civil fines and penalties, are the direct consequences of material misstatements and omissions in the entity's financial reports or deficiencies in the financial reporting process. Others are indirect risks associated with corporate decisions based on inaccurate or incomplete financial information or misrepresentations of the entity's true financial condition.

Exhibit 5.1 lists various direct and indirect risks applicable to public and nonpublic companies. The following sections describe certain of these risks in greater detail.

EXHIBIT 5.1

Risks of Failing to Meet Reporting Objectives

	DIRECT	INDIRECT
Public companies	• Financial statement audit failure and restatement • Internal control audit failure • Civil fines and penalties • Criminal fines and imprisonment • Shareholder litigation	• Fraudulent conveyances • Illegal dividends • Breach of loan covenants • Rescission of directors and officers (D&O) insurance policies • Damage to reputation resulting in lower stock prices and higher costs of capital
Nonpublic companies	• Financial statement audit failure and restatement • Shareholder litigation	• Same as for public companies • Barriers to future sale, public registration, or recapitalization of the company's securities

3 *United States v. O'Hagan*, 521 U.S. 642, 658 (1997).

(a) AUDIT FAILURE

As set forth in Statement of Auditing Standards No. 58, "Reports on Audited Financial Statements," an auditor's standard unqualified opinion states that the financial statements present fairly, in all material respects, an entity's financial position, results of operations, and cash flows in conformity with generally accepted accounting principles. This conclusion may be expressed only when the auditor has formed such an opinion on the basis of an audit performed in accordance with generally accepted auditing standards.

Certain circumstances may require a qualified opinion. A qualified opinion states that, *except for the effects of the matter to which the qualification relates,* the financial statements present fairly, in all material respects, the financial position, results of operations, and cash flows of the entity in conformity with generally accepted accounting principles. A qualified opinion is appropriate when:

- There is a lack of sufficient competent evidential matter or there are restrictions on the scope of the audit that have led the auditor to conclude that he or she cannot express an unqualified opinion, but he or she has concluded not to disclaim an opinion.
- The auditor believes, on the basis of his or her audit, that the financial statements contain a departure from GAAP, the effect of which is material, but he or she has concluded not to express an adverse opinion.
- The auditor encounters restrictions on the scope of the audit, whether imposed by the client or by circumstances, such as the timing of his or her work, the inability to obtain sufficient competent evidential matter, or an inadequacy in the accounting records, that require the auditor to qualify his or her opinion or to disclaim an opinion.

An adverse opinion states that the financial statements do not fairly present the financial position, results of operations, or cash flows of the entity in conformity with GAAP. Such an opinion is required when, in the auditor's judgment, the financial statements taken as a whole are not presented fairly in conformity with GAAP.

Under Rule 2-02 of SEC Regulation S-X, public companies are required to include in their periodic SEC reports:

- The opinion of the entity's independent financial auditor with respect to the financial statements covered by the report and the accounting principles and practices reflected therein;
- The opinion of the independent financial auditor as to the consistency of the application of the accounting principles, or as to any changes in such principles that have a material effect on the financial statements; and
- Any matters to which the independent financial auditor takes exception and the effect of each such exception on the financial statements.

(i) RESTATEMENT OF FINANCIAL STATEMENTS

A *financial statement restatement* occurs when a company, either voluntarily or under prompting by its auditors or regulators, revises financial statements that were previously reported to the SEC. Under Rule 4-01 of SEC Regulation S-X, public companies must present their financial statements in accordance with GAAP. Financial statements that are found to contain material misstatements due to error or fraud must be restated.

Fraud, as defined in Statement of Auditing Standards No. 99, "Consideration of Fraud in a Financial Statement Audit," is an intentional act that results in a material misstatement in financial statements (see § 26.2(d)). SAS 47 defines *errors* as unintentional misstatements or omissions of amounts or disclosures in financial statements. This includes mistakes in gathering or processing accounting data from which the financial statements are prepared, incorrect accounting estimates arising from misinterpretation or oversight of facts, and mistakes in application of accounting principles relating to amount, classification, and manner of presentation or disclosure.

The determination of whether an inaccuracy in the financial statements is material is not based solely on financial magnitude. An intentional accounting irregularity may be considered material even though an unintentional error of the same magnitude would be considered immaterial. This is because of the importance of advising investors of the intentional nature of the company's conduct (see § 12.2(b)(iii)).

Environmental financial reporting involves accounting estimates. Changes in estimates are not the same as error or fraud. A change in an estimate is generally the result of new information, or new circumstances, causing a change in the assumptions underlying the estimate. Pending or probable claims for Superfund liability, for example, are generally reported as an estimate of expected future remediation costs. The sudden bankruptcy of a significant participating PRP, or other new circumstances causing management to increase its estimated share of the remediation costs, would be considered a change in estimate. Changes in estimates are treated as accounting adjustments in the year in which new information causes the estimate to be changed. Financial statements for prior periods are not restated.

A change in estimate, however, may call into question the use of the estimate in a prior reporting period, particularly if the change is material. If the change in estimate is based on information that was known, or should have been known, by the company during the prior period, a restatement of the prior-period financial statements may be required. For example, if management failed to implement appropriate procedures to identify, assess, measure, and report environmental-related asset retirement obligations in the prior period, and then subsequently reports preexisting but previously unidentified obligations, the prior omissions may be considered erroneous. If management intentionally used erroneous estimates or failed to develop estimates for known environmental obligations to deceive investors, this may be considered fraud.

The issuance of a restatement can have far-reaching effects on a public company, potentially leading to declines in stock prices, investigations by the SEC or the Department of Justice, other criminal investigations, private securities litigation, or SEC civil litigation. A 2002 GAO report noted that from the trading day before the initial restatement announcement to the trading day after the announcement, the stock prices of companies issuing restatements of financial statements fell, on average, almost 10 percent.[4]

In addition, if an issuer is required to restate its financial statements due to noncompliance with the federal securities laws, section 304 of Sarbanes-Oxley requires that the CEO and CFO may be required to reimburse the company for certain forms of compensation and profits realized from the sale of issuer securities.

(ii) REPORTABLE CONTROL DEFICIENCIES

As discussed in Chapter 27, section 404 of Sarbanes-Oxley requires the independent financial auditor to render an attestation as to the design and operational effectiveness of the entity's internal control over financial reporting. The purpose of the independent review and attestation is to identify control deficiencies that could lead to misstatements in the entity's financial reports. Public companies are required to disclose in their annual Forms 10-K any material weaknesses in internal control identified by the auditor. Market reaction to disclosure of material weaknesses in internal control can be significant. In addition, disclosure of material weaknesses can call into question the validity of prior certifications by the CEO and CFO under section 302 of Sarbanes-Oxley regarding the effectiveness of the entity's disclosure controls and procedures (see § 5.5(b)(i)).

(b) CIVIL AND CRIMINAL LIABILITY FOR FALSE CERTIFICATIONS

(i) SARBANES-OXLEY SECTION 302

SEC rules promulgated under section 302 of Sarbanes-Oxley require the chief executive officer (CEO) and chief financial officer (CFO) of public companies to sign and certify the issuer's SEC periodic reports and disclosure controls and procedures. False certifications are subject to civil penalties of up to $100,000 for individuals and up to $500,000 for the company. In addition, the SEC has the authority to permanently bar a violator from serving as an officer or director of a public company.

(ii) SARBANES-OXLEY SECTION 906

Section 906 of the Act requires an issuer's CEO and CFO to certify that the financial statements contained in the issuer's periodic reports fully comply with the requirements of section 13(a) or section 15(d) of the Exchange Act,

---

[4] Government Accountability Office, Financial Statement Restatements: Trends, Market Impacts, Regulatory Responses, and Remaining Challenges, GAO-03-138 (2002).

and that information contained in the periodic reports fairly presents, in all material respects, the financial condition and results of operations of the issuer (see § 7.2(b)).[5]

False certifications under section 906 are subject to stiff criminal penalties. A certifying officer who *knowingly* certifies a periodic report that does not fairly present, in all material respects, the financial condition and results of operations of the issuer can be fined not more than $1 million, or imprisoned for up to 10 years. An officer who *willfully* makes the certification, knowing that the accompanying periodic report does not fairly present, in all material respects, the financial condition and results of operations of the issuer, can be fined not more than $5 million, or imprisoned not more than 20 years, or both.

Like most federal criminal statutes, section 906 contains a *mens rea* or mental-state requirement. Section 906 requires that the certifying officer have knowledge that he or she is giving a false certification. Nonetheless, under various legal theories, mental-state elements may be established through something other than proof of actual knowledge on the part of corporate officers themselves. These legal theories include:

- *The responsible corporate officer doctrine.* This doctrine seeks to impose criminal liability on corporate officers solely by virtue of their position within the corporation, without the necessity of establishing knowledge. This doctrine is generally limited to misdemeanor prosecutions under strict liability statutes.
- *Establishing knowledge by reference to a corporate officer's title and duties.* Prosecutors have won felony convictions of corporate managers and executives in cases where the proof establishing criminal knowledge was based on little more than the executive's title and scope of responsibility. In prosecutions brought under federal environmental criminal laws, for example, jurors have inferred criminal knowledge based on a corporate officer's title and the duties shown to accompany such a title. In essence, the defendant is held accountable for what he or she should have known given his or her title within the organization and the duties that accompany that position in the context of a regulatory scheme.
- *The willful blindness doctrine.* This doctrine provides that a finding of criminal knowledge may not be avoided by a showing that the defendants closed their eyes to what was going on around them.

The section 906 certification makes an issuer's most senior officers responsible for the accuracy of the issuer's financial statements, and creates a duty, within the scope of that prescribed responsibility, to ensure personally that the issuer's reports to the SEC fairly present the issuer's financial condition. These relationships and responsibilities are further reinforced by the certification requirements under section 302 of the Act, which require the certifying officers to assume personal responsibility for the design and operational effectiveness of the issuer's financial reporting system.

---

5 18 U.S.C. § 1350.

Based on existing legal doctrines, certifying officers could face criminal prosecution for providing a false certification under section 906, even in the absence of intentional fraud. Reliance on the issuer's securities counsel and accountants may not ensure protection for certifying officers. The defense of *reliance on experts* has been held to apply only when the defendant can demonstrate that his or her accountant or attorney was presented with all relevant facts, and when the defendant was "specifically advised" as to "the course of conduct taken."[6] In this regard, the potential failure to provide the entity's attorneys and accountants with all relevant facts concerning known or reasonably suspected pollution conditions is of particular concern. Failure to fully inform the issuer's independent auditors can also give rise to criminal liability under section 303 of Sarbanes-Oxley.

(c) PERSONAL LIABILITY FOR IMPROPER DISTRIBUTIONS

Payment of stock dividends and other distributions or conveyances at a time when the corporation is insolvent, or nearly insolvent, may be prohibited under state corporation laws and state and federal bankruptcy laws. Corporate directors who authorize dividends, distributions, or other significant transactions without considering the effect of unreported or understated environmental liabilities on the solvency of the company run the risk of being held liable retroactively for any resulting damages to creditors.[7]

---

6 *United States v. McLennan*, 563 F.2d 943, 946 (9th Cir. 1977); *see United States v. Johnson*, 730 F.2d 683, 686 (11th Cir. 1984) (to "succeed [in establishing defense of good faith reliance on expert advice], the defendant must show that (1) he fully disclosed all relevant facts to the expert and (2) that he relied in good faith on the expert's advice").

7 *See, e.g., Pereira v. Cogan*, 2003 WL 21039976 (S.D.N.Y. 2003); *see also In re W.R. Grace & Co.*, 281 B.R. 852 (Bankr. D. Del. 2002).

PART TWO

Sarbanes-Oxley

CHAPTER SIX

Sarbanes-Oxley: Overview

6.1 INTRODUCTION

On July 30, 2002, President Bush signed the Sarbanes-Oxley Act of 2002[1] (Sarbanes-Oxley or Act). Congress rushed passage of the legislation to restore investor confidence in the stock markets following the Enron and Worldcom accounting scandals by improving the accuracy and reliability of corporate disclosures made pursuant to the federal securities laws. Among other things, Sarbanes-Oxley amends the Securities Act of 1933 and the Securities Exchange Act of 1934. Sarbanes-Oxley is implemented in large part through rules adopted by the SEC.

This chapter contains an overview of the Act. Chapters 7 through 11 discuss in greater depth those provisions in Sarbanes-Oxley most relevant to environmental financial reporting.

6.2 APPLICABILITY

Sarbanes-Oxley is generally applicable to all entities, including non-U.S. companies, required to file reports with the SEC under the Exchange Act or that have a registration statement on file with the SEC under the Securities Act, in each case

[1] H.R. 3763, Pub. L. No.107-204, 116 Stat. 745 (2002).

regardless of size (collectively, *public companies* or *issuers*). Some of the legislation's provisions apply only to companies listed on a national securities exchange (*listed companies*) such as the New York Stock Exchange (NYSE) or the NASDAQ Stock Market (NASDAQ).

Small business issuers (generally entities with total assets of $5 million or less) generally are subject to Sarbanes-Oxley in the same ways as larger companies, although some specifics vary. Sarbanes-Oxley is applicable in many, but not all, respects to registered investment companies and foreign issuers.

Non-U.S. companies having no securities listed on a U.S. exchange may nonetheless be subject to the Act's criminal provisions (e.g., mail and wire fraud, obstruction of justice, and whistleblower provisions). Additionally, companies with securities that trade over the counter or who have American Depository Receipts (ADRs) are also required to comply with the criminal provisions and whistleblower provisions of the Act. An *ADR* is a stock that trades on a U.S. exchange or association and is issued by a U.S. bank for the purpose of representing a specified number of shares in the non-U.S. company.

Sarbanes-Oxley is not directly applicable to private companies. Lenders, institutional investors, and insurers, however, may require private companies to comply with some or all of the corporate governance provisions contained in the Act. In addition, private companies that contemplate an initial public offering, seek financing from investors whose exit strategy is a public offering, or wish to be acquired by a public company may find it advantageous or necessary to implement many aspects of the legislative requirements.

6.3 PUBLIC COMPANY ACCOUNTING OVERSIGHT BOARD

One of the most far-reaching aspects of Sarbanes-Oxley is the creation of the federal Public Company Accounting Oversight Board (PCAOB) to oversee the activities of the public accounting firms that audit the financial statements and financial reporting systems of public companies. The PCAOB is also responsible for establishing auditing standards, including standards for auditing internal control over financial reporting (see Chapters 8 and 27). The PCAOB is a private, nonprofit corporation funded by assessments charged to public companies based on their market capitalization. The SEC appoints PCAOB board members and the board has authority to conduct investigations of public companies in coordination with the SEC's enforcement division. PCAOB oversight is intended to avoid a repeat of the high-profile audit failures associated with the Enron and Worldcom scandals by pressuring audit firms to increase the rigor of their auditing processes and assume greater accountability for detection and disclosure of financial reporting fraud—a gatekeeper role that the SEC has long advocated for accounting firms.

6.4 CEO/CFO CERTIFICATIONS

Sarbanes-Oxley contains two different provisions that require the CEO and CFO of each reporting company to certify the issuer's SEC periodic reports and disclosure controls and procedures, subject to possible criminal and civil penalties for false statements. These certification provisions are described further in Chapter 7.

6.5 INTERNAL CONTROL

As directed by the Act, the SEC has adopted rules mandating inclusion of an internal control report and assessment in Form 10-K annual reports. The internal control report is required to assert the responsibility of management for establishing and maintaining an adequate internal control structure and procedures for financial reporting; and include an assessment, as of the end of the most recent fiscal year of the issuer, of the effectiveness of the internal control structure and procedures of the issuer for financial reporting. Sarbanes-Oxley further requires the public accounting firm that issues the audit report to attest to, and report on, the assessment made by corporate management of internal control. The internal control provisions in Sarbanes-Oxley are examined further in Chapter 8.

6.6 IMPROPERLY INFLUENCING AUDITORS

Pursuant to the Act, the SEC has adopted a rule that specifically prohibits officers and directors and persons acting under their direction (which could include environmental attorneys, managers, and consultants), from coercing, manipulating, misleading, or fraudulently influencing an auditor engaged in the performance of an audit of the issuer's financial statements when the officer, director, or other person knew or should have known that the action, if successful, could result in rendering the issuer's financial statements materially misleading. This prohibition is covered in greater detail in Chapter 9.

6.7 INCREASED DISCLOSURE

Public companies are required to disclose in plain English additional information concerning material changes in their financial condition or operations on a real-time basis. SEC rulemaking defines the specific requirements of the enhanced reporting in several areas, including

- Form 10-K and 10-Q disclosure of all material off-balance-sheet arrangements with unconsolidated entities that may have a material effect on the financial status of an issuer (see Chapter 10).
- Enhanced accelerated disclosure on Form 8-K (see Chapter 11).
- Use of non-GAAP financial measures (see § 4.10).

6.8 RESTRICTIONS ON NONAUDIT SERVICES

To increase the independence of public accounting firms, Sarbanes-Oxley and SEC rules restrict the nonaudit services accounting firms may offer to their audit clients. Among the services that audit firms may not provide for their audit clients are:

- Bookkeeping or other services related to the accounting records or financial statements of the audit client.
- Financial information system design and implementation.
- Appraisal or valuation services, fairness opinions, or contribution-in-kind reports.
- Actuarial services.
- Internal audit outsourcing services.
- Management functions or human resources.
- Broker/dealer, investment adviser, or investment banking services.
- Legal services.
- Expert services unrelated to the audit.

Accounting firms generally may provide tax services to their audit clients, but may not represent those clients in tax litigation.

6.9 NEW AUDIT COMMITTEE REQUIREMENTS

Sarbanes-Oxley and SEC rules establish new requirements and create new responsibilities for audit committees of listed companies. Audit committees of listed companies:

- Must have direct responsibility for the appointment, compensation, and oversight (including the resolution of disagreements between management and the auditors regarding financial reporting) of the auditors.
- Must be comprised solely of independent directors.
- Are responsible for establishing procedures for the handling of complaints regarding financial reporting matters.
- Must establish a confidential, anonymous complaint system for employees of the issuer (*whistleblowers*) regarding questionable financial reporting matters.

Issuers are required to disclose the names of the members of the audit committee and whether the audit committee has an audit committee financial expert; if there is such an expert, the issuer must also disclose his or her name.

The Act requires that the independent auditors report to the audit committee regarding critical accounting policies (see §§ 12.5 and 24.5(e)) and alternative treatments of financial information under GAAP that have been discussed with management. The Act also requires the audit committee or its designees to preapprove all auditing services and nonaudit services provided by the issuer's independent auditor.

6.10 PROFESSIONAL RESPONSIBILITIES OF LAWYERS

New SEC rules under Sarbanes-Oxley require lawyers practicing before the SEC (which includes environmental lawyers involved in any of the activities related to financial disclosure of environmental costs, liabilities, and risks) to report evidence of a material violation of any federal law or fiduciary duty to the chief legal officer (CLO) or the CEO of the company. If corporate executives do not respond appropriately, the lawyers must report to an appropriate committee of independent directors or to the board of directors. This rule applies to both inside and outside legal counsel.

6.11 CEO/CFO REIMBURSEMENT TO ISSUER

If an issuer is required to restate its financial statements because of the issuer's material noncompliance as a result of misconduct as to any financial reporting requirements under the federal securities laws, section 304 of Sarbanes-Oxley requires that the CEO and CFO reimburse the company for any bonus or incentive or equity-based compensation received during the 12-month period following the first public issuance or filing with the SEC (whichever first occurs) of the financial document embodying such financial reporting requirement, and any profits realized from the sale of securities of the issuer during that 12-month period.

6.12 INSIDER TRADING FREEZE DURING PLAN BLACKOUT

The Act prohibits public company executives and directors from trading stock during periods when employees cannot trade company stock held in a retirement fund (*blackout periods*). The prohibition applies to transactions in any equity security of the issuer during any blackout period when at least half of the issuer's individual account plan participants are not permitted to purchase, sell, or otherwise transfer their interests in that security.

6.13 INSIDER LOANS

Subject to certain limited exceptions, Sarbanes-Oxley prohibits public companies from making loans to their directors or executive officers.

6.14 CODES OF ETHICS

The SEC has adopted rules requiring public companies to disclose, on Form 10-K, whether the issuer has adopted a code of ethics that applies to the issuer's CEO, CFO, principal accounting officer or controller, or persons performing similar functions. If the issuer has not done so, it must state why.

6.15 RECORD RETENTION

Sarbanes-Oxley and SEC rules prohibit destroying, altering, concealing, or falsifying records with the intent to obstruct or influence an investigation in a matter in federal jurisdiction or in bankruptcy. Those same rules require auditors to maintain, for a seven-year period, all audit or review work papers pertaining to a public company audit client.

6.16 CRIMINAL AND CIVIL SANCTIONS

Sarbanes-Oxley increased maximum prison sentences, fines, and civil penalties for unlawful acts relating to accounting and securities fraud. The Act also restricts the discharge of such obligations in bankruptcy.

CHAPTER SEVEN

Certifications

7.1 INTRODUCTION

By the passage of Sarbanes-Oxley, Congress sought to restore investor confidence in the reliability of reported financial information by increasing the accountability of senior executives for the accuracy and completeness of such information. Under new certification provisions, the CEO and CFO of entities subject to the Act are required to personally attest to both the reliability of reported financial information and the effectiveness of the reporting systems used to generate that information. By knowingly making false certifications, certifying officers expose themselves to civil and criminal liability.

Faced with this level of personal accountability, it is not surprising that many certifying officers have sought to push accountability down the management hierarchy by using subcertifications (sometimes called *cascading certifications*). Cascading certifications may require finance directors, business unit leaders, staff directors, and mid-level managers to attest to the reliability of that portion of the financial information within their area of responsibility. Environmental managers may, for example, be asked to certify the accuracy and completeness of the issuer's reported environmental financial information.

Certifying officers, as well as environmental managers who are required to sign cascading certifications, must be especially concerned about the reliability of environmental financial information, for the following reasons:

- Environmental financial information is largely based on estimates and assumptions that involve high levels of subjectivity and judgment, and that are susceptible to future changes in facts, law, or science.

- Generally accepted accounting principles, as they relate to accounting for environmental asset retirement obligations and environmental indemnities, have changed significantly in recent years with the adoption of FAS 143, FIN 47, and FIN 45. Current accounting standards under GAAP sharply contrast with historical practices at many entities.
- Because of certain limitations in FAS 5 and FIN 14, full compliance with GAAP may not ensure the fair presentation of the financial condition of the entity as required by Sarbanes-Oxley.
- There is significant controversy among investors and special interest groups regarding the criteria for assessing the materiality of environmental financial information.
- Many entities lack effective systems and procedures to initiate, authorize, record, process, or report environmental financial information.
- Environmental financial reporting is frequently attended by the three risk factors for fraud identified in Statement of Auditing Standards No. 99, "Consideration of Fraud in a Financial Statement Audit" (SAS 99). SAS 99 is discussed in § 26.2(d).

7.2 FINANCIAL STATEMENT CERTIFICATIONS

(a) SECTION 302

Section 302(a) of the Act directs the SEC to adopt rules requiring the certifying officers of issuers filing periodic reports with the SEC to certify, in each annual or quarterly report, that:

- The officer has reviewed the report;
- Based on the officer's knowledge, the report does not contain any untrue statement of a material fact or omit to state a material fact necessary to make the statements made, in light of the circumstances under which such statements were made, not misleading; and
- Based on such officer's knowledge, the financial statements, and other financial information included in the report, fairly present in all material respects the financial condition and results of operations of the issuer as of, and for, the periods presented in the report.

SEC rules implementing section 302(a) of the Act now require the following financial statement certification to be included as an exhibit with each periodic report filed with the SEC:

I, [identify the certifying individual], certify that:

1. I have reviewed this [specify report] of [identify registrant];
2. Based on my knowledge, this report does not contain any untrue statement of a *material* fact or omit to state a material fact necessary to make the statements made, in light of the circumstances under

which such statements were made, not misleading with respect to the period covered by this report;

3. Based on my knowledge, the financial statements, and other financial information included in this report, fairly present in all material respects the financial condition, results of operations and cash flows of the registrant as of, and for, the periods presented in this report [items 4 and 5, pertaining to disclosure controls and procedures and internal control, have been omitted here, but are covered in § 7.3].[1]

The section 302 financial statement certification contains two distinct representations. The certification statement concerning the material accuracy and completeness of the periodic reports (paragraph 2 above) mirrors preexisting statutory disclosure standards for material accuracy and completeness of information contained in reports (see § 12.2). This certification applies to both financial and nonfinancial information contained in periodic reports.

The section 302 certification statement regarding fair presentation of financial statements and other financial information (paragraph 3 above) applies to the financial statements (including the notes to the financial statements), selected financial data, management's discussion and analysis of financial condition and results of operations, and other financial information in a report.

The *fair-presentation* certification is not limited by reference to GAAP. As stated by the SEC in the section 302 rulemaking:

> The certification statement regarding fair presentation of financial statements and other financial information is not limited to a representation that the financial statements and other financial information have been presented in accordance with "generally accepted accounting principles" and is not otherwise limited by reference to generally accepted accounting principles. We believe that Congress intended this statement to provide assurances that the financial information disclosed in a report, viewed in its entirety, meets a standard of overall material accuracy and completeness that is broader than financial reporting requirements under generally accepted accounting principles. In our view, a "fair presentation" of an issuer's financial condition, results of operations and cash flows encompasses the selection of appropriate accounting policies, proper application of appropriate accounting policies, disclosure of financial information that is informative and reasonably reflects the underlying transactions and events and the inclusion of any additional disclosure necessary to provide investors with a materially accurate and complete picture of an issuer's financial condition, results of operations and cash flows.[2]

---

1 17 C.F.R. § 229.601(b)(31).

2 Securities Act Release No. 33-8124, 67 Fed. Reg. 57,276, 57,279 (Sept. 9, 2002). Case law existing prior to the passage of Sarbanes-Oxley had already established precedent for the SEC's interpretation of section 302. *See United States v. Simon*, 425 F.2d 796 (2d Cir. 1969); *see also In re* Caterpillar, Inc., Release No. 34-30532 (Mar. 31, 1992); Edison Schs., Inc., Release No. 34-45925 (May 14, 2002) (presenting financial information in accordance with GAAP might not satisfy an issuer's obligations under the antifraud provisions of the federal securities laws).

Under generally accepted auditing standards (predating Sarbanes-Oxley), a determination of whether financial statements are presented fairly in conformance with GAAP is to be based on the following factors:

- The accounting principles selected and applied have general acceptance.
- The accounting principles are appropriate in the circumstances.
- The financial statements and related notes are informative of matters that may affect their use, understanding, and interpretation.
- The information presented in the financial statements is classified and summarized in a reasonable manner.
- The financial statements reflect the underlying transactions and events in a manner that presents financial position, results of operations, and cash flows within a range of acceptable limits based on the concept of materiality.[3]

These factors, without being limited by reference to GAAP, provide guidance in determining whether an issuer's financial information, taken as a whole, provides a fair presentation of its financial condition and results of operations.[4] Consideration of these factors with respect to environmental financial information appears in § 7.2(c).

(b) SECTION 906

Section 906 of the Act contains a financial statement certification that is separate and distinct from the certification mandated by section 302. The section 906 certification became effective immediately upon passage of the Act. Similar to section 302(a) of the Act, section 906 requires the issuer's certifying officers to certify that the financial statements contained in the issuer's periodic reports fully comply with the requirements of section 13(a) or 15(d) of the Exchange Act and that information contained in the periodic reports fairly presents, in all material respects, the financial condition and results of operations of the issuer.[5] False certifications under section 906 are subject to stiff criminal penalties (see § 5.5(b)(ii)).

(c) CERTIFYING ENVIRONMENTAL FINANCIAL INFORMATION

As noted at the beginning of this chapter, certification of environmental financial information can present special concerns for certifying officers and lower-level managers who are asked to sign subcertifications *(cascading certifications)*. The fair-presentation certification required by Section 302 of the Act may be of particular concern because this certification is not limited to a representation that the financial statements and other financial information have been presented in accordance with GAAP and is not otherwise limited by reference to

---

3 Codification of Statements on Auditing Standards, AU § 411.04.

4 Securities Act Release No. 33-8124, 67 Fed. Reg. 57,276, 57,279, n.56 (Sept. 9, 2002).

5 18 U.S.C. § 1350.

GAAP. This means that anyone making the fair-presentation certification under section 302 cannot merely rely on the independent financial auditor's opinion that the issuer's financial statements are presented fairly in conformity with GAAP. The same concern is also likely to apply to the fair-presentation certification required by section 906 of the Act, but with the added risk of possible criminal sanctions.

To the extent that GAAP may fail to ensure reliable reporting of material environmental financial information, issuers must take extra precautions in order for the certifying officers to have reasonable assurance that the requirements of the fair-presentation standard under sections 302 and 906 are met. Issuers for whom environmental financial information could be regarded by reasonable investors as material should focus on two principal areas: (1) critical accounting policies, and (2) effective internal control.

(i) CRITICAL ACCOUNTING POLICIES

The SEC considers *critical accounting policies* to be those accounting policies that have a material impact on an entity's financial presentation upon their initial adoption, and that involve critical accounting estimates.[6] As discussed in § 24.5(e), *critical accounting estimates*, for purposes of MD&A disclosure, are accounting estimates and assumptions that may be material due to the levels of subjectivity and judgment necessary to account for highly uncertain matters or the susceptibility of such matters to change, and that have a material impact on financial condition or operating performance. Environmental financial information is to a large extent based on subjective estimates and assumptions. To the extent that environmental financial information may have a *material* impact on an issuer's financial condition and operating performance, the issuer's environmental accounting policies can be considered critical accounting policies.

Examples of critical environmental accounting policies include:

- *Criteria and procedures for assessing materiality.* As an initial matter, the entity must undertake a reasonable process to determine whether environmental financial information is potentially material to the entity's present or future financial condition or operating performance. If environmental information is determined to be potentially material, development of critical environmental accounting policies will be warranted. Important policy decisions regarding the assessment of materiality include whether and to what degree the entity will consider the aggregate impact of individually immaterial environmental matters, and nonquantitative factors. The highly complex issue of materiality is examined in detail in § 12.2.
- *Accounting for environmental loss contingencies.* As discussed in Chapter 19, accounting for environmental loss contingencies requires accounting estimates and assumptions that involve high levels of subjectivity and

---

6 Securities Act Release No. 33-8098, 67 Fed. Reg. 35,620, 35,621 (May 10, 2002).

judgment. Accounting policies of special importance with respect to environmental loss contingencies include:

- Criteria for classification of environmental loss contingencies as either liabilities or asset impairments.
- Policies governing accrual and disclosure regarding unasserted environmental claims.
- Policies governing accrual and disclosure regarding environmental obligations relating to previously owned and operated sites.
- Procedures for assessing the probability that a liability has been incurred or that an asset has been impaired.
- Methodologies used to estimate the loss associated with environmental loss contingencies, including criteria for determining when a loss cannot be reasonably estimated.
- Valuation of accruals for environmental loss contingencies and environmental remediation liabilities. In particular, issuers should consider whether valuation at the low end of the range of estimates, as permitted under FIN 14, fairly presents the entity's financial condition (see § 7.2(a)).
- Disclosure of assumptions and other information regarding critical accounting estimates pursuant to Item 303 of Regulation S-K (see § 24.5(e)).

- *Accounting for environmental guarantees.* FIN 45 requires entities to recognize a liability for the noncontingent component of environmental guarantees and indemnities granted in connection with the sale or lease of properties with known or suspected historical pollution conditions. Entities must develop appropriate accounting policies to govern identification, valuation, accrual, and disclosure of these liabilities. Accounting for environmental guarantees is covered in Chapter 21.

- *Accounting for rights of recovery.* FIN 39 sets forth rules governing offsetting of rights of recovery against related liabilities. Although rights of recovery may be considered in assessing the materiality of environmental liabilities for purposes of Regulation S-K disclosure, netting of environmental liabilities and rights of recovery generally is not permissible under GAAP. Accounting for rights of recovery is covered in Chapter 16.

- *Accounting for environmental-related asset retirement obligations.* The adoption of FIN 47 on conditional asset retirement obligations under FAS 143 (see Chapter 22) represents a marked departure from preexisting generally accepted accounting practices regarding unasserted claims associated with historical pollution conditions. Accordingly, issuers now need to pay special attention to the selection and application of appropriate accounting policies to comply with FAS 143. Accounting policies of special importance with respect to environmental-related asset retirement obligations include:

  - The categories of long-lived assets (e.g., property, plant, and equipment) for which environmental-related asset retirement obligations will be recognized.
  - Procedures for identifying and evaluating legal obligations to perform environmental-related asset retirement activities that are conditional on one or more future events.
  - Criteria for distinguishing between *normal operation* and *improper operation* of a long-lived asset.
  - Procedures for measuring environmental asset retirement obligations.
  - Disclosure of assumptions and other information regarding critical accounting estimates pursuant to Item 303 of Regulation S-K (see § 24.5(e)).
- *Accounting for environmental-related asset impairments.* Accounting policies of special importance with respect to environmental-related asset impairments (Chapter 23) include:
  - Identification of triggers for conducting an impairment test on long-lived assets affected by known or suspected pollution conditions.
  - Methodologies for valuation of environmental impairments.
  - Criteria for determining and evaluating management's intent regarding future use of the asset.
- *Data collection and analysis.* The "don't ask, don't tell" strategy described in § 5.4(b) creates a substantial risk that material environmental financial information will go unreported. The timely collection and analysis of environmental financial information is the subject of internal control (discussed in § 7.3 and Chapter 8). Effective internal control over financial reporting provides certifying officers with reasonable assurance that potentially material environmental matters are identified and evaluated on a timely basis.

Issuers should adopt environmental accounting policies that reflect the entity's environmental financial reporting objectives, as discussed in Chapter 5.

(ii) EFFECTIVE INTERNAL CONTROL

Selection and application of appropriate environmental accounting policies (see § 7.2(c)(i)) is an important aspect of ensuring that an issuer's reported financial information is reliable. Much more, however, is required if certifying officers are to have reasonable assurance that the requirements of the financial statement certifications under sections 302 and 906 are met. Such assurance requires a system of effective internal control (see Chapter 8).

Recognizing this reality, in addition to the financial statement certifications mandated by sections 302 and 906 of the Act, Congress included in section 302 a second category of certification requirements pertaining to internal control. Thus, while the financial statement certifications give certifying officers a compelling reason to ensure that the issuer has an effective system of internal control, these certifying officers must further attest to their personal knowledge of the design and operational effectiveness of such systems. In effect, Congress sought to eliminate the "Ken Lay defense" (Ken Lay, the former CEO and chairman of Enron, claimed that he was unaware of the fraudulent activities of subordinates) by forcing certifying officers to acknowledge that they are personally responsible for ensuring effective internal control. The internal control certification requirements under section 302 of the Act are discussed in the following section.

7.3 INTERNAL CONTROL CERTIFICATIONS

Sections 302 and 404 of the Act contain provisions requiring management to vouch for the effectiveness of the management system designed to ensure the reliability of the issuer's financial reports. Section 302 requires the issuer's certifying officers to give assurances as to the effectiveness of the issuer's disclosure controls and procedures (see § 8.4) on a quarterly basis. Section 404 requires the issuer's management to provide an annual report on the effectiveness of the entity's internal control over financial reporting (see § 8.3). Because the scope of disclosure controls and procedures and internal control over financial reporting overlap to a large extent, the quarterly and annual representations by the issuer's management also overlap.

(a) SECTION 302

Under new rules adopted by the SEC, which implement section 302(a)(4) of the Act, each periodic report filed with the SEC by the issuer must contain the following statement by each certifying officer:

> "I, [identify the certifying individual], certify that: . . .
>
> 4. The registrant's other certifying officer(s) and I are responsible for establishing and maintaining disclosure controls and procedures (as defined in Exchange Act Rules 13a-15(e) and 15d-15(e)) and internal control over financial reporting (as defined in Exchange Act Rules 13a-15(f) and 15d-15(f)) for the registrant and have:
>
>   a. Designed such *disclosure controls and procedures*, or caused such disclosure controls and procedures to be designed under our supervision, to ensure that material information relating to the registrant, including its consolidated subsidiaries, is made known to us by others within those entities, particularly during the period in which this report is being prepared;
>
>   b. Designed such *internal control over financial reporting*, or caused such internal control over financial reporting to be designed under our supervision, to provide reasonable assurance regarding the reliability of financial reporting and the preparation of financial statements for external purposes in accordance with generally accepted accounting principles;

c. Evaluated the effectiveness of the registrant's disclosure controls and procedures and presented in this report our conclusions about the effectiveness of the disclosure controls and procedures, as of the end of the period covered by this report based on such evaluation; and

d. Disclosed in this report any change in the registrant's internal control over financial reporting that occurred during the registrant's most recent fiscal quarter (the registrant's fourth fiscal quarter in the case of an annual report) that has materially affected, or is reasonably likely to materially affect, the registrant's internal control over financial reporting; and

5. The registrant's other certifying officer(s) and I have disclosed, based on our most recent evaluation of internal control over financial reporting, to the registrant's auditors and the audit committee of the registrant's board of directors (or persons performing the equivalent functions):

a. All significant deficiencies and material weaknesses in the design or operation of internal control over financial reporting which are reasonably likely to adversely affect the registrant's ability to record, process, summarize and report financial information; and

b. Any fraud, whether or not material, that involves management or other employees who have a significant role in the registrant's internal control over financial reporting."[7]

The section 302 certification is intended to ensure that the senior management assumes responsibility for the design and effective operation of the issuer's financial reporting system.

Disclosure controls and procedures are discussed in § 8.4.

(b) SECTION 404

Under section 404, issuers are required to include in their annual reports a report by management on the issuer's internal control over financial reporting. The internal control report must include the following four statements:

1. A statement of management's responsibility for establishing and maintaining adequate internal control over financial reporting for the issuer.
2. Management's assessment of the effectiveness of the issuer's internal control over financial reporting as of the end of the issuer's most recent fiscal year.
3. A statement identifying the framework used by management to evaluate the effectiveness of the issuer's internal control over financial reporting.

[7] 17 C.F.R. § 229.601(b)(31) (emphasis added). Paragraphs 1 to 3 of this statement are discussed in § 7.2(a).

4. A statement that the registered public accounting firm that audited the issuer's financial statements included in the annual report has issued an attestation report on management's assessment of the issuer's internal control over financial reporting.

Internal control over financial reporting is discussed in greater detail in § 8.3. The standards for auditing an issuer's internal control over financial reporting and management's assessment of the issuer's internal control over financial reporting are covered in Chapter 27.

CHAPTER EIGHT

Internal Control

8.1 INTRODUCTION

A revolutionary aspect of Sarbanes-Oxley is its focus on increased accountability of management for the design and operation of effective financial reporting systems. Sections 302 and 404 of the Act each contain provisions requiring management to vouch for the design and operational effectiveness of the financial reporting system used to generate the issuer's financial reports. Section 302 requires the issuer's certifying officers to give assurances as to the effectiveness of the issuer's *disclosure controls and procedures* (see § 8.4) on a quarterly basis. Section 404 requires the issuer's management to provide an annual report on the effectiveness of the entity's *internal control over financial reporting* (see § 8.3(b)(i)). Even more significant, section 404 requires the issuer's independent financial auditor to attest to the effectiveness of the issuer's internal control over financial reporting (see § 8.3(b)(ii)). Although the federal securities laws have required issuers to maintain effective internal control systems for many years (see § 8.5), sections 302 and 404 of the Act have greatly increased management's accountability to ensure compliance with these requirements.

The leading standard for internal control in the United States is the Internal Control—Integrated Framework developed by the Committee of Sponsoring Organizations of the Treadway Commission (COSO Framework). An understanding of the COSO Framework is essential to understanding the application of internal control under Sarbanes-Oxley for the following reasons:

- Rulemaking by the SEC and PCAOB on internal control under section 404 of Sarbanes-Oxley is largely based on, and repeatedly references, the COSO Framework.
- The COSO Framework and accompanying evaluation tools provide the background and detail necessary to understand the principles and application of internal control under section 404 of Sarbanes-Oxley.
- The COSO Framework is the de facto standard in the United States for evaluation of internal control over financial reporting by management under section 404 of Sarbanes-Oxley.

8.2 COSO FRAMEWORK

In 1992, the Committee of Sponsoring Organizations of the Treadway Commission (COSO)—including the AICPA, the American Accounting Association, the Financial Executives International, the Institute of Internal Auditors, and the Institute of Management Accountants—published the Internal Control—Integrated Framework. The COSO Framework defines *internal control* as "a process, effected by an entity's board of directors, management and other personnel, designed to provide reasonable assurance regarding the achievement of objectives" in three categories:

1. Reliability of financial reporting.
2. Compliance with applicable laws and regulations.
3. Effectiveness and efficiency of operations.

As depicted in Exhibit 8.1, these three categories often overlap to a significant extent. The controls that management designs and implements may achieve more than one objective. For example, the achievement of a financial reporting objective, such as fairly presenting the financial condition of the entity, may also achieve an operational objective (e.g., identification and assessment of environmental conditions posing a significant risk to the future financial condition of the enterprise).

In situations where objectives overlap, the component elements of internal control are also likely to overlap. Thus, many of the same control activities needed to ensure full compliance with the federal securities laws are also needed to ensure that the entity achieves its financial reporting objectives. In other situations, dual control objectives may be in conflict. For example, an entity's objective to reduce operational costs may motivate managers to circumvent legal requirements.

EXHIBIT 8.1

Scope of Internal Control

In such situations, control activities must be designed to ensure that operating objectives do not improperly encourage illegal behavior.

The COSO Framework does not specifically address environmental concerns. The three categories of objectives identified in the COSO Framework, however, are all relevant to environmental management. Following are examples of environmental matters and how they might relate to the COSO internal control objectives. The examples below correlate to the numbered areas shown in Exhibit 8.1:

Area 1: Regulatory compliance matters that are unrelated to operational objectives and for which it is not reasonably possible that noncompliance will result in a material loss to the entity (e.g., clerical errors in reported emissions of hazardous air pollutants).

Area 2: Environmental financial reporting matters that are unrelated to compliance or operational objectives (e.g., asset retirement obligations for historical pollution conditions resulting from legal waste disposal activities).

Area 3: Operational objectives that are unrelated to legal compliance or financial reporting (e.g., voluntary waste reduction programs intended to reduce waste disposal costs, avoidance of certain assets and activities because of their inherent environmental risk, and so forth).

Area 4: Operational objectives that are coextensive with environmental regulatory requirements (e.g., raw material substitutions that both reduce operating costs and enable compliance with applicable Clean Air Act emission limits).

Area 5: Regulatory compliance matters for which it is reasonably possible, given the nature of the business, that noncompliance could result in a material contingent liability reportable under FAS 5 (e.g., failure to maintain compliance with air emissions and wastewater discharge permits).

Area 6: Operational objectives that are coextensive with financial reporting objectives (e.g., identification and assessment of environmental conditions posing a significant risk to the future financial condition of the enterprise).

Area 7: Financial reporting objectives that are coextensive with operational and regulatory compliance objectives (e.g., prevention and detection of illegal waste disposal activities).

In 1995, the AICPA incorporated the definition of *internal control* set forth in the COSO Framework in Statement on Auditing Standards No. 78, "Consideration of Internal Control in a Financial Statement Audit: An Amendment to Statement on Auditing Standards No. 55" (SAS 78) (codified in the AICPA Professional Standards as AU § 319).

Internal control comprises attitudes, policies, plans, procedures, processes, systems, activities, functions, projects, initiatives, and endeavors of all types at all levels of an enterprise. The COSO Framework classifies these various components into five basic elements of internal control: (1) control environment, (2) risk assessment, (3) control activities, (4) information and communication, and (5) monitoring.

(a) CONTROL ENVIRONMENT

The control environment sets the tone of an organization. Relevant factors include, among other things, the attention and direction provided by the board of directors. With regard to environmental financial reporting, evidence that the audit committee of the board of directors and senior management are committed to transparent reporting of environmental financial information is indicative of a positive control environment.

(b) RISK ASSESSMENT

Risk assessment is the identification and analysis of relevant risks to achievement of the company's objectives. This element requires the entity to establish environmental financial reporting objectives (see Chapter 5) and identify the various risks to achievement of these objectives (e.g., failure to identify pollution conditions that could give rise to a material environmental liability).

(c) CONTROL ACTIVITIES

Control activities are the policies and procedures that help ensure that necessary actions are taken to address risks to achievement of the entity's objectives. They include a range of activities as diverse as approvals, authorizations, verifications, reconciliations, reviews of operating performance, security of assets, and segregation of duties. With respect to environmental financial reporting, relevant control activities include procedures to identify, assess, measure, and report pollution conditions that could give rise to reportable environmental liabilities.

(d) INFORMATION AND COMMUNICATION

The company must identify, capture, and communicate relevant information in a form and time frame that enables people to carry out their responsibilities. For example, the entity must have mechanisms for capturing environmental assessment data that will be used by others to measure environmental liabilities.

(e) MONITORING

The quality of the performance of the internal control system over time must be monitored. This is accomplished through a combination of ongoing monitoring activities and separate evaluations. For example, the entity might conduct ongoing internal assessments of the effectiveness of its environmental financial reporting system and arrange for periodic audits by an independent specialist.

As discussed in the following section, the SEC and the PCAOB have interpreted section 404 of Sarbanes-Oxley to include many, but not all aspects, of the COSO Framework.

8.3 INTERNAL CONTROL OVER FINANCIAL REPORTING

(a) SCOPE OF INTERNAL CONTROL OVER FINANCIAL REPORTING

The SEC intended the scope of internal control, for purposes of section 404 of the Act, to be consistent with the existing description of internal accounting controls under Exchange Act section 14(b)(2)(B).[1] In its rulemaking, the SEC uses the term *internal control over financial reporting* to implement section 404, as well as the section 302 certification requirements and forms of certification. The rules define *internal control over financial reporting* as:

> A process designed by, or under the supervision of, the registrant's principal executive and principal financial officers, or persons performing similar functions, and effected by the registrant's board of directors, management and other personnel, to provide reasonable assurance regarding the reliability of financial reporting and the preparation of financial statements for external purposes in accordance with generally accepted accounting principles and includes those policies and procedures that:
>
> 1. Pertain to the maintenance of records that in reasonable detail accurately and fairly reflect the transactions and dispositions of the assets of the registrant;
> 2. Provide reasonable assurance that transactions are recorded as necessary to permit preparation of financial statements in

---

[1] Securities Act Release No. 33-8238, 68 Fed. Reg. 36,636, 36,640 (June 18, 2002).

accordance with generally accepted accounting principles, and that receipts and expenditures of the registrant are being made only in accordance with authorizations of management and directors of the registrant; and

3. Provide reasonable assurance regarding prevention or timely detection of unauthorized acquisition, use or disposition of the registrant's assets that could have a material effect on the financial statements.[2]

Exhibit 8.2 depicts the scope of internal control over financial reporting with respect to the three objectives identified in the COSO Framework: reliability of financial reporting, compliance with applicable laws and regulations, and effectiveness and efficiency of operations. Clearly, internal control over financial reporting encompasses environmental financial information to the extent necessary to permit preparation of financial statements in accordance with GAAP. An important, but less obvious, issue is the extent to which internal control over financial reporting encompasses the COSO Framework objectives of compliance with applicable laws and regulations, and effectiveness and efficiency of operations. The following sections discuss the circumstances in which internal control over environmental financial reporting overlaps with environmental operations and compliance management.

(i) *ENVIRONMENTAL COMPLIANCE MANAGEMENT*

The SEC's definition of *internal control over financial reporting* does not encompass the elements of the COSO Framework definition that relate to a company's com-

EXHIBIT 8.2

Internal Control over Financial Reporting

[2] 17 C.F.R. §§ 240.13a-15(f), 240.15d-15(f).

pliance with applicable laws and regulations, with the exception of compliance with the applicable laws and regulations directly related to preparation of financial statements (e.g., the SEC's financial reporting requirements).[3] For public companies, however, legal compliance and financial reporting are closely intertwined. As discussed in Chapter 1, financial reporting by public companies is subject to the federal securities laws and SEC regulations. According to SEC rulemaking under section 404 of Sarbanes-Oxley, the definition of *internal control over financial reporting* "does not encompass . . . a company's compliance with applicable laws and regulations, with the exception of compliance with the applicable laws and regulations directly related to the preparation of financial statements, such as the [SEC's] financial reporting requirements."[4]

Of course, it might be possible to connect the violation of nearly any law to the financial statements by observing that if the violation is significant enough, it could have a material impact on the issuer's financial statements. The SEC, however, has clarified that internal control over financial reporting does not extend to compliance with all laws.[5] For example, although compliance with many of the requirements of Sarbanes-Oxley is relevant to the preparation of the entity's financial statements, rules requiring disclosure of the existence of a code of ethics or disclosure of the existence of an audit committee financial expert are not.

The SEC's position on internal control over legal compliance appears to be generally consistent with Statement of Auditing Standards No. 54, "Illegal Acts by Clients" (SAS 54), which requires financial statement auditors to consider laws and regulations that are generally recognized by auditors to have "a direct and material effect on the determination of financial statement amounts." SAS 54 states that tax laws, for example, have a direct effect on specific line items in the issuer's financial statements and that applicable laws may affect the amount of revenue accrued under government contracts.

Unlike securities laws and tax laws, environmental laws relate more to an entity's operations than to its financial accounting, and the impact of compliance or noncompliance with such laws on the issuer's financial statements, if any, is indirect—typically the result of the need to disclose a contingent liability relating to a pending or threatened regulatory enforcement action. Although the direct effects of a regulatory violation, such as failure to obtain a wastewater discharge permit, may be properly recorded (e.g., the additional net income achieved by avoiding the costs of obtaining and complying with the permit), the indirect effect (the contingent liability for fines and penalties or business interruptions) may not be appropriately reported in the financial statements. The question then becomes to what extent, if any, is compliance with environmental laws encompassed by internal control over financial reporting?

As discussed below, the PCAOB has expressed an opinion on this issue that appears to be more expansive than the position taken by the SEC. Section 404(b)

---

3 Securities Act Release No. 33-8238, 68 Fed. Reg. 36,636, 36,640 (June 18, 2002).

4 *Id.*

5 *See* SEC Staff Guidance, *Office of the Chief Accountant and Division of Corporation Finance: Management's Report on Internal Control over Financial Reporting and Certification of Disclosure in Exchange Act Periodic Reports, Frequently Asked Questions,* Question 10 (June 23, 2004; as amended Oct. 6, 2004).

of Sarbanes-Oxley requires the issuer's independent financial auditor to attest to, and report on, management's internal control assessment pursuant to rules developed by the PCAOB. Paragraph 15 of PCAOB Auditing Standard No. 2, "An Audit of Internal Control over Financial Reporting Performed in Conjunction with an Audit of Financial Statements" (PAS 2), states in part:

> The COSO framework identifies three primary objectives of internal control: efficiency and effectiveness of operations, financial reporting, and compliance with laws and regulations. The COSO perspective on internal control over financial reporting does not ordinarily include the other two objectives of internal control, which are the effectiveness and efficiency of operations and compliance with laws and regulations. However, the controls that management designs and implements may achieve more than one objective. Also, operations and compliance with laws and regulations directly related to the presentation of and required disclosures in financial statements are encompassed in internal control over financial reporting. Additionally, not all controls relevant to financial reporting are accounting controls. *Accordingly, all controls that could materially affect financial reporting, including controls that focus primarily on the effectiveness and efficiency of operations or compliance with laws and regulations and also have a material effect on the reliability of financial reporting, are a part of internal control over financial reporting.*[6]

In an October 6, 2004, guidance document, the PCAOB staff clarified the intended meaning of Paragraph 15, stating that:

> Auditing Standard No. 2 encompasses controls over compliance with laws and regulations that have a material effect on the reliability of financial reporting. Therefore, *internal control over financial reporting encompasses controls over the identification, measurement, and reporting of all material actual loss events which have occurred, including controls over the monitoring and risk assessment of areas in which, given the nature of the company's operations, such actual loss events are reasonably possible.* For example, internal control over financial reporting at a waste disposal company ordinarily would encompass controls for identifying and measuring environmental liabilities for existing and newly acquired landfills, even if there is no governmental investigation or enforcement proceeding underway.[7]

The term *reasonably possible* is defined under FAS 5 (and incorporated into the PCAOB's rulemaking) and used to assess the likelihood of a loss contingency resulting in a liability or impairment. A contingency is reasonably possible when the chance of the future event or events occurring is more than remote but less than likely.

---

6 Exchange Act Release No. 34-49544, 69 Fed. Reg. 20,672, 20,675 (Apr. 16, 2004) (emphasis added).

7 *See* PCAOB, *Staff Questions and Answers: Auditing Internal Control over Financial Reporting,* Question 27 (Oct. 6, 2004) (emphasis added).

The PCAOB appears to have extended the scope of internal control over financial reporting further into the realm of environmental compliance management than previously indicated by the SEC. Arguably, in picking the example of a waste management company, the PCAOB intentionally limited the guidance to situations in which business operations and compliance with environmental law are coextensive. However, there are many types of businesses other than waste management companies for which historical or future material environmental loss events are reasonably possible.

(ii) *ENVIRONMENTAL OPERATIONS*

According to the SEC, internal control over financial reporting "does not encompass the elements of the COSO Report definition that relate to effectiveness and efficiency of a company's operations."[8] As discussed in § 8.3(a)(i), however, the PCAOB has stated that "operations ... directly related to the presentation of and required disclosures in financial statements are encompassed in internal control over financial reporting."[9]

For example, an issuer may have established an ISO 14000 environmental management system (EMS) for the purpose of improving the effectiveness and efficiency of its operations. As part of the ongoing risk identification and assessment process under its EMS, the company looks for evidence of pollution conditions resulting from its operations. Such conditions might or might not be a violation of environmental law. For example, a release of hazardous substances into a public drinking water resource as a result of a transportation accident might represent a contingent environmental liability to the company for bodily injury, property damage, and natural resource damage claims, even though the unintended release was not unlawful. To the extent that an EMS, even though primarily intended to achieve operational objectives, serves to identify and evaluate pollution conditions that could reasonably be expected to meet the criteria for recognition or disclosure of a material environmental liability, those components of the EMS are directly related to the presentation of, and required disclosures in, financial statements.

(iii) *SEC DISCLOSURES*

Internal control over financial reporting is concerned with preparation of financial statements in accordance with GAAP. Accordingly, internal control over financial reporting encompasses those elements of the COSO Framework related to the preparation of reliable financial statements and accompanying notes. Internal control over financial reporting does not encompass SEC disclosure requirements under Regulation S-K. By contrast, *disclosure controls and procedures* do encompass SEC disclosure requirements under Regulation S-K. The similarities and differences between internal control over financial reporting and disclosure controls and procedures are discussed in § 8.4(c).

---

8 Securities Act Release No. 33-8238, 68 Fed. Reg. 36,636, 36,640 (June 18, 2002).

9 Exchange Act Release No. 34-49544, 69 Fed. Reg. 20,672, 20,675 (Apr. 16, 2004).

EXHIBIT 8.3

Section 404 and Regulation S-K

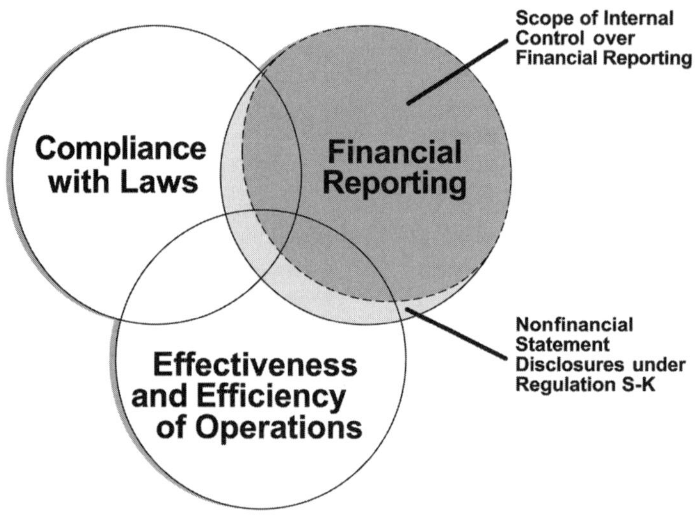

Exhibit 8.3 illustrates the relationship of internal control over financial reporting to environmental disclosures required under Regulation S-K. The shaded portion of the financial reporting circle—representing the financial statements and notes—is within the scope of internal control over financial reporting and is subject to independent review by the issuer's financial auditor under section 404 of Sarbanes-Oxley. The unshaded portions of the financial reporting circle—representing the nonfinancial statement information required under Regulation S-K—is outside the scope of section 404 and is not subject to independent review by the issuer's financial auditor.

(iv) ENVIRONMENTAL FINANCIAL REPORTING PROCESS

The scope of internal control over financial reporting, for purposes of section 404 of Sarbanes-Oxley (and perhaps section 302 of the Act as well), appears to encompass the entirety of the environmental financial reporting process (see Chapter 1)—including identification, assessment, measurement, and reporting—when it is at least *reasonably possible* (as that term is defined in FAS 5), given the nature of the company's current and historical assets and operations, that the entity has incurred or will incur in the future material environmental losses. This conclusion is based on the following points:

- A material weakness in internal control (as defined in § 27.3(b)) exists when one or more control deficiencies results in more than a remote likelihood that a material misstatement of the annual or interim financial statements will not be prevented or detected.
- The failure to identify and assess transactions, conditions, and events having environmental consequences potentially can result in a material

misstatement of an entity's financial condition and results of operations. If a material asset retirement obligation, for example, is not identified and assessed, it cannot be measured and properly reported.

- To provide reasonable assurance of compliance with SEC regulations, internal control over financial reporting must encompass procedures to identify and assess transactions, conditions, and events that have a reasonable possibility of giving rise to material environmental financial information.
- Although the PCAOB's guidance regarding the applicability of internal control over financial reporting to environmental legal compliance and operations uses a waste disposal company as an example (see § 8.3(a)(i)), companies other than waste disposal companies can incur material environmental losses. A company's potential exposure to material environmental losses requires an in-depth understanding of the nature of the company's current and historical assets and operations.
- Although the PCAOB's guidance regarding the applicability of internal control over financial reporting to environmental legal compliance and operations expressly addresses FAS 5 loss contingencies (see § 8.3(a)(i)), the PCAOB's rationale is equally applicable to other types of environmental financial information (e.g., asset retirement obligations, environmental guarantees, and environmental-related asset impairments).

Management and independent financial auditors of public companies, with guidance and oversight from the PCAOB, must determine the extent to which internal control over financial reporting encompasses the environmental financial reporting process. Pending issuance and widespread adoption of uniform standards for the scope and quality of internal control over environmental financial reporting, such determinations will necessarily involve considerable judgment.

(b) EVALUATION OF INTERNAL CONTROL

(i) MANAGEMENT'S REPORT

As discussed in § 7.3(b), issuers are required by section 404(a) of the Act to include in their annual reports a report of management on the issuer's internal control over financial reporting. Applicable SEC rules require that management base its evaluation of the effectiveness of the issuer's internal control over financial reporting on a suitable, recognized control framework that is established by a body or group that has followed due-process procedures, including broad distribution of the framework for public comment. The SEC has acknowledged that the COSO Framework satisfies this criterion and may be used as an evaluation framework for purposes of management's annual internal control evaluation and disclosure requirements. In recognition of the fact that other evaluation standards exist outside of the United States, and that frameworks other than COSO may be developed within the United States in the future, SEC rules do not mandate use of the COSO Framework. Today, however, the COSO Framework is the de facto standard for U.S. companies implementing and evaluating internal control over financial reporting.

(ii) INDEPENDENT ATTESTATION

Section 404(b) of the Act requires the issuer's independent financial auditor to attest to, and report on, management's internal control assessment pursuant to rules developed by the PCAOB.

Based on the PCAOB's rules (see Chapter 27), the outside auditor must now render three opinions in connection with the year-end financial statements:

1. An opinion as to whether the issuer's financial statements fairly present the issuer's financial position, results of operations, and cash flows in accordance with GAAP.
2. An opinion on whether management's assessment of the effectiveness of the issuer's internal control over financial reporting is fairly stated.
3. An opinion on whether the issuer maintained, in all material respects, effective internal control over financial reporting as of the end of the fiscal year.

Section 404(b) is arguably the most significant provision in the Act. Although the federal securities laws have required issuers to maintain effective internal control over financial reporting for several decades, the accounting fraud perpetrated by Enron, Worldcom, and others provided ample evidence that some leading U.S. companies in fact did not have effective internal control. In the spirit of "trust but verify," section 404(b) for the first time requires an independent review and assessment of the financial reporting *system*, not just the financial statements. For the first time under the federal securities laws, management is now graded against an objective standard for its ability to effectively manage the risks inherent in financial reporting, including the risk that material environmental financial information will not be identified, assessed, measured, and reported in a timely manner.

Section 404(b) has particular significance for environmental financial reporting, because companies may lack adequate procedures and controls for the identification, assessment, measurement, and reporting of certain types of environmental financial information required by recently adopted financial reporting standards (e.g., asset retirement obligations and environmental guarantees). Moreover, the competing objectives discussed in § 5.4 have encouraged some companies to avoid implementation of rigorous environmental financial reporting processes and controls. Issuers that have historically adopted a "don't ask, don't tell" policy (see § 5.4(b)) must now subject these policies and practices to an independent assessment. Whereas historically the odds of a material misstatement of environmental financial information resulting in an SEC enforcement action have been low, the chances that an independent auditor will object to policies and practices knowingly intended to understate, or having the unintended effect of understating, environmental liabilities are now considerably higher.

Effective internal control is a particular concern with respect to environmental financial reporting, for reasons such as the following:

- Conditions giving rise to material environmental liabilities may be invisible to directors, officers, shareholders, and auditors; identification, assessment, and measurement of environmental liabilities typically require proactive due diligence by management.
- New financial accounting standards, such as FAS 143 and FIN 47 (see Chapter 22), and FIN 45 (see Chapter 21) require entities to develop controls and procedures not previously required for conformance with GAAP.
- Measurement of environmental liabilities involves critical accounting estimates that are subject to special scrutiny (see §§ 7.2(c)(i), 12.5, and 26.3(b)).
- Under recently adopted auditing standards, intentional failure to identify, assess, measure, and report material environmental financial information, even when management has plausible arguments supporting its actions, may be considered to constitute financial reporting fraud (see § 26.2(d)).

(c) CONCEPT OF REASONABLE ASSURANCE

Internal control cannot provide absolute assurance of the reliability of financial reporting. No system will always do what it is intended to do. Reasonable assurance that the entity's financial reporting objectives will be achieved is the best that can be expected from any internal control system. The concept of *reasonable assurance* is built into the definition of *internal control over financial reporting* under section 404 of Sarbanes-Oxley.

Reasonable assurance does not imply that internal control systems will fail frequently. Many factors, individually and collectively, strengthen the concept of reasonable assurance. The cumulative effect of overlapping and reinforcing controls at various levels in the organization greatly reduces the risk that an entity will not achieve its financial reporting objectives.

Of course, no internal control system will be effective in achieving objectives that it was not designed to achieve. An otherwise effective internal control system will thus provide no assurance that the entity will achieve compliance with the federal securities laws, if management has not established full legal compliance as an objective. Because of strong competing objectives (described in § 5.4), it is imperative that senior management and the board of directors have a clear understanding of the legal requirements pertaining to environmental financial reporting and, at a minimum, establish full compliance with these legal requirements as a nondiscretionary financial reporting objective.

8.4 DISCLOSURE CONTROLS AND PROCEDURES

Section 302(a)(4) of the Act directs the SEC to adopt rules to require the issuer's certifying officers to certify that they:

- Are responsible for establishing and maintaining internal controls.
- Have designed such internal controls to ensure that material information relating to the issuer and its consolidated subsidiaries is made known to such officers by others within those entities, particularly during the period in which the periodic reports are being prepared.
- Have evaluated the effectiveness of the issuer's internal controls as of a date within 90 days prior to the report.
- Have presented in the report their conclusions about the effectiveness of their internal controls based on their evaluation as of that date.

The SEC adopted rules implementing section 302(a) of the Act effective August 29, 2002.[10] The rules apply to all issuers that file periodic reports under section 13(a) or 15(d) of the Exchange Act, including foreign private issuers, banks and savings associations, issuers of asset-backed securities, small business issuers, and registered investment companies.

As discussed in § 8.5, internal control historically has been understood to encompass those processes intended to provide reasonable assurance as to the reliability of financial reporting and the preparation of financial statements in accordance with GAAP. With this historical context in mind, the SEC observed that, although section 302 requires various certifications regarding controls and procedures for financial reporting under GAAP, it does not directly address the issuer's responsibility for controls and procedures related to the issuer's reporting obligations under the federal securities laws, which include financial and nonfinancial reporting requirements beyond GAAP. Accordingly, the SEC defined the term *disclosure controls and procedures* to make it explicit that the controls contemplated by section 302(a) of the Act are intended to incorporate a broader concept of controls and procedures designed to ensure compliance with disclosure requirements under the federal securities laws. In the SEC's words:

> We make this distinction [between internal control over financial reporting and disclosure controls and procedures] based on our review of Section 302 of the Act as well as to effectuate what we believe to be Congress' intent to have senior officers certify that required material nonfinancial information, as well as financial information, is included in an issuer's quarterly and annual reports. Under this interpretation, we maintain the pre-existing concept of internal controls without expanding it by relating it to nonfinancial information.[11]

---

[10] Securities Act Release No. 33-8124, 67 Fed. Reg. 57,276 (Sept. 9, 2002).

[11] *Id.*, 67 Fed. Reg. at 57,280.

(a) SEC RULEMAKING ON DISCLOSURE CONTROLS AND PROCEDURES

Under new rules 13a-14(a)(4) and 15d-14(a)(4), which implement section 302(a)(4) of the Act, each periodic report filed by the issuer must contain a statement by each certifying officer that he or she and the other certifying officers are responsible for establishing and maintaining disclosure controls and procedures for the issuer, and that they have:

- Designed such disclosure controls and procedures to ensure that material information relating to the issuer, including its consolidated subsidiaries, is made known to them by others within those entities, particularly during the period in which the periodic reports are being prepared.
- Evaluated the effectiveness of the issuer's disclosure controls and procedures as of a date within 90 days prior to the filing date of the report (Evaluation Date).
- Presented in the report their conclusions about the effectiveness of the disclosure controls and procedures based on their evaluation as of the Evaluation Date.[12]

(b) DEFINITION OF DISCLOSURE CONTROLS AND PROCEDURES

The rules implementing section 302(a) of the Act define *disclosure controls and procedures* to mean:

> [C]ontrols and other procedures of an issuer that are designed to ensure that information required to be disclosed by the issuer in the reports that it files or submits under the [Exchange Act] is recorded, processed, summarized and reported within the time periods specified in the [SEC's] rules and forms. Disclosure controls and procedures include, without limitation, controls and procedures designed to ensure that information required to be disclosed by an issuer in the reports that it files or submits under the [Exchange Act] is accumulated and communicated to the issuer's management, including its principal executive officer or officers and principal financial officer or officers, or persons performing similar functions, as appropriate to allow timely decisions regarding required disclosure.[13]

(c) DISTINGUISHED FROM INTERNAL CONTROL

There is substantial overlap between disclosure controls and procedures and internal control over financial reporting, but the two concepts are not identical. There are elements of disclosure controls and procedures that are not subsumed by internal control over financial reporting and some elements of internal control that are not subsumed by disclosure controls and procedures. Exhibit 8.4

---

12 17 C.F.R. §§ 240.13a-14(b)(4), 240.15d-14(b)(4).
13 17 C.F.R. §§ 240.13a-14(c), 240.15d-14(c).

EXHIBIT 8.4

Overlap of Control Definitions

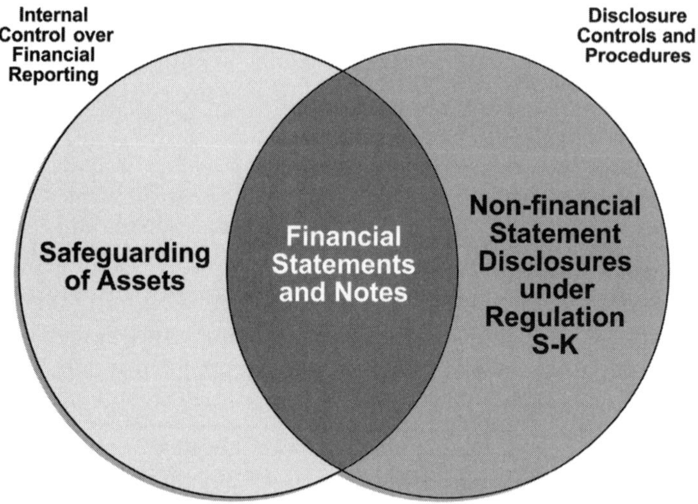

illustrates the overlap and distinctions between disclosure controls and procedures and internal control over financial reporting.

As discussed in § 8.3, internal control over financial reporting encompasses those policies and procedures that:

1. Pertain to the maintenance of records that in reasonable detail accurately and fairly reflect the transactions and dispositions of the assets of the entity;
2. Provide reasonable assurance that transactions are recorded as necessary to permit preparation of financial statements in accordance with generally accepted accounting principles, and that receipts and expenditures of the entity are being made only in accordance with authorizations of management and directors of the entity; and
3. Provide reasonable assurance regarding prevention or timely detection of unauthorized acquisition, use, or disposition of the entity's assets that could have a material effect on the financial statements.

According to the SEC, disclosure controls and procedures include those components of internal control over financial reporting that provide reasonable assurance that transactions are recorded as necessary to permit preparation of financial statements in accordance with GAAP.[14] Disclosure controls and procedures thus appear to encompass those elements of internal control over financial reporting included in paragraphs (1) and (2) above, while excluding those elements contained in paragraph (3). To the extent that internal control policies and

[14] Securities Act Release No. 33-8238, 68 Fed. Reg. 36,636, 36,645 (June 18, 2003).

procedures address the prevention and detection of unauthorized acquisition, use, or disposition of the entity's assets, internal control over financial reporting is a broader concept than disclosure controls and procedures.

Disclosure controls and procedures include controls and procedures designed to ensure timely and reliable reporting of financial and nonfinancial information in periodic reports filed under the Exchange Act. Whereas internal control over financial reporting applies only to financial information presented in the financial statements and the notes to the financial statements, disclosure controls and procedures encompass both financial information presented in the financial statements and the notes to the financial statements and financial and nonfinancial information disclosed pursuant to Regulation S-K. To the extent that disclosure controls and procedures address the accurate and timely reporting of financial and nonfinancial information outside of the financial statements and the notes to the financial statements, disclosure controls and procedures is a broader concept than internal control over financial reporting.

The scope of disclosure controls and procedures and internal control over financial reporting overlap with respect to compliance with applicable laws to the extent that controls are needed to ensure that the effects of noncompliance with environmental laws are recorded in the issuer's financial statements. For example, controls necessary to ensure timely identification, assessment, measurement, and reporting of material environmental loss contingencies arising from noncompliance with environmental laws are encompassed within both disclosure controls and procedures and internal control over financial reporting.[15]

(d) APPLICATION TO ENVIRONMENTAL FINANCIAL REPORTING

With respect to environmental financial reporting, the only significant difference between the scope of disclosure controls and procedures and internal control over financial reporting is nonfinancial statement disclosures required under Regulation S-K. Exhibit 8.3 illustrates the subset of environmental regulatory compliance and environmental operations management that is subject to financial reporting requirements under Regulation S-K.

To the extent that environmental regulatory compliance and environmental operations matters are subject to financial reporting requirements under Regulation S-K, both are within the scope of the section 302 certification pertaining to disclosure controls and procedures. Examples of environmental regulatory compliance and environmental operations management matters are shown in Exhibit 4.3.

As part of management's evaluation of disclosure controls and procedures, management must appropriately consider the issuer's exposure to environmental risks and compliance with environmental laws. Such consideration should include assessing whether the issuer adequately monitors environmental risks and compliance with environmental laws, and has appropriate disclosure

15 *See* SEC Staff Guidance, *Office of the Chief Accountant and Division of Corporation Finance: Management's Report on Internal Control over Financial Reporting and Certification of Disclosure in Exchange Act Periodic Reports, Frequently Asked Questions,* Question 10 (June 23, 2004; as amended Oct. 6, 2004).

controls and procedures to ensure timely disclosure of material environmental risks and legal matters.

8.5 PRIOR LEGISLATION AND CASE LAW

The Foreign Corrupt Practices Act of 1977 (FCPA) amended section 13(b)(2) of the Exchange Act to include provisions requiring public companies to keep books, records, and accounts that, in reasonable detail, accurately and fairly reflect transactions and dispositions of the issuer's assets, and to devise and maintain a system of internal accounting controls sufficient to provide reasonable assurance that the objectives of internal control (e.g., reliable financial reports) are being met. Section 13(b)(5) of the Exchange Act makes knowing circumvention or failure to implement a system of internal accounting controls or knowing falsification of any book, record, or account a criminal act.

The Omnibus Trade and Competitiveness Act of 1988 (1988 Trade Act) further amended the FCPA's accounting provisions and clarified the terms *reasonable assurances* and *reasonable detail* as used in section 13(b)(2) of the Exchange Act. The 1988 Trade Act clarified these provisions by stating that these terms mean "such level of detail and degree of assurance as would satisfy prudent officials in the conduct of their affairs."[16]

Even before Sarbanes-Oxley, the internal control requirements in the federal securities laws were recognized as relevant to environmental financial reporting. In a 1998 administrative proceeding,[17] the SEC addressed the relationship between internal control and the estimation of environmental liabilities.

The case involved Lee Pharmaceuticals and several of the company's officers and directors. In 1987, Lee first learned of high levels of contamination in the soil and groundwater at one of its operating facilities. The California Regional Water Quality Control Board subsequently ordered Lee, both in 1988 and in 1989, to investigate the contamination, but Lee replied that it had not caused any contamination. Lee's consultants then performed tests, and confirmed the presence of contamination to Henry Lee, Lee's board chairman, in a 1989 letter and two 1990 reports. Lee, however, failed to complete its investigation of the contamination and, according to the SEC, misled investors about the nature and extent of its environmental responsibilities and liabilities in its SEC reports from 1991 through 1996.

In October 1991, Henry Lee received an estimate of $465,200 for environmental investigation and cleanup costs. Management believed the estimate was unreliable and failed to disclose it in Lee's 1991 Form 10-K. Lee further misrepresented in that Form 10-K that it was conducting further tests. Also, notwithstanding confirmation that Lee's property was contaminated, Lee nevertheless falsely reported in its 1991 Form 10-K that Lee had "some potential contamination," but that the environmental tests were "inconclusive." Lee continued to materially understate the seriousness of its environmental obligations in future

[16] 15 U.S.C. § 78m(b)(7).

[17] *In re* Lee Pharms., 66 SEC Docket 2134 (Apr. 9, 1998) (Exchange Act Release No. 34-39843).

SEC filings. For example, Lee falsely stated in its 1992 Form 10-K that it had no information about the cleanup costs for its property, even though in May 1992, Henry Lee, in a letter to Lee's insurance carrier, had estimated Lee's environmental investigation and cleanup costs at $700,000.

Among other violations of the federal securities laws, the SEC addressed Lee's violation of the internal control provisions of Exchange Act section 13(b)(2)(B). The SEC found that Lee lacked the required internal accounting controls necessary to properly report its environmental liabilities. Noting that Lee's CFO, Michael Agresti, was primarily responsible for devising and implementing Lee's system of internal accounting controls, the SEC concluded that Agresti "did not develop internal controls for Lee's environmental liabilities that would assure that Lee would obtain estimates of its range of environmental costs, and accrue the minimum of the range as a loss in Lee's financial statements as required by GAAP. Agresti, therefore, willfully aided and abetted and caused Lee's violations of the internal control provisions of section 13(b)(2)(B) of the Exchange Act."[18] The SEC further found that Henry Lee had violated Rule 13b2-2 by failing to inform Lee's auditors about the $465,200 estimate for cleanup costs that he received in 1991, and the $700,000 estimate he made in 1992 for insurance purposes. (See Chapter 9 for a discussion of new standards and penalties under Sarbanes-Oxley for failing to share information with auditors.)

For willfully aiding and abetting and causing violations of sections 13(a), 13(b)(2)(A), and 13(b)(2)(B) of the Exchange Act, and Rules 12b-20 and 13a-1, the SEC revoked Agresti's privilege of appearing or practicing before the SEC as an accountant for three years. Henry Lee settled the charges against him and was ordered to cease and desist from committing or causing any current or future violation of the federal securities laws.

---

[18] *Id.*

CHAPTER NINE

Improper Influence on the Audit

9.1 INTRODUCTION

Section 303(a) of Sarbanes-Oxley states:

> It shall be unlawful, in contravention of such rules or regulations as the [SEC] shall prescribe as necessary or appropriate in the public interest and for the protection of investors, for any officer or director of an issuer, or any other person acting under the direction thereof, to take any action to fraudulently influence, coerce, manipulate, or mislead any independent public or certified accountant engaged in the performance of an audit of the financial statements of that issuer for the purpose of rendering such financial statements materially misleading.[1]

Before enactment of section 303 of the Act, SEC rule 132-2 already prohibited officers and directors from directly or indirectly making or causing to be made materially misleading statements to auditors. For example, it was unlawful before section 303, and continues thereafter to be unlawful, for an officer or director entering into an arrangement with a third party to send a misleading confirmation or to provide other misleading information or data to the auditor of the issuer's financial statements. Section 303, however, significantly expanded the scope of preexisting SEC prohibitions.

In response to section 303, the SEC adopted new rules supplementing Regulation 13B-2, which addresses the falsification of books, records, and accounts and false or misleading statements, or omissions to make certain statements, to accountants. Effective June 27, 2003, new rule 13b2-2(b)(1) specifically prohibits officers and directors, and persons acting under their direction, from coercing, manipulating, misleading, or fraudulently influencing (collectively referred to

[1] 107 P.L. 204, Title III, § 303, 116 Stat. 745 (July 30, 2002).

as *improperly influencing*) the auditor of the issuer's financial statements when such person knew or should have known that the action, if successful, could result in rendering the issuer's financial statements materially misleading.

9.2 DEFINITION OF *OFFICER*

The term *officer* includes the company's president, vice president, secretary, treasurer or principal financial officer, comptroller or principal accounting officer, and any person routinely performing corresponding functions with respect to any organization, whether incorporated or unincorporated.

9.3 ACTING UNDER THE DIRECTION OF

The SEC interprets Congress' use of the term *direction* to encompass a broader category of behavior than *supervision*. A person may be *acting under the direction* of an officer or director even if the person is not under the supervision or control of that officer or director. Such persons might include not only the issuer's employees, but also customers, vendors (e.g., environmental consultants), or creditors who, under the direction of an officer or director, provide false or misleading confirmations or other false or misleading information to auditors, or who enter into side agreements that enable the issuer to mislead the auditor.

In appropriate circumstances, persons acting under the direction of officers and directors also may include partners or employees of the issuer's accounting firm (such as consultants or forensic accounting specialists retained by counsel for the issuer) and attorneys, securities professionals, or other advisers. Such persons may be in violation of section 303 when they pressure an auditor to:

- Limit the scope of the audit.
- Issue an unqualified report on the financial statements when such a report is unwarranted.
- Not object to an inappropriate accounting treatment.
- Not to withdraw an issued audit report on the issuer's financial statements.

In the case of an investment company, persons acting under the direction of officers and directors of a registered investment company may include, among others, officers, directors, and employees of the investment company's investment adviser, sponsor, depositor, administrator, principal underwriter, custodian, transfer agent, or other service providers.

9.4 EXAMPLES OF IMPROPER INFLUENCE

The SEC has identified several types of conduct that could constitute improper influence (if the person engaging in that conduct knows or should know that the conduct, if successful, could result in rendering the issuer's financial statements materially misleading). These include, but are not limited to, directly or indirectly:

- Offering or paying bribes or other financial incentives, including offering future employment or contracts for nonaudit services.
- Providing an auditor with an inaccurate or misleading legal analysis.
- Threatening to cancel, or canceling, existing nonaudit or audit engagements if the auditor objects to the issuer's accounting.
- Seeking to have a partner removed from the audit engagement because the partner objects to the issuer's accounting.
- Blackmailing.
- Making physical threats.

Whether the conduct would violate section 303 will depend on an analysis of the facts and circumstances of each case.

9.5 RENDERING FINANCIAL STATEMENTS MATERIALLY MISLEADING

For the improper influence on the auditor to be actionable under section 303, it must be for the purpose of rendering the issuer's financial statements materially misleading. Because management prepares the financial statements and the auditor conducts an audit or review of those financial statements, the auditor would not directly render the financial statements materially misleading. Rather, the auditor might be improperly influenced to, among other things:

- Issue an unwarranted report on the financial statements, including suggesting or acquiescing in the use of inappropriate accounting treatments or not proposing adjustments required for the financial statements to conform with GAAP.
- Refrain from performing audit or review procedures that, if performed, might divulge material misstatements in the financial statements.
- Not withdraw a previously issued audit report when required by generally accepted auditing standards.
- Refrain from communicating appropriate matters to the audit committee.

9.6 KNEW OR SHOULD HAVE KNOWN

Section 303(a) of the Act provides that improper influence of the issuer's financial auditor is actionable if undertaken "for the purpose of rendering [the issuer's] financial statements materially misleading." The SEC interprets this to mean that a person who engages in conduct to improperly influence an auditor will be culpable only if he or she *knew or should have known* that the improper influence, if successful, could result in rendering financial statements materially misleading. This constructive knowledge standard in effect establishes a negligence standard.

Fraudulent intent is not required. For example, an officer of an issuer may coerce an auditor not to conduct certain audit procedures required by generally accepted auditing standards in order to conceal the officer's embezzlement of funds from the issuer. Such actions might not be for the purpose of rendering the financial statements misleading. If that officer, however, knew or should have known that not performing the procedures could result in the auditor not detecting and seeking correction of material errors in the financial statements, then the officer's conduct is subject to the rule.

9.7 ENVIRONMENTAL CONCERNS

Section 303 of the Act and new SEC Regulation 13B-2 present particular cause for concern for employees and other professionals involved in the identification, assessment, measurement, and reporting of environmental financial information. Failure of such persons to recognize recent changes in historical financial reporting practices relating to environmental legal obligations and impairments, or aggressive interpretation of new financial reporting standards so as to avoid full disclosure of environmental financial information, for example, could be found to constitute improper influence under the Act. Environmental matters are of particular concern for several reasons:

- Competing objectives that may have resulted in past under reporting of environmental obligations (see § 5.4).
- The significant complexity and uncertainty involved in measuring environmental liabilities.
- The high degree of judgment and subjectivity involved in assessments of probability and materiality of environmental loss contingencies.
- The introduction of new financial reporting standards representing a marked departure from the historical environmental financial reporting framework (e.g., conditional asset retirement obligations and environmental guarantees).

The following scenario illustrates one example of how employees and professional advisors can inadvertently run afoul of section 303. In the course of an audit, independent accountants generally rely on company employees to disclose known environmental liabilities. Depending on the questions asked by the auditor, however, employees may not provide the auditor with a comprehensive list. For decades prior to the issuance of FIN 47, GAAP was understood to require accrual or disclosure only of pending or threatened legal claims. When asked to provide a list of known environmental liabilities, impairments, and asset retirement obligations, employees may not understand that it is necessary to identify historical pollution conditions affecting company-owned facilities even though these matters are not subject to pending or threatened legal action. The auditor may or may not conduct independent investigation to verify the completeness of the entity's disclosure, other than to send inquiry letters to the entity's lawyers (see § 26.3(i)). Audit inquiry letters, however, are unlikely to fill in all the gaps.

Audit inquiry letters generally ask the reporting entity's lawyers to describe both pending legal matters and unasserted claims. According to American Bar Association guidelines, however, attorneys are instructed not to provide the auditor with information about unasserted claims unless, and only to the extent that, the client has requested the attorney to comment on specific unasserted claims.[2] In general practice, reporting entities do not ask their outside legal counsel to comment on specific unasserted claims relating to known or suspected historical pollution conditions in audit inquiry letters. Accordingly, attorneys do not discuss such matters in their response to the auditors. This raises the very real possibility that the auditor will not be informed of potentially material environmental obligations (e.g., conditional asset retirement obligations), which though legally enforceable are not the subject of pending legal action. In response to Sarbanes-Oxley, many law firms are adjusting the standard language in their audit inquiry response letters to limit the scope of the response specifically so they do not run afoul of section 303 of the Act.

Failure to fully inform the company's independent auditor of all material environmental matters—including conditional asset retirement obligations—could be deemed improper influence on the conduct of an audit. In such event, a broad range of individuals could be subject to civil and criminal liability under section 303 of the Act, including:

- *Directors and officers.* The entity's directors and officers may be culpable for having failed to establish appropriate financial reporting policies and procedures that would ensure full disclosure of all potentially material environmental matters to the entity's auditors.
- *Environmental managers.* Environmental managers often will be responsible for assembling the list of environmental matters to be disclosed to the auditors. Environmental managers are also the most likely persons within the organization to have direct knowledge of known or suspected historical pollution conditions, including those that are not subject to pending or threatened legal action.
- *Environmental consultants.* Independent environmental consultants may be aware of historical pollution conditions that the entity has decided not to investigate in order to avoid or delay potential cleanup costs. If called upon by the issuer's financial auditor to discuss known or suspected historical pollution conditions for which the issuer might be responsible, the consultant may be constrained from disclosing such matters by confidentiality agreements entered into with the issuer. If the consultant fails to disclose matters that the consultant knew or should have known could result in rendering the issuer's financial statements materially misleading, the con-

2 *American Bar Association Statement of Policy Regarding Lawyers' Responses to Auditors' Requests for Information,* § 5, pp. 8-9, 31 Bus. Law. (no. 3, Apr. 1976).

sultant could be in violation of section 303. The SEC has clearly indicated that rule 13b2-2(b)(1) applies not only to the issuer's employees, but also to vendors who provide false or misleading confirmations or other false or misleading information to auditors under the direction of an officer or director.

- *General counsel.* Rule 13b2-2(b)(1) applies to lawyers who provide an auditor with an inaccurate or misleading legal analysis. As illustrated by the law and accounting sandwich metaphor discussed in Chapter 2, environmental financial reporting to a large extent rests on interpretations of environmental law. Corporate attorneys may run afoul of section 303, for example, by providing to the auditor an inaccurate or misleading analysis of the issuer's environmental loss contingencies and legal obligations under FAS 5, FAS 143, FIN 47, and FIN 45.
- *Outside legal counsel.* Outside legal counsel for the issuer could violate rule 13b2-2(b)(1) by providing their client's auditor with an inaccurate or misleading legal analysis of the issuer's environmental loss contingencies and legal obligations. For example, issuers may pressure their outside legal counsel to opine that assertion of unasserted claims associated with known pollution conditions is not probable, even though the circumstances indicate otherwise. If the attorneys comply with their client's wishes, when they knew or should have known that their legal analysis could result in rendering the issuer's financial statements materially misleading, they face potential civil and criminal liability under section 303.

CHAPTER TEN

Off-Balance-Sheet Arrangements

10.1 INTRODUCTION

Section 401(a) of Sarbanes-Oxley added section 13(j) to the Exchange Act. The new section required the SEC to adopt final rules to require periodic SEC reports (Forms 10-Q and 10-K) to disclose "all material off-balance sheet transactions, arrangements, obligations (including contingent obligations), and other relationships of the issuer with unconsolidated entities or other persons, that may have a material current or future effect on financial condition, changes in financial condition, results of operations, liquidity, capital expenditures, capital resources, or significant components of revenues or expenses."

In February 2003, the SEC issued final rules implementing the requirements of section 401(a). Release No. 33-8182[1] amends Item 303 of Regulation S-K (MD&A). According to the SEC, Item 303 already required disclosure of off-balance-sheet arrangements if necessary for understanding of a registrant's financial condition, changes in financial condition, or results of operations. The amendments thus clarify disclosures that registrants must make with regard to off-balance-sheet arrangements, require registrants to set apart disclosures relating to off-balance-sheet arrangements in a designated section of the MD&A, and (except in the case of small business issuers) require tabular disclosure of aggregate contractual obligations.

10.2 DEFINITION OF *OFF-BALANCE-SHEET ARRANGEMENTS*

For purposes of MD&A disclosure, the new rule defines *off-balance-sheet arrangements* as any transaction, agreement, or other contractual arrangement to which an entity unconsolidated with the registrant is a party, under which the registrant has:

1 Securities Act Release No. 33-8182, 68 Fed. Reg. 5982 (Feb. 5, 2003).

- Any obligation under a guarantee contract that has any of the characteristics identified in paragraph 3 of FIN 45, and that is not excluded from the initial recognition and measurement provisions of FIN 45 pursuant to paragraphs 6 or 7 of that Interpretation;
- A retained or contingent interest in assets transferred to an unconsolidated entity or similar arrangement that serves as credit, liquidity, or market risk support to such entity for such assets;
- Any obligation, including a contingent obligation, under a contract that would be accounted for as a derivative instrument, except that it is both indexed to the registrant's own stock and classified in stockholders' equity in the registrant's statement of financial position, and therefore excluded from the scope of FASB Statement of Financial Accounting Standards No. 133, "Accounting for Derivative Instruments and Hedging Activities," pursuant to paragraph 11(a) of that Statement, as may be modified or supplemented; or
- Any obligation, including a contingent obligation, arising out of a variable interest (as referenced in FASB Interpretation No. 46, "Consolidation of Variable Interest Entities," as may be modified or supplemented) in an unconsolidated entity that is held by, and material to, the registrant, where such entity provides financing, liquidity, market risk, or credit risk support to, or engages in leasing, hedging, or research and development services with, the registrant.[2]

The definition is intended to encompass the means through which companies typically structure off-balance-sheet transactions or otherwise incur risks of loss that are not fully transparent to investors.

The definition specifically excludes contingent liabilities arising out of litigation, arbitration, or regulatory actions, a notable change from the SEC's proposed rulemaking. In the view of the SEC, meaningful disclosure of contingent liabilities and commitments is not necessarily best accomplished by an aggregated disclosure format (either tabular or textual), because such a format would inevitably omit important information about the operative facts and circumstances of contingent liabilities and commitments (e.g., triggering events, probability of occurrence, or recourse provisions). The SEC has stated, however, that it will continue to assess the costs and benefits of an MD&A disclosure requirement for aggregate contingent liabilities and commitments in connection with its ongoing review of the MD&A. Pending future SEC action on the subject, registrants should refer to the existing guidance in Release No. 33-8056[3] to consider whether it would be beneficial to investors to include tabular disclosure of aggregate commercial commitments.

---

2 17 C.F.R. § 229.303((a)(4)(ii).

3 Securities Act Release No. 33-8056, 67 Fed. Reg. 3746 (Jan. 25, 2002).

10.3 MATERIALITY THRESHOLD

The new rule requires disclosure of off-balance-sheet arrangements that are "reasonably likely" to have a current or future material effect on the registrant's financial condition, changes in financial condition, revenues or expenses, results of operations, liquidity, capital expenditures, or capital resources. The concept of *materiality* is discussed in § 12.2. The *reasonably likely* probability standard used for off-balance-sheet arrangements is the same standard applicable to other portions of MD&A disclosure (see § 12.2(c)(iii)).

10.4 DISCLOSURE REQUIREMENTS

(a) TEXTUAL DISCLOSURE

As amended, Item 303 requires disclosure of the following information to the extent necessary for an understanding of a registrant's off-balance-sheet arrangements and their effects:

- The nature and business purpose of the registrant's off-balance-sheet arrangements;
- The importance of the off-balance-sheet arrangements to the registrant for liquidity, capital resources, market risk or credit risk support, or other benefits;
- The financial impact of the arrangement on the registrant (e.g., revenues, expenses, cash flows, or securities issued) and the registrant's exposure to risk as a result of the arrangements (e.g., retained interests or contingent liabilities); and
- Known events, demands, commitments, trends, or uncertainties that affect the availability or benefits to the registrant of material off-balance-sheet arrangements.

In addition to these enumerated items, the amendments contain a principles-based requirement that the registrant disclose any additional information that it believes is necessary for an understanding of its off-balance-sheet arrangements and the specified material effects.

There is no obligation to disclose an off-balance-sheet arrangement until a definitive agreement that is unconditionally binding or subject only to customary closing conditions exists or, if there is no such agreement, when settlement of the transaction occurs.

(b) AGGREGATED TABULAR DISCLOSURE

In addition to textual disclosure, the amendments require registrants to disclose, in a tabular format, the amounts of payments due under specified contractual obligations, aggregated by category of contractual obligations, for specified time periods. The amendments specify that the following categories of contractual obligations must be included within the table:

- Long-term debt obligations
- Capital lease obligations
- Operating lease obligations
- Purchase obligations
- Other long-term liabilities reflected on the registrant's balance sheet under GAAP

The amendments define the first four categories of contractual obligations. The fifth category captures all other long-term liabilities that are reflected on the registrant's balance sheet.

10.5 ENVIRONMENTAL MATTERS

(a) ENVIRONMENTAL LOSS CONTINGENCIES

The exclusion of "contingent liabilities arising out of litigation, arbitration, or regulatory actions" under the definition of *off-balance-sheet arrangements* effectively excludes most environmental loss contingencies from the new disclosure requirements under section 401(a) of the Act. For example, pending or threatened claims associated with historical pollution conditions falling within the scope of FAS 5 are not subject to the amended Item 303 disclosure requirements.

(b) ENVIRONMENTAL GUARANTEES

The definition of *off-balance-sheet arrangements* addresses certain guarantees that may be a source of potential risk to a registrant's future liquidity, capital resources, and results of operations, regardless of whether they are recorded as liabilities. The definition is designed so that a registrant's application of FIN 45 will provide the basis for determining the guaranteed contracts that are subject to disclosure under the amendments.

Environmental guarantees are contracts that contingently require the guarantor to make payments to the guaranteed party upon the future occurrence of specified events or conditions giving rise to environmental losses on the part of the guaranteed party. As discussed in § 21.2(a), environmental guarantees are within the scope of FIN 45. Accordingly, environmental guarantees are subject to the amended Item 303 textual disclosure requirements if they are *reasonably likely* to have a current or future material effect on the registrant's financial condition, changes in financial condition, revenues or expenses, results of operations, liquidity, capital expenditures, or capital resources. In addition, to the extent that the registrant's various environmental guarantees are reflected as liabilities on the registrant's balance sheet pursuant to FIN 45, these liabilities must be presented in the registrant's aggregated tabular disclosure under the category for "other long-term liabilities" reflected on the registrant's balance sheet under GAAP.

CHAPTER ELEVEN

Accelerated Reporting

11.1 INTRODUCTION

Prior to Sarbanes-Oxley, issuers were required to report very few significant corporate events. The limited number of Form 8-K disclosure items permitted issuers to delay disclosure of many significant events until the due date of the next periodic report. During such a delay, the market was unable to assimilate such undisclosed information into the value of the issuer's securities.

Section 409 of the Act, entitled "Real Time Issuer Disclosures," states that:

> Each issuer reporting under section 13(a) or 15(d) shall disclose to the public on a rapid and current basis such additional information concerning material changes in the financial condition or operations of the issuer, in plain English, which may include trend and qualitative information and graphic presentations, as the [SEC] determines, by rule, is necessary or useful for the protection of investors and in the public interest.

Effective August 23, 2004, new SEC rules adopted pursuant to section 409 of the Act accelerate the deadline for filing Form 8-K reports for most items to four business days after a "reportable event" occurs. The rules also significantly expand the scope of events that issuers must report on Form 8-K.

11.2 REPORTABLE EVENTS

The amendments to Form 8-K significantly expand the scope of events subject to mandatory reporting and reorganize the reporting requirements into various topics. In addition to creating eight new disclosure requirements, the SEC amendments moved two existing reporting requirements from other reports into Form 8-K and expanded two other existing Form 8-K requirements.

The amendments organize the Form 8-K items under the following section headings and with the following new numbering system:

- Section 1—Registrant's Business and Operations
  - Item 1.01 Entry into a Material Definitive Agreement
  - Item 1.02 Termination of a Material Definitive Agreement
  - Item 1.03 Bankruptcy or Receivership
- Section 2—Financial Information
  - Item 2.01 Completion of Acquisition or Disposition of Assets
  - Item 2.02 Results of Operations and Financial Condition
  - Item 2.03 Creation of a Direct Financial Obligation or an Obligation under an Off-Balance-Sheet Arrangement of a Registrant
  - Item 2.04 Triggering Events that Accelerate or Increase a Direct Financial Obligation or an Obligation under an Off-Balance-Sheet Arrangement
  - Item 2.05 Costs Associated with Exit or Disposal Activities
  - Item 2.06 Material Impairments
- Section 3—Securities and Trading Markets
  - Item 3.01 Notice of Delisting or Failure to Satisfy a Continued Listing Rule or Standard; Transfer of Listing
  - Item 3.02 Unregistered Sales of Equity Securities
  - Item 3.03 Material Modifications to Rights of Security Holder
- Section 4—Matters Related to Accountants and Financial Statements
  - Item 4.01 Changes in Registrant's Certifying Accountant
  - Item 4.02 Non-Reliance on Previously Issued Financial Statements or a Related Audit Report or Completed Interim Review
- Section 5—Corporate Governance and Management
  - Item 5.01 Changes in Control of Registrant
  - Item 5.02 Departure of Directors or Principal Officers; Election of Directors; Appointment of Principal Officers
  - Item 5.03 Amendments to Articles of Incorporation or Bylaws; Change in Fiscal Year
  - Item 5.04 Temporary Suspension of Trading Under Registrant's Employee Benefit Plans
  - Item 5.05 Amendments to the Registrant's Code of Ethics, or Waiver of a Provision of the Code of Ethics

- Section 6—[Reserved]

- Section 7—Regulation FD
  - Item 7.01 Regulation FD Disclosure

- Section 8—Other Events
  - Item 8.01 Other Events

- Section 9—Financial Statements and Exhibits
  - Item 9.01 Financial Statements and Exhibits

11.3 REPORTABLE ENVIRONMENTAL EVENTS

Environmental matters subject to accelerated reporting on Form 8-K may include environmental indemnities, environmental loss contingencies, and environmental asset impairments.

(a) ENVIRONMENTAL GUARANTEES UNDER ITEM 2.03

New Item 2.03 requires disclosure on Form 8-K if an entity becomes obligated under a material direct financial obligation, or directly or contingently liable for a material obligation arising out of an off-balance-sheet arrangement. Direct financial obligations include long-term debt obligations, capital lease obligations, operating lease obligations, and short-term debt obligations that arise other than in the ordinary course of business.

Item 2.03 refers to Item 303(a)(4)(ii) of Regulation S-K for the definition of the term *off-balance-sheet arrangements*. As discussed in § 10.5(b), environmental guarantees are considered off-balance-sheet arrangements. Environmental guarantees and indemnity agreements (Chapter 21) are thus subject to accelerated reporting on Form 8-K if they are *material* to the registrant. The concept of materiality is discussed in § 12.2.

If a registrant becomes directly or contingently liable for an environmental indemnity obligation that is material to the entity, it must disclose the following information on Form 8-K:

- The date on which the registrant becomes directly or contingently liable on the obligation and a brief description of the transaction or agreement creating the arrangement and obligation.
- A brief description of the nature and amount of the registrant's obligation under the arrangement, including the material terms under which it may become a direct obligation, if applicable, or may be accelerated or increased, and the nature of any recourse provisions that would enable the registrant to recover from third parties.
- The maximum potential amount of future payments (undiscounted) that the registrant may be required to make, if different (without reduction for

the effect of any amounts that may possibly be recovered under any recourse provisions).

- A brief description of the other terms and conditions of the obligation or arrangement that are material to the company.

Disclosure regarding an environmental indemnity is required under Item 2.03 even if the registrant is not a party to the transaction or agreement creating such obligation. In the event that neither the registrant nor any affiliate of the registrant is a party to the transaction or agreement creating the contingent obligation on the part of the registrant, the four-business-day period for reporting the event begins on the earlier of the fourth business day after the contingent obligation is created or arises or the day on which an executive officer becomes aware of the contingent obligation.

(b) ENVIRONMENTAL GUARANTEES UNDER ITEM 2.04

New Item 2.04 requires disclosure on Form 8-K if a triggering event occurs, causing any of the following, and the consequences of the event are material to the registrant:

- The increase or acceleration of a direct financial obligation of the registrant.
- The increase or acceleration of an obligation of the registrant under an off-balance-sheet arrangement.
- A contingent obligation of the registrant under an off-balance-sheet arrangement to become a direct financial obligation of the registrant.

A *triggering event* is an event, including an event of default, event of acceleration, or similar event, as a result of which a direct financial obligation of the registrant or an obligation of the registrant arising under an off-balance-sheet arrangement is increased or becomes accelerated or as a result of which a contingent obligation of the registrant arising out of an off-balance-sheet arrangement becomes a direct financial obligation of the registrant.

For purposes of Item 2.04, an *off-balance-sheet arrangement* has the meaning stated in Item 2.03 (see § 11.3(a)). The term *direct financial obligation* is also defined by reference to Item 2.03, but for the purposes of Item 2.04 also includes obligations arising out of off-balance-sheet arrangements that are accrued under FAS 5 as probable loss contingencies.

As discussed in § 11.3(a), environmental guarantees are considered off-balance-sheet arrangements. In addition, for purposes of Item 2.04, the contingent component of environmental guarantees, to the extent recognized as liabilities under FAS 5 and FIN 45, are direct financial obligations. Consequently, the following events, if material to the registrant, are subject to accelerated reporting under Item 2.04:

- Events causing an increase or acceleration of the contingent component of an environmental indemnity previously recognized as a liability.
- Events causing an increase in the recognized liability for the noncontingent component of an environmental indemnity.
- Events making it necessary to recognize as a liability the contingent component of an environmental indemnity not previously recognized as a liability.

Environmental guarantees are thus subject to accelerated reporting under both Item 2.03 and Item 2.04. The creation of an environmental guarantee that is material to the registrant is reported under Item 2.03. Disclosure under Item 2.04 is required upon the subsequent occurrence of events that increase or accelerate the registrant's obligations under the guarantee (e.g., the occurrence of events or conditions specified in the guarantee causing the contingent obligation to become a direct financial obligation of the registrant to make payments to the indemnified party). Accounting for environmental guarantees under FIN 45 is discussed in Chapter 21.

When events affecting an environmental guarantee are subject to Item 2.04, the registrant must disclose the following information:

- The date of the triggering event and a brief description of the environmental guarantee.
- A brief description of the triggering event.
- The nature and amount of the obligation, as increased if applicable, and the applicable terms of payment or acceleration.
- Any other material obligations of the registrant that may arise, increase, be accelerated, or become direct financial obligations as a result of the triggering event or the increase or acceleration of the obligation under the environmental guarantee, or its becoming a direct financial obligation of the registrant.

(c) EXIT AND DISPOSAL COSTS

New Item 2.05 requires disclosure on Form 8-K when the board of directors, a committee of the board of directors, or an authorized officer or officers (if board action is not required) commits the company to an exit or disposal plan or otherwise disposes of a long-lived asset or terminates employees under a plan of termination, under which material charges will be incurred under GAAP.

Item 2.05 requires issuers to disclose:

- The date of the commitment to the course of action and a description of the course of action, including the facts and circumstances leading to the expected action and the expected completion date.
- For each major type of cost associated with the course of action (for example, one-time termination benefits, contract termination costs, and other

associated costs), an estimate of the total amount or range of amounts expected to be incurred in connection with the action.

- An estimate of the total amount or range of amounts expected to be incurred in connection with the action.
- The issuer's estimate of the amount or range of amounts of the charge that will result in future cash expenditures.

Charges for environmental exit costs (e.g., asset retirement obligations) associated with the entity's exit or disposal plan may be subject to accelerated reporting under Item 2.05.

(d) ENVIRONMENTAL ASSET IMPAIRMENTS

New Item 2.06 requires disclosure on Form 8-K when a registrant's board of directors, a committee of the board of directors, or an authorized officer (if board action is not required) concludes that a material charge for impairment to one or more of the registrant's assets is required under GAAP. Specifically, the registrant must:

- Disclose the date of the conclusion that a material charge is required and describe the impaired asset or assets and the facts and circumstances leading to the conclusion that the charge for impairment is required.
- Disclose the registrant's estimate of the amount or range of amounts of the impairment charge.
- Disclose the registrant's estimate of the amount or range of amounts of the impairment charge that will result in future cash expenditures.

Environmental asset impairments are discussed in Chapter 23. Tests for impairment or recoverability of environmental asset impairments often occur in conjunction with the preparation, review, or audit of financial statements. In such cases, information regarding the impairment will be forthcoming on the registrant's periodic report. No Form 8-K disclosure is required under Item 2.06 if the conclusion regarding the material charge is made in connection with the preparation, review, or audit of financial statements at the end of a fiscal quarter or year and the plan is disclosed in the registrant's periodic report (e.g., Form 10-Q or Form 10-K) for that period.

Sudden and accidential pollution conditions (e.g., a catastrophic industrial accident) could give rise to the need for accelerated Form 8-K disclosure under Item 2.06.

11.4 SAFE HARBOR

The SEC has provided a limited safe harbor from public and private claims under Exchange Act section 10(b) and rule 10b-5 for failure to timely file a Form 8-K regarding Items 1.01, 1.02, 2.03, 2.04, 2.05, 2.06, and 4.02(a). The safe harbor provides that failure to file a report on Form 8-K for these items is not a violation of section 10(b) and rule 10b-5 under the Exchange Act. The safe harbor applies only to a failure to file. If the registrant files a Form 8-K, any material misstatements or omissions in the report continue to be subject to section 10(b) and rule 10b-5 liability. The safe harbor does not limit the SEC's ability to enforce any of the Form 8-K filing requirements under these items.

If the registrant has a separate duty to disclose information covered by the safe harbor other than Form 8-K, the registrant will not be protected from section 10(b) and rule 10b-5 liability for failure to satisfy such separate disclosure obligations. For example, if a registrant publicly sells or repurchases its own securities while in possession of material nonpublic information that is required to be disclosed on Form 8-K pursuant to an item that is covered by the safe harbor, the safe harbor will not protect the registrant from section 10(b) and rule 10b-5 liability regarding its separate disclosure obligation pursuant to the offering of securities.

The new safe harbor extends only until the due date of the registrant's next periodic report. If the registrant fails to file a required Form 8-K report, it must provide the disclosure prescribed by the relevant Form 8-K item in its next periodic report. Failure to do so voids the Form 8-K safe harbor, in addition to subjecting the registrant to potential liability for filing a false or misleading Form 10-Q or Form 10-K.

Failure to timely file a Form 8-K required by Items 1.01, 1.02, 2.03, 2.04, 2.05, 2.06, or 4.02(a) will not result in a loss of eligibility to use Form S-2 or Form S-3. However, the registrant must be current in its Form 8-K filings with respect to these items at the actual time of a Form S-2 or Form S-3 filing. Thus, a registrant must have filed the disclosure required by any of these Form 8-K items on or before the date that it files a Form S-2 or Form S-3-registration statement.

PART THREE

Financial Reporting Standards

CHAPTER TWELVE

General Principles of Financial Reporting

12.1 INTRODUCTION

Several general concepts of financial accounting have particular relevance to environmental financial reporting, because of the uncertain nature of environmental costs, liabilities, and risks. These general concepts include:

- Materiality
- Probability

- Reasonable estimation
- Significant risks and uncertainties
- Change in accounting estimates

These general concepts and related principles apply under a variety of different financial reporting standards covering both financial and nonfinancial information contained in the financial statements and nonfinancial statement disclosures.

12.2 MATERIALITY

The concept of materiality is a fundamental principle of financial reporting. It is a primary consideration in every aspect of financial reporting, including:

- Design and implementation of internal control systems.
- Application of generally accepted accounting principles.
- Compliance with SEC financial reporting requirements.
- Auditing of financial statements and internal control systems.
- Antifraud provisions of the federal securities laws.

Generally, the concept of materiality recognizes that some matters, either individually or in the aggregate, are important to the fair presentation of an entity's financial condition and performance, whereas other matters are not. The meaning of *materiality*, however, can vary depending on the circumstances and the particular application.

A significant and increasingly vocal minority of investors and environmental advocacy groups consider materiality to be an unworkable standard for environmental matters, in part because the SEC has not sought to compel public companies to consider qualitative factors and aggregate impacts in assessing materiality. A 2004 SEC enforcement action against KPMG (discussed in § 12.2(b)(ii)), however, may cause independent financial auditors to apply greater scrutiny to procedures and controls for assessing materiality generally. This in turn may lead auditors and reporting entities to focus greater attention on the criteria used to assess the materiality of environmental matters.

(a) MATERIALITY UNDER THE ANTIFRAUD PROVISIONS OF THE FEDERAL SECURITIES LAWS

The federal securities laws contain several provisions concerning the materiality of misstatements and omissions in SEC reports. These provisions, combined with judicial interpretations, form the basis for assessing materiality under the antifraud provisions of the federal securities laws.

(i) REGULATORY REFERENCES

Regulations promulgated under the federal securities laws contain the following provisions concerning the *material* accuracy and completeness of information contained in SEC reports:

RULE	CONTENT
Rule 12b-2	The term *material,* when used to qualify a requirement for the furnishing of information as to any subject, limits the information required to those matters as to which there is "a substantial likelihood that a reasonable investor would attach importance in determining whether to buy or sell the securities registered."[1]
Rule 12b-20	In addition to the information expressly required to be included in a statement or report, there shall be added such further *material* information, if any, as may be necessary to make the required statements, in the light of the circumstances under which they are made not misleading.[2]
Rule 10b-5	It shall be unlawful for any person, directly or indirectly, by the use of any means or instrumentality of interstate commerce, or of the mails or of any facility of any national securities exchange, i) To employ any device, scheme, or artifice to defraud, ii) To make any untrue statement of a *material* fact or to omit to state a *material* fact necessary in order to make the statements made, in the light of the circumstances under which they were made, not misleading, or iii) To engage in any act, practice, or course of business which operates or would operate as a fraud or deceit upon any person, in connection with the purchase or sale of any security.[3]
Rule 210.1-02 (Regulation S-X)	The term *material,* when used to qualify a requirement for the furnishing of information as to any subject, limits the information required to those matters about which an average prudent investor ought reasonably to be informed.[4]
Rule 210.4-01(a) (Regulation S-X)	Financial statements should be filed in such form and order, and should use such generally accepted terminology, as will best indicate their significance and character in the light of the provisions applicable thereto. The information required with respect to any statement shall be furnished as a minimum requirement *to which shall be added such further material information as is necessary to make the required statements, in the light of the circumstances under which they are made, not misleading.*[5]
Rule 210.4-02 (Regulation S-X)	If the amount that would otherwise be required to be shown with respect to any item is not *material,* it need not be separately set forth. The combination of insignificant amounts is permitted.[6]

1 17 C.F.R. § 240.12b-2.
2 17 C.F.R. § 240.12b-20 (emphasis added).
3 17 C.F.R. § 230.10b-5(b) (emphasis added).
4 17 C.F.R. § 2101.1-02(o).
5 17 C.F.R. § 240.4-01(a) (emphasis added).
6 17 C.F.R. § 240.4-02 (emphasis added).

(ii) JUDICIAL INTERPRETATIONS

The federal courts have interpreted the meaning of materiality in the context of shareholder litigation accusing registrants of material misstatements and omissions. *Basic Inc. v. Levinson*[7] is the seminal U.S. Supreme Court case on materiality. In December 1978, Combustion Engineering, Inc., and Basic Incorporated agreed to merge. During the preceding two years, representatives of the two companies had various meetings and conversations regarding the possibility of a merger. During that time, Basic made three public statements denying that any merger negotiations were taking place or that it knew of any corporate developments that would account for heavy trading activity in its stock. The plaintiffs had sold their stock in Basic in the open market shortly before a public announcement of the merger. They alleged that Basic's statements had been false or misleading, in violation of section 10(b) of the Exchange Act and rule 10b-5, and that the plaintiffs were injured by selling their shares at prices artificially depressed by those statements. Basic countered that the merger discussions were not material as of the date the plaintiffs sold their shares.

The Supreme Court's opinion in *Basic* with regard to materiality under rule 10b-5 established three important principles:

1. *Contingent or speculative events are not immaterial simply because they are contingent or speculative.* There is "no valid justification for artificially excluding from the definition of materiality information concerning merger discussions, which would otherwise be considered significant to the trading decision of a reasonable investor, merely because agreement-in-principle as to price and structure has not yet been reached by the parties or their representatives."[8]
2. *The materiality of contingent or speculative events depends on the significance the reasonable investor would place on the withheld or misrepresented information.* An omitted fact is material if there is "a substantial likelihood that the disclosure of the omitted fact would have been viewed by the reasonable investor as having significantly altered the 'total mix' of information made available."[9]
3. *The significance of contingent or speculative events to investors depends on both the likelihood of occurrence and the magnitude of potential impact.* When the event is contingent or speculative in nature, it is difficult to ascertain whether the reasonable investor would have considered the omitted information significant at the time. Under such circumstances, materiality "will depend at any given time upon a balancing of both the indicated probability that the event will occur and the anticipated magnitude of the event in light of the totality of the company activity."[10]

---

[7] 485 U.S. 224 (1988).

[8] *Basic*, 485 U.S. at 236.

[9] *Basic*, 485 U.S. at 231-32, *quoting* TSC Indus., Inc. v. Northway, Inc., 426 U.S. 438, 449 (1976).

[10] *Basic*, 485 U.S. at 238, *quoting* SEC v. Texas Gulf Sulphur Co., 401 F.2d 833, 849 (2d Cir. 1968) (en banc).

The Supreme Court's analysis of materiality in *Basic* is particularly relevant to environmental matters, which are often contingent or speculative in nature. The *Basic* test for determining materiality can be applied to environmental matters as follows:

- Environmental matters, such as environmental loss contingencies (Chapter 19), environmental remediation liabilities (Chapter 20), and conditional asset retirement obligations (Chapter 22), are not immaterial solely because they are contingent or speculative.
- The materiality of contingent or speculative environmental matters depends on the significance a reasonable investor would place on the withheld or misrepresented information.
- The significance of contingent or speculative environmental matters to investors depends on both the indicated probability of occurrence and the magnitude of potential impact in light of the totality of the company activity.

(iii) RIGHTS OF RECOVERY

The availability of insurance, indemnification, or contribution often will be relevant in assessing the magnitude of potential impact of a loss contingency to the entity. How rights of recovery may be considered in assessing materiality depends on the specific context, as follows:

- For purposes of disclosure of environmental matters under Regulation S-K, potential rights of recovery may be considered in assessing materiality.
- For purposes of reporting of environmental matters under GAAP, potential rights of recovery may not be considered in assessing materiality.

Consistent with the Supreme Court's analysis in *Basic*, if a potential loss to the enterprise is fully or partially insured, a reasonable investor would consider the loss contingency to be less significant than if it were wholly uninsured. The SEC has expressly recognized that it is appropriate to consider the availability of insurance, indemnification, or contribution when determining whether an environmental loss contingency is material for purposes of MD&A disclosure.[11] The registrant's assessment in this regard should include consideration of facts such as the periods in which claims for recovery may be realized, the likelihood that the claims may be contested, and the financial condition of third parties from which recovery is expected.

Considerations of rights of recovery under GAAP are discussed in Chapter 16.

(b) MATERIALITY UNDER GAAP AND GAAS

Authoritative accounting pronouncements typically state that they are applicable only to material items. FASB Statements of Financial Accounting Standards,

---

[11] Securities Act Release No. 33-6835, 54 Fed. Reg. 22427 (May 24, 1989).

for example, generally provide that "[t]he provisions of this Statement need not be applied to immaterial items"—yet these pronouncements generally provide few, if any, specific guidelines for assessing materiality.

The primary definition of *materiality* for purposes of GAAP is contained in AICPA Statement on Auditing Standards No. 47, "Audit Risk and Materiality in Conducting an Audit" (SAS 47). SAS 47 and subsequent amendments to it are incorporated into AICPA Professional Standards section AU 312.

Section AU 312 describes three key materiality concepts with respect to auditing of financial statements prepared in accordance with GAAP:

1. The concept of materiality recognizes that some matters, either individually or in the aggregate, are important for fair presentation of financial statements in conformity with GAAP, whereas other matters are not important.
2. Financial statements are materially misstated when they contain misstatements whose effect, individually or in the aggregate, is important enough to cause them not to be presented fairly, in all material respects, in conformity with GAAP. Misstatements can result from errors or fraud.
3. In planning the audit, the auditor is concerned with matters that could be material to the financial statements. The auditor has no responsibility to plan and perform the audit to obtain reasonable assurance that misstatements, whether caused by errors or fraud, that are not material to the financial statements are detected.[12]

SAS 47 recognizes that materiality is not a constant. It varies among entities of different size and nature. It also can vary for the same entity from year to year. Section AU 312.10 states that "consideration of materiality is a matter of professional judgment and is influenced by [the auditor's] perception of the needs of a reasonable person who will rely on the financial statements."

(i) QUANTITATIVE CONSIDERATIONS

The quantitative materiality of environmental liabilities depends on the amount of the liabilities, both individually and in the aggregate; the amount of the entity's total liabilities; and the amount of the entity's total assets. The materiality of environmental liabilities increases as the financial solvency of the entity decreases.

Environmental liabilities tend to extend across numerous accounting periods. Whereas misstatements of net income may be transitory in nature, misstatements of environmental liabilities are persistent. Over time, understatements of environmental liabilities may become increasingly significant to the overall financial health of the entity, as the entity's liabilities increase relative to its assets.

A determination that environmental liabilities are immaterial may be reasonable at a time when the entity is financially strong and unreasonable in sub-

[12] AU §§ 312.03–312.05.

sequent years when the financial condition of the entity has deteriorated. Companies that choose not to identify, assess, measure, and report environmental liabilities based on materiality considerations thus may face the future obligation to report preexisting liabilities for the first time just when shareholders and creditors are making judgments about the viability of the company as a going concern.

The SEC is expected soon to issue additional guidance on materiality that will instruct issuers that recurring items that have a bigger impact on the balance sheet than the income statement cannot be deemed immaterial simply because they have only a small impact on the income statement. The SEC believes that issuers must look at both balance sheet and income statement in isolation, as well as consider the cumulative impact of recurring items.[13]

(ii) QUALITATIVE CONSIDERATIONS

SAS 47 discusses the perceived needs of financial statement users by quoting FASB Statement of Financial Accounting Concepts No. 2, "Qualitative Characteristics of Accounting Information" (SFAC 2). That concepts statement defines materiality as:

> the magnitude of an omission or misstatement of accounting information that, in the light of surrounding circumstances, makes it probable that the judgment of a reasonable person relying on the information would have been changed or influenced by the omission or misstatement.[14]

This formulation is in substance identical to the formulation used by the courts in interpreting the antifraud provisions in the federal securities laws (see § 12.2(a)). It is also consistent with the financial accounting provisions in Regulation S-X of the federal securities laws, which defines *material* information as "the information . . . about which an average prudent investor ought reasonably to be informed."[15]

SAS 47 also references SFAC 2 for the notion that materiality judgments are made in light of surrounding circumstances and necessarily involve both quantitative and qualitative considerations. It reminds accountants and auditors that misstatements of relatively small amounts sometimes can have a material effect on the financial statements. For example, the illegal payment of an otherwise immaterial amount could be material if there is a reasonable possibility that it could lead to a material loss contingency.

Reporting entities and auditors routinely apply simplistic rules of thumb (e.g., less than 5 percent of income or assets) as per se standards in assessing materiality. Though commonplace, there is no basis in the accounting literature or the law for exclusive reliance on a numerical threshold. The practice also contradicts guidance from the SEC, which favors consideration of *all relevant*

---

13 See e.g., statements of SEC Deputy Chief Accountant Scott Taub, reported in "And the Magic Number is. . .Yes," CFO.com, May 5, 2005.

14 Statement of Financial Accounting Concepts No. 2, Qualitative Characteristics of Accounting Information, Glossary of Terms (May 1980).

15 17 C.F.R. § 2101.1-02(o).

considerations—including qualitative factors and the aggregate effect of multiple, individually immaterial, omissions.

SEC Staff Accounting Bulletin No. 99 (SAB 99) expresses the SEC's opinion that exclusive reliance on certain quantitative benchmarks to assess materiality in preparing financial statements and performing audits of those financial statements is inappropriate. SAB 99 rejects the use of numerical thresholds—in particular, a threshold of less than 5 percent—as a per se standard for immateriality:

> The [SEC] staff is aware that certain registrants [and their auditors] . . . have developed quantitative thresholds as "rules of thumb" to assist in the preparation of their financial statements. One [such] rule of thumb . . . suggests that the misstatement or omission of an item that falls under a 5% threshold is not material in the absence of particularly egregious circumstances, such as self-dealing or misappropriation by senior management . . . . [In the view of the SEC staff,] exclusive reliance on this or any percentage or numerical threshold has no basis in the accounting literature or the law.[16]

The SEC supports the use of rule-of-thumb percentage thresholds, such as 5 percent, as an initial step in assessing materiality, but reminds reporting entities and auditors that quantifying, in percentage terms, the magnitude of a misstatement is only the first step in an analysis of materiality. According to the SEC, percentage thresholds cannot appropriately be used as a substitute for a full analysis of all relevant considerations, based on the Supreme Court's holding that a fact is material if there is "a substantial likelihood that the . . . fact would have been viewed by the reasonable investor as having significantly altered the 'total mix' of information made available."[17] According to the SEC staff:

> Under the governing principles, an assessment of materiality requires that one views the facts in the context of the "surrounding circumstances," as the accounting literature puts it, or the "total mix" of information, in the words of the Supreme Court. In the context of a misstatement of a financial statement item, while the "total mix" includes the size in numerical or percentage terms of the misstatement, it also includes the factual context in which the user of financial statements would view the financial statement item. The shorthand in the accounting and auditing literature for this analysis is that financial management and the auditor must consider both "quantitative" and "qualitative" factors in assessing an item's materiality.[18]

The SEC staff also contends that misstatements of relatively small amounts can have a material effect on the financial statements as a result of the interaction of quantitative and qualitative factors. Considerations that may render material a quantitatively small item include, but are not limited to the following:

---

16 Release No. SAB 99, 64 Fed. Reg. 45,150, 45,151 (Aug. 19, 1999).

17 *See* TSC Indus. v. Northway, Inc., 426 U.S. 438 (1976); Basic, Inc. v. Levinson, 485 U.S. 224 (1988). See § 12.2(a).

18 Release No. SAB 99, 64 Fed. Reg. 45,150, 45,151 (Aug. 19, 1999) (footnotes omitted).

- Whether the misstatement arises from an item capable of precise measurement or whether it arises from an estimate and, if so, the degree of imprecision inherent in the estimate
- Whether the misstatement masks a change in earnings or other trends
- Whether the misstatement hides a failure to meet analysts' consensus expectations for the enterprise
- Whether the misstatement changes a loss into income or vice versa
- Whether the misstatement concerns a segment or other portion of the registrant's business that has been identified as playing a significant role in the registrant's operations or profitability
- Whether the misstatement affects the registrant's compliance with regulatory requirements
- Whether misstatement affects the registrant's compliance with loan covenants or other contractual requirements
- Whether the misstatement has the effect of increasing management's compensation (e.g., by satisfying requirements for the award of bonuses or other forms of incentive compensation)
- Whether the misstatement involves concealment of an unlawful transaction
- Whether the misstatement is expected to have a significant positive or negative market reaction on the registrant's securities

Note: When management or the independent auditor expects (based, for example, on a pattern of market performance) that a known misstatement may result in a significant positive or negative market reaction, that expected reaction should be taken into account when considering whether a misstatement is material.

An enforcement action against national accounting firm KPMG LLP indicates that the SEC is serious about qualitative materiality. In October 2004, the SEC sanctioned KPMG LLP, two former KPMG partners, and a current partner and senior manager for engaging in improper professional conduct as auditors for Gemstar-TV Guide International, Inc. The SEC claimed that despite indications of Gemstar's improper accounting and disclosure, KPMG issued unqualified audit reports representing that KPMG had conducted its audits in accordance with generally accepted auditing standards and that Gemstar's financial statements fairly presented its financial results in accordance with GAAP. The SEC alleged that in reaching these conclusions, the auditors unreasonably decided that the unsupported revenues were immaterial to Gemstar's financial statements. According to the SEC, the auditors' materiality determinations were unreasonable in that they were based on a quantitative analysis and failed to consider whether the revenues at issue were qualitatively material.

As part of the settlement, KPMG was censured and agreed to pay $10 million to harmed Gemstar shareholders. At the time, this represented the largest payment ever made by an accounting firm in an SEC action. The auditors, all of whom were certified public accountants, agreed to suspensions from practicing before the SEC. In addition to the censure and the $10 million payment by KPMG, the firm agreed to conduct training for its partners and managers on qualitative materiality.

Qualitative factors can be particularly important with regard to the materiality of environmental matters. Reporting entities may wish to consider, for example, the following qualitative factors when assessing the materiality of environmental financial information:

- Environmental financial information often is based on estimates that are incapable of precise measurement.
- Reasonable worst-case outcomes of environmental matters can have a significant adverse impact on the entity's financial condition, sometimes resulting in bankruptcy.
- In some industries, negative publicity regarding an entity's environmental stewardship can have a significant adverse impact on the entity's reputation with customers, employees, business partners, and suppliers.
- Environmental matters are generally closely tied to regulatory requirements that can give rise to civil or criminal prosecution of the entity and its directors, officers, and employees.
- Environmental performance is an important investment consideration for many socially responsible investment (SRI) funds. SRI funds currently represent several hundred million dollars of invested capital and continue to grow in popularity.
- An entity's management of environmental liabilities, including the accurate and complete reporting of such liabilities in the entity's financial statements, is regarded as a proxy of the quality of the entity's management team and corporate governance by an increasing number of SRI and non-SRI investors and fiduciaries.

(iii) INTENTIONAL MISSTATEMENTS

The intent of management may provide significant evidence of materiality (e.g., when management intentionally misstates items in the financial statements to "manage" reported earnings). Management's intentional misstatement of earnings is evidence of management's belief that the misstatement(s) would be significant to users of the entity's financial statements. The SEC advises reporting entities and auditors not to assume that even small intentional misstatements in financial statements are immaterial. SAB 99's statements regarding the materiality of intentional misstatements is also consistent with prior SEC assertions that the "integrity of . . . management . . . is always a material factor."[19]

FASB Statements of Financial Accounting Standards generally provide that they need not be applied to immaterial items. In theory, this qualification could be interpreted to mean that the entity is free to intentionally display (or not)

[19] *In re* Franchard Corp., 42 S.E.C. 163, 1964 WL 67454 at *7 (July 31, 1964).

immaterial items in financial statements in a manner that plainly would be contrary to GAAP if the misstatement were material. The SEC staff believes that the FASB did not intend this result.

In certain circumstances, intentional misstatements are unlawful even though immaterial. For example, as discussed in § 12.2(d), registrants must comply with sections 13(b)(2)–(7) of the Exchange Act,[20] even if misstatements are immaterial.

Section 10A(b) of the Exchange Act requires auditors to take certain actions upon discovery of an illegal act. The statute specifies that these obligations are triggered whether or not the illegal acts are perceived to have a material effect on the issuer's financial statements. Among other things, section 10A(b)(1) requires the auditor to inform the appropriate level of management of an illegal act (unless clearly inconsequential) and ensure that the registrant's audit committee is adequately informed with respect to the illegal act. (For more information on consideration of fraud in a financial statement audit, see § 26.2(d).)

Intentional misstatements also may signal the existence of control environment deficiencies in the registrant's system of internal control designed to detect and deter improper accounting and financial reporting. (For more information on the implementation and auditing of internal control systems, see Chapters 8 and 27.)

(iv) BUSINESS SEGMENTS

SAB 99 advises that where a misstatement appears in the financial statements may determine whether it is material. For example, a misstatement may relate to a segment of the entity's operations. In assessing the materiality of the misstatement to the financial statements taken as a whole, entities and their auditors should consider not only the size of the misstatement but also the significance of the segment information to the financial statements taken as a whole. Situations may arise in practice in which an environmental matter relating to segment information is qualitatively material even though it is quantitatively immaterial to the financial statements taken as a whole.

(v) AGGREGATION OF INDIVIDUALLY IMMATERIAL ITEMS

The materiality of environmental costs and liabilities should be evaluated on both an individual and aggregate basis. As previously noted, SAS 47 recognizes that:

- Some matters, either individually *or in the aggregate,* are important for fair presentation of financial statements in conformity with generally accepted accounting principles.
- Financial statements are materially misstated when they contain misstatements whose effect, individually *or in the aggregate,* is important enough to cause them not to be presented fairly, in all material respects, in conformity with GAAP.

---

[20] 15 U.S.C. §§ 78m(b)(2)–(7).

Generally accepted auditing standards also preclude *netting* of misstatements. For example, a material understatement of environmental liabilities is not rendered immaterial by a material understatement of rights of recovery from environmental insurance, even if the net result of the two overstatements is that balance sheet equity is correctly stated.

As described in SAB 99, assessment of materiality is a two-step process. Entities should first consider each misstatement separately and secondarily consider the aggregate effect of multiple misstatements within the same category.

Step 1—Assess individual materiality. Entities should consider whether each misstatement is material, irrespective of its effect when combined with other misstatements. The analysis should consider whether the misstatement of individual amounts causes a material misstatement of the financial statements taken as a whole. This analysis requires consideration of both quantitative and qualitative factors.

Quantitative materiality assessments often involve comparison of adjustments to revenues, gross profit, pretax and net income, total assets, stockholders' equity, or individual line items in the financial statements. The particular items in the financial statements used as a basis for the materiality determination depend on the proposed adjustment to be made and other factors. For example, an adjustment to environmental liabilities that is immaterial to pretax income or net income may be material to the financial statements because it may affect a working capital ratio or cause the entity to be in default of a loan covenant.

If the misstatement of an individual amount causes the financial statements as a whole to be materially misstated, that effect cannot be eliminated by other misstatements whose effect may be to diminish or entirely offset the impact of the misstatement on other financial statement items. For example, if the entity's environmental liabilities are materially understated, the financial statements taken as a whole will be materially misleading even if the effect on owner's equity is completely offset by an equivalent understatement of environmental assets.

Step 2—Assess aggregate materiality. Even though an individual misstatement may not cause the financial statements taken as a whole to be materially misstated, it may nonetheless, when aggregated with other misstatements, render the financial statements taken as a whole to be materially misleading. Entities must therefore consider the effect of the misstatement on financial statement subtotals or totals. The entity should aggregate all misstatements that affect each subtotal (e.g., environmental remediation liabilities) or total (e.g., long-term liabilities) and consider whether the misstatements in the aggregate affect the subtotal or total in a way that causes the financial statements taken as a whole to be materially misleading.

For example, an entity that has numerous environmental remediation liabilities relating to different Superfund sites may reasonably conclude under step 1 that no single liability would be material to the financial statements as a whole. Thus, the misstatement or nonrecognition of any single environmental remediation liability would be immaterial. Under step 2, however, the entity must determine whether its aggregate environmental remediation liabilities are material, such that the aggregate effect of misstating or failing to record its entire portfolio of environmental remediation liabilities would cause its financial statements taken as a whole to be materially misleading.

In considering the aggregate effect of multiple misstatements on a financial statement subtotal or total, entities should exercise particular care when considering whether to offset (or the appropriateness of offsetting) a misstatement of an estimated amount with a misstatement of an item capable of precise measurement. For example, entities should carefully consider whether it is appropriate to offset the failure to record a recognized liability for an asset retirement obligation (an estimate) by a corresponding failure to record an environmental insurance asset relating to the liability (an item capable of precise measurement). Given the imprecision inherent in estimates, there is by definition a corresponding imprecision in the aggregation of misstatements involving estimates with those that do not involve estimates. Entities should also be aware that FIN 39 (endorsed by the SEC in SAB 92) generally prohibits netting of liabilities and rights of recovery (see § 16.4(a)).

Entities and their auditors are also directed by SAB 99 to consider the effect of misstatements from prior periods on the current financial statements. For example, environmental liabilities not recorded by the entity might be immaterial to the current financial statements based on the entity's current financial condition. Such misstatements, however, could potentially cause future financial statements to be materially misstated if the entity's financial condition deteriorates. The same concerns exist when immaterial misstatements recur in several years and the cumulative effect becomes material in the current year. For example, failure to recognize incremental asset retirement obligations that occur over several years (see Chapter 22) may eventually result in a material misstatement, even though each individual annual increment standing alone is immaterial.

Consideration of the aggregate materiality of environmental liabilities is recommended in ASTM E 2173, "Standard Guide for Disclosure of Environmental Liabilities" (see § 25.3). This supplemental reporting standard states that disclosure should be made when an entity believes its environmental liability for an individual circumstance or its environmental liability in the aggregate is material. The standard broadly defines *environmental liabilities* to include damages attributed to the entity's products or processes, environmental cleanups, reclamation costs, fines, and litigation costs.

At its March 9, 2005 board meeting, the FASB considered a request made by The Rose Foundation to reconsider the accounting and reporting standards for contingent environmental liabilities. Specifically, FASB considered whether contingent environmental liabilities of a similar nature should be aggregated for purposes of assessing materiality as required under ASTM E 2173 (see Section 25.3). FASB rejected the request, finding that the current accounting literature already provides that contingent environmental liabilities of a similar nature should be aggregated for purposes of assessing materiality and that the problems identified by The Rose Foundation are related to compliance with the literature, rather than deficiencies in the literature.[21]

---

[21] Minutes of March 9, 2005 FASB board meeting (available at www.fasb.org).

(c) MATERIALITY UNDER REGULATION S-K

(i) *ITEM 101*

Item 101 of Regulation S-K requires issuers to disclose, among other things, the material effects of compliance with environmental laws on their capital expenditures, earnings, and competitive position (see § 24.3). Materiality, for purposes of Item 101, is determined using the Supreme Court's analysis in *Basic* (see § 12.2(a)(ii)).

(ii) *ITEM 103*

Item 103 of Regulation S-K requires registrants to describe certain administrative or judicial legal proceedings arising from environmental laws (see § 24.4). Materiality, for purposes of Item 103, generally is determined using the Supreme Court's analysis in *Basic* (see § 12.2(a)(ii)). Item 103, however, contains two specific materiality thresholds in Instructions 2 and 5:

Instruction 2: A proceeding (including a proceeding arising under environmental laws) that involves primarily a claim for damages is not material if the amount involved, exclusive of interest and costs, does not exceed 10 percent of the current assets of the registrant and its subsidiaries on a consolidated basis. Multiple proceedings presenting in large degree the same legal and factual issues should be aggregated in computing this percentage. The availability of insurance, indemnification, or contribution may be considered in determining whether this materiality threshold has been met. The registrant's assessment in this regard should include consideration of facts such as the periods in which claims for recovery may be realized, the likelihood that the claims may be contested, and the financial condition of third parties from which recovery is expected.[22]

Instruction 5: Certain types of administrative or judicial proceedings arising under environmental laws—namely, legal proceedings involving governmental authorities and potential monetary sanctions (e.g., EPA enforcement of a Clean Air Act permit violation)—are material for purposes of Item 103, unless the registrant *reasonably believes* that such proceeding will result in no monetary sanctions or in monetary sanctions, exclusive of interest and costs, of less than $100,000. The availability of insurance, indemnification, or contribution cannot be considered in determining whether this materiality threshold has been met.[23] Though the $100,000 threshold appears at first to be an objective bright-line standard, the reasonable-belief criterion renders the application of the standard highly subjective.

---

22 Securities Act Release No. 33-6835, 54 Fed. Reg. 22427 (May 24, 1989).
23 *Id.*

(iii) ITEM 303

In its broadest sense, Item 303 of Regulation S-K, "Management Discussion and Analysis" (MD&A), is intended to give investors a "look at the company through the eyes of management."[24] Among other things, Item 303 requires registrants to disclose known trends, events, or uncertainties that have affected, will affect, or that are reasonably likely to affect the registrant's liquidity, capital resources, or results of operations (see § 24.5). Materiality, for purposes of Item 303, generally is determined using the Supreme Court's analysis in *Basic* (see § 12.2(a)(ii)).

When applying the probability component of the two-part probability/magnitude test in *Basic* for purposes of Item 303, registrants must determine whether the trend, event, or uncertainty is *reasonably likely* to have a material effect on the registrant's financial condition, changes in financial condition, or results of operations. If management concludes that the known trend, demand, commitment, event, or uncertainty is not reasonably likely to occur, then no MD&A disclosure is required.[25]

When applying the magnitude component of the two-part probability/magnitude test in *Basic*, for purposes of Item 303, the availability of insurance, indemnification, or contribution may be considered. The registrant's assessment in this regard should include consideration of facts such as the periods in which claims for recovery may be realized, the likelihood that the claims may be contested, and the financial condition of third parties from which recovery is expected.[26]

(d) MATERIALITY FOR PURPOSES OF INTERNAL CONTROL

(i) EXCHANGE ACT SECTION 13(B)

Entities may be tempted to simply presume that environmental matters are not material to the enterprise, without collecting the information necessary to adequately assess materiality. The presumed immateriality of environmental matters may sometimes legitimately justify management's decision not to design and implement effective controls and procedures for environmental financial reporting. Whether omitted or misstated environmental financial information would be significant to investors, however, is not the test for determining whether an entity must implement controls and procedures sufficient to provide reasonable assurance of the reliability of its reported environmental financial information. Rather, under the federal securities laws, registrants must maintain internal accounting controls for environmental matters at the level of detail and degree of assurance that would satisfy prudent officials in the conduct of their own affairs.

---

24 Remarks of Richard Y. Roberts, SEC Commissioner, at Annual SEC/FASB Accounting & Reporting Conference, New York, New York, December 14, 1994.

25 *See* 17 C.F.R. § 229.303(a)(4)(i); *see also* Securities Act Release No. 33-8182, 68 Fed. Reg. 5982 (Feb. 5, 2003).

26 Securities Act Release No. 33-6835, 54 Fed. Reg. 22427 (May 24, 1989).

The books-and-records provisions of section 13(b) of the Exchange Act originally were passed as part of the Foreign Corrupt Practices Act. Under these provisions, each registrant with securities registered pursuant to section 12 of the Exchange Act, or required to file reports pursuant to section 15(d), must:

- Make and keep books, records, and accounts, which, in reasonable detail, accurately and fairly reflect the transactions and dispositions of assets of the registrant; and
- Maintain internal accounting controls that are sufficient to provide reasonable assurances that, among other things, transactions are recorded as necessary to permit the preparation of financial statements in conformity with GAAP.

A person who knowingly circumvents or knowingly fails to implement a system of internal accounting controls or knowingly falsifies books, records, or accounts is subject to criminal liability.[27]

In this context, determinations of what constitutes *reasonable assurance* and *reasonable detail* are based not on a materiality analysis but on the level of detail and degree of assurance that would satisfy prudent officials in the conduct of their own affairs.[28] In the conference committee report regarding the 1988 amendments to the FCPA, the committee stated, "The conference committee adopted the prudent man qualification in order to clarify that the current standard does not connote an unrealistic degree of exactitude or precision. The concept of reasonableness of necessity contemplates the weighing of a number of relevant factors, including the costs of compliance."[29]

Like materiality, reasonableness is not an absolute standard of exactitude for corporate records. Unlike materiality, however, reasonableness is not solely a measure of the significance of a financial statement item to investors. Reasonableness, in this context, reflects a judgment as to whether an issuer's failure to correct a known misstatement implicates the purposes underlying the accounting provisions of sections 13(b)(2)–(7) of the Exchange Act.[30]

There is only limited case law discussing section 13(b)(2) of the Exchange Act in any detail, and the courts generally have found that no private right of action exists under the accounting and books-and-records provisions of the Exchange Act.[31]

---

[27] 5 U.S.C. § 78m(4), (5). *See also* rule 13b2-1 under the Exchange Act, 17 C.F.R. § 240.13b2-1, which states, "No person shall, directly or indirectly, falsify or cause to be falsified, any book, record or account subject to Section 13(b)(2)(A) of the Securities Exchange Act."

[28] 5 U.S.C. § 78m(b)(7).

[29] Cong. Rec. H2116 (daily ed. Apr. 20, 1988).

[30] *See* Securities Exchange Act Release No. 17500, 46 Fed. Reg. 11,544 (Feb. 9, 1981).

[31] *See* SEC v. World-Wide Coin Invs., Ltd., 567 F. Supp. 724 (N.D. Ga. 1983); *see also* Lamb v. Phillip Morris Inc., 915 F.2d 1024 (6th Cir. 1990); JS Serv. Ctr. Corp. v. General Elec. Technical Servs. Co., 937 F. Supp. 216 (S.D.N.Y. 1996).

SAB 99 sets forth several factors for registrants and their auditors to consider in assessing whether a misstatement results in a violation of a registrant's obligation to keep books and records that are accurate in reasonable detail:

- The significance of the misstatement
  Note: Though the SEC does not believe that registrants need to make finely calibrated determinations of significance with respect to immaterial items, plainly it is reasonable to treat misstatements whose effects are clearly inconsequential differently than more significant ones.
- How the misstatement arose
  Note: It is unlikely that it is ever reasonable for registrants to record misstatements or not to correct known misstatements—even immaterial ones—as part of an ongoing effort directed by or known to senior management for the purposes of managing earnings. However, insignificant misstatements that arise from the operation of systems or recurring processes in the normal course of business generally will not cause a registrant's books to be inaccurate in reasonable detail.
- The cost of correcting the misstatement
  Note: The books-and-records provisions of the Exchange Act do not require registrants to make major expenditures to correct small misstatements. Conversely, when little cost or delay is involved in correcting a misstatement, failing to do so is unlikely to be reasonable.
- The clarity of authoritative accounting guidance with respect to the misstatement
  Note: Where reasonable minds may differ about the appropriate accounting treatment of a financial statement item, a failure to correct it may not render the registrant's financial statements inaccurate in reasonable detail. Where, however, there is little ground for reasonable disagreement, the case for leaving a misstatement uncorrected is correspondingly weaker.

Because the judgment as to reasonableness is not mechanical, the SEC will generally defer to judgments that allow a business, acting in good faith, to comply with the Exchange Act's books-and-records provisions in an innovative and cost-effective way.

(ii) SARBANES-OXLEY SECTION 404

As discussed in Chapter 27, section 404 of Sarbanes-Oxley requires the independent financial auditor to render an attestation as to the design and operational effectiveness of the entity's internal control over financial reporting. The purpose of the independent review and attestation is to identify control deficiencies that could lead to misstatements in the entity's financial reports. The magnitude of a potential misstatement is measured in terms of materiality, assessed at both the financial-statement level and at the individual account-balance level (see § 27.3(e)).

For purposes of an internal control audit, the magnitude of a potential misstatement arising from a control deficiency is measured on a scale that ranges from *inconsequential*, to *more than inconsequential*, to *material*. A misstatement is *inconsequential* if a reasonable person would conclude, after considering the possibility of further undetected misstatements, that the misstatement, either individually or when aggregated with other misstatements, would be clearly immaterial to the financial statements.

- A *significant deficiency* is a control deficiency, or combination of control deficiencies, that adversely affects the entity's ability to initiate, authorize, record, process, or report external financial data reliably in accordance with GAAP such that there is more than a remote likelihood that a misstatement of the entity's annual or interim financial statements that is more than inconsequential will not be prevented or detected. Significant deficiencies must be reported to the issuer's audit committee.
- A *material weakness* is a significant deficiency, or combination of significant deficiencies, that results in more than a remote likelihood that a material misstatement of the annual or interim financial statements will not be prevented or detected. Material weaknesses must be reported in the issuer's Form 10-K.

The low threshold for significant deficiencies (more than a remote likelihood of a misstatement that is not clearly immaterial) reinforces the need for issuers to maintain effective internal accounting controls for environmental matters unless the probability of material unreported environmental liabilities can safely be presumed to be highly unlikely. Indeed, the PCAOB has issued guidance stating that public companies must maintain controls over the identification, assessment, measurement, and reporting of environmental matters unless, given the nature of the company's operations, the likelihood of material unreported environmental liabilities is remote (see § 8.3(a)).

(e) THE REASONABLE INVESTOR

According to the U.S. Supreme Court, an omitted fact is material if there is "a substantial likelihood that the disclosure of the omitted fact would have been viewed by the *reasonable investor* as having significantly altered the total mix of information made available."[32] Generally accepted auditing standards adopt a similar standard for materiality, but reference the "reasonable person" instead of the "reasonable investor." These standards raise two important questions. First, who are these reasonable investors? Second, what environmental financial information is important to them?

The Supreme Court's definition of *materiality* precludes the views of fringe environmental activists from setting the standard of disclosure for corporate America. In recent years, however, institutional investors and socially responsible investment funds, representing trillions of dollars in invested assets, have become increasingly concerned about the perceived inadequacy of reported environmental financial information. Given their size and sophistication, these investors are clearly something other than fringe environmental activists.

---

[32] *Basic*, 485 U.S. at 231–32 (emphasis added).

Institutional investors and fiduciaries are increasingly looking at environmental factors as indicators of the quality of management and the sustainability of the enterprise, and they have expressed frustration with the quantity and quality of environmental disclosure. In 2004, a coalition of pension fund leaders collectively representing more than $1 trillion in assets issued a public demand for tough new steps by the SEC, corporate boards, and Wall Street firms to increase corporate disclosure of environmental liabilities and risks, including the risks posed to investors by climate change.[33] Apparently, these investors believe that information significant to their investment decisions is being withheld.

Whether the views of the growing minority of institutional investors and fiduciaries calling for increased environmental transparency are sufficiently representative of the overall market to be considered objectively reasonable for purposes of establishing financial reporting standards remains an open question. Nonetheless, because these investors represent trillions of dollars in assets and are becoming increasingly active in class action securities litigation, reporting entities should carefully evaluate the criteria in SAB 99 before disregarding the demands of these investors for greater environmental disclosure.

12.3 PROBABILITY

The concept of probability is an integral factor when assessing the significance of financial information associated with contingent or speculative matters. For example, § 12.2 describes how the probability of occurrence of future events or conditions is considered in the assessment of materiality. Chapter 19 describes how the likelihood of occurrence of future events or conditions is considered in determining whether a liability should be recognized for a loss contingency under FAS 5. Section 22.2(c) describes how the probability of occurrence of future events or conditions is considered in the fair value measurement of a conditional asset retirement obligation.

Because environmental matters tend to be inherently contingent or speculative in nature, the concept of probability is one of the most significant aspects of environmental financial reporting. It is also one of the most confusing and contentious aspects of environmental financial reporting.

Probability is important because it bears directly on three critical elements of financial reporting: materiality, recognition, and measurement.

- *Materiality*. Probability is an inseparable aspect of materiality because the significance of contingent or speculative environmental matters to investors depends on both the indicated probability of occurrence and the magnitude of potential impact.
- *Recognition*. Probability is the primary consideration in determining whether contingent liabilities should be recorded on the balance sheet pursuant to FAS 5. Interestingly, FAS 5, which requires recognition of loss

[33] *See* www.incr.com.

contingencies only when it is probable that a liability has been incurred, does not consider the magnitude of the potential loss. Thus, although a contingent liability of overwhelming magnitude but only a reasonable possibility of occurrence might be considered material, it would not be subject to recognition as a liability under FAS 5.

- *Measurement*. Uncertainty is an inherent challenge in estimating the financial value of contingent or speculative matters. More robust measurement techniques are designed specifically to address high degrees of uncertainty by utilizing probabilistic analysis and statistics.

Probability is confusing largely because (as discussed above) it has so many different meanings and applications in environmental financial reporting. In addition, the use of inconsistent terminology and definitions among various accounting and disclosure standards has exacerbated the problem. For example, as described below, the terms *probable* and *probability* have different meanings when used in different financial reporting contexts:

- Under FAS 5, a liability for a loss contingency will be recognized if it is *probable* that an asset has been impaired or a liability has been incurred and the amount of loss can be reasonably estimated. For purposes of FAS 5, *probable* means that the future event or events in question are *likely to occur*. FAS 5 also uses the terms *remote* and *reasonably possible* to represent degrees of likelihood less than probable.
- Liabilities are defined as *probable* future sacrifices of economic benefits arising from present obligations of a particular entity to transfer assets or provide services to other entities in the future as a result of past transactions or events. In this context, *probable* is used with its usual general meaning, rather than in a specific accounting or technical sense (such as that in FAS 5), and refers to that which can reasonably be expected or believed on the basis of available evidence or logic but is neither certain nor proved. As used in FAS 5, *probable* requires a high degree of expectation. As used in the definition of a liability, however, the term is intended to acknowledge that business and other economic activities occur in an environment characterized by uncertainty in which few outcomes are certain (see Chapter 18).
- In the context of determining whether a known trend, event, or uncertainty is *probable* of occurrence, and therefore potentially material for purposes of Item 303 of Regulation S-K, the probability standard is whether the trend, event, or uncertainty is *reasonably likely* to have a material effect on the registrant's financial condition, changes in financial condition, or results of operations.
- For purposes of fair value measurement (e.g., measurement of conditional asset retirement obligations under FAS 143 and impairments to long-lived assets under FAS 144), the concept of probability takes on a different meaning and purpose. Instead of being used as a criterion for recognition of a liability or asset impairment (i.e., Is an asset impaired or

does a liability exist?), probability is used in this context to measure the amount of a loss or liability (i.e., How much is the loss or the liability?). The critical distinction in the way probability is used in determining the fair value of an impairment or liability, as opposed to its use in triggering the initial recognition of an impairment or liability, is discussed further below.

The concept of *probability* can be contentious because assessments of probability are inherently subjective and therefore difficult to objectively verify and enforce. Consequently, reporting entities have a great deal of flexibility—many would argue too much flexibility—in determining what environmental matters are material, what environmental liabilities must be recognized in the balance sheet, and the value to be assigned to such liabilities.

As noted above, the concept of probability is used for purposes of materiality, recognition, and measurement. The following sections examine more closely the distinctions among these different applications.

(a) FOR PURPOSES OF MATERIALITY

For purposes of assessing materiality (see § 12.2), *probability* refers to the likelihood that a future speculative or contingent event will occur. In this context, probability represents a range of certainty from zero to 100 percent, rather than a particular point within that range (e.g., remote, reasonably possible, probable, or certain). Materiality is a function of both probability and magnitude. Thus, a contingency that is nearly certain to occur, but which is expected to have an insignificant financial impact, is nonetheless immaterial. Conversely, a contingency that is only reasonably likely to occur, but which would have a devastating financial impact on the reporting entity if it were to occur, is material.

(b) FOR PURPOSES OF RECOGNITION

The use of *probable* in the first recognition criterion of FAS 5 (Is it *probable* that an asset had been impaired or a liability had been incurred?) refers to the likelihood that an asset has been impaired or a liability incurred. The term does not reference the individual cash flows or factors that would be considered in estimating the fair value of the asset or liability. FAS 5 is primarily concerned with determining whether loss contingencies should be recognized, and devotes little attention to measurement beyond the requirement that the amount of a loss be reasonably estimated. Similarly, a probability standard is used in Item 303 of Regulation S-K (MD&A) to determine whether disclosure of information about a known trend, event, or uncertainty is required (see § 12.2(c)(iii)).

In contrast, FAS 143 requires that all asset retirement obligations within the scope of the standard be recognized when a reasonable estimate of fair value can be made. The first recognition criterion of FAS 5 is not applicable to liabilities that are to be measured at fair value (e.g., conditional asset retirement obligations). That is because, for purposes of initial recognition under FAS 5, uncertainty is used to decide whether to recognize a liability, whereas for purposes of fair value measurement uncertainties in the amount and timing of settlement are incorporated into the estimate of the recognized liability. Uncertainty, therefore, does not affect the decision to recognize a liability when the objective is to measure that liability at fair value, unless the degree of uncertainty is so great that a reasonable estimate of fair value cannot be made.

(c) FOR PURPOSES OF MEASUREMENT

The second recognition criterion in FAS 5 focuses on the ability to estimate the amount of the loss. When describing contingent liabilities and asset impairments, the amount of the loss often is derived from an estimate of a single most likely (most probable) outcome and the accumulation of cash flows associated with that outcome. By contrast, measurement of the fair value of an asset retirement obligation under FAS 143 does not aim to determine a single most probable outcome, but rather entails a much more robust analysis of uncertainty and probability. Fair value measurements involve the estimate of:

- Future cash flows;
- A *probabilistic* assessment of their possible variability;
- The time value of money; and
- The price that marketplace participants demand for bearing the uncertainty inherent in those cash flows.

Similarly, the amount that a third party would charge to assume an uncertain liability necessarily incorporates expectations about future events that are not probable, as that term is used in FAS 5 (e.g., the likelihood that actual cleanup costs for an environmental remediation project will exceed estimated amounts due to the discovery of previously unidentified contamination).

12.4 REASONABLY ESTIMABLE

Generally accepted accounting principles consistently recognize the possibility that reasonable estimation of a liability or impairment may not be possible. Furthermore, both FAS 5 and FAS 143 preclude recognition of a liability that cannot be reasonably estimated.

The reasonable-estimation criterion raises several important questions that should be addressed in connection with the entity's policies regarding critical accounting estimates (see §§ 12.5 and 24.5(e)):

- What are the criteria for determining that a liability or impairment cannot be reasonably estimated?
- If the inability to reasonably estimate a loss is due to a lack of obtainable data, what is the obligation of the entity to collect additional data?
- What disclosure obligations exist when the entity determines that a loss cannot be reasonably estimated?

(a) CRITERIA

FAS 5, FIN 14, and FAS 143 provide the following limited criteria for determining when a liability can or cannot be reasonably estimated:

- The condition that a loss be reasonably estimated should not delay accrual of a loss until only a single most-likely amount can be reasonably estimated.
- When available information indicates that the estimated amount of a loss is within a range of amounts, it follows that some amount of loss has occurred and can be reasonably estimated.
- If an asset has an indeterminate useful life, sufficient information to estimate a range of potential settlement dates for an asset retirement obligation might not be available.
- Uncertainty about performance of conditional obligations shall not prevent the determination of a reasonable estimate of fair value for a conditional asset retirement obligation.

FIN 47 provides additional criteria for determining whether an asset retirement obligation (ARO) can be reasonably estimated. According to paragraph 4 of FIN 47, an ARO is reasonably estimable if one of the following three conditions exists:

1. It is evident that the amount of the obligation is embedded in the acquisition price of the asset.
2. An active market exists for transfer of the obligation.
3. Sufficient information exists to apply an expected present value technique.

If conditions 1 or 2 above exist, fair value is deemed to be reasonably estimable. Paragraph 17 of FASB Concepts Statement No. 7, "Using Cash Flow Information and Present Value in Accounting Measurements," states, "If a price for an asset or liability or an essentially similar asset or liability can be observed in the marketplace, there is no need to use present value measurements. The marketplace assessment of present value is already embodied in such prices."

If neither condition 1 nor condition 2 exists, the entity must determine whether sufficient information exists to develop an expected present value estimate. FIN 47 states that an entity would have sufficient information to apply an expected present value technique (and therefore an ARO would be reasonably estimable) if either of the following conditions exists:

1. The settlement date and method of settlement for the obligation have been specified by others (e.g., the law, regulation, or contract that gives rise to the legal obligation specifies the settlement date and method of settlement).

2. Information is available to reasonably estimate (a) the settlement date or the range of potential settlement dates, (b) the method of settlement or potential methods of settlement, and (c) the probabilities associated with the potential settlement dates and potential methods of settlement.

In situations in which the date and method of settlement of an ARO are certain, there are only two possible outcomes: either the entity will be required to perform or the entity will not be required to perform. If no information is available about which outcome is more probable, paragraph 5 of FIN 47 and paragraph A23 of FAS 143 require a 50 percent likelihood for each outcome to be used until additional information is available.

It will rarely be the case that the settlement date and method of settlement for an environmental legal obligation will be specified by the law, regulation, or contract that gives rise to the legal obligation or otherwise known with certainty. Therefore, in situations in which the amount of the obligation is not embedded in the acquisition price of the asset and an active market does not exist for transfer of the obligation, it generally will be necessary to determine whether sufficient information exists to reasonably estimate the range of settlement dates, costs associated with alternative potential methods of settlement, and the associated probabilities. FIN 47 states that relevant sources of information include, but are not limited to:

- The entity's past practice
- Industry practice
- Management's intent
- The estimated economic life of the asset

The determination of whether sufficient information exists to reasonably estimate the fair value of an ARO using an expected present value technique is a matter of judgment that depends on the relevant facts and circumstances.

(b) DATA COLLECTION

If the inability to reasonably estimate a loss is due to a lack of data that is attainable but not readily available, what is the obligation of the entity to collect additional data? For example, does a reporting entity have an obligation under GAAP to identify and assess historical pollution conditions in order to measure and report the liabilities associated with these conditions?

Generally, financial accounting standards assume that the entity is aware of the transactions, conditions, or events giving rise to environmental financial reporting obligations. Thus, for example, they tend to address the sufficiency of available information to measure an environmental liability, while being silent as to the entity's obligation to identify the transaction, condition, or event giving rise to the liability in the first place. One notable exception is FIN 47, "Accounting for Conditional Asset Retirement Obligations." Paragraph 4 of FIN 47 imposes an affirmative duty of investigation on reporting entities, stating that "[a]n entity shall identify all its asset retirement obligations." Information indicating the existence of an environmental liability, however, may be insufficient to support the measurement of that liability. In such cases, additional assessment may be necessary.

It is a general principle of financial reporting that the benefits of financial information should be expected to equal or exceed the cost of obtaining such information. Because the relative cost-benefit of financial information is usually difficult or impossible to measure objectively, however, reasonable persons can be expected to disagree about whether the benefits of environmental financial information justify its costs.

FAS 5 and FIN 14 state that the entity should consider "information *available* prior to issuance of the financial statements." These standards do not elaborate on the cost-benefit of efforts to obtain information that is not readily available.

For purposes of measuring the fair value of an asset retirement obligation under FAS 143 or an asset impairment under FAS 144, SFAC 7 requires entities to use assumptions regarding cash-flow estimates that marketplace participants would use in their estimates of fair value when that information is available "without undue cost or effort." This standard is consistent with the general cost-benefit principle described above. The FASB, however, appears prepared to remove the *undue cost or effort* criterion from the determination of fair value.

As of the date of publication of this book, the FASB was deliberating comments on a June 23, 2004 Exposure Draft of a proposed Statement, "Fair Value Measurements." In the Exposure Draft, the FASB allowed for situations in which the information necessary to apply a valuation technique is not available without *undue cost and effort*. During the comment period, some respondents contended that "undue cost and effort" should not be a basis for determining whether to apply a valuation technique that is otherwise relevant, arguing that in some cases, the most relevant valuation technique might also be the most costly valuation technique. The respondents also expressed concerns that an *undue cost and effort* criterion could result in entities failing to complete the requisite estimates when doing so becomes "overly burdensome" and, in that regard, likely would be inconsistently applied. As of May 2005, the FASB agreed, and removed the *undue cost and effort* criterion. Pending formal adoption of the Standard, the FASB's decision is tentative, but the FASB's deliberations on this subject send a strong signal that reporting entities should be proceed cautiously in relying on the *undue cost and effort* criterion.

Financial accounting standards generally do not identify the sources of information that must be considered. Again, a notable exception is FIN 47, which specifies that the entity must consider relevant sources of information (e.g., the entity's past practice, industry practice, management's intent, and the estimated economic life of the asset) when determining whether sufficient information exists to develop an expected present value estimate of an ARO. Supplemental standards ASTM E 2137 and ASTM E 2173 also specify sources of information to be considered.

In some cases, the obligation to collect data may arise under environmental laws rather than financial accounting standards. For example, the costs to characterize contamination associated with pollution conditions is a component of the legal obligation imposed on PRPs under CERCLA and corresponding state environmental cleanup laws (see § 3.2(a)). In some situations, therefore, the costs of environmental investigation are not merely administrative costs incurred solely for the purpose of providing a more accurate estimate of a liability or impairment. Such costs are independently mandated under environmental laws. In other situations (e.g., company-owned properties and facilities with known or reasonably suspected historical pollution conditions), the legal obligation under environmental law to collect data in the absence of government enforcement action or other legal proceedings, if any, may be less certain.

For public companies, additional data collection standards are imposed by SEC regulations. For example, Instruction 2 to Item 303 of Regulation S-K (see § 24.5) formerly provided that "information provided pursuant to this Item need only include that which is available to the registrant without undue effort or expense and which does not clearly appear in the registrant's financial statements."[34] The SEC, in connection with new rules promulgated pursuant to section 401 of Sarbanes-Oxley, eliminated this limitation.[35] The rulemaking notice does not discuss the SEC's decision to remove this sentence from the instructions. By negative implication, however, the SEC has thereby indicated that public companies cannot avoid disclosure of material information that is available to them on the basis that obtaining such information would be difficult or expensive.

Data collection to support accounting estimates by public companies is also subject to the standards for internal control (see § 12.2(d) and Chapter 8). These standards require public companies to maintain books and records with a level of detail and degree of assurance that would satisfy prudent officials in the conduct of their own affairs.

(c) DISCLOSURE

In circumstances in which it is not possible to reasonably estimate a loss, the entity nonetheless may be required to provide information describing the nature of the contingency, and the reasons why an amount cannot be reasonably estimated.

Under FAS 5, disclosure is required if it is *probable* that an asset had been impaired or a liability had been incurred as of the date of the financial statements, but the loss is not accrued because the amount of loss cannot be reasonably estimated (see § 19.4(d)(ii)).

In circumstances in which the liability for an asset retirement obligation under FAS 143 cannot be reasonably estimated, the entity is required to disclose a description of the obligation, the fact that a liability has not been recognized because the fair value cannot be reasonably estimated, and the reasons why fair value cannot be reasonably estimated.

---

[34] 17 C.F.R. § 229.303, Instruction 2 to ¶ 303(a) (2002 ed.).

[35] Securities Act Release No. 33-8182, 68 Fed. Reg. 5982, 5999 (Feb. 5, 2003).

12.5 SIGNIFICANT RISKS AND UNCERTAINTIES

SOP 94-6, "Disclosure of Certain Significant Risks and Uncertainties" (SOP 94-6), requires disclosures regarding estimates used in valuing assets, liabilities, or gain or loss contingencies if both of the following conditions are met:

1. It is at least *reasonably possible* (as that term is defined in FAS 5) that the estimate of the effect on the financial statements of a condition, situation, or set of circumstances that existed at the date of the financial statements will change in the near term due to one or more future confirming events; and
2. The effect of the change would be material to the financial statements.

The disclosure should describe the nature of the uncertainty and include an indication that it is at least reasonably possible that a change in the estimate will occur in the near term (a period of time not to exceed one year from the date of the financial statements). The determination of whether a change in estimate is *reasonably possible* to occur is the most challenging aspect of implementing SOP 94-6. The judgments of both financial statement preparers and auditors play a significant role in determining whether the occurrence of something is reasonably possible, and there may be differences of opinion regarding what constitutes a reasonable possibility.

SOP 94-6 is separate from and does not modify FAS 5. For example, the disclosure for an estimate of an environmental loss contingency under FAS 5 should include an estimate of the possible range of loss, or state that an estimate cannot be made. SOP 94-6 encourages but does not require disclosure of factors that would make an estimate sensitive to change.

Environmental remediation-related obligations are specifically identified in SOP 94-6 as an example of items that may be based on estimates that are particularly sensitive to change in the near term. For the purposes of determining materiality, it is the effect of a change to an estimate and not the amount of an estimate itself that determines whether an item is material and must be disclosed. For example, the fact that there is a reasonable possibility of a near-term change in the estimate for a material environmental loss contingency does not trigger disclosure requirements, unless the change in estimate would itself be material. Conversely, simply because an estimate resulted in the recognition of an immaterial financial statement amount, or no amount, does not necessarily mean that disclosure is not required under SOP 94-6.

Many entities use risk-reduction techniques, such as environmental insurance, to mitigate losses. If the effect of a change in environmental liability estimate is unlikely to be material because of risk-reduction techniques, the entity is encouraged, but not required, to disclose the uncertainty as well as the relevant risk-reduction techniques.

See also § 24.5(e) regarding disclosure requirements for critical accounting estimates under Item 303 of Regulation S-K.

12.6 CHANGE IN ACCOUNTING ESTIMATES

Environmental financial reporting involves frequent use of estimates for such items as environmental loss contingencies, environmental remediation liabilities, environmental guarantees, asset retirement obligations, and asset impairments. Future conditions and events that affect these estimates cannot be estimated with certainty. Changes in estimates are inevitable as new information and more experience are obtained. FASB Statement of Financial Accounting Standards No. 154, "Accounting Changes and Error Corrections, a replacement of APB Opinion No. 20 and FASB Statement No. 3," (FAS 154) requires that changes in estimates be handled currently and prospectively. The effect of a change in accounting estimate is accounted for in the period of change if the change affects that period only, or the period of change and future periods, if the change affects both.

A permanent impairment affecting the recoverability of an asset (see Chapter 23) is not a change in accounting estimate. Rather, it is treated as an operating expense of the period in which it is incurred (in effect, an impairment loss is treated as additional depreciation).

A change in accounting estimate that is caused by a change in accounting principle is reported as a change in accounting estimate. The reasoning is that the effect of the change in accounting principle is inseparable from the effect of the change in estimate.

SAS 57, "Auditing Accounting Estimates," states that accounting estimates are appropriate when either the measurement of some amounts or the valuation of some accounts is uncertain, pending the outcome of *future* events, or relevant data concerning events that have already occurred cannot be accumulated on a timely, cost-effective basis. If the change in estimate is based on information that was known, or should have been known, by the company during the prior period, a restatement of the prior-period financial statements may be required. For more information on the evaluation of changes in estimates during a financial statement audit, see § 26.3(d).

CHAPTER THIRTEEN

Environmental Costs

13.1 INTRODUCTION

Environmental costs are the costs of steps taken to manage an enterprise in an environmentally responsible manner, including compliance with environmental laws, as well as other costs driven by the environmental objectives and requirements of the enterprise. Environmental costs include cleanup costs, environmental exit costs, pollution control costs, and environmental damages. Issues relating to environmental costs center on the period or periods in which costs should be recognized, and whether they should be capitalized or charged to income.

13.2 RECOGNITION

Environmental costs generally should be recognized in the period in which cash is spent or liabilities are incurred for environmental-related goods and services. Environmental expense (or loss) may also be recognized when it becomes evident that previously recognized future economic benefits of an asset have been reduced or eliminated (see Chapter 23), or that an environmental liability has been incurred or increased, without associated economic benefits (see Chapter 18).

In some cases, environmental costs may relate to pollution conditions that first commenced in a prior period. Examples include environmental damage to property that occurred prior to acquisition, an accident or other activities in a prior period that now require cleanup, cleanup of property divested in a prior period, and costs of disposing or treating hazardous waste created in a prior period. Accounting standards, however, generally preclude treatment of environmental costs as prior-period adjustments unless there is a change in accounting policy or unless there was a fundamental error. The preceding examples would, therefore, generally not qualify as prior-period adjustments.

(a) CLEANUP COSTS

Cleanup costs are expenses, including legal expenses, incurred for the investigation, removal, remediation (including associated monitoring), or disposal of soil, surface water, groundwater, or other contamination as required by environmental laws, contract, or company policy; plus costs incurred to repair, replace, or restore real or personal property damaged in the course of such activities. Cleanup costs include environmental exit costs. Specific elements of cleanup costs for Superfund and RCRA remediation efforts are described in § 20.3(a).

Cleanup costs generally should be charged to current operations, unless such costs satisfy the criteria for capitalization as an asset (see Chapter 14).

(b) ENVIRONMENTAL EXIT COSTS

Environmental exit costs include site restoration costs, postclosure and monitoring costs, and other environmental cleanup costs incurred when a property or facility is sold, abandoned, or ceases operations. Environmental exit costs are generally incurred to comply with environmental laws, such as RCRA (see § 3.2(b)), that contemplate an acceptable level of environmental contamination associated with normal operation of the facility (see § 22.2(d)(v)(D) for a discussion of normal operation in the context of asset retirement obligations). Environmental exit costs may be incurred to comply with state environmental laws that require cleanup of historical pollution conditions prior to the sale of real property (see § 3.2(d)). Environmental exit costs also may be incurred to comply with contractual obligations or nonbinding company policies.

Environmental exit costs are an element of cleanup costs and are differentiated from other cleanup costs that are not incurred in connection with the sale, abandonment, or discontinuation of operation of properties and facilities. Generally, the obligation to incur future environmental exit costs upon retirement of a company-owned property or facility is recognized as an asset retirement obligation under FAS 143, "Accounting for Asset Retirement Obligations" (Chapter 22). The obligation to incur future environmental exit costs upon retirement of properties or facilities not owned by the entity may be recognized as an environmental remediation liability under FAS 5, "Accounting for Contingencies," and/or FIN 45 (see Chapters 20 and 21). Obligations for future environmental exit costs not otherwise covered by FAS 5 or FAS 143 may also be recognized as liabilities under FAS 146, "Accounting for Costs Associated with Exit or Disposal Activities."

Environmental exit costs generally should be charged to current operations, unless such costs satisfy the criteria for capitalization as an asset (see Chapter 14).

(c) POLLUTION CONTROL COSTS

Pollution control costs are expenditures other than cleanup costs incurred to reduce the negative impact of the entity's activities on the environment. Pollution control costs may be incurred voluntarily or involuntarily. Examples of pollution control costs include expenditures for environmental permits, personnel salaries and training, environmental information management systems, compliance audits, secondary containment systems, and end-of-pipe control technology.

Pollution control costs generally should be charged to current operations, unless such costs satisfy the criteria for capitalization as an asset (see Chapter 14).

(d) ENVIRONMENTAL DAMAGES

Environmental damages are costs associated with noncompliance with environmental laws or breach of a duty owed to others under principles of common law. Noncompliance with pollution control laws can result in administrative, civil, and criminal enforcement. In some cases, noncompliance can result in a government-ordered shutdown of operations. In addition, historical pollution conditions and accidents resulting in the release of hazardous substances can give rise to common law and statutory claims for cleanup costs, bodily injury, and property damage.

Environmental damages are different from other types of environmental costs in that they provide no benefit or return to the enterprise. Environmental damages include:

- Monetary awards or settlements of compensatory damages.
- Punitive, exemplary, or multiple damages.
- Natural resource damages.
- Civil fines, penalties, or assessments for bodily injury or property damage.
- Costs, charges, and expenses incurred in the defense, investigation, or adjustment of claims.

Environmental damages generally should be charged to current operations as a nonextraordinary expense.

13.3 MEASUREMENT

Environmental costs incurred for environmental-related goods and services are recorded for the exchange amount. Environmental expense (or loss) recognized in connection with changes in environmental assets (Chapter 14) or liabilities (Chapter 18) generally involves measurement based on estimates.

13.4 DISPLAY AND DISCLOSURE

(a) BALANCE SHEET DISPLAY

If the criteria for recognition as an asset have been met (Chapter 14), environmental costs should be capitalized and amortized to the income statement over the estimated useful life of the asset.

(b) INCOME STATEMENT DISPLAY

Unless the criteria for recognition as an asset have been met (Chapter 14), environmental costs should be charged to net income immediately. If the criteria for recognition as an asset have been met, they should be capitalized and amortized to the income statement over the estimated useful life of the asset.

Environmental costs generally should be classified as a component of operating expenses. Because the events underlying the incurrence of environmental costs typically relate to an entity's operations, such costs should be charged against operations. Although charging cleanup costs and environmental damages relating to past environmental impacts against current operations may seem questionable, because of the time between the underlying cause and the subsequent incurrence of costs, environmental-related expenses have become a regular cost of conducting economic activity in many industries. Accordingly, environmental costs generally should be reported as a component of operating income in income statements that classify items as operating or nonoperating.

(c) DISCLOSURE OF ACCOUNTING PRINCIPLES

APB Opinion 22, "Disclosure of Accounting Policies," provides guidance regarding accounting principles that should be described in the accounting policies note to the financial statements. APB Opinion 22, paragraph 12, states that entities should disclose those accounting principles that "materially affect the determination of financial position or results of operations." In particular, entities should disclose accounting principles and the methods of applying those principles when alternatives exist. With respect to environmental costs, entities should disclose the criteria used for determining when to expense and when to capitalize such costs (see Chapter 15).

(d) DISCLOSURES FOR ENVIRONMENTAL COSTS

According to SOP 96-1, entities are encouraged but not required to disclose the amount of expenditures for environmental cleanup costs charged to income and the following related information:

- The amount recognized for environmental remediation liabilities (see Chapter 20) in each period.
- The amount of any recovery from third parties that is credited to environmental cleanup costs in each period (see Chapter 16).
- The income statement caption in which environmental cleanup costs and credits are included

(e) ADDITIONAL CONSIDERATIONS FOR PUBLIC COMPANIES

Public companies are required to disclose information regarding the material effects of pollution control costs under Item 101 of Regulation S-K (see § 24.3), and legal proceedings that could give rise to environmental damages under Item 103 of Regulation S-K (see § 24.4).

CHAPTER FOURTEEN

Environmental Assets

14.1 INTRODUCTION

Statement of Financial Accounting Concepts No. 6, "Elements of Financial Statements" (SFAC 6), defines *assets* as probable future economic benefits obtained or controlled by a particular entity as a result of past transactions or events. As used in this definition, *probable* is used with its usual general meaning, rather than in a specific accounting or technical sense such as that in FAS 5 (see § 19.2(a)(iii)), and refers to that which can reasonably be expected or believed on the basis of available evidence or logic but is neither certain nor proved. Its inclusion in the definition is intended to acknowledge that business and other economic activities occur in an environment characterized by uncertainty in which few outcomes are certain.

Identifiable environmental assets fall into three categories: (1) capitalized environmental costs (Chapter 15), (2) environmental-related rights of recovery (Chapter 16), and (3) emission credits (Chapter 17). In addition, if such matters are considered material to investors, an entity may elect to disclose nonfinancial information regarding positive environmental-related achievements (e.g., ISO 14001 certification or company-wide reductions in toxic air emissions or greenhouse gas emissions) that would not qualify as assets in the accounting sense.

An entity may also possess certain other types of intangible environmental assets that are expected to have future economic benefits. Such assets may include, for example:

- A company's reputation with consumers for environmentally friendly products or environmental stewardship.
- A company's relationship of trust with regulatory agencies, employees, and communities.

- Legal rights to operate in certain geographic locations or to maintain certain types of operations that are otherwise unavailable to competitors or new market entrants.
- Lower operating costs due to minimization of waste and related waste management costs.

Positive environmental attributes, such as those listed above, can significantly increase the value of a business enterprise. However, it generally is not possible to separately identify and assign a determinable fair value to such assets. Accordingly, they are typically recognized as goodwill in connection with a business combination and are not separately identified in the financial statements.

14.2 RECOGNITION

(a) CHARACTERISTICS OF ASSETS

Paragraph 26 of Statement of Financial Accounting Concepts No. 6, "Elements of Financial Statements" (SFAC 6), states that an asset has three essential characteristics:

- It embodies a probable future benefit that involves a capacity, singly or in combination with other assets, to contribute directly or indirectly to future net cash inflows.
- A particular entity can obtain the benefit and control others' access to it.
- The transaction or other event giving rise to the entity's right to or control of the benefit has already occurred.

Although assets generally share other characteristics, the absence of such characteristics is not sufficient to preclude an item from qualifying as an asset. Assets may be acquired at a cost or without cost. They may be tangible or intangible, exchangeable or nonexchangeable. Although assets generally are legally enforceable, legal enforceability of a claim to the benefit is not a prerequisite for a benefit to qualify as an asset if the entity has the ability to obtain and control the benefit in other ways.

Once acquired, an asset continues as an asset of the entity until the entity collects it, transfers it to another entity, or uses it up, or some other event or circumstance destroys the future benefit or removes the entity's ability to obtain it.

Assets can be subdivided into two basic types: tangible and intangible.

(b) TANGIBLE ENVIRONMENTAL ASSETS

Tangible assets have physical substance. They include *long-lived assets,* which are assets that provide an economic benefit to the enterprise for a number of future accounting periods (e.g., property, plant, and equipment). Tangible environmental assets may be separate assets or components of other capital assets. For example, the removal of asbestos from a building does not in itself result in a future economic or environmental benefit; it is the building that receives the benefit. It would therefore be inappropriate to recognize asbestos removal as a separate asset. A piece of machinery that removes pollution from the water or atmosphere, however, could have a specific or separate future benefit and might properly be recognized as a separate asset.

(c) INTANGIBLE ENVIRONMENTAL ASSETS

Intangible assets have no physical substance. Their value is based on the rights or privileges that they grant to the business enterprise. Intangible assets include rights that are expected to have future economic benefits and purchased goodwill. *Goodwill* is the reputation of an entity with its customers. Goodwill that is purchased in a business combination is recognized, internally generated goodwill is not. Patents, copyrights, logos, and trademarks are examples of rights that are recognized as intangible assets. Examples of intangible environmental assets include:

- Potential recoveries (Chapter 16)
- Emission credits (Chapter 17)
- Goodwill associated with a company's environmental performance or risk profile

Intangible assets are often recognized for the first time as the result of a business acquisition or merger. Intangible assets that can be separately identified at a determinable fair value should be assigned a portion of the total purchase price and should be amortized over their estimated lives. Any portion of the purchase price that cannot be identified with specific tangible and intangible assets (less liabilities assumed) is assigned to goodwill.

14.3 MEASUREMENT

Measurement of environmental assets is discussed in subsequent chapters in the context of capitalized environmental costs (Chapter 15), rights of recovery (Chapter 16), and emission credits (Chapter 17).

14.4 DISPLAY AND DISCLOSURE

Display and disclosure issues for environmental assets are discussed in subsequent chapters in the context of capitalized environmental costs (Chapter 15), rights of recovery (Chapter 16), and emission credits (Chapter 17).

CHAPTER FIFTEEN

Capitalized Environmental Costs

15.1 INTRODUCTION

As discussed in Chapter 13, unless the criteria for recognition as an asset have been met (Chapter 14), environmental costs should be expensed in the current period. Alternatively, if the criteria for recognition as an asset have been met, environmental costs should be capitalized. This chapter discusses the recognition, measurement, display, and disclosure of environmental costs that are capitalized as environmental assets.

15.2 RECOGNITION

EITF 90-8, "Capitalization of Costs to Treat Environmental Contamination," provides that environmental costs should be capitalized as assets when they relate, directly or indirectly, to future economic benefits that will flow to the enterprise, as evidenced by meeting one or more of the following criteria:

- The costs increase the capacity or improve the safety or efficiency of other assets owned by the enterprise.
- The costs mitigate or prevent future environmental contamination while also improving the property.
- The costs are incurred in preparing for sale a property that is currently held for sale.

Some environmental costs may not directly increase economic benefits to the enterprise, but may be necessary if the enterprise is to benefit from its other assets. For example, costs to obtain an operating permit required under environmental law are necessary if the enterprise is to benefit from the facility to be permitted. Such costs are appropriately capitalized.

Exhibit 15.1 provides several examples from EITF 90-8 illustrating when environmental costs should and should not be capitalized.

EXHIBIT 15.1

Capitalized Environmental Costs

ENVIRONMENTAL CONDITIONS AND COSTS	EVALUATION OF CRITERIA FOR CAPITALIZATION
• Tanker Oil Spill:	
(a) Clean up waterway and beachfront	1. Costs to clean up the waterway and beachfront are not eligible for consideration under the first criterion because the oil company does not own the property. 2. The cleanup of the waterway and beachfront does not mitigate or prevent a future oil spill from future operations. 3. The waterway and beachfront are not owned assets; therefore, the third criterion does not apply. *Conclusion*: Costs incurred for cleanup and restoration in connection with the oil spill should be charged to expense.[a]
(b) Reinforce tanker's hull to reduce risk of future spill	1. Reinforcing the hull improves the tanker's safety compared to when the tanker was originally constructed or acquired. 2. Reinforcing the hull mitigates the risk that the tanker will experience a similar oil spill during future operations and improves the tanker's safety compared to when the tanker was originally constructed or acquired. *Conclusion*: The costs incurred in connection with reinforcing the tanker's hull may be capitalized under either the first or second criterion.
• Rusty Chemical Storage Tank:	
(a) Remove rust that developed during ownership	1. Removing the rust has not improved the tank compared with its condition when built or acquired. 2. Removing the rust has mitigated the possibility of future leaks. However, removing the rust has not improved the tank compared with its condition when built or acquired. *Conclusion*: Rust removal costs should be expensed unless the tank is currently held for sale and the costs were incurred to prepare the tank for sale.

[a] This consensus does not require that tangible assets acquired to clean a particular spill be charged to expense immediately. Rather, to the extent that those tangible assets have future uses, they may be capitalized and depreciated over their remaining useful lives.

EXHIBIT 15.1 *(CONTINUED)*

Capitalized Environmental Costs	
(b) Apply rust prevention chemicals	1. The application of rust prevention chemicals has improved the tank's condition compared with its condition when built or acquired. 2. Rust prevention chemicals mitigate the possibility that future rust will cause leaks and also improve the tank's condition compared with its condition when built or acquired. *Conclusion*: The costs of applying the rust prevention chemicals may be capitalized under either the first or second criterion.
• Air Pollution Caused by Manufacturing Activities:	
(a) Acquire and install pollution control equipment	1. The pollution control equipment improves the safety of the plant compared with its condition when built or acquired. 2. The pollution control equipment mitigates or prevents air pollution that has yet to occur but that may otherwise result from future operation of the plant and improves the safety of the plant compared with its condition when built or acquired. *Conclusion*: Costs associated with acquisition and installation of the pollution control equipment may be capitalized under either the first or second criterion.
(b) Pay fines for violations of the Clean Air Act	1. Payment of fines does not extend the plant's life, increase its capacity, or improve its efficiency or safety. 2. Payment of fines does not mitigate or prevent pollution that has yet to occur but that may otherwise result from future operation of the plant. *Conclusion*: Fines paid in connection with violations of the Clean Air Act should be charged to expense. Even if the plant is currently held for sale, the fines should be charged to expense because the costs would not have been incurred to prepare the plant for sale.
• Lead Pipes in Office Building Contaminate Drinking Water:	
(a) Remove lead pipes and replace with copper pipes	1. Removing the lead pipes has improved the safety of the building's water system compared with its condition when the water system was built or acquired. 2. By removing the lead pipes, the building's owner eliminated an existing environmental problem and prevented any further contamination from that lead. However, by removing the existing pipes, the building's owner has not mitigated or prevented environmental problems yet to occur, if any, from future operation of the building.

EXHIBIT 15.1 *(CONTINUED)*

Capitalized Environmental Costs	
	Conclusion: Costs to remove the lead pipes and install copper pipes may be capitalized under the first criterion. The book value of the lead pipes should be charged to expense when removed.
• Soil Contamination Caused by an Operating Garbage Dump:	
(a) Remediate soil on dump property	1. The life of a garbage dump is not extended by remediating its soil. Further, the condition of the soil after remediating will not be improved over its condition when the garbage dump was constructed or acquired. Removal of the toxic waste restores the soil to its original uncontaminated condition. 2. Removal of toxic waste from the soil addresses an existing environmental concern. It also prevents that waste from leaching in the future. However, removing the waste does not mitigate or prevent future operations from creating future toxic waste. The risk will continue regardless of how much of the existing soil is remediated. *Conclusion*: Soil remediation costs should be charged to expense unless the garbage dump is currently held for sale and the costs were incurred to prepare the garbage dump for sale.
(b) Install liner	1. The liner does not extend the useful life or improve the efficiency or capacity of the garbage dump. However, the liner has improved the garbage dump's safety compared to when the dump was constructed or acquired. 2. The liner addresses an existing and potential future problem. In this example, the garbage dump contains toxic waste from past operations and will likely generate toxic waste during future operations. The liner partly addresses the existing environmental problem by preventing future leaching of existing toxic waste into the soil. The liner also mitigates or prevents leaching of toxic waste that may result from garbage dumping in a future period and has improved the garbage dump's safety compared to when the dump was constructed or acquired. *Conclusion*: The liner may be capitalized under either the first or second criterion.
• Water Well Contamination Caused by Chemicals that Leaked into Wells Containing Water that Will Be Used in Future Beer Production:	

EXHIBIT 15.1 *(CONTINUED)*

Capitalized Environmental Costs	
(a) Decontaminate water in wells	1. The treatment does not extend the life of the wells, increase their capacity, or improve efficiency. The condition of the water is not safer after the treatment compared to when the wells were initially acquired. 2. By decontaminating the water, the possibility of future contamination of the wells from future operations has not been mitigated or prevented. *Conclusion*: Costs incurred to neutralize well water should be charged to expense unless the wells were held for sale and the costs were incurred to prepare the wells for sale.
(b) Install water filters	1. The water filters improve the safety of the wells compared with their uncontaminated state when built or acquired. 2. The water filters address future problems that may result from future operations. Because the water filters are effective in filtering environmental contamination, they mitigate the effect of spilling new contaminants into the wells during future operations. In addition, the water filters represent an improvement compared with the wells' original condition without water filters. *Conclusion*: The water filtering system may be capitalized under either the first or the second criterion.
• Underground Gasoline Storage Tanks Leak and Contaminate the Company's Property:	
(a) Remediate soil	1. Soil remediation does not extend the useful life, increase the capacity, or improve the efficiency or safety of the land relative to its unpolluted state when acquired. 2. By remediating the contaminated soil, the oil company has addressed an existing problem. However, the company has not mitigated or eliminated future leaks during future operations. *Conclusion*: Soil remediation costs should be charged to expense unless the property is currently held for sale and the costs were incurred to prepare the property for sale.
(b) Encase tanks so as to prevent future leaks from contaminating surrounding soils	1. In some cases, encasement may increase the life of the tanks because of their increased resistance to corrosion, leaking, and so on. In other situations, the treatment does not increase the life of the tanks. However, the encasement has improved the tanks' safety compared with their condition when built or acquired.

EXHIBIT 15.1 *(CONTINUED)*

Capitalized Environmental Costs	
	2. Encasement has mitigated or prevented future leakage and soil contamination that might otherwise result from future operations. In addition, the encasement has improved the tanks' safety compared with their condition when built or acquired. *Conclusion*: The cost of encasement may be capitalized under either the first or the second criterion.
• Air in Office Building Contaminated with Asbestos Fibers:	
(a) Remove asbestos	1. Removal of the asbestos improves the building's safety over its original condition, because the environmental contamination (asbestos) existed when the building was constructed or acquired. 2. By removing the asbestos, the building's owner has eliminated an existing environmental problem and has prevented any further contamination from that asbestos. However, by removing the existing asbestos, the building's owner has not mitigated or prevented new environmental problems, if any, that might result from future operation of the building. *Conclusion*: Asbestos removal costs may be capitalized as a betterment under the first criterion.

15.3 MEASUREMENT

The scope of capitalized environmental costs may include incremental direct costs (e.g., for materials, equipments, labor and consulting services, and so forth) and costs of compensation and benefits for those employees who are expected to devote a significant amount of time directly to the capital project, to the extent of the time expected to be spent directly on the project.

Capitalized environmental costs generally are measured based on current exchange prices at the date of recognition (*historical cost*). Once an asset is recognized, it continues to be measured at the amount initially recognized until an event that changes the asset or its amount occurs and meets the recognition criteria.

15.4 DISPLAY AND DISCLOSURE

(a) BALANCE SHEET DISPLAY

In most instances, capitalized environmental costs are related to another asset and should be included as an integral part of that asset, rather than being recognized separately. For example, it would be inappropriate to recognize the cost of asbestos abatement as a separate asset, as it does not result in a separate future economic benefit. Alternatively, a piece of machinery that removes pollution from the water or atmosphere has a specific or separate future benefit and therefore should be recognized separately.

Before an environmental cost is capitalized and included as an integral part of another asset, the combined asset should be tested for impairment (Chapter 23). The integration of capitalized environmental costs with the related asset can result in recordation of a combined asset that is not recoverable. For example, the capitalization of $1 million of cleanup costs incurred to remediate a contaminated company-owned property with a carrying cost and post-cleanup value of $100,000 will result in the combined asset ($1,100,000) being recorded above its fair value (and most likely above its recoverable amount). If environmental costs are not recoverable, they should be expensed immediately. Similarly, environmental costs recognized as a separate asset should also be tested for impairment.

(b) INCOME STATEMENT DISPLAY

Capitalized environmental costs are depreciated (amortized) to the income statement over the current and appropriate future periods in the same manner as other long-lived assets.

(c) DISCLOSURE OF ACCOUNTING PRINCIPLES

APB Opinion 22, "Disclosure of Accounting Policies," provides guidance regarding accounting principles that should be described in the accounting policies note to the financial statements. APB Opinion 22, paragraph 12, indicates that entities should disclose those accounting principles that "materially affect the determination of financial position or results of operations." In particular, entities should disclose accounting principles and the methods of applying those principles when alternatives exist. With respect to capitalized environmental costs, entities should disclose the criteria used for determining when to expense and when to capitalize environmental costs.

(d) DISCLOSURES FOR CAPITALIZED ENVIRONMENTAL COSTS

There are no specific disclosure requirements under GAAP applicable to capitalized environmental costs.

(e) ADDITIONAL CONSIDERATIONS FOR PUBLIC COMPANIES

Section 404 of Sarbanes-Oxley imposes requirements on public companies to design, implement, and periodically assess the operational effectiveness of internal control over financial reporting (see Chapter 8). In addition, section 404 requires the reporting entity's independent financial auditor to examine the entity's internal control over financial reporting and annually attest to its design and operational effectiveness (see Chapter 27).

Exhibit 15.2

Process and Control Considerations for Capitalized Environmental Costs

Process Area	Process and Control Considerations
Identification	• Identification of capital projects with environmental costs • Tracking of environmental costs
Assessment	• Evaluation of criteria for capitalization • Evaluation of criteria for impairment testing
Measurement	• Determination of direct and indirect costs
Reporting	• Selection and application of criteria for separate asset recognition

Internal control over financial reporting of capitalized environmental costs will require appropriate processes to identify, assess, measure, and report such costs. Exhibit 15.2 identifies certain process and control issues that may warrant special attention for reporting entities and financial auditors.

Notwithstanding an effective internal control system design, the operational effectiveness of the system will largely depend on the performance of employees and contractors in carrying out established policies and procedures. Employee and contractor performance in turn will depend largely on the company's control environment with respect to environmental financial reporting (see § 8.2(a)) and personnel qualifications, training, and incentives (or disincentives).

CHAPTER SIXTEEN

Rights of Recovery

16.1 INTRODUCTION

Rights of recovery include legal claims against other parties (e.g., other PRPs at a Superfund site), environmental guarantees owed to the entity, environmental insurance, and other forms of financial assurance designed to offset existing environmental liabilities and loss contingencies. Rights of recovery can be subdivided into two categories: (1) recoveries under contractual risk transfer mechanisms (e.g. insurance, guarantees, and indemnification agreements) and (2) statutory and common law rights under environmental laws to recover losses from other responsible persons. Contractual risk-transfer mechanisms are generally used to manage environmental loss exposures prospectively (with the notable exception of retroactive insurance contracts), whereas legal rights of recovery are typically used to mitigate environmental losses already incurred by the entity.

Entities may seek to transfer risks for a wide range of environmental loss exposures, including:

- Litigation, claims, and assessments for cleanup costs and environmental damages relating to preexisting but unknown pollution conditions.
- Litigation, claims, and assessments for cleanup costs and environmental damages relating to future onsite or offsite pollution conditions.
- Diminution in the value of company-owned property resulting from future pollution conditions.
- Risk of loss from business interruptions or regulatory-imposed reductions/caps on manufacturing capacity.
- Environmental-related product liability.

Many entities purchase environmental insurance policies to cover a variety of environmental loss exposures. Frequently, multiple parties are beneficiaries of the policy, including past and present property owners, tenants, lenders, and contractors.

Today, most environmental insurance policies are issued on a claims-made basis. (There are still substantial rights of recovery relating to historical pollution conditions for environmental claims under pre-1986 occurrence-based general liability policies, particularly for personal injury and disease with long latency periods.) Under a claims-made insurance policy, an entity is insured for any claims reported during the term of the policy, in many cases including those that occurred prior to the policy effective date, but after the specified retroactive date.

Environmental insurance is underwritten on a claims-made basis because occurrence dates are often difficult to determine, and the "occurrence" may span a long period of time. A claims-made policy mitigates potential coverage disputes because the occurrence date generally is not relevant to the determination of coverage.

Entities purchasing a claims-made policy must renew the policy following the expiration of the policy term to maintain coverage. The amount of coverage purchased may change over time to meet current needs (e.g., changing levels of environmental risk within the entity). When operations cease or are divested, an entity may purchases *tail coverage* to insure itself against any previously unasserted claims. Presuming the entity can renew the claims-made policy each year and can obtain tail coverage when desired, such a strategy effectively converts the claims-made policy into an occurrence-based policy covering the entity for any claim made against it.

Many entities that purchase environmental claims-made insurance policies have no knowledge of unasserted outstanding claims or, because their environmental loss contingencies have not met the recognition criteria contained in FAS 5 (Chapter 19), have no recognized liability for claims, including incurred but not reported (IBNR) claims. In other situations, however, entities that purchase environmental claims-made insurance policies are aware of potential claims based on known preexisting pollution conditions. In those situations, unasserted claims can be either specifically excluded from or specifically included in the coverage.

16.2 RECOGNITION

Any claim for recovery should be estimated and evaluated independent of the related liability. An asset relating to a right of recovery should be recognized when (and only when) realization of the claim for recovery is deemed *probable* (as the term is defined in FAS 5) (see § 19.2(a)(iii)). A claim is presumed not to be probable if the claim is disputed or the subject of litigation. In most circumstances, the point in time at which an environmental loss contingency is both probable and reasonably estimable will precede the point in time at which any related recovery is probable of realization.

(a) INSURANCE CONTRACTS

Purchasers of claims-made environmental insurance must consider whether the insurance contract (1) transfers risk to the insurance company and (2) is retroactive or prospective. EITF 03-8, "Accounting for Claims-Made Insurance and Retroactive Contracts by the Insured Entity," explains how an entity should analyze insurance contracts when determining whether the contracts should be treated as retroactive or prospective. EITF 03-8 also describes the accounting that is required for each type of contract.

A retroactive contract provides indemnification against loss or liability relating to liabilities that have been incurred as a result of a past event (e.g., environmental remediation liabilities). A retroactive contract may apply to asserted claims, known unasserted claims, and any known prior conditions that might result in a specific claim (whether asserted or unasserted), regardless of whether the insured has recognized a loss contingency for those claims. It also includes claims that were not reported, but would have been reportable had a claims-made policy been in place in a prior period. A recognized liability for IBNR claims (claims for losses related to events that the insured is not specifically aware of but expects to be reported) generally would not be determinative in concluding that the claims-made insurance policy contains a retroactive provision. (i.e., liability for IBNR claims could arise from either prior or prospective events and circumstances).

A prospective contract transfers risk associated with future events. Some insurance contracts have both retroactive and prospective elements.

The following factors indicate that a claims-made insurance policy does *not* contain a retroactive provision (i.e., it does not provide coverage for previously reportable claims) and, therefore, should be accounted for on a prospective basis:

- The insured consistently purchases claims-made insurance policies as part of its risk management program for the specific type of risk being insured, and tail coverage for both prior periods and prior policies is readily available and not excessively priced as compared to tail coverage, offered to similar companies, that do not contain retroactive provisions.
- The claims-made insurance policy is responsive to unknown risks for a finite or limited period of time, as evidenced by the facts that the type of

risk being insured is inherently short-tailed (i.e., the claims are incurred during the policy period and paid out in their entirety shortly after the end of the policy period), the policy term is for a limited period of time (e.g., one-year coverage), claims-made coverage is the most readily available coverage for this type of insurance risk, and the occurrence date of the type of risk covered by the policy is unclear (i.e., the causal event that gives rise to an insured claim is difficult to determine).

- The claims-made insurance policy contains an unambiguous trigger indicating that a claim is covered by the policy. That contract trigger should not be subject to interpretation, negotiation, or manipulation. An example of an unambiguous trigger that indicates that a claim is covered by a claims-made insurance policy is the following:
    - The insured notifies the insurance carrier during the policy term that a claim has been asserted, or that an incident has occurred, and
    - The insured must represent that it was not aware of any such incident when the claims-made policy was purchased.
- The premium charged for the claims-made insurance policy is not significantly in excess of the premium that would be charged for a claims-made insurance policy that could be purchased by a similar entity with similar insurance risks and that has no knowledge of any circumstances or events that would result in any claims, excluding any anticipated amounts for a typical number of claims for which the insured is not aware to have specifically occurred, but that it expects would be reported (IBNR claims).
- The insurer may base the premium for the claims-made insurance policy on estimates and predictions that are based on the past experience of the insured, but the premium is not based on settlement estimates of specific, known events that are expected to be recovered under the policy.
- The premium charged for the policy in the current year is not significantly in excess of that charged in previous years, other than for increases in the amount or type of coverage. An anticipated increase in premiums that is expected to occur because the insured entity is advancing toward the mature stage of premiums for claims-made insurance would not be considered in making that determination.
- The claims-made insurance policy is primarily intended to cover insurance risk and is not a financing arrangement. Claims-made insurance policies that are intended to cover insurance risk typically include features such as an absence of adjustment features based on experience and coverage of the ultimate loss from the claim, once made, regardless of period of settlement.
- If the claims-made insurance policy has a specified retroactive date prior to inception of the claims-made relationship with the insurer, the period from that specified retroactive date to the inception of the claims-made relationship with that insurer is either short or covered by other insurance policies.

The determination must be made upon the specific facts and circumstances, and no one factor is determinative in this evaluation.

Environmental insurance may contain prospective provisions, retroactive provisions, or a combination of both. Following are the three basic scenarios involving the use of environmental insurance:

- Coverage for known preexisting pollution conditions.
- Coverage for unknown preexisting pollution conditions.
- Coverage for future pollution conditions.

(i) KNOWN PREEXISTING POLLUTION CONDITIONS

The following examples demonstrate the application of the factors in EITF 03-8 to environmental insurance for known preexisting pollution conditions.

Example 1: On February 20, 20XX, Universal Industries determined that it needed to recognize a $100 million contingent liability under FAS 5 for cleanup costs and property damage claims as a result of an accident at one of its manufacturing plants that caused significant environmental contamination. Universal initially believed that it would manage the cleanup and any lawsuits arising from the accident through an internal self-insurance program. Subsequently, Universal decided to purchase a claims-made insurance policy that would include all claims arising from the incident. Universal decided that it should purchase the policy because it would be more efficient to transfer the risk associated with the development and timing of claims to a third party, and because representing that the risk associated with all claims had been transferred to a third party would reduce Universal's risk profile to its shareholders and other potential investors. On April 1, 20XX, Universal pays InsureAll $60 million for a claims-made insurance policy covering cleanup costs, bodily injury, and property damage claims with $100 million in limits and no exclusions for known preexisting conditions. Universal and InsureAll expect the claims related to the incident to be settled over a ten-year period after the purchase of the policy.

Evaluation: Based on an evaluation of the factors in EITF 03-8, Universal determines that its claims-made insurance policy contains a retroactive provision. In making that determination, Universal specifically considered the following:

- The claims-made policy was purchased specifically to cover known claims for which a liability had been recognized.
- The claims-made policy effectively represented a financing of the liability previously recognized by Universal.
- The premium charged was primarily based on expected payouts for an event that had already occurred.

Example 2: Assume the same facts as in Example 1, except that Universal books a $10 million environmental remediation liability for expected cleanup costs, but concludes that property damage claims are reasonably possible but not probable. Universal decides to manage the cleanup itself and buy insurance for potential tort claims. Universal pays InsureAll $300,000 for a 10-year claims-made insurance policy with limits of $20 million covering bodily injury and property damage claims, with no exclusions for known preexisting conditions. The policy specifically excludes cleanup cost coverage for known preexisting conditions.

Evaluation: Based on an evaluation of the factors in EITF 03-8, Universal determines that its claims-made insurance policy does not contain a retroactive provision. In making that determination, Universal specifically considered the following:

- The claims-made policy was purchased to cover unasserted claims for which no liability had been recognized.
- The claims-made insurance policy was primarily intended to cover insurance risk and was not a financing arrangement.
- The premium was not based on settlement estimates of specific, known events that were expected to be recovered under the policy.

The foregoing example can be distinguished from a claims-made environmental insurance policy providing coverage for *unknown* preexisting pollution conditions. In that case, the insured must represent that it is not aware of any such incident when the claims-made policy is purchased and the policy is responsive to unknown risks (see example 3 below).

(ii) UNKNOWN PREEXISTING POLLUTION CONDITIONS

The following example demonstrates the application of the factors in EITF 03-8 to environmental insurance for unknown preexisting pollution conditions.

Example 3: Universal enters into a purchase and sale agreement to acquire a property historically used for industrial operations. As part of its preacquisition due diligence, Universal conducts an environmental assessment of the property and finds no soil or groundwater contamination. Universal nonetheless decides to pay InsureAll $125,000 for a 10-year claims-made insurance policy with coverage of $10 million for unknown preexisting pollution conditions.

Evaluation: Based on an evaluation of the factors in EITF 03-8, Universal determines that its claims-made insurance policy does not contain a retroactive provision. In making that determination, Universal specifically considered the following:

- The claims-made insurance policy is responsive to unknown risks for a finite or limited period of time.
- The claims-made insurance policy was primarily intended to cover insurance risk and was not a financing arrangement.
- The premium was not based on settlement estimates of specific, known events expected to be recovered under the policy.

(iii) *FUTURE POLLUTION CONDITIONS*

The following example demonstrates the application of the factors in EITF 03-8 to environmental insurance for future pollution conditions.

Example 4: Assume the same facts as in example 3, except that the claims-made insurance policy purchased by Universal also contains coverage for pollution conditions first commencing after inception of the policy.

Evaluation: Based on an evaluation of the factors in EITF 03-8, Universal determines that the coverage for new pollution conditions under its claims-made insurance policy does not contain a retroactive provision. In making that determination, Universal specifically considered the following:

- The claims-made insurance policy is responsive to unknown risks for a finite or limited period of time.
- The claims-made insurance policy was primarily intended to cover insurance risk and was not a financing arrangement.
- The premium was not based on settlement estimates of specific, known events expected to be recovered under the policy.

(b) RETROACTIVE INSURANCE CONTRACTS

Because a retroactive insurance policy does not extinguish the entity's environmental liability, the premium paid for a retroactive policy should be reported separately as a receivable immediately upon payment. If the purchased insurance contract includes coverage for legal and other costs, the accounting for legal and other costs should be consistent between the asset and the liability (see § 20.3(a) regarding the scope of included costs for environmental remediation liabilities). Accordingly, if the entity's accounting policy is to include legal and other categories of costs in the accrual for an environmental liability, the insurance receivable also should reflect those costs if they are covered under the terms of the insurance policy. If an entity's accounting policy is not to accrue for those costs, the insurance receivable should not reflect those costs on an accrual basis.

(c) PROSPECTIVE INSURANCE CONTRACTS

The premium paid for prospective coverage under a claims-made environmental insurance policy should be recognized as a prepaid expense and amortized ratably over the policy period (or using another amortization method that is appropriate under the circumstances).

An asset relating to a right of recovery under a prospective environmental insurance provision should be recognized when realization of the claim for recovery is deemed probable.

(d) COMBINED CONTRACTS

If a claims-made environmental insurance policy contains both prospective and retroactive elements, the retroactive and prospective provisions of the policy should be accounted for separately, if practicable. If it is not practicable to separate the retroactive and prospective provisions, the claims-made insurance policy should be accounted for entirely as a retroactive contract. A claims-made insurance policy that contains no retroactive provisions should be accounted for on a prospective basis.

16.3 MEASUREMENT

Generally, rights of recovery should be measured at fair value. The concept of fair value requires consideration of both transaction costs related to receipt of the recovery and the time value of money. Transaction costs, such as litigation costs involved with potential recoveries, should be charged to expense as incurred until realization of the claim for recovery is considered probable and an asset relating to the recovery is recognized, at which time future legal costs should be considered in the measurement of the recovery.

The time value of money should not be considered in the determination of the fair value of a potential recovery if the associated liability is not discounted and the timing of the recovery is dependent on the timing of the payment of the liability (e.g., receipt of insurance proceeds depends on the settlement of a loss covered by the insurance policy). For example, if there is an insured environmental loss, the entity's insurance policy covers the insured loss and costs, and the timing of the recovery depends on the cost and timing of the related liability payment, the entity must base its recorded insurance receivable on the same assumptions used to measure the associated liability. If the receivable does not depend on the timing of the liability payment, the receivable should be discounted. The appropriate discount rate generally will be the risk-free rate of monetary assets that have comparable maturities.

(a) RETROACTIVE INSURANCE CONTRACTS

The amount of the receivable recognized for a retroactive environmental insurance provision should not exceed the lesser of the recorded liabilities relating to the underlying insured event (e.g., the amount of the recognized liability for an environmental loss contingency) or the limits of the insurance policy. If the recorded liabilities exceed the amounts paid for the insurance, the insurance receivable should be increased to reflect the resulting deferred gain (i.e., an insurance receivable is established in an amount equal to the recorded liability and a deferred gain is established in an amount equal to the difference between the premium paid for the policy and the recorded liability). If the amount of the liability is subsequently adjusted upward, the amount of the insurance receivable is adjusted upward by a corresponding amount, up to the limits of the policy.

(b) PROSPECTIVE INSURANCE CONTRACTS

Recoveries from prospective environmental insurance contracts generally should be measured at fair value, as described above. For any insurance recoverable recognized, either related to IBNR liability or to a specific incurred claim, the entity should evaluate those assets and adjust them, if necessary, based on changes in circumstances.

16.4 DISPLAY AND DISCLOSURE

(a) BALANCE SHEET DISPLAY

Regardless of whether the entity has transferred risk through an insurance policy or other risk-transfer mechanism, the company generally retains the primary obligation with respect to any environmental losses. Accordingly, financial reporting standards require separate presentation of the gross liability and the corresponding right of recovery.

FIN 39 recognizes the general principle of accounting that the offsetting of assets and liabilities in the balance sheet is improper except when a right of setoff exists. A *right of setoff* is a debtor's legal right, by contract or otherwise, to discharge all or a portion of the debt owed to another party by applying against the debt an amount that the other party owes to the debtor. A debtor having a right of setoff may offset the related asset against the liability and report the net amount.

Paragraph 5 of FIN 39 states that a right of setoff exists when all of the following conditions are satisfied:

- Each of two parties owes the other determinable amounts.
- The reporting entity has the right to set off the amount owed against the amount owed by the other party.
- The reporting entity intends to set off.
- The right of setoff is enforceable at law.

Potential sources of recovery, such as insurance, contribution, and indemnification, would rarely, if ever, constitute a right of setoff against an environmental liability or loss contingency. Liabilities for environmental cleanup are not the assets of identifiable individuals. The obligation or debt is instead typically owed to the government (or third party) and the government (or third party) owes no offsetting obligation or debt to the reporting entity.

Any unusual claims and incidents that have occurred prior to the end of an interim period, but will probably be reported prior to year-end, should not affect net income if they will be insured under the existing claims-made insurance policy. However, both the asset (under the insurance claim) and the liability (for the incident) will be reflected on the balance sheet.

If the receivable established for a retroactive environmental insurance provision exceeds the amounts paid for the insurance, the difference is recorded as a deferred gain. Immediate gain recognition and liability derecognition are not appropriate because the liability has not been extinguished (the entity is not entirely relieved of its obligation). Additionally, as discussed above, the liability incurred as a result of a past insurable event and amounts receivable under the insurance contract generally do not meet the criteria for offsetting under FIN 39.

(b) INCOME STATEMENT DISPLAY

Insurance premiums are typically amortized over the policy period on a straight-line basis as a means of matching the cost to the period benefited. In the case of a claims-made policy, however, occurrences in the early part of the year are normally more likely to result in a claim by year-end (and thus be covered by the policy) than occurrences later in the year. Therefore, an accelerated method of amortization may achieve a better matching of costs to the interim period benefited. The method selected should be appropriate in light of the relevant facts and circumstances and consistently applied.

Amounts paid for retroactive insurance should be expensed immediately. If the amounts and timing of the insurance recoveries can be reasonably estimated, any deferred gain should be amortized using the interest method over the estimated period during which the entity expects to recover substantially all amounts due under the terms of the insurance contract. If the amounts and timing of the insurance recoveries cannot be reasonably estimated, then the proportion of actual recoveries to total estimated recoveries should be used to determine the amount of the amortization. Immediate gain recognition is not appropriate because the liability has not been extinguished (the entity is not entirely relieved of its obligation).

(c) DISCLOSURE OF ACCOUNTING PRINCIPLES

APB Opinion 22, "Disclosure of Accounting Policies," provides guidance regarding accounting principles that should be described in the accounting policies note to the financial statements. APB Opinion 22, paragraph 12, states that entities should disclose those accounting principles that "materially affect the determination of financial position or results of operations." In particular, entities should disclose accounting principles and the methods of applying those principles when alternatives exist.

With respect to potential recoveries, financial statements should disclose the means used to determine fair value and whether the asset is measured on a discounted basis. SOP 96-1 encourages but does not require entities to disclose their policies concerning the timing of recognition of recoveries.

(d) DISCLOSURES FOR RIGHTS OF RECOVERY

Entities should ensure that environmental liabilities and associated rights of recovery are properly disclosed in accordance with FAS 5 (see § 19.4(d)(i)) and SOP 94-6, "Disclosure of Certain Significant Risks and Uncertainties" (see § 12.5). Companies also should disclose the amount of recorded recoveries that are being contested and discuss the reasons for concluding that the amounts are probable of recovery.

(e) ADDITIONAL CONSIDERATIONS FOR PUBLIC COMPANIES

The SEC has provided guidance regarding accounting for potential recoveries related to loss contingencies (see § 19.4(e)). The SEC staff has indicated in SAB 92 that, pursuant to FIN 39, environmental liabilities and loss contingencies should not be netted against potential claims for recovery. Each item should instead be presented separately on the balance sheet.

Facts as to whether insurance coverage may be contested, and whether and to what extent potential sources of contribution or indemnification constitute reliable sources of recovery, may be factored into the determination of whether a material future effect is reasonably likely to occur for MD&A disclosure purposes (see § 12.2(c)(iii)). Significant uncertainties may exist regarding both the timing and the ultimate realization of claims made to recover amounts from environmental insurance carriers and other third parties, as evidenced by litigation over insurance policy coverage of environmental liabilities and financial failures in the insurance industry. The issuer's assessment of materiality, therefore, should include consideration of facts such as the periods in which claims for recovery may be realized, the likelihood that the claims may be contested, and the financial condition of third parties from which recovery is expected.

It is important to note that the SEC's netting guidance with respect to materiality for MD&A purposes (see § 12.2(c)(iii)) does not supersede the accounting principle, reflected in SOP 96-1 and SAB 92, that offsetting recoveries from other responsible parties or insurance carriers may not be directly netted out in a registrant's financial statements, or considered in determining whether a contingent liability is material for financial statement reporting purposes.

Section 404 of Sarbanes-Oxley imposes requirements on public companies to design, implement, and periodically assess the operational effectiveness of internal control over financial reporting (see Chapter 8). In addition, section 404 requires the reporting entity's independent financial auditor to examine the entity's internal control over financial reporting and annually attest to its design and operational effectiveness (see Chapter 27).

Internal control over financial reporting of environmental loss contingencies and associated rights of recovery involves a complex formulation of policies, procedures, controls, and communication and information systems. Designing, implementing, monitoring, and auditing the control system can require significant effort and diligence on both an initial and sustained basis. Exhibit 16.1

EXHIBIT 16.1

Process and Control Considerations for Environmental Rights of Recovery

PROCESS AREA	PROCESS AND CONTROL CONSIDERATIONS
Identification	• Identification of potential rights of recovery associated with environmental loss contingencies
Assessment	• Assessment of likelihood of recovery • Application of criteria for rights of setoff
Measurement	• Use of actuaries and other specialists • Classification and measurement of retroactive, prospective, and blended insurance contracts
Reporting	• Amortization of prospective insurance contracts • Accounting for environmental liability transfers using finite risk insurance mechanisms • Disclosures relating to rights of recovery

identifies certain process and control issues with regard to financial reporting of rights of recovery. Internal control considerations for environmental loss contingencies and environmental remediation liabilities are discussed in Chapters 19 and 20.

Notwithstanding an effective internal control system design, the operational effectiveness of the system will largely depend on the performance of employees and contractors in carrying out established policies and procedures. Employee and contractor performance in turn will depend largely on the company's control environment with respect to environmental financial reporting (see § 8.2(a)) and personnel qualifications, training, and incentives (or disincentives).

CHAPTER SEVENTEEN

Emission Credits

17.1 INTRODUCTION

Several governments around the world have developed, or are in the process of developing, schemes to encourage reduced emissions of pollutants, especially greenhouse gases. Many of these regulatory schemes, such as the European Union Emissions Trading Directive, are *cap-and-trade* programs modeled after the pioneering SO_2 (acid rain) program under the U.S. Clean Air Act. In a cap-and-trade model, participants are allocated emission rights (also called *credits* or *allowances*) equal to a cap (i.e., a target level of emissions) and are permitted to trade those credits. If the company is able to reduce its emissions of the pollutant such that it does not need the credit, it can sell the credit to another entity that has a need to emit greater amounts of the pollutant.

Cap-and-trade programs operate over defined (often annual) compliance periods. Credits are allocated (or auctioned) to the participants at the beginning of the compliance period. During the period, participants may buy or sell allowances directly with other participants or through a broker or on an exchange. At the end of a compliance period, the participant must deliver emissions credits equal to its actual emissions. If a participant fails to deliver the required credits, it may be required to pay fines (or receive a smaller financial incentive) and it may receive a smaller allocation of emissions allowances in the future. In some cases, unused (or excess) credits may be carried forward to future compliance periods.

For a compliance period, a participant has three options:

1. It may emit designated pollutants to the level of its allocated credits.
2. It may emit pollutants to a lower level than is represented by the allocated credits and it may sell or bank the excess credits.
3. It may emit pollutants to a higher level than is represented by the allocated credits and either buy additional credits or pay a penalty.

In the extreme, a participant may sell all of its credits at the beginning of the compliance period with the expectation of either buying credits to cover emissions at a later date, or ceasing emissions, or paying regulatory penalties. Typically, brokers and other nonparticipants are also allowed to buy and sell emissions credits, which may increase market liquidity.

Currently, in the United States there is no consensus under GAAP on how entities should account for their participation in emission control schemes that use marketable credits. In 2003, the FASB Emerging Issue Task Force added Issue 03-14, "Participants' Accounting for Emissions Allowances under a "Cap and Trade" Program," to its agenda. The task force's objective was to provide a comprehensive accounting model for participants in cap-and-trade emissions reduction programs—ultimately addressing asset recognition, measurement and impairment, cost allocation, liability recognition, presentation (gross versus net), and disclosures.

In November 2003, the task force dropped the emission credit project from its agenda with no plans for further discussion. The task force cited various reasons for ending the project, including concerns about implications beyond cap-and-trade programs (e.g., the impact on accounting for governmental licenses and permits); concerns about the prospect of an accounting model that might permit immediate recognition of income upon receipt of the emissions credits, with the costs of complying with the related regulations being recognized subsequently as an expense; and perceptions that there was not a sufficient practice issue or diversity in the accounting for emissions trading programs to warrant further effort.

In December 2004, the International Financial Reporting Interpretations Committee (IFRIC), an arm of the International Accounting Standards Board (IASB) based in London, moved forward with issuance of an interpretation explaining how accounting standards should be applied to cap-and-trade schemes. IFRIC 3, "Emission Rights," specifies the accounting for participants in GHG cap-and-trade schemes. Given the absence of a consensus in the United States, the provisions of IFRIC 3 are described in this chapter and compared with alternative accounting approaches under GAAP.

17.2 RECOGNITION

Under GAAP, emission credits meet the definition of *intangible assets* under Statement of Financial Accounting Standards No. 142, "Goodwill and Other Intangible Assets" (FAS 142). Intangible assets include both current and noncurrent assets that lack physical substance. Intangible assets are recognized separately from goodwill if they meet either of the following criteria:

- *Legal/contractual criterion.* Control over the future economic benefits of the asset is obtained through contractual or other legal rights irrespective of whether those rights are transferable or separable from other rights and obligations.

- *Separability criterion.* The asset is capable of being separated or divided and sold, transferred, licensed, rented, or exchanged irrespective of whether the acquirer intends to do so. This criterion is met if the asset can be sold, transferred, licensed, rented, or exchanged along with a related contract, asset, or liability.

Emission credits purchased or obtained from a government under a cap-and-trade program generally satisfy both of these criteria. Hence, a basis exists under GAAP for recognition of emission credits as identifiable intangible assets separate from goodwill.

Although a participant's emission credits constitute an intangible asset, the participant's obligation to deliver credits to cover its actual emissions at the end of the compliance period constitutes a corresponding liability. In the absence of a specific accounting standard for emission credits, the obligation to deliver credits would appear to be most appropriately accounted for as a contingent liability under FAS 5 (see Chapter 19).

IFRIC 3 recognizes emission credits as intangible assets and also requires recognition of a corresponding liability. IFRIC 3 requires participants to initially record the emission credits they purchase or receive from governments as an intangible asset in accordance with International Accounting Standard No. 38, "Intangible Assets" (IAS 38) (comparable to FAS 142). The standard also requires participants, as they generate emissions throughout the compliance period, to recognize a liability for the obligation to deliver credits to cover those emissions in accordance with International Accounting Standard No. 37, "Provisions, Contingent Liabilities and Contingent Assets" (IAS 37) (comparable to FAS 5). The asset and the liability are recognized separately without netting.

17.3 MEASUREMENT

Under both FAS 142 and IFRIC 3, emission credits are initially recognized and measured at fair value. The fair value of an emission credit is the amount at which the credit could be bought (or incurred) or sold (or settled) in a current transaction between willing parties (i.e., other than in a forced or liquidation sale).

Under IFRIC 3, the corresponding liability for the participant's obligation to deliver credits at the conclusion of the compliance period would be measured at the best estimate of the expenditure required to settle the present obligation at the balance sheet date. This will normally be the present market price of the number of credits required to cover emissions made up to the balance sheet date. However, if the participant's best estimate is that some or all of the obligation will be settled by incurring a cash penalty, it would measure that part of its obligation at the cost of the penalty rather than at the market price of the relevant number of credits.

17.4 DISPLAY AND DISCLOSURE

(a) BALANCE SHEET DISPLAY

Under both FAS 142 and IFRIC 3, emission credits are presented on the balance sheet at their assigned fair value. When credits are allocated for less than fair value, IFRIC 3 requires the difference between the amount paid and fair value to be accounted for as a government grant under IAS 20, "Accounting for Government Grants and Disclosure of Government Assistance." The grant is initially recognized as deferred income in the balance sheet and subsequently recognized as income on a systematic basis over the compliance period.

Under FAS 142, an identifiable intangible asset generally is amortized over its expected useful economic life (i.e., the compliance period). By contrast, emission credits are not amortized under IFRIC 3. Instead, a corresponding liability is gradually recognized to offset the asset.

Under IFRIC 3, as actual emissions occur, a contingent liability is recognized for the obligation to deliver credits equal to actual emissions. The liability is settled by delivering credits, incurring a government-imposed penalty, or a combination of both.

Under both FAS 142 and IFRIC 3, emission credits should be evaluated for recoverability, when necessitated by changes in facts and circumstances, in the same manner as set forth in FAS 144 for tangible long-lived assets (see Chapter 23). As an aside, the existence of an emission rights scheme may also cause other assets of the participant to become impaired. For example, the cap-and-trade program may result in the need to reduce hours of operation or throughput at some of the participant's production facilities. This could in turn lead to a reduction of expected cash flows from those assets.

(b) INCOME STATEMENT DISPLAY

Under FAS 142, intangible assets generally are amortized over their expected useful economic lives. The useful life of an emission credit is the compliance period—most often, one year. Emission credits under regulatory schemes with indefinite compliance periods would not be subject to amortization. Amortization expense and impairment losses are presented in the income statement under continuing operations.

Under IFRIC 3, impairment losses are applied to owner's equity rather than the income statement. Accruals for contingent liabilities reflecting the participant's obligation to deliver credits for actual emission are charged to income.

(c) DISCLOSURE OF ACCOUNTING PRINCIPLES

APB Opinion 22, "Disclosure of Accounting Policies," provides guidance regarding accounting principles that should be described in the accounting policies note to the financial statements. APB Opinion 22, paragraph 12, indicates that entities should disclose those accounting principles that "materially affect the determination of financial position or results of operations." In particular, entities should disclose accounting principles and the methods of applying those principles when alternatives exist. With regard to emission credits, entities should disclose the valuation methods used in measuring emission credits and related liabilities.

(d) DISCLOSURES FOR EMISSION CREDITS

For intangible assets, acquired either individually or with a group of assets, paragraph 44 of FAS 142 calls for the following information to be disclosed in the notes to the financial statements in the period of acquisition.

- For intangible assets subject to amortization: the total amount assigned and the amount assigned to any major intangible asset class (e.g., emission credits); the amount of any significant residual value, in total and by major intangible asset class; and the weighted-average amortization period, in total and by major intangible asset class.
- For intangible assets not subject to amortization, the total amount assigned and the amount assigned to any major intangible asset class.

Paragraph 45 of FAS 142 states that the following information should be disclosed in the financial statements or the notes to the financial statements for each period for which a statement of financial position is presented:

- For intangible assets subject to amortization: the gross carrying amount and accumulated amortization, in total and by major intangible asset class; the aggregate amortization expense for the period; and the estimated aggregate amortization expense for each of the five succeeding fiscal years.
- For intangible assets not subject to amortization, the total carrying amount and the carrying amount for each major intangible asset class.

Paragraph 46 of FAS 142 states that for each impairment loss recognized related to an intangible asset, the following information should be disclosed in the notes to the financial statements that include the period in which the impairment loss is recognized:

- A description of the impaired intangible asset and the facts and circumstances leading to the impairment.
- The amount of the impairment loss and the method for determining fair value.
- The caption in the income statement or the statement of activities in which the impairment loss is aggregated.
- If applicable, the segment in which the impaired intangible asset is reported under Statement of Financial Accounting Standards No. 131, "Disclosures about Segments of Enterprise and Related Information."

(e) ADDITIONAL CONSIDERATIONS FOR PUBLIC COMPANIES

Section 404 of Sarbanes-Oxley imposes requirements on public companies to design, implement, and periodically assess the operational effectiveness of internal control over financial reporting (see Chapter 8). In addition, section 404 requires the reporting entity's independent financial auditor to examine the entity's internal control over financial reporting and annually attest to its design and operational effectiveness (see Chapter 27).

Emission credits and corresponding liabilities under the EU Emission Trading Directive have been shown to represent a material element of some companies' financial statements. If a cap-and-trade program is established in the United States to address greenhouse gases and global warming, internal control over financial reporting of emission credits will become an increasingly important consideration. Exhibit 17.1 identifies certain process and control issues with regard to financial reporting of emission credits.

EXHIBIT 17.1

Process and Control Considerations for Emission Credits

PROCESS AREA	PROCESS AND CONTROL CONSIDERATIONS
Identification	• Identification of contractual or other legal rights to emit pollutants that offer future economic benefits • Identification and tracking of actual emissions subject to cap-and-trade programs • Identification of conditions and events triggering the need for an impairment test
Assessment	• Assessment of whether the asset is capable of being separated or divided and sold, transferred, licensed, rented, or exchanged • Evaluation of the company's strategy for settling obligations at the end of the compliance period under a cap-and-trade system
Measurement	• Determination of fair value • Estimation of contingent liabilities to deliver credits for actual emissions
Reporting	• Analysis of compliance periods and useful life • Disclosures relating to intangible assets

CHAPTER EIGHTEEN

Environmental Liabilities

18.1 INTRODUCTION

FASB Statement of Financial Accounting Concepts No. 6, "Elements of Financial Statements" (SFAC 6), defines *liabilities* as probable future sacrifices of economic benefits arising from present obligations of a particular entity to transfer assets or provide services to other entities in the future as a result of past transactions or events.

As used in this definition, *probable* has its usual general meaning, rather than a specific accounting or technical meaning such as that in FAS 5 (see § 19.2(a)(iii)), and refers to that which can reasonably be expected or believed on the basis of available evidence or logic but is neither certain nor proved. Its inclusion in the definition is intended to acknowledge that business and other economic activities occur in an environment characterized by uncertainty in which few outcomes are certain.

The term *obligations* is used with its usual general meaning to refer to duties imposed legally or socially; to that which one is bound to do by contract, promise, moral responsibility, and so on. It includes equitable and constructive obligations as well as legal obligations. *Legal obligations* are obligations that a party is required to settle as a result of an existing or enacted law, statute, ordinance, or written or oral contract, or by legal construction of a contract under the doctrine of promissory estoppel.

Most liabilities are obligations of only one entity. Some liabilities, however, are shared. For example, two or more entities may be *jointly and severally* liable for environmental cleanup costs and environmental damages under CERCLA (see § 3.2(a)). In contrast to CERCLA liability, liabilities that bind two or more entities are often ranked rather than shared. For example, the current property owner and a guarantor may both be obligated for environmental cleanup costs, but they do not have the same obligation. The guarantor must pay only if the property owner fails to pay; thus, the guarantor has a contingent or secondary obligation.

The definition of *liabilities* for purposes of GAAP is not a legal definition and does not necessarily comport with legal definitions of the term or related terms (e.g., *debt* and *liability on a claim*), which have diverse meanings depending on the context or the branch of law involved. This point is illustrated by judicial decisions in bankruptcy proceedings, which often involve determinations and valuation of the debtor's legal obligations (see § 2.2(b)(v)).

Environmental liabilities are obligations relating to future environmental costs that meet the criteria for recognition as a liability. Environmental liabilities can arise from legal or equitable obligations associated with environmental transactions, conditions, or events. Environmental liabilities may be recognized in connection with environmental loss contingencies (Chapter 19), environmental remediation liabilities (Chapter 20), environmental guarantees (Chapter 21), and asset retirement obligations (Chapter 22).

Environmental liabilities generally represent estimated future obligations for cleanup costs (environmental remediation liabilities) and/or environmental damages (environmental loss contingencies). The underlying cause of an environmental remediation liability is the past or present ownership or operation of a contaminated site, or the contribution or transportation of waste to a site, at which investigation or corrective action must take place. The underlying cause of an environmental loss contingency is the past or present release of hazardous substances or other pollutants in the workplace or to the external environment, resulting in injury to human health, private property, publicly owned natural resources, or economic activity. Such liabilities may or may not involve environmental remediation.

Environmental liabilities frequently are imposed on entities by government agencies or private parties enforcing rights established under environmental laws, or are accepted by the entity to avoid government enforcement or other legal action. Environmental legal obligations often arise under CERCLA or related state Superfund laws for cleanup costs associated with historical pollution conditions. Other environmental liabilities are imposed on entities by courts (e.g., "toxic tort" claims for bodily injury caused by exposure to hazardous materials), or are accepted by the entity to avoid enforcement by the courts. Environmental liabilities may also result from agreements between entities.

Legal obligations arising under environmental laws may include, for example:

- Superfund liability for cleanup of nonowned disposed sites (see § 3.2(a)).
- Obligations for corrective action, site restoration, postclosure care, and monitoring under the remediation provisions in RCRA (see § 3.2(b)).
- Obligations to compensate the United States for damage to natural resources (see § 3.2(a)(viii)).
- Obligations to report and respond to sudden and accidental releases of hazardous substances (see § 3.2(a)(ix)).
- Monetary awards or settlements for environmental damages for bodily injury or property damages under tort laws (see § 3.4).

Environmental liabilities may also arise under contractual agreements between two or more business entities. Environmental guarantees are commonly used in connection with real estate and business transfers as a means to contractually allocate the risk associated with uncertain future environmental costs. Such agreements can give rise to liabilities for the obligation to stand ready to perform, as well as a contingent obligation to transfer resources in the future (see Chapter 21).

18.2 RECOGNITION

(a) CHARACTERISTICS OF A LIABILITY

As set forth in paragraph 36 of SFAC 6, a liability has three essential characteristics:

1. It embodies a present duty or responsibility to one or more other entities that entails settlement by probable future transfer or use of assets at a specified or determinable date, on occurrence of a specified event, or on demand.
2. The duty or responsibility obligates a particular entity, leaving it little or no discretion to avoid the future sacrifice.
3. The transaction or other event obligating the entity has already happened.

Although liabilities generally share other characteristics, the absence of such characteristics is not sufficient to preclude an item from qualifying as a liability. For example, most liabilities require the obligated entity to pay cash to one or more identified other entities and are legally enforceable. Those features, however, are not essential characteristics of liabilities.

- Environmental liabilities may not require an entity to pay cash but to convey other assets, provide services (e.g., environmental remediation), provide access to a contaminated area, provide the use of assets, or stand ready to do any or all of these.
- The identity of the recipient need not be known to the obligated entity before the time of settlement (e.g., an environmental liability may exist before an injured party asserts a claim against a party responsible for pollution conditions).
- Existence of a legally enforceable claim is not a prerequisite for an obligation to qualify as a liability if for other reasons the entity has the duty or responsibility to pay cash, to transfer other assets, or to provide services to another entity (e.g., an enterprise may have an established policy to clean up environmental contamination in foreign countries to U.S. standards even if such standards are more stringent than legally required).

Once incurred by an entity, a liability remains a liability until it is satisfied (settled) in another transaction or other event or circumstance affecting the entity. Most liabilities are settled by cash payments. Others are settled by transferring assets or providing services to other entities. Liabilities are also sometimes settled by forgiveness, compromise, incurrence of another liability, or changed circumstances.

(b) CONDITIONAL LEGAL OBLIGATIONS

That pollution conditions can give rise to legal obligations under environmental laws is unquestionable. However, the matter of when such obligations accrue is often less certain. In some cases, the legal obligation is absolute and unconditional. In other cases, the obligation is conditional on the future occurrence of events or circumstances that will obligate the entity to pay cash, transfer other assets, or provide services to other entities to settle the obligation. When obligations are conditional on future events, such future events may be either outside the entity's control (e.g., assertion of a legal claim against the entity for environmental damages) or within the entity's control (e.g., the decision to demolish a building containing asbestos).

Environmental guarantees (Chapter 21) illustrate the difference between conditional and unconditional legal obligations. Environmental guarantees involve two distinct obligations. The first is the obligation to stand ready to perform over the term of the guarantee in case the specified triggering events or conditions occur. This obligation comes into existence upon execution of the guarantee. The obligation to stand ready is unconditional in that it does not depend upon the occurrence of future events or conditions. The second obligation is the obligation to make payments in the event the specified triggering events or conditions occur. This obligation is contingent upon the occurrence of specified future events or conditions.

Obligations giving rise to environmental liabilities are typically conditional on the future occurrence of events or circumstances that will require the entity to pay cash, transfer other assets, or provide services to other entities to settle the obligation. The underlying cause of liabilities arising under environmental laws (i.e., the transactions, conditions, or events that result in legal remedies) are often specified or inherent in the nature of the particular statute or regulation. For example, administrative fines and penalties may be incurred for failure to install and maintain required pollution control technology; restoring the land after strip-mining a mineral deposit is a consequence of removing the ground cover or overburden and ore; cleanup obligations result from the past or present ownership or operation of a site, or the contribution or transportation of waste to a site, at which investigation or corrective action must take place.

SFAC 6 provides that, for obligations imposed under statutes and regulations, as for obligations resulting from contractual agreements in connection with exchange transactions, no liability is incurred under GAAP until the occurrence of an event or circumstance that *obligates* an entity to pay cash, transfer other assets, or provide services to other entities in the future. This raises an important question: What is the event or circumstance that creates the obligation? For example:

- Is the obligating event the release of hazardous substances to the environment, the initiation of government action to compel investigation and cleanup of the resulting contamination, or the determination of a court that the costs of such investigation and cleanup are properly attributable to the entity that was the subject of the government action?

- Is the obligating event the purchase of a building containing asbestos that must be abated prior to demolition of the building, or the decision to demolish the building?

Identification of the obligating event for purposes of determining whether a liability exists is addressed in the following sections.

(i) CONDITIONS WITHIN THE ENTITY'S CONTROL

SFAC 6 states that an entity is not obligated to sacrifice assets in the future if it can avoid the future sacrifice at its discretion without significant penalty. For example, an entity might have a policy of returning contaminated property to prerelease background conditions, but might freely elect instead to clean up a particular property to risk-based levels under applicable environmental laws at considerably lower cost. An entity also may have the ability to defer indefinitely settlement of environmental cleanup obligations associated with company-owned properties. The ability to defer settlement of such obligations, however, does not necessarily allow the entity to avoid the future sacrifice of assets, nor does it relieve the entity of the obligation.

The ability to *defer* the future sacrifice of assets to settle an obligation is not the same as the ability to *avoid* the future sacrifice entirely. It is generally not within the entity's discretion to avoid obligations imposed under environmental laws, even though it may be within the entity's discretion to defer the future sacrifice of assets or to choose the manner in which the obligation will be settled (e.g., supplemental environmental projects). FASB has carefully considered the question of when an entity can avoid a future sacrifice associated with legal obligations in the context of asset retirement obligations. Paragraph B11 of FIN 47, "Accounting for Conditional Asset Retirement Obligations," states that the ability to indefinitely *defer* settlement of a legal obligation associated with the future retirement of an asset or the ability to sell the asset does not provide the entity discretion to *avoid* the future sacrifice, nor does it relieve the entity of the obligation.

FASB's analysis of conditional legal obligations in the context of asset retirement obligations is supported by an analysis of the possible alternatives for environmentally impaired assets. Consider, for example, a building containing regulated asbestos-containing material (RACM). Environmental laws require that RACM be properly maintained during the life of the building and completely removed before the building is demolished (see § 3.3(d)). Economically, the owner of a building containing RACM has only five options available:

1. Sell the asset subject to the obligation to remove and dispose of the RACM (in which case the owner must accept a lower price from a buyer in return for the buyer's assumption of the obligation).
2. Sell the building at a higher price, but promise to reimburse the buyer for the costs to remove and dispose of the RACM.

3. Remove and dispose of the RACM before sale of the building.
4. Maintain the building until the end of its useful life and then remove and dispose of the RACM.
5. Abandon the building with the RACM in place, thereby sacrificing the residual value of the land and the building while incurring a perpetual obligation to pay taxes, insurance, maintenance, and security on a nonproductive asset.

In each case, the existence of the environmental legal obligation directly affects the owner's exit strategy for the building. Under scenarios 1 through 4, only the timing and amount of the liability are in question. Under scenario 5, though it is conceivable that the owner of the building can indefinitely defer abatement of the RACM through active maintenance and other techniques, such as encapsulation, events outside the control of the owner (e.g., fires, boiler explosions, water damage, natural disaster, etc.) could require that RACM be removed from the building at any time.

The foregoing economic analysis can be applied to obligations to investigate and clean up historical pollution conditions affecting soil and groundwater on company-owned properties (or properties operated under a capital lease). The analysis does not apply equally to pollution conditions affecting properties that the entity does not own (e.g., leased properties, formerly owned properties, nonowned disposal sites, nonowned natural resources, and migration of contamination from company-owned sites onto adjacent properties). It also does not apply to environmental conditions causing injury to humans. In such cases, future events or circumstances that will create an obligation for the entity to pay cash, transfer other assets, or provide services to other entities are outside the entity's control and may or may not occur.

When environmental legal obligations are conditional on future events or circumstances that are largely or entirely within the entity's control, the obligating event is the entity's determination to settle the obligation, unless the entity cannot avoid the future sacrifice without significant penalty. When environmental legal obligations attach directly to company-owned assets, it is rarely the case, if ever, that the entity can permanently avoid settling the obligation without penalty. Consequently, in such cases, the obligating event generally is either the acquisition of an asset subject to existing obligations; the transactions, conditions, or events specified or inherent in the nature of the environmental law involved; or the enactment of an environmental law with retroactive effect (as was the case with CERCLA) (see § 3.2(a)(i)(B)).

(ii) CONDITIONS OUTSIDE THE ENTITY'S CONTROL

In situations in which the obligation for the entity to pay cash, transfer other assets, or provide services to other entities is conditional on future events or circumstances outside the entity's control, there will be a degree of uncertainty as to whether such events or circumstances will occur. For example, government environmental protection agencies may or may not initiate legal action against an entity for violation of environmental laws. Similarly, persons suffering bodily injury or property damages caused by environmental contamination may or may not file a lawsuit to recover environmental damages. Furthermore, even if legal action is brought against the entity to enforce an alleged legal obligation, the outcome may be highly uncertain.

When environmental legal obligations are conditional on future events or circumstances that are outside the entity's control, the obligating event is the event or circumstance that obligates the entity to settle the obligation by paying cash, transferring other assets, or providing services to one or more other entities. In most such cases, the obligating event is the final resolution of formal legal proceedings to enforce the obligation or the contractual agreement by the entity to settle an alleged obligation in order to avoid enforcement by government agencies or the courts. As discussed in Chapter 19, however, for purposes of financial reporting, GAAP requires recognition of a liability prior to final resolution of a conditional legal obligation when it is sufficiently likely that the entity will not be able to avoid the future sacrifice of assets to settle the obligation.

(iii) ENVIRONMENTAL LIABILITY MATRIX

As illustrated by the discussion of conditional legal obligations in the foregoing sections, the determination of when an environmental obligation satisfies the three essential characteristics of a liability set forth in SFAC 6 depends on three key variables. These variables are: (1) the nature of the future environmental costs represented by the obligation (i.e., cleanup costs or environmental damages); (2) the relationship, if any, of the underlying pollution condition giving rise to the obligation to a tangible long-lived asset (e.g., property, plant, and equipment); and (3) the entity's ownership (or nonownership) of that asset. As depicted in Exhibit 18.1, these three variables determine the classification of liabilities associated with environmental obligations as either:

1. Environmental loss contingencies (Chapter 19);
2. Environmental remediation liabilities (Chapter 20); or
3. Environmental asset retirement obligations (Chapter 22).

Liabilities under environmental guarantees or indemnities may be incurred under any of the four scenarios shown in Exhibit 18.1.

18.3 MEASUREMENT

Measurement of environmental liabilities is discussed in subsequent chapters in the context of environmental loss contingencies (Chapter 19), environmental remediation liabilities (Chapter 20), environmental guarantees (Chapter 21), and asset retirement obligations (Chapter 22).

EXHIBIT 18.1

Environmental Liability Matrix

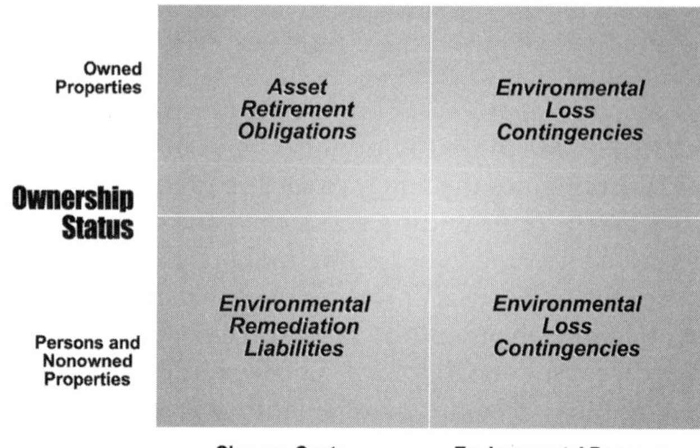

18.4 DISPLAY AND DISCLOSURE

Display and disclosure issues for environmental liabilities are discussed in subsequent chapters in the context of environmental loss contingencies (Chapter 19), environmental remediation liabilities (Chapter 20), environmental guarantees (Chapter 21), and asset retirement obligations (Chapter 22).

CHAPTER NINETEEN

Environmental Loss Contingencies

19.1 INTRODUCTION

An *environmental loss contingency* is an existing condition, situation, or set of circumstances involving uncertainty as to possible environmental loss to an enterprise that will ultimately be resolved when one or more future events occur or fail to occur. Resolution of the uncertainty may confirm the loss or impairment of an asset (an *environmental asset impairment*) or the incurrence of a liability (an *environmental liability*). Environmental loss contingencies include environmental remediation liabilities, which are the subject of specific guidance under SOP 96-1 and are covered in Chapter 20. Environmental remediation liabilities pertain solely to contingent liabilities for cleanup costs associated with historical pollution conditions, generally involving Superfund liability at nonowned waste disposal sites. This chapter discusses environmental loss contingencies other than environmental remediation liabilities, which include contingent liabilities for environmental damages (e.g., liability for bodily injury, property damage, and natural resource damage), and cleanup costs associated with sudden and accidental pollution conditions.

19.2 RECOGNITION

FAS 5 defines a *contingency* as an existing condition, situation, or set of circumstances involving uncertainty as to possible gain (*gain contingency*) or loss (*loss contingency*) to an enterprise that will ultimately be resolved when one or more future events occur or fail to occur. In the case of a gain contingency, resolution of the uncertainty may confirm the acquisition of an asset or the reduction of a liability. In the case of a loss contingency, resolution of the uncertainty may confirm the loss or impairment of an asset or the incurrence of a liability.

Paragraph 8 of FAS 5 requires accrual of a liability for the estimated loss from a loss contingency if both of the following conditions are met: (1) information available prior to issuance of the financial statements indicates that it is probable that an asset had been impaired or a liability had been incurred at the date of the financial statements; and (2) the amount of loss can be reasonably estimated.

Although FAS 5 encompasses asset impairments arising from loss contingencies, FAS 5 rarely will be applicable to environmental-related impairments, which typically affect tangible long-lived assets. Environmental-related impairments of tangible long-lived assets (e.g., property, plant, and equipment) are covered under FAS 144 (Chapter 23). For reasons discussed below, however, clear evidence of an environmental impairment may in some circumstances provide a reasonable basis for recognition of a contingent environmental liability under FAS 5.

(a) PROBABILITY TEST

A loss contingency has two primary elements. The first element is an existing condition, situation, or set of circumstances involving uncertainty as to a possible loss. The second element is a future event or nonevent that will ultimately resolve the uncertainty.

(i) EXISTING CONDITIONS GIVING RISE TO UNCERTAINTY

The first element of a loss contingency is an existing condition, situation, or set of circumstances involving uncertainty as to a possible loss. For purposes of FAS 5, the uncertainty in question is whether a loss will ultimately be incurred at all, rather than uncertainty as to the amount of the loss. The fact that an estimate is involved does not of itself constitute the type of uncertainty required for a loss contingency to exist.

Uncertainty as to a possible environmental loss may arise from an existing condition, situation, or set of circumstances that either presents a risk of loss to the entity that may arise solely as a result of future events (e.g., a possible future industrial accident); or presents a risk of loss to the entity that may arise as a result of events that have already taken place.

A risk of loss arising solely as a result of future events does not satisfy the condition for accrual of a liability. Exposure to environmental risks from future events does not indicate that a liability *has been* incurred. FAS 5 requires accrual of a liability only when events giving rise to a possible loss have taken place prior to the date of the financial statements.

For example, an enterprise may choose not to purchase environmental insurance against risk of loss for cleanup costs, property damage, and bodily injury resulting from future releases of pollutants to the environment. Exposure to environmental risks associated with the entity's operations constitutes an existing condition involving uncertainty about the amount and timing of any losses that may occur as a result of future events, such as an industrial accident. Thus, a loss contingency exists.

Mere exposure to environmental risks, however, does not mean that a liability has been incurred. The condition for accrual is not met with respect to environmental losses arising from an industrial accident that may occur after the date of an enterprise's financial statements. Such losses do not relate to the current or a prior period but rather to the future period in which they might occur. Thus, the enterprise should not recognize a liability for environmental losses that may be caused by future pollution conditions even if the amount of those losses may be reasonably estimable.

However, the conditions for accrual would be met with respect to an uninsured environmental loss resulting from an industrial accident that took place prior to the date of the financial statements. This is so even though the company may not become aware of the loss until after that date, if, prior to the date of its financial statements, the experience of the company or other information enables it to make a reasonable estimate of the loss.

Examples of underlying conditions and events giving rise to uncertainty as to a possible environmental loss include:

- Historical pollution conditions resulting from the entity's operations.
- Past or present exposures of employees to hazardous substances in the workplace.
- Past or present exposures of humans to hazardous materials in contaminated environmental media (e.g., soil, groundwater, surface water).
- Sale and distribution of products containing hazardous substances.
- The past or present ownership or operation of a contaminated site.
- The contribution or transportation of waste to a site at which investigation or corrective action must take place.

(ii) FUTURE EVENTS WILL RESOLVE UNCERTAINTY AS TO WHETHER A LOSS HAS BEEN INCURRED

The second element of a loss contingency is a future event (or nonevent) that will ultimately resolve the uncertainty as to whether a loss has been incurred. As discussed in § 18.2(b), many environmental obligations arise from transactions or events that are specified or inherent in the nature of the environmental law involved (e.g., fines and penalties incurred for failure to comply with provisions of laws or regulations). For obligations imposed under environmental laws, governmental or private-party efforts to enforce available remedies under such laws (or the absence of any such efforts within applicable limitations periods) generally will resolve the uncertainty as to whether a loss has been incurred (see § 18.2(b)).

(iii) DEGREES OF UNCERTAINTY

When a loss contingency exists, the probability that the future event or events will confirm the impairment of an asset or the incurrence of a liability can range from zero to 100 percent. FAS 5 uses the terms *probable*, *reasonably possible*, and *remote* to identify three points within that range. These terms are defined in paragraph 3 of FAS 5 as follows:

- *Probable.* The future event or events are likely to occur.
- *Reasonably possible.* The chance of the future event or events occurring is more than remote but less than likely.
- *Remote.* The chance of the future event or events occurring is slight.

Entities and their accountants and legal counsel must analyze all relevant and available information concerning the uncertain set of circumstances to determine the probability of the future event (or nonevent).

(b) REASONABLY ESTIMABLE TEST

The two conditions for accrual of an estimated loss from a loss contingency are that: (1) information available prior to issuance of the financial statements indicates that it is probable that a liability had been incurred at the date of the financial statements, and (2) the amount of loss can be reasonably estimated. In some situations in which condition 1 is met, a range of loss can be reasonably estimated but no single amount within the range appears at the time to be a better estimate than any other amount within the range. According to FIN 14, "Reasonable Estimation of the Amount of a Loss," accrual of a contingent liability should not be delayed until only a single amount can be reasonably estimated. Rather, condition 2 is met when a range of loss can be reasonably estimated. This approach was developed to address measurement of losses in situations in which a single *best estimate* is not available.

(c) ENVIRONMENTAL CLAIMS AND LOSSES

Examples of transactions, conditions, and events giving rise to environmental loss contingencies include:

- Potential claims for cleanup costs for historical pollution conditions under federal or state Superfund laws.
- Sudden and accidental pollution conditions resulting from casualty losses (e.g., fire, wind, or flood), transportation and industrial accidents, or other hazards.

- Pending or threatened enforcement or litigation.
- Actual or probable claims and assessments by environmental regulatory agencies.
- Environmental guarantees given in connection with the sale of assets.
- Risk of loss from asbestos and environmental claims assumed by property and casualty insurance companies, including reinsurance companies.

For accounting purposes, there are two major categories of environmental loss contingencies:

1. *Asserted claims* (claims that have been filed with or against the entity).
2. *Unasserted claims* (incidents that have not yet resulted in a claim but may lead to a claim in the future).

(i) ASSERTED CLAIMS

Asserted environmental claims create uncertainty as to a possible loss. In determining whether accrual and/or disclosure are required with respect to asserted claims, paragraph 33 of FAS 5 states that the following factors, among others, must be considered:

- The period in which the underlying events giving rise to the claim occurred.
- The degree of probability of an unfavorable outcome.
- The ability to make a reasonable estimate of the amount of loss.

As a condition for accrual of an environmental loss contingency, information must be available prior to the issuance of the financial statements indicating that it is probable that a liability had been incurred as of the date of the financial statements. Accrual would clearly be inappropriate for cases in which the claim accrued after the date of the financial statements but before the financial statements are issued. Disclosure, however, may be required in such cases (see § 19.4(d)(iv)).

Accrual may be required for claims whose underlying cause is an environmental transaction, condition, or event occurring on or before the date of the financial statements. In such cases, the probability of an outcome unfavorable to the enterprise must be assessed to determine whether it is probable that a liability had been incurred as of the date of the financial statements. According to paragraph 36 of FAS 5, factors that should be considered in this analysis include:

- Nature of the litigation, claim, or assessment.
- Progress of the case (including progress after the date of the financial statements but before those statements are issued).
- Opinions or views of legal counsel and other advisers.
- Experience of the company in similar cases.

- Experience of other entities.
- Any decision of the entity's management as to how the entity intends to respond (e.g., a decision to contest the case vigorously or a decision to seek an out-of-court settlement).

The fact that legal counsel is unable to express an opinion that the outcome will be favorable to the enterprise does not necessarily mean that the condition for accrual of a loss is met. Similarly, the mere filing of a suit or formal assertion of a claim or assessment does not automatically require accrual of a loss. Rather, the probability of an unfavorable outcome must be assessed. If legal counsel determines that an unfavorable outcome is probable, then it is probable that an asset has been impaired or a liability has been incurred. If legal counsel determines that an unfavorable outcome is reasonably possible but not probable, or if the amount of loss cannot be reasonably estimated, accrual would be inappropriate, but disclosure would be required (see § 19.4(d)).

(ii) *UNASSERTED CLAIMS AND ASSESSMENTS*

Legal claims arising from environmental transactions, conditions, or events may not be brought until years after the underlying cause of the obligation, if at all. Long delays may be due to several factors, including:

- Historical pollution conditions often go undiscovered for long periods.
- The cause or source of historical pollution conditions may be difficult to determine.
- Physical manifestations of bodily injury caused by exposure to toxic substances may take long periods to develop.
- Persons harmed by pollution conditions may have incentives to delay legal action. For example, workers exposed to hazardous substances in the workplace may wish to retire before filing suit to avoid limitations imposed under workers' compensation laws.

With respect to unasserted environmental claims, the entity must determine the likelihood that a claim will be asserted, and the likelihood of an unfavorable outcome. If the entity determines that assertion of a claim is not probable, no accrual or disclosure is required. If the entity determines that assertion is probable, then a second judgment must be made as to the likelihood of an unfavorable outcome. If an unfavorable outcome is probable and the amount of loss can be reasonably estimated, accrual of a loss is required. If an unfavorable outcome is reasonably possible but not probable, disclosure, but not accrual, is required (see § 19.4(d)(i)).

Unasserted environmental claims can be subdivided into two categories: (1) reported incidents (incidents that the entity has determined—usually under a risk-management reporting system of some kind—are events that might result in a claim); and (2) unreported incidents (incidents that occurred before the reporting period ended but that have yet to be specifically identified by the entity).

(A) Reported Incidents

A catastrophe, accident, or other similar physical occurrence predictably engenders claims for redress, and in such circumstances their assertion may be probable. Similarly, an investigation of an enterprise by a governmental agency, if enforcement proceedings have been or are likely to be instituted, is sometimes followed by private claims for redress; the probability of their assertion and the possibility of loss should be considered in each case.

(B) Unreported Incidents

The consensus reached in FASB Emerging Issues Task Force 03-8, "Accounting for Claims-Made Insurance and Retroactive Insurance Contracts by the Insured Entity" (EITF 03-8) is that entities must recognize a liability for the probable losses from incurred but not reported (IBNR) claims and incidents if both of the recognition criteria of FAS 5 are met (i.e., if the loss is both probable and reasonably estimable). Losses arising from IBNR claims are sometimes both probable and reasonably estimable. For example, with regard to loss exposures in a large population (e.g., asbestos personal injury claims), it is often possible, based on historical company and industry experience, to determine a reasonable estimate of the amount of the losses associated with claims and incidents that have occurred but that have not yet been reported. When the probable losses from IBNR claims and incidents cannot be reasonably estimated, no liability should be accrued, regardless of whether such losses may be insured.

Unasserted environmental claims also can be subclassified as: unasserted claims for cleanup costs and environmental damages related to an entity's tangible long-lived assets (i.e., environmental impairments of property, plant, and equipment); and unasserted claims for cleanup costs and environmental damages unrelated to an entity's tangible long-lived assets (e.g., toxic tort and property damage claims). Special issues associated with each category of unasserted claims are discussed below.

(C) Asset-Related Claims

Uncertainties associated with unasserted environmental claims can result in the current diminution in value of long-lived assets (i.e., buildings and real estate). Environmental impairments of this sort can arise when potential environmental liabilities are directly associated with the asset. Current owners and operators of contaminated properties and facilities face potential strict liability for cleanup costs under state and federal Superfund laws, even though they did not cause or contribute to the pollution conditions (see § 3.2(a)(i)(A)). Prospective purchasers, tenants, and lenders may be concerned that they too will be exposed to such liability if they buy, lease, or lend against the property.

Concern over environmental liability continues to have a significant impact on the commercial real estate market. Environmental liability concerns, for example, continue to discourage the redevelopment of brownfields. *Brownfields* are abandoned, idled, or underused industrial and commercial sites where expansion or redevelopment is complicated by real or perceived historical pollution conditions that can add cost, time, or uncertainty to a redevelopment project. The EPA estimates that there are more than 400,000 brownfields in the United States.

Real or perceived pollution conditions negatively affect the marketability and value of land and buildings. In some cases, the value of contaminated real estate can be significantly less than zero. The loss in marketability and value derives from several factors, including estimated cleanup costs, potential cleanup cost overruns, and uncertainty regarding potential future liability for property damage and bodily injury claims. Loss in value may persist even after sites have been cleaned up. For example, some courts have held that remediated sites continue to bear *stigma damages* even after they have been cleaned up to government-approved standards.

Enforceable, though unasserted, obligations for environmental cleanup costs, as well as contingent liability for potential property damage and bodily injury claims, are routinely factored into real estate and business transactions. Frequently, such matters kill the deal. More often, the parties allocate environmental loss contingencies through a combination of price reductions, property carve-outs, affirmative covenants, indemnifications, escrows, and insurance.

In such situations, there is uncertainty as to whether existing environmental conditions will give rise to the assertion of future environmental claims, but there is no uncertainty as to whether the economic value of the affected property has been impaired (see § 18.2(b)(i)). Accordingly, there are no future events that will resolve uncertainty as to whether a loss has been incurred. A loss *has* been incurred. The only uncertainty is the amount of the loss (i.e., the price that marketplace participants would demand for bearing the inherent uncertainty regarding potential future expenditures to settle environmental claims).

Environmental impairments often consist of three components: (1) the estimated cleanup costs needed to meet applicable standards under environmental laws; (2) a risk premium to account for possible cleanup cost overruns; and (3) a risk premium to account for unasserted claims for environmental damages. The determination of the risk premium is independent of the FAS 5 probability criterion, in that market participants may demand a risk premium for unasserted claims that are not probable of assertion. Depending on the circumstances, the risk premium related to environmental damages can be significant, potentially far exceeding the estimate of cleanup costs (e.g., when an existing source of contamination on the entity's property has contaminated a public drinking water supply).

The fair values of these impairment elements are routinely measured in the context of real estate transactions involving contaminated properties. Valuation of these impairments elements is also a central issue in determining property damages in environmental litigation, in the underwriting of environmental insurance and adjustment of environmental insurance claims, and in the valuation of environmental guarantees (Chapter 21).

When environmental loss contingencies are directly associated with, and directly affect the value of, an entity's tangible long-lived assets, as is the case with contaminated real estate, such contingencies may satisfy the conditions for accrual under FAS 5: information available prior to issuance of the financial statements indicates that it is probable that an asset had been impaired or a lia-

EXHIBIT 19.1

Accounting for Environmental Impairments

STANDARD	ISSUES AND UNCERTAINTIES
FAS 5	• FAS 5 does not apply to impairments of tangible long-lived assets • FAS 5 generally does not apply to environmental liabilities associated with unasserted claims that are not probable of assertion
FAS 143	• FAS 143 applies to unasserted claims for cleanup costs and other environmental exit costs associated with tangible long-lived assets • FAS 143 does not encompass contingent liabilities for environmental damages (e.g., bodily injury, property damage, and natural resource damage claims)
FAS 144	• The criteria for recognition of an impairment under FAS 144 are dissimilar from the criteria in FAS 5 • FAS 144 does not contemplate reductions in the carrying value of impaired assets below zero

bility had been incurred at the date of the financial statements; and the amount of loss can be reasonably estimated.

As shown in Exhibit 19.1, there are various issues and uncertainties regarding accounting principles applicable to environmental impairments. In most cases, the estimated cleanup costs needed to meet applicable standards under environmental laws and a risk premium to account for possible cleanup cost overruns will be recorded as an asset retirement obligation (ARO) under FAS 143 (Chapter 22). However, FAS 143 does not contemplate obligations for environmental damages. Accordingly, it may be appropriate in some situations to record an ARO for cleanup costs, and either record a separate contingent liability relating to unasserted claims for environmental damages, or test the asset for recoverability under FAS 144 (Chapter 23).

(D) Nonasset-Related Claims

Unasserted claims for environmental damages unrelated to the entity's tangible long-lived assets may exist under a variety of circumstances:

- Unasserted personal injury claims for asbestos exposure.
- Unasserted toxic tort claims relating to the entity's operations at a leased or formerly owned site.
- Unasserted claims for bodily injury and property damages relating to a release of toxic substances in a transportation accident.
- Unasserted claims for noncompliance with environmental laws.
- Unasserted claims associated with environmental indemnity agreements provided by the entity in connection with prior asset divestitures.

Because these claims are not associated with the entity's tangible long-lived assets, it is unlikely that the entity will incur a loss (e.g., pay cash, transfer other assets, or provide services to other entities in settlement of the obligation) unless the government or an injured party initiates formal legal action to enforce the claim. Here, the two-prong test in FAS 5 closely approximates the economic reality of the situation. The likelihood that the entity will incur a loss is unlikely, unless it is probable (1) that such unasserted claims will be asserted in the future, and (2) an unfavorable outcome is probable.

Because these criteria are so subjective, reporting entities and their legal counsel must carefully evaluate each situation on an individual basis to determine whether accrual and/or disclosure of unasserted claims is appropriate or necessary. In making this assessment, the findings and conclusions of a 2002 federal bankruptcy court case (covered in § 2.2(b)(v)) are instructive. That case, *Official Committee of Asbestos Personal Injury Claimants v. Sealed Air Corp.*,[1] illustrates the point that unasserted environmental claims can meet the two-prong test for liability recognition under FAS 5.

19.3 MEASUREMENT

Once an entity has determined that it is probable that an environmental liability has been incurred and the loss can be reasonably estimated, the entity should estimate the liability based on available information. According to FIN 14, when some amount within a range of possible outcomes appears at the time to be a better estimate than any other amount within the range (*most likely value*), that best estimate amount should be accrued. When no amount within the range is a better estimate than any other amount, however, the minimum amount in the range (*known minimum*) should be accrued.

In some cases, the range of possible loss may be wide. For example, an enterprise may be litigating an environmental toxic tort matter. In preparation for the trial, the entity may determine that, based on recent decisions involving one aspect of the litigation, it is probable that it will have to pay damages of $20 million to the plaintiffs. However, depending on the court's interpretation of another important aspect of the case, the enterprise may have to pay $80 million over and above the $20 million. FIN 14 requires accrual of $20 million as the known minimum. Disclosure of the additional $80 million loss exposure is required if there is a reasonable possibility that the court will award these damages (see § 19.4(d)(i)).

In estimating the amount of a contingent liability, the entity should consider all relevant factors, including the experience that both the entity and its industry have had with that type of claim, as well as any known unasserted claims or reasonably suspected unreported incidents. For claims involving a large population (e.g., asbestos injury claims) (see § 19.2(c)(ii)(D)), a best estimate usually can be reached. For unusual claims (e.g., unique toxic tort or property damage litigation situations) that a company has no history of dealing with, it generally would be appropriate for the entity to accrue the known minimum amount under FIN 14.

---

[1] 281 B.R. 852 (Bankr. D. Del. 2002).

If no amount or range of loss can be determined for a particular category (e.g., asserted claims, reported incidents, or unreported incidents), no loss should be accrued for that category. However, the contingency should be disclosed in the notes to the financial statements, as required by FAS 5.

There is no definitive guidance on whether an accrual must be made for legal costs that the entity expects to incur in connection with a loss contingency. Some argue that legal fees should be recognized as incurred, which is when the legal services are provided, and therefore should not be recognized as part of a FAS 5 accrual. Others argue that the accrual of the loss should factor in all costs and that if the legal costs are reasonably estimable, they should be accrued in accordance with FAS 5 and FIN 14, regardless of whether a liability can be estimated for the contingency itself. With respect to legal costs associated with environmental remediation, SOP 96-1 requires that entities include legal costs in the measurement of the environmental remediation liability (see § 20.3(a)).

Entities may discount recorded loss contingencies (whether they were established for settled, reported, or unreported losses) when certain criteria are met. Discounting is acceptable when the aggregate amount of the liability and the timing of cash payments for the liability are fixed or reliably determinable. For example, discounting is generally appropriate for loss exposures that result in a large volume of relatively small claims that have a highly predictable settlement pattern (such as claims for workers' compensation and employee medical coverage) and for settled claims that represent an obligation to pay a specific sum on fixed or determinable dates. In contrast, discounting is generally inappropriate for exposures that result in erratic and unpredictable loss experience, such as most environmental claims.

Adherence to FIN 14, which generally leads to accrual of the known minimum value or most likely value, can result in significant understatement of environmental loss contingencies when compared to more robust measurement techniques such as fair value and expected value. For certifying officers of public companies, this may raise concerns that the reporting entity has not fairly presented the financial condition of the company as required by Sarbanes-Oxley section 302 (see § 7.2(a)). To address these concerns, reporting entities may choose to replace FIN 14 with the supplemental guidance on estimation of environmental costs and liabilities contained in ASTM E 2137, "Standard Guide for Estimating Monetary Costs and Liabilities for Environmental Matters," which is covered in Chapter 25.

At its March 9, 2005 board meeting, the FASB considered a request made by The Rose Foundation to reconsider the accounting and reporting standards for contingent environmental liabilities. Specifically, FASB considered whether environmental loss contingencies that meet the recognition criteria in paragraph 8 of FAS 5 should be recognized at expected value pursuant to ASTM E 2137. FASB rejected the request, choosing not to reconsider FAS 5 and FIN 14 solely in the context of environmental liabilities, and noting that an ongoing FASB project to reconsider the conceptual framework may result in changes to the accounting and reporting of contingent liabilities.[2]

---

2 Minutes of March 9, 2005 FASB board meeting (available at www.fasb.org).

19.4 DISPLAY AND DISCLOSURE

(a) BALANCE SHEET DISPLAY

Recognized liabilities for environmental loss contingencies are recorded on the entity's balance sheet. Recorded liabilities are reduced (or increased) as new information results in a change in estimate or as expenditures are incurred to settle the obligation.

An entity's balance sheet also may include assets that relate to an environmental obligation, such as recoveries from insurers, indemnitors, or other responsible parties. (Chapter 16 addresses recognition and measurement of potential recoveries related to environmental liabilities.) In summary, FIN 39 requires separate presentation of environmental liabilities and related rights of recovery, unless a right of setoff exists. A right of setoff exists only when all of the following conditions are met: each of two parties owes the other determinable amounts; the reporting party has the right to set off the amounts owed with the amount owed to the other party; the reporting party intends to set off; and the right of setoff is enforceable at law.

A debtor that has a right of setoff that meets all these conditions may offset the related asset and liability and report the net amount. SOP 96-1 notes, however, that the facts and circumstances surrounding environmental remediation liabilities and related receivables and potential recoveries would rarely, if ever, meet all these conditions.

(b) INCOME STATEMENT DISPLAY

Generally, recording an environmental liability under FAS 5 results in a corresponding charge to income as an operating expense. In certain situations, such as those described in Chapter 15, it may be appropriate to capitalize environmental costs. However, because environmental damages should not be capitalized, it will rarely be the case that an environmental loss contingency (other than environmental remediation liabilities affecting company-owned properties) should be capitalized.

Also, in conjunction with the initial recording of a purchase business combination or the final estimate of a preacquisition contingency at the end of the allocation period, a contingent environmental liability is considered in the determination and allocation of the purchase price, according to the guidance in Accounting Principles Board Opinion 16, "Business Combinations," and FASB Statement of Financial Accounting Standards No. 38, "Accounting for Preacquisition Contingencies of Purchased Enterprises." By analogy to the accounting for a purchase business combination, the recording of a contingent environmental liability in conjunction with the acquisition of property would affect the amount recorded as an asset. Finally, the recording of the receipt of property as a contribution received, following the guidance in FAS 116, "Accounting for Contributions Received and Contributions Made," should include the effect of the environmental remediation liability that is recorded in conjunction with contribution.

APB Opinion 30, "Reporting the Results of Operations," sets forth the criteria for reporting extraordinary items. The incurrence of environmental loss contingencies may or may not be considered an event that is unusual in nature. As such, the related costs and recoveries may or may not meet the criteria for classification as extraordinary.

Furthermore, it is extremely difficult to substantiate the classification of environmental damages as a component of nonoperating expenses. Because the events underlying the incurrence of the obligation relate to an entity's operations, environmental damages should be charged against operations. Accordingly, environmental-related expenses should be reported as a component of operating income in income statements that classify items as operating or nonoperating. Credits arising from recoveries of environmental losses from other parties should be reflected in the same income statement line. Any earnings on assets that are reflected on the entity's financial statements and are earmarked for funding its environmental liabilities should be reported as investment income.

Environmental-related expenses and related recoveries attributable to discontinued operations that were accounted for as such in accordance with APB Opinion 30 should be classified as discontinued operations.

(c) DISCLOSURE OF ACCOUNTING PRINCIPLES

APB Opinion 22, "Disclosure of Accounting Policies," provides guidance regarding accounting principles that should be described in the accounting policies note to the financial statements. APB Opinion 22, paragraph 12, indicates that entities should disclose those accounting principles that "materially affect the determination of financial position or results of operations." In particular, entities should disclose accounting principles and the methods of applying those principles when alternatives exist. With respect to environmental loss contingencies, financial statements should disclose whether the accrual for environmental liabilities is measured on a discounted basis. If an entity utilizes present value measurement techniques, additional disclosures are appropriate (see § 19.4(d)(i)).

Entities are encouraged, but not required, to disclose the event, situation, or set of circumstances, if any, that generally trigger recognition of environmental loss contingencies. Also, entities are encouraged to disclose their policies concerning the timing of recognition of recoveries.

(d) DISCLOSURES FOR ENVIRONMENTAL LOSS CONTINGENCIES

Uncertainties associated with environmental loss contingencies are pervasive, and they often result in wide ranges of reasonably possible losses with respect to such contingencies. Further, resolution of the uncertainties and the cash-flow effects of the loss contingencies often occur over a span of many years. GAAP encourages, but does not require, entities to provide additional specific disclosures with respect to environmental loss contingencies that would further the understanding of the entity's financial statements.

FAS 5, SOP 96-1, "Environmental Remediation Liabilities" (Chapter 20); and SOP 94-6, "Disclosure of Certain Significant Risks and Uncertainties" (see § 12.5), contain rules and guidelines relevant to disclosure of environmental loss contingencies.

Paragraphs 9 and 10 of FAS 5 set forth the following rules and guidelines for disclosure for loss contingencies:

- Disclosure is required if it is probable that an asset had been impaired or a liability had been incurred as of the date of the financial statements but the loss is not accrued because the amount of loss cannot be reasonably estimated.
- Disclosure is required if there is a reasonable possibility that a loss may have been incurred even though information may not indicate that it is probable that an asset had been impaired or a liability had been incurred at the date of the financial statements.
- Disclosure is not required of a loss contingency involving an unasserted claim or assessment when there has been no manifestation by a potential claimant of an awareness of a possible claim or assessment unless it is considered probable that a claim will be asserted and there is a reasonable possibility that the outcome will be unfavorable.
- Disclosure of the nature and the amount of an accrual for a loss contingency may be necessary for the financial statements not to be misleading.

While focusing on environmental remediation obligations, SOP 96-1 provides interpretative guidance that is generally applicable to all environmental loss contingencies. FAS 5 and SOP 96-1 contemplate disclosures for loss contingencies in four different scenarios: (1) recognized losses and reasonably possible (additional) loss exposures, (2) probable but not reasonably estimable losses, (3) unasserted claims, and (4) post-period events.

(i) RECOGNIZED LOSSES AND RECOVERIES, AND REASONABLY POSSIBLE LOSS EXPOSURES

If the degrees of uncertainty used in the FAS 5 probability test (i.e., remote, reasonably possible, and probable) were mapped onto a range of likelihood of the existence of a loss spanning from zero to 100 percent, the reasonably possible portion would span a significant breadth of the range starting from remote and ending with probable. The potential outcomes of environmental loss contingencies often span a wide range of possibilities. If a loss is deemed probable and it is reasonably estimable, it is recognized; however, beyond the recognized losses, there may be additional exposure to loss that is reasonably possible. This often happens in situations in which a range of possible outcomes is identified and, in accordance with FIN 14 (see § 19.3), the entity records either a best estimate within the range or the known minimum amount, thus leaving unrecorded amounts of additional possible loss for the higher-cost outcomes. In other situations, no loss may be probable, but a loss is reasonably possible. There may also be situations in which a loss is probable, but no amount that would be material to the entity is reasonably estimable (see § 19.4(d)(ii)).

Paragraph 7.20 of SOP 96-1 states that with respect to recorded accruals for environmental loss contingencies and assets for third-party recoveries related to environmental obligations, financial statements should disclose the following:

- The nature of the accruals, if such disclosure is necessary for the financial statements not to be misleading, and, in situations in which disclosure of the nature of the accruals is necessary, the total amount accrued for the obligation, if such disclosure is also necessary for the financial statements not to be misleading.
- If any portion of the accrued obligation is discounted, the undiscounted amount of the obligation and the discount rate used in the present value determinations.
- If the criteria of SOP 94-6 (see § 12.5) are met with respect to the accrued obligation or to any recognized asset for third-party recoveries, an indication that it is at least reasonably possible that a change in the estimate of the obligation or of the asset will occur in the near term.

With respect to reasonably possible loss contingencies, including reasonably possible loss exposures in excess of the amount accrued, financial statements should disclose the following:

- The nature of the reasonably possible loss contingency; that is, a description of the reasonably possible obligation, and an estimate of the possible loss exposure or the fact that such an estimate cannot be made.
- If the criteria of SOP 94-6 are met with respect to estimated loss (or gain) contingencies, an indication that it is at least reasonably possible that a change in the estimate will occur in the near term.

Entities also are encouraged, but not required, to disclose the following:

- The estimated time frame of disbursements for recorded amounts if expenditures are expected to continue over the long term.
- The estimated time frame for realization of recognized probable recoveries, if realization is not expected in the near term.
- If the criteria of SOP 94-6 are met with respect to the accrued obligation, to any recognized asset for third-party recoveries, or to reasonably possible loss exposures or disclosed gain contingencies, the factors that cause the estimate to be sensitive to change.
- If an estimate of the probable or reasonably possible loss or range of loss cannot be made, the reasons why it cannot be made.
- If information about the reasonably possible loss or the recognized and additional reasonably possible loss for an environmental obligation related to an individual location or site is relevant to an understanding of

the financial position, cash flows, or results of operations of the entity, the following with respect to the site:

- The total amount accrued for the site.
- The nature of any reasonably possible loss contingency or additional loss, and an estimate of the possible loss or the fact that an estimate cannot be made and the reasons why it cannot be made.
- Whether other potentially responsible parties are involved and the entity's estimated share of the obligation.
- The status of regulatory proceedings.
- The estimated time frame for resolution of the contingency.

(ii) PROBABLE BUT NOT REASONABLY ESTIMABLE LOSSES

An entity often is able to determine, early in the process of assessing an environmental loss contingency, that it is probable that the entity has an obligation, even though the determination of a reasonable estimate of the total cost of that obligation may take additional time (e.g., due to the necessity of identifying and organizing other potentially responsible parties, studying and evaluating the pollution conditions, or negotiating the scope of required response actions with the regulatory authorities and other stakeholders). In situations in which a probable obligation exists, FAS 5 and FIN 14 require that the best estimate of the loss be recorded or, if the reasonable estimate of the loss is a range and there is no best estimate within the range, that the minimum amount in the range be disclosed. However, it may be that there is no best estimate and the minimum amount in the range of the overall liability is not a material amount.

Even though an entity may not be able to establish a reasonable estimate of a material loss or a range of reasonably estimable material loss exposure that must be recorded, in many cases it can determine early in the investigation whether the costs, in fact, may be material (i.e., the upper end of the range of the reasonable estimate of the loss is material) (see § 12.2). If an entity's probable but not reasonably estimable environmental obligations may be material, the financial statements should disclose the nature of the probable contingency (i.e., a description of the obligation, and the fact that a reasonable estimate cannot currently be made). Entities also are encouraged, but not required, to disclose the estimated time frame for resolution of the uncertainty as to the amount of the loss.

(iii) UNASSERTED CLAIMS

Whether notification by regulatory authorities or private claimants in relation to particular environmental laws constitutes the assertion of a claim is a matter of legal judgment. Simultaneous legal determinations may be required in multiple contexts, which may or may not be mutually binding. For example, notification of the entity's insurance carrier of a possible claim does not necessarily mean that a claim has been asserted. If an entity concludes that it has no current legal obligation to address a situation of probable or possible environmental impact, then (in accordance with FAS 5) no disclosure is required.

(iv) POST-PERIOD EVENTS

After the date of an enterprise's financial statements but before those financial statements are issued, information may become available indicating that an asset was impaired or a liability was incurred after the date of the financial statements, or that there is at least a reasonable possibility that an asset was impaired or a liability was incurred after that date. The information may relate to an environmental loss contingency that existed at the date of the financial statements (e.g., unasserted claims for environmental damages relating to a release of hazardous substances prior to the date of the financial statements). Alternatively, the information may relate to a loss contingency that did not exist at the date of the financial statements (e.g., a release of hazardous substances that occurred after the date of the financial statements).

In these situations, the conditions for accrual of a liability are not met. Disclosure of those kinds of losses or loss contingencies may be necessary, however, to keep the financial statements from being misleading. If disclosure is deemed necessary, the financial statements should indicate the nature of the loss or loss contingency and give an estimate of the amount or range of loss or possible loss or state that such an estimate cannot be made.

Occasionally, in the case of a loss arising after the date of the financial statements for which the amount of asset impairment or liability can be reasonably estimated, disclosure may best be made by supplementing the historical financial statements with pro forma financial data giving effect to the loss as if it had occurred at the date of the financial statements. It may be desirable to present pro forma statements, usually a balance sheet only, in columnar form on the face of the historical financial statements.

(v) CONCLUSIONS ON LOSS CONTINGENCIES AND OTHER MATTERS

Financial statements may include a contingency conclusion that addresses the estimated total unrecognized exposure to environmental loss contingencies. Such contingency conclusions may state, for example, that "management believes that the outcome of these uncertainties should not have [or "may have"] a material adverse effect on the financial condition, cash flows, or operating results of the enterprise." Alternatively, the disclosure may indicate that the adverse effect could be material to a particular financial statement or to results and cash flows of a quarterly or annual reporting period. Although potentially useful information, these conclusions are not a substitute for the required disclosures of SOP 96-1 and FAS 5, such as the requirement to disclose the amounts of material reasonably possible additional losses or to state that such an estimate cannot be made. Also, the assertion that the outcome should not have a material adverse effect must be supportable. If the entity is unable to estimate the maximum end of the range of possible outcomes, it may be difficult to support an assertion that the outcome should not have a material adverse effect.

Entities may wish to provide a description of the general applicability and impact of environmental laws upon their businesses and how the existence of such laws may give rise to environmental loss contingencies. Such disclosures often acknowledge the uncertainty of the effect of possible future changes to environmental laws and their application, and they are frequently made on an aggregated basis, considering the entity's total exposures for all environmental matters.

(e) ADDITIONAL CONSIDERATIONS FOR PUBLIC COMPANIES

Public companies must also consider the directives and guidance of the SEC regarding disclosure of environmental loss contingencies contained in SAB 92 (as updated and recodified by SAB 103). SAB 92 states that:

> [P]roduct and environmental liabilities typically are of such significance that detailed disclosures regarding the judgments and assumptions underlying the recognition and measurement of the liabilities are necessary to prevent the financial statements from being misleading and to inform readers fully regarding the range of reasonably possible outcomes that could have a material effect on the registrant's financial condition, results of operations, or liquidity.[3]

The SEC has identified the following examples of disclosures that may be necessary:

- Circumstances affecting the reliability and precision of loss estimates.
- The extent to which unasserted claims are reflected in any accrual or may affect the magnitude of the contingency.
- Uncertainties with respect to joint and several liability that may affect the magnitude of the contingency.
- Disclosure of the nature and terms of cost-sharing arrangements with other potentially responsible parties.
- The extent to which disclosed but unrecognized contingent losses are expected to be recoverable through insurance, indemnification arrangements, or other sources, with disclosure of any material limitations of that recovery.
- Uncertainties regarding the legal sufficiency of insurance claims or solvency of insurance carriers.
- The time frame over which the accrued or presently unrecognized amounts may be paid out.
- Material components of the accruals and significant assumptions underlying estimates.

Measurement of environmental loss contingencies in accordance with FIN 14 can result in estimates that are significantly lower than estimates developed using the more robust measurement techniques described in ASTM E 2137 (Chapter 25). This raises the question of whether the understatement of environmental loss contingencies, although reported in conformance with GAAP, may

---

[3] Release No. SAB 92, 58 Fed. Reg. 32,843, 32,845 (June 14, 1993).

nonetheless result in a failure to fairly present the financial condition of the entity (see § 7.2(a)).

Public companies are required to disclose additional information regarding critical accounting estimates (see § 24.5(e)) in the MD&A section of their periodic SEC reports. These disclosures are in addition to the disclosures described above and the financial statement footnote disclosures described in § 19.4(d).

Section 404 of Sarbanes-Oxley imposes requirements on public companies to design, implement, and periodically assess the operational effectiveness of internal control over financial reporting (see Chapter 8). In addition, section 404 requires the reporting entity's independent financial auditor to examine the entity's internal control over financial reporting and annually attest to its design and operational effectiveness (see Chapter 27).

Internal control over financial reporting of environmental loss contingencies is fraught with potential pitfalls, in part because of complex accounting standards; significant challenges in data collection, assessment, and measurement; and the high degree of subjectivity involved in the application of applicable financial reporting standards. Even more than other areas of environmental financial reporting, it involves a complex formulation of policies, procedures, controls, and communication and information systems. Designing, implementing, monitoring, and auditing the control system can require significant effort and diligence on an initial and ongoing basis. For large public companies, especially those engaged in frequent acquisitions, consistent application of policies and procedures across the entire organization is a great challenge in itself.

Financial reporting of environmental loss contingencies is also a highly sensitive matter because of the competing objectives discussed in Chapter 5. This raises increased concerns about the potential for management override of stated policies and procedures.

Exhibit 19.2 identifies certain process and control issues with regard to financial reporting of environmental loss contingencies that may warrant special attention for reporting entities and financial auditors.

Notwithstanding an effective internal control system design, the operational effectiveness of the system will largely depend on the performance of employees and contractors in carrying out established policies and procedures. Employee and contractor performance in turn will depend largely on the company's control environment with respect to environmental financial reporting (see § 8.2(a)) and personnel qualifications, training, and incentives (or disincentives).

Exhibit 19.2

Process and Control Considerations for Environmental Loss Contingencies

Process Area	Process and Control Considerations
Identification	• Identification of asserted and unasserted claims associated with current and former assets and operations, nonowned disposal sites, and transportation-related incidents • Use of environmental specialists
Assessment	• Selection and application of criteria for assessment of the probability of a future loss from identified contingencies • Policies and procedures for investigation and additional data gathering • Evaluation of environmental loss contingencies separate from related recoveries • Reliance on determinations of legal counsel
Measurement	• Selection and application of measurement techniques • Use of actuaries and other specialists • Determination of ability to reasonably estimate • Evaluation of potential for significant near-term changes in estimated amounts
Reporting	• Selection and application of criteria for assessment of materiality • Balance sheet display of liabilities and related rights of set off • Disclosures relating to loss contingencies • Disclosures related to significant risks and uncertainties

CHAPTER TWENTY

Environmental Remediation Liabilities

20.1 INTRODUCTION

Environmental remediation liabilities are a subset of environmental loss contingencies (Chapter 19) that relate to obligations for cleanup costs. SOP 96-1, "Environmental Remediation Liabilities," provides extensive guidance on the application of FAS 5 to environmental remediation liabilities arising under Superfund (§ 3.2(a)) and the corrective action provisions of RCRA (§ 3.2(b)). Although SOP 96-1 focuses almost entirely on Superfund and RCRA corrective action liabilities, remediation obligations can and often do arise under other federal environmental laws, including the RCRA underground storage tank program (with respect to petroleum products; § 3.2(c)) and TSCA (with respect to asbestos, PCBs, and lead; § 3.3(d)). Environmental remediation liabilities may also arise under analogous state and foreign laws.

For purposes of this book and SOP 96-1, environmental remediation liabilities do not include:

- Cleanup costs incurred in connection with environmental remediation actions that are undertaken at the sole discretion of management and that are not induced by the threat, by governments or other parties, of litigation or of assertion of a claim or an assessment—for example, remediation under a state voluntary cleanup program (see § 3.2(f)).
- Pollution control costs with respect to current operations (see § 13.2(c)).
- Liabilities for environmental damages other than cleanup costs, such as toxic tort and natural resource damages (see § 13.2(d)).
- Environmental guarantees (Chapter 21).
- Environmental exit costs (see § 13.2(b)) and asset retirement obligations (Chapter 22).
- Asset impairments (Chapter 23).

The following sections closely parallel the guidance in SOP 96-1. Readers should bear in mind that this guidance, though heavily focused on Superfund liability (with analogies drawn to RCRA corrective action), may be equally applicable to other types of environmental cleanup obligations that are not described in the SOP.

20.2 RECOGNITION

FAS 5 requires the accrual of a liability if information available prior to issuance of the financial statements indicates that it is probable that an asset has been impaired or a liability has been incurred at the date of the financial statements and the amount of the loss can be reasonably estimated.

An environmental cleanup obligation arising from a pending or threatened claim or assessment generally does not become determinable as a distinct event, nor is the amount of the liability generally fixed and determinable at a specific point in time. Rather, the existence of a liability for cleanup costs becomes determinable and the amount of the liability becomes estimable over a continuum of events and activities that help to frame, define, and verify the liability.

The underlying cause of an environmental remediation liability is the past or present ownership or operation of a site affected by historical pollution conditions, or the contribution or transportation of waste to such a site, at which remedial actions (at a minimum, investigation) must take place. For a liability to be recognized in the financial statements, this underlying cause must have occurred on or before the date of the financial statements. The obligating event of an environmental remediation liability, as distinguished from the underlying cause, is generally the threat or assertion of a legal claim to compel the entity to incur cleanup costs (see § 18.2(b)(ii)).

(a) PROBABILITY TEST

SOP 96-1 provides that the probability criterion under FAS 5 is met if the following two conditions are met:

1. Litigation seeking to hold the entity responsible for participating in the remediation process has commenced; such a claim against the issuer has been asserted, or, based on available information, such a litigation or claim is probable; and
2. Based on available information, it is probable that the outcome of such litigation or claim will be unfavorable, such that the entity will be held responsible for participating in a remediation process.

Legal analysis and judgment may be required to determine whether the probability criterion has been met with respect to a given site under applicable environmental laws. However, there is a presumption that the outcome of any litigation, claim, or assessment will be unfavorable if litigation has commenced, or a claim or an assessment has been asserted; or if commencement of litigation or assertion of a claim or assessment is probable, and the reporting entity is associated with the site (i.e., it in fact arranged for the disposal of hazardous substances found at a site or transported hazardous substances to the site or is the current or previous owner or operator of the site).

(b) REASONABLY ESTIMABLE TEST

Remediation cost estimates can be difficult to estimate because of a variety of factors, including:

- Incomplete information to fully characterize the nature and extent of hazardous substances (or petroleum substances or other hazardous materials) at a site.
- The range of technologies that can be used to remediate the site.
- Evolving risk-based remediation standards under applicable environmental laws.
- The number and financial condition of other potentially responsible parties at multiparty sites and the extent of their responsibility for the remediation.

FIN 14, "Reasonable Estimation of the Amount of a Loss," concludes that the reasonable estimation test for recognition of a loss contingency under FAS 5 is met when a range of loss can be reasonably estimated. FIN 14 further provides that when no amount within the range of loss is a better estimate than any other amount, the minimum value in the range (*known minimum value*) should be recorded. This approach was developed to address measurement of losses in situations in which a single most likely amount is not available.

At the early stages of a remediation process, environmental remediation liabilities are not easily quantified. The amount of the liability is defined and refined as the remediation process unfolds. Estimating the range of an entity's environmental remediation liability requires an analysis of the various stages of the overall remediation process, including site assessment, development of a response action plan, soil cleanup, groundwater cleanup, and postclosure care. Estimated costs (or ranges of costs) for each phase are combined to arrive at an estimate (or range of estimates) of total cleanup costs.

For some elements of the cleanup, some cost estimates may seem more probable than any others within the range of possibilities. For other elements of the cleanup, there may be no estimate that is more likely than any other. Accordingly, the overall liability that is recorded may be based on amounts representing the known minimum value for some elements of the liability and on the most likely value for other components of the liability.

Early in the remediation process, particular components of the overall liability may not be reasonably estimable at all. According to SOP 96-1, this fact should not preclude the recognition of a liability. Instead, the components of the liability that can be reasonably estimated should be viewed as a surrogate for the known minimum value in the range of the overall liability. For example, a sole PRP that has confirmed that it sent waste to a Superfund site and agrees to perform a remedial investigation and feasibility study (RI/FS) may know that it will incur costs related to the RI/FS. The PRP, although aware that total costs associated with the site will be greater than the cost of the RI/FS, may be unable to reasonably estimate the overall liability. The inability to quantify the total costs of the overall liability should not preclude recognition of the estimated cost of the RI/FS. In this situation, SOP 96-1 provides that a liability for the best estimate (or, if no such estimate is available, the known minimum value) of the cost of the RI/FS, and for any other remediation components that can be reasonably estimated, should be recognized as a liability.

Additional uncertainties arise if other PRPs are involved at the site. The costs of the remediation ultimately will be assigned and allocated among the various PRPs. The final allocation of costs may not be known, however, until the remediation effort is nearly complete. An entity's allocated share of the costs may or may not be based on its relative direct responsibility at a site (i.e., the amount and toxicity of wastes contributed by the various PRPs). An entity's final allocation of costs may depend on several factors, including, among other things, the willingness of the PRPs to negotiate a cost allocation, the results of the negotiation, the ability of the other PRPs to fund their share of remediation costs, and the entity's share of any orphan costs.

According to SOP 96-1, uncertainties relating to the relative share of the total remediation costs at a site should not preclude the entity from recognizing as a liability the best estimate of its share of the costs or, if no best estimate can be made, the minimum estimate of its share of the costs.

Changes in estimates of the entity's remediation liability, including revisions to the entity's estimate of its share of the liability due to negotiation or identification of other PRPs, should be accounted for as changes in estimates, in consonance with FAS 154, "Accounting Changes and Error Corrections" (see § 12.6).

(c) MILESTONES

Certain stages of the remediation process (§ 3.2(a)(vi)) and of PRP involvement (§ 3.2(a)(vii)) act as milestones that should be considered when evaluating the probability that a loss has been incurred and the extent to which the loss is reasonably estimable. At a minimum, the estimate of a Superfund (or RCRA) remediation liability should be evaluated at each of these milestones.

(i) IDENTIFICATION AND VERIFICATION OF AN ENTITY AS A PRP

Receipt of notification or otherwise becoming aware that an entity may be a PRP at a Superfund site compels the entity to action. If the site is not owned or operated by the entity, the entity must examine its records to determine whether it is associated with the site. If, based on a review and evaluation of its records and all other available information, the entity determines that it is associated with the site, it is probable that a liability has been incurred. If all or a portion of the liability is reasonably estimable, a liability should be recognized.

In some cases, an entity will be able to reasonably estimate a range of its liability very early in the process because the site situation is comparable to situations at other sites (e.g., the cleanup involves only the removal of underground storage tanks in accordance with the UST program). In such cases, the criteria for recognition under FAS 5 would be met and the liability should be recognized. In other cases, however, the entity may have insufficient information to reasonably estimate the minimum amount in the range of its liability. In these cases, the criteria for recognition would not be met at this stage.

The RCRA equivalent to being identified as a PRP under CERCLA occurs when a facility is subject to RCRA permit requirements, in particular, investigation and cleanup of so-called solid waste management units, which may be currently used as part of the facility's waste storage and handling plan, or may be purely historical in nature.

(ii) RECEIPT OF UNILATERAL ADMINISTRATIVE ORDER

An entity may receive a unilateral administrative order compelling it to take a response action at a Superfund site or risk penalties of up to four times the cost of the response action. Such response actions may be relatively limited actions, such as the performance of a RI/FS or performance of a removal action. Alternatively, a unilateral order may demand full remediation of the site.

Under section 106 of Superfund, the EPA must find that an "imminent and substantial endangerment" exists at a site before such an order may be issued. Preenforcement review by a court is not available to an entity wishing to challenge a unilateral administrative order. Receipt of a unilateral order therefore indicates that it is probable that a liability has been incurred.

The ability to estimate costs resulting from unilateral administrative orders varies with factors such as site complexity and the nature and extent of the work to be performed. The milestones that follow should be considered in evaluating the ability to estimate such costs insofar as the actions required by the unilateral administrative order involve these milestones. The cost of performing the requisite work generally is estimable within a range, and recognition of an environmental remediation liability for costs of removal actions generally should not be delayed.

The requirement to conduct interim corrective measures under RCRA to address an imminent hazard is generally equivalent to receipt of a CERCLA section 106 order.

(iii) PARTICIPATION AS A PRP IN THE RI/FS

At this stage, the entity has been identified as a PRP and has agreed, individually or with other PRPs, to pay the costs of an investigation. The total cost of the RI/FS generally is estimable within a reasonable range and the identification of other PRPs and their agreement to participate in funding the RI/FS typically provides a reasonable basis for determining the entity's allocable share of the cost of the RI/FS. At this stage, additional information may be available regarding the extent of environmental impact and possible remediation alternatives. This additional information may not, however, be sufficient to provide a basis for reasonable estimation of the entity's allocable share of the total cleanup costs. At a minimum, the entity should recognize its share of the estimated total cost of the RI/FS.

As the RI/FS proceeds, the entity may be able to better estimate other components of the liability. For example, an entity may be able to estimate the extent of environmental impact and identify alternative remediation technologies. An entity may also be able to better assess the extent of its involvement at the site relative to other PRPs.

The RCRA equivalent to participation as a PRP in the RI/FS is the RCRA facility investigation.

(iv) COMPLETION OF FEASIBILITY STUDY

Upon substantial completion of the feasibility study, both a minimum remediation liability and the entity's allocated share generally will be reasonably estimable. The FS should be considered substantially complete no later than the point at which the PRPs recommend a proposed course of action to the EPA. If the entity has previously recognized an estimate of its remediation liability, recognition should not be delayed beyond this point, even if uncertainties remain (e.g., about allocations to individual PRPs and potential recoveries from third parties).

The RCRA equivalent to completion of the FS under CERCLA is completion of the corrective measures study.

(v) ISSUANCE OF RECORD OF DECISION

At this point, the EPA has issued its determination specifying a preferred remedy. Normally, the entity and other PRPs have begun, or perhaps completed, negotiations, litigation, or both to determine their allocated share of the remediation liability. The entity's estimate usually can be refined at this stage, based on the specified preferred remedy and a preliminary allocation of the total cleanup costs.

The RCRA equivalent to issuance of a record of decision (ROD) at a Superfund site is approval of the corrective measures study.

(vi) REMEDIAL DESIGN, INSTALLATION AND STARTUP; OPERATION AND MAINTENANCE; CLOSURE; POSTCLOSURE CARE, AND MONITORING

The bulk of cleanup costs typically are incurred during this phase of activity. During the design phase of the remediation, engineers develop a better sense of the work to be done and are able to provide more precise estimates of total cleanup costs. Further information likely will become available at various points until the site is delisted from the NPL, subject only to postremediation monitoring. The entity should continue to refine and adjust its best estimate of its final liability as this additional information becomes available.

The RCRA equivalent to this CERCLA activity is corrective measures implementation.

20.3 MEASUREMENT

Once an entity has determined that it is probable that an environmental remediation liability has been incurred, the entity should estimate that liability based on available information. The estimate of the liability includes the entity's allocable share of the liability for a specific site plus the entity's share of amounts related to the site that will not be paid by other PRPs or the government (*orphan share*).

SOP 96-1 incorporates the measurement guidance contained in FIN 14. As discussed in Chapter 19, adherence to FIN 14, which generally leads to accrual of the known minimum value or most likely value, can result in significant understatement of environmental remediation liabilities when compared to more robust measurement techniques such as fair value and expected value. For certifying officers of public companies, this may raise concerns that the reporting entity has not fairly presented the financial condition of the company as required by Sarbanes-Oxley section 302 (see § 7.2(a)). To address these concerns, reporting entities may choose to replace FIN 14 with the supplemental guidance on estimation of environmental costs and liabilities contained in ASTM E 2137, "Standard Guide for Estimating Monetary Costs and Liabilities for Environmental Matters," which is covered in Chapter 25.

At its March 9, 2005 board meeting, the FASB considered a request made by The Rose Foundation to reconsider the accounting and reporting for contingent environmental liabilities. Specifically, FASB considered whether environmental loss contingencies that meet the recognition criteria in paragraph 8 of FAS 5 should be recognized at expected value pursuant to ASTM E 2137. FASB rejected the request, choosing not to reconsider FAS 5 and FIN 14 solely in the context of environmental liabilities, and noting that an ongoing FASB project to reconsider the conceptual framework may result in changes to the accounting and reporting of contingent liabilities.

Once the entity has determined the appropriate measurement technique to be used, measurement of remediation liabilities involves the following additional issues:

- Costs that should be included in the measurement.
- Whether the measurement should consider the effects of expected future events or developments, including discounting considerations.
- How the measurement should be affected by the existence of other PRPs.
- How the measurement should be affected by potential recoveries.

(a) SCOPE OF INCLUDED CLEANUP COSTS

As noted at the beginning of this chapter, environmental remediation liabilities relate to asserted or probable legal claims for cleanup costs. Although contingent liabilities for environmental damages, including natural resource damages and toxic torts, may arise from the same set of environmental conditions or events giving rise to an environmental remediation liability, such exposures were considered too case-specific by the AICPA for general guidance under SOP 96-1.

Cleanup costs to be included in the measurement include the incremental direct costs of the remediation effort, and costs of compensation and benefits for those employees who are expected to devote a significant amount of time directly to the remediation effort, to the extent of the time expected to be spent directly on the remediation effort. The *remediation effort*, which is to be considered on a site-by-site basis, includes:

- Precleanup activities, such as the performance of a remedial investigation, risk assessment, or feasibility study and the preparation of a remedial action plan and remedial designs for a Superfund site; or the performance of a RCRA facility assessment, RCRA facility investigation, or RCRA corrective measures studies.
- Performance of remedial actions under Superfund, corrective actions under RCRA, and analogous actions under state and foreign laws.
- Government oversight and enforcement-related activities.
- Operation and maintenance of the remedy, including required postremediation monitoring.

(i) INCREMENTAL DIRECT COSTS

Determining the extent of remedial actions that are required, the type of remedial actions to be used, and the allocation of costs among PRPs is part of the remediation effort, and the costs of making such determinations, including legal costs, are to be included in the measurement of the remediation liability. Examples of incremental direct costs of the remediation effort include:

- Fees to outside law firms for work related to determining the extent of remedial actions that are required, the type of remedial actions to be used, or the allocation of costs among PRPs.
- Costs related to completing the RI/FS.
- Fees to outside engineering and consulting firms for site investigations and the development of remedial action plans and remedial designs.
- Costs of contractors performing remedial actions.
- Government oversight costs.
- Past costs incurred by a governmental authority dealing with the site.
- The cost of machinery and equipment that is dedicated to the remedial actions and that does not have an alternative use.
- Assessments by a PRP group covering costs incurred by the group in dealing with a site.
- Costs of operation and maintenance of the remedial action, including the costs of postremediation monitoring required by the remedial action plan.

The costs of services related to routine environmental compliance matters and litigation costs involved with potential rights of recovery are not part of the remediation effort. Litigation costs involved with potential recoveries should be charged to expense as incurred until realization of the claim for recovery is considered probable and an asset relating to the recovery is recognized, at which time any remaining legal costs should be considered in the measurement of the recovery. The determination of what legal costs are for potential recoveries rather than for determining the allocation of costs among PRPs will depend on the specific facts and circumstances of each situation.

(ii) EMPLOYEE COSTS

Examples of employees who may devote a significant amount of time directly to the remediation effort include:

- The internal legal staff that is involved with the determination of the extent of required remedial actions, the type of remedial action to be used, and the allocation of costs among PRPs.
- Technical employees who are involved with the remediation effort.

Estimates of the compensation and benefits costs to be incurred for a specific site should be made in connection with the initial recording of the liability and subsequently adjusted at each reporting date to reflect the current estimate of such costs to be incurred in the future.

(b) EFFECT OF EXPECTED FUTURE EVENTS OR DEVELOPMENTS

Remediation of a Superfund or RCRA site may take several years or even decades. During this span of time, the applicable legal standards and available remediation technology may change. Such changes can significantly affect the ultimate cost of the remediation effort. Additionally, inflation and productivity improvements over a span of several years can change the estimates of costs to be incurred. Finally, litigation or negotiations among the PRPs, or between the PRPs and the government, based on new technical findings at the site, may substantially alter the cost allocation (see § 20.3(c)(ii)).

The measurement of environmental remediation liabilities should be based on enacted laws and adopted regulations and policies. The impact of changes in laws, regulations, and policies should be recognized when such changes are enacted or adopted.

Remediation technology continues to evolve. In many instances, new technologies have affected the costs of a remediation effort. The remedial action plan that is used to develop the estimate of the liability should be based on the methodology that is expected to be approved to complete the cleanup. Once a methodology has been approved, that methodology and the technology available therefore should be the basis for estimating the liability until it is probable that there will be formal acceptance of a revised methodology.

Measurement of environmental remediation liabilities should be based on the entity's estimate of the cost to perform the various elements of the remediation effort *at the time such activities are expected to be performed*. This allows the reporting entity to consider the future effects of inflation and other factors, such as expected increases in productivity due to experience with similar sites. In situations in which it is not practicable to estimate inflation and other cost factors, because of uncertainty about the timing of expenditures, SOP 96-1 instructs entities to record the known minimum value of current-cost estimates until such time as those cost effects can be reasonably estimated.

SOP 96-1 provides that cost estimates may be discounted to reflect the time value of money only when the amount and timing of future payments are fixed and determinable. Discounting is not allowed when the entity cannot reasonably estimate the future impact of inflation and other cost factors because of uncertainty about the timing of expenditures. For this purpose, the amount of the aggregate liability or component thereof is the reporting entity's allocable share of the undiscounted joint and several liability for the remediation effort (or of an element thereof). For public companies, SAB 92 (as recodified and updated in SAB 103) provides that the discount rate to be used is the rate that will produce an amount at which the liability theoretically could be settled in an arm's-length transaction with a third party, and should not exceed the rate on risk-free monetary assets with comparable maturities.

(c) ALLOCATION OF LIABILITY AMONG PRPs

The environmental remediation liability recorded by an entity should be based on that entity's estimate of its allocable share of the joint and several remediation liability. The estimation of an entity's allocable share of the joint and several remediation liability for a site requires an entity to identify the PRPs for the site, assess the likelihood that other PRPs will pay their full allocable share of the liability, and determine the percentage of the liability that will be allocated to the entity.

(i) IDENTIFICATION OF PRPs

For purposes of estimating an entity's allocable share of the joint and several remediation liability for a site, those parties that are potentially responsible for paying the remediation liability belong to one of the following five PRP categories: (1) participating PRPs, (2) recalcitrant PRPs, (3) unproven PRPs, (4) parties that have not yet been identified as PRPs, and (5) parties that are PRPs but cannot be located or have no assets. Over the duration of a remediation project, individual entities may move from one PRP category to another.

Participating PRPs acknowledge their potential involvement with respect to a site. Some may participate in the various administrative negotiation, monitoring, and remediation activities related to the site. Others may simply monitor the activities and decisions of the more involved PRPs. This more passive approach may be motivated by a variety of factors, such as the entity's lack of experience, limited internal resources, or relative involvement at a site.

Recalcitrant PRPs, or *nonparticipating PRPs*, seek to delay or deny their involvement in the entire remediation effort even though evidence exists that they are, in fact, involved. Some may adopt this attitude out of ignorance of the law; others may do so in the hope that they will be considered a nuisance and therefore be ignored. Typically, parties in this category must be sued in order to collect their allocable share of the remediation liability; however, it may be that it is not economical to bring such suits because the party's assets are limited.

Unproven PRPs are parties that have been identified as PRPs by the EPA but do not acknowledge their potential involvement because there is currently no substantive evidence to link them to the site. Some ultimately may be dropped from the PRP list because no substantive evidence is found to link them to the site. For others, substantive evidence eventually may be found that confirms their liability. At early stages of the remediation process, the list of PRPs may be limited to a handful of entities that either were significant contributors of waste to the site or were easy to identify (for example, because of their proximity to the site or because of labeled material found at the site). As further investigation of the site occurs and as remediation activities take place, additional PRPs may be identified. Once identified, the additional PRPs would be reclassified from the unproven category to either the participating PRP or recalcitrant PRP category. The total number of parties in this category and their aggregate allocable share of the remediation liability vary by site and cannot be reliably determined prior to the specific identification of individual PRPs. This category of PRPs is sometimes referred to as *unknown PRPs*.

Parties that are PRPs but cannot be located or have no assets will never contribute to the remediation effort. This category of PRPs is sometimes referred to as the *orphan share.*

(ii) ALLOCATION PROCESS

In estimating allocable shares of the joint and several remediation liability for a site, there is a rebuttable presumption that costs will be allocated only among participating PRPs, as that category exists at the date of issuance of the financial statements. There are numerous ways to allocate liabilities among PRPs. The four principal factors considered in a typical allocation process are:

1. Elements of fair share (e.g., the amount of waste based on volume, the amount of waste based on mass, the type of waste, the toxicity of waste, the degree to which contamination from one source is divisible from other sources, the length of time the site was used).
2. Classification of PRP (e.g., site owner, site operator, transporter of waste, generator of waste).
3. Limitations on payments (e.g., statutory or regulatory defenses or limitations on contributions that may be applicable to a PRP).
4. Degree of care (i.e., the degree of care exercised in selecting the site or in selecting a transporter).

PRPs may reach an agreement among themselves as to the allocation method and percentages to be used, they may hire an allocation consultant whose conclusions may or may not be binding, or they may request a nonbinding allocation of responsibility from the EPA. The allocation method or percentages used may change as the remediation project moves forward. An agreement to reallocate the preliminarily allocated liability at the end of the remediation project may exist, or the allocation percentages may be adjusted during the project to reflect prior allocations that subsequently are agreed to have been inequitable.

An entity should determine its allocable share of the joint and several remediation liability for a site based on its estimate of the allocation method and percentage that ultimately will be used for the entire remediation effort. The primary sources for this estimate should be the allocation method and percentages that the PRPs have agreed to (whether that agreement applies to the entire remediation effort or to the costs incurred in the current phase of the remediation process), has been assigned by a consultant, or has been determined by the EPA. If the entity's estimate of the ultimate allocation method and percentage differs significantly from the method or percentage from these primary sources, the entity's estimate should be based on objective, verifiable information. Examples of objective, verifiable information include existing data about the kinds and quantities of waste at the site, experience with allocation approaches in comparable situations, reports of environmental specialists (internal or external), and internal data refuting EPA allegations about the entity's contribution of waste (kind, volume, etc.) to the site.

An entity should assess the likelihood that each PRP will pay its allocable share of the joint and several remediation liability. That assessment should be based primarily on the financial condition of the participating PRP. This assessment requires the entity to gain an understanding of the financial condition of the other participating PRPs and to update and monitor this information as the remediation progresses. The entity should include in its liability its share of amounts related to the site that will not be paid by other PRPs or the government.

(d) IMPACT OF POTENTIAL RECOVERIES

Potential recoveries of amounts expended for environmental remediation are distinguishable from the allocation of costs subject to joint and several liability. Potential recoveries may be claimed from a number of different parties or sources, including insurers, PRPs other than participating PRPs, and governmental or third-party funds. The amount of an environmental remediation liability should be determined independent of any potential claim for recovery, and an asset relating to the recovery should be recognized only when realization of the claim for recovery is deemed probable (under the FAS 5 probability test). If the claim is the subject of litigation, a rebuttable presumption exists that realization of the claim is not probable.

Rights of recovery should be measured at their fair value. The concept of fair value requires consideration of both transaction costs related to time receipt of the recovery and the time value of money. However, the time value of money should not be considered in the determination of the recorded amount of a potential recovery if the liability is not discounted and the timing of the recovery is dependent on the timing of payment of the liability. In most circumstances, the point in time at which a liability for environmental remediation is both probable and reasonably estimable will precede the point in time at which any related recovery is probable of realization.

20.4 DISPLAY AND DISCLOSURE

(a) BALANCE SHEET DISPLAY

Recognized liabilities for environmental remediation liabilities are recorded on the entity's balance sheet. Recorded liabilities are reduced (or increased) as new information results in a change in estimate or as expenditures are incurred to settle the obligation.

An entity's balance sheet may include several assets that relate to an environmental remediation obligation. Among them are:

- Receivables from other PRPs that are not providing initial funding.
- Anticipated recoveries from insurers.
- Anticipated recoveries from prior owners or others as a result of indemnification agreements.

Chapter 16 addresses recognition and measurement of potential recoveries related to environmental liabilities. In summary, FIN 39 requires separate presentation of environmental liabilities and related rights of recovery, unless a right of setoff exists. A right of setoff exists only when all of the following conditions are met: each of two parties owes the other determinable amounts; the reporting party has the right to set off the amounts owed with the amount owed to the other party; the reporting party intends to set off; and the right of setoff is enforceable at law.

A debtor that has a right of setoff that meets all these conditions may offset the related asset and liability and report the net amount. Rarely, if ever, will the facts and circumstances surrounding environmental remediation liabilities and related receivables and potential recoveries meet all these conditions.

(b) INCOME STATEMENT DISPLAY

Generally, recording an environmental remediation liability under SOP 96-1 results in a corresponding charge to income as an operating expense. In certain situations, such as those described in Chapter 15, however, it may be appropriate to capitalize environmental cleanup costs (e.g., in situations in which the remediation effort will mitigate or prevent future environmental contamination affecting a company-owned property while also enhancing the value of that property).

Also, in conjunction with the initial recording of a purchase business combination or the final estimate of a preacquisition contingency at the end of the allocation period, the environmental remediation liability is considered in the determination and allocation of the purchase price, according to the guidance in APB Opinion 16, "Business Combinations," and FASB Statement of Financial Accounting Standards No. 38, "Accounting for Preacquisition Contingencies of Purchased Enterprises." By analogy to the accounting for a purchase business combination, the recording of an environmental remediation liability in conjunction with the acquisition of property would affect the amount recorded as an asset. Finally, the recording of the receipt of property as a contribution received, following the guidance in FAS 116, "Accounting for Contributions Received and Contributions Made," should include the effect of the environmental remediation liability that is recorded in conjunction with contribution.

APB Opinion 30, "Reporting the Results of Operations," sets forth the criteria for reporting extraordinary items. The incurrence of environmental remediation obligations is not an event that is unusual in nature. As such, the related costs and recoveries do not meet the criteria for classification as extraordinary.

SOP 96-1 states that it is extremely difficult to substantiate the classification of environmental cleanup costs as a component of nonoperating expenses when the events underlying the incurrence of the obligation (e.g., waste disposal activities) relate to an entity's operations. Accordingly, such remediation costs should be charged against operations. Although charging the costs of remediating past environmental impacts against current operations may appear debatable, because of the time between the contribution or transportation of waste materials to a site and the subsequent incurrence of remediation costs, environmental remediation-related expenses have become a regular cost of conducting economic activity. Although not addressed by SOP 96-1, environmental remediation liabilities unrelated to the company's waste disposal activities (e.g., obligations incurred solely by virtue of current ownership of a site) might appropriately be reported as a component of nonoperating income.

Credits arising from recoveries of environmental losses from other parties should be reflected in the same income statement line. Any earnings on assets that are reflected on the entity's financial statements and are earmarked for funding its environmental liabilities should be reported as investment income.

Environmental remediation-related expenses and related recoveries attributable to discontinued operations that were accounted for as such in accordance with APB Opinion 30 should be classified as discontinued operations.

(c) DISCLOSURE OF ACCOUNTING PRINCIPLES

APB Opinion 22, "Disclosure of Accounting Policies," provides guidance regarding accounting principles that should be described in the accounting policies note to the financial statements. APB Opinion 22, paragraph 12, indicates that entities should disclose those accounting principles that "materially affect the determination of financial position or results of operations." In particular, entities should disclose accounting principles and the methods of applying those principles when alternatives exist. With respect to environmental remediation obligations, financial statements should disclose whether the accrual for environmental remediation liabilities is measured on a discounted basis. If an entity utilizes present value measurement techniques, additional disclosures are appropriate (see § 19.4(d)(i)).

SOP 96-1 encourages, but does not require, disclosure of the event, situation, or set of circumstances that generally triggers recognition of environmental remediation liabilities (e.g., during or upon completion of the feasibility study for a Superfund site). SOP 96-1 also encourages disclosure of policies concerning the timing of recognition of recoveries.

An illustration of an accounting policies note disclosure for environmental remediation-related costs follows (italicized information is not required):

> Environmental cleanup costs—*Enterprise A accrues for losses associated with environmental remediation obligations when such losses are probable and reasonably estimable. Accruals for estimated losses from environmental remediation obligations generally are recognized no later than completion of the remedial feasibility study. Such accruals are adjusted as further information develops or circumstances change.* Costs of future expenditures for environmental remediation obligations are not discounted to their present value. *Recoveries of environmental cleanup costs from other parties are recorded as assets when their receipt is deemed probable.*

(d) DISCLOSURES FOR ENVIRONMENTAL REMEDIATION LIABILITIES

The FAS 5 provisions regarding disclosures for loss contingencies are applicable to loss contingencies for environmental cleanup costs covered by SOP 96-1. The disclosure requirements of SOP 94-6, "Disclosure of Certain Significant Risks and Uncertainties," also apply to environmental remediation liabilities (see § 12.5).

Rules and guidance contained in FAS 5 and SOP 96-1 that are generally applicable to disclosures for all environmental loss contingencies are included in § 19.4(d). In addition to the general disclosure requirements for environmental loss contingencies, SOP 96-1 provides the following examples of disclosures for environmental remediation liabilities (italicized information in the examples is encouraged but not required).

Example 1: Site-specific disclosures. Following is an illustration of disclosure for a situation in which—(1) an entity is involved in a single environmental site at which a number of potential outcomes may occur; (2) there is a probable, reasonably estimable recovery from a third party; (3) the entity has accrued for the most likely outcome within a range of possible outcomes for each component; (4) the nature of the amounts accrued for remediation and the related probable recovery must be disclosed for the financial statements not to be misleading; and (5) there is a reasonably possible loss exposure in excess of the amount accrued that is material and it is reasonably possible that a change in estimate that would be material to the financial statements will occur in the near term.

> Enterprise A has been notified by the United States Environmental Protection Agency (EPA) that it is a potentially responsible party (PRP) under Superfund legislation *with respect to XYZ site in Sometown, USA, a disposal site previously used in its chemical fertilizer business. The EPA has also identified ten other PRPs for XYZ. A remedial investigation and feasibility study has been completed, and the results of that study have been forwarded to the EPA. The study indicates a range of viable remedial approaches, but agreement has not yet been reached with the EPA on the final remediation approach. The PRP group has preliminarily agreed to an allocation that sets Enterprise A's share of the cost of remediating XYZ site at 6 percent.* Enterprise A has accrued its best estimate of its obligation with respect to the site at December 31, 20XX, *which is $10 million and which is included in long-term liabilities and is expected to be disbursed over the next ten years. If certain of the PRPs are ultimately not able to fund their allocable share or the EPA insists on a more expensive remediation approach,* Enterprise A could incur additional obligations of up to *$7 million.* It is reasonably possible that Enterprise A's recorded estimate of its obligation may change in the near term.
>
> With respect to the environmental obligation discussed above, the site was acquired in *1982*, and, in connection with that acquisition, the former owner partially indemnified Enterprise A for environmental impacts occurring prior to the acquisition. *Based on the existing documentation indicating the years the business shipped wastes to XYZ and the terms of the indemnification in the acquisition agreement,* Enterprise A *believes it is probable that it will recover from the prior*

owners 50 percent of its allocated remediation costs for XYZ, and accordingly, has recorded a receivable of *$5 million* at *December 31, 20XX.*

Example 2: Disclosures for a probable but not reasonably estimable environmental remediation loss contingency.

> Enterprise A has been notified by the U.S. Environmental Protection Agency (EPA) that it is a potentially responsible party (PRP) with respect to environmental impacts *identified at the XYZ site in Sometown, USA. Several meetings have been held with the EPA and the other identified PRPs, and a remedial investigation has recently commenced.* Although a loss is probable, it is not possible at this time to reasonably estimate the amount of any obligation for remediation that would be material to Enterprise A's financial statements *because the extent of environmental impact, allocation among the PRPs, remediation alternatives (which could involve no or minimal efforts), and concurrence of the regulatory authorities have not yet advanced to the stage where a reasonable estimate of any loss that would be material to the enterprise can be made. A reasonable estimate of a material obligation, if any, is expected to be possible in 20XX.*

(e) DISCLOSURES FOR ENVIRONMENTAL CLEANUP COSTS

SOP 96-1 encourages but does not require disclosure of the amount of expenditures for environmental cleanup costs charged to income and the following related information:

- The amount recognized for environmental remediation loss contingencies in each period.
- The amount of any recovery from third parties that is credited to environmental cleanup costs in each period (see Chapter 16).
- The income statement caption in which environmental cleanup costs and credits are included.

(f) ADDITIONAL CONSIDERATIONS FOR PUBLIC COMPANIES

Public companies must adhere to various SEC guidance, particularly SAB 92 (as updated and recodified at SAB 103); Regulation S-K Rules 101, 103, and 303; and Financial Reporting Release No. 36.[1]

As previously noted, measurement of environmental remediation liabilities in accordance with FIN 14 can result in estimates that are significantly lower than estimates developed using the more robust measurement techniques described in ASTM E 2137 (Chapter 25). This raises the question of whether the understatement of environmental remediation liabilities, although reported in conformance with GAAP, may nonetheless result in a failure to fairly present the financial condition of the entity (see § 7.2(a)).

Public companies are required to disclose additional information regarding critical accounting policies (see § 24.5(e)) in the MD&A section of their periodic

[1] Securities Act Release No. 33-6835, 54 Fed. Reg. 22427 (May 24, 1989).

SEC reports. These disclosures are in addition to the financial statement footnote disclosures described in § 20.4(d).

Public companies are also subject to section 404 of Sarbanes-Oxley, which requires entities to design, implement, and periodically assess the operational effectiveness of internal control over financial reporting (see Chapter 8). In addition, section 404 requires the reporting entity's independent financial auditor to examine the entity's internal control over financial reporting and annually attest to its design and operational effectiveness (see Chapter 27).

Internal control over financial reporting of environmental remediation liabilities involves many of the same considerations set forth in § 19.4(e) (internal control over financial reporting of environmental loss contingencies). Exhibit 20.1 lists additional process and control issues that may warrant special attention.

EXHIBIT 20.1

Process and Control Considerations for Environmental Remediation Liabilities

PROCESS AREA	PROCESS AND CONTROL CONSIDERATIONS
Identification	• Identification of asserted and unasserted claims for remediation associated with current and former assets and operations, nonowned disposal sites, and transportation-related incidents • Use of environmental specialists
Assessment	• Determination of milestones for assessment of probability of loss • Evaluation of environmental remediation liabilities separate from related recoveries • Reliance on determinations of legal counsel
Measurement	• Selection and application of measurement techniques • Use of actuaries and other specialists • Determination of ability to reasonably estimate • Evaluation of potential for significant near-term changes in estimated amounts
Reporting	• Selection and application of criteria for assessment of materiality • Display of liabilities and related rights of set off • Disclosures relating to environmental remediation liabilities • Disclosure of environmental cleanup costs • Disclosures related to significant risks and uncertainties

Notwithstanding an effective internal control system design, the operational effectiveness of the system will largely depend on the performance of employees and contractors in carrying out established policies and procedures. Employee and contractor performance in turn will depend largely on the company's control environment with respect to environmental financial reporting (see § 8.2(a)) and personnel qualifications, training, and incentives (or disincentives).

CHAPTER TWENTY-ONE

Environmental Guarantees

21.1 INTRODUCTION

Guarantees are contractual agreements that contingently require the guarantor to make payments (either in cash, financial instruments, other assets, shares of its stock, or provision of services) to the guaranteed party upon the future occurrence of specified events or conditions. *Environmental guarantees* often take the form of indemnity agreements that contingently require the indemnitor to make payments to the indemnified party upon the future occurrence of specified events or conditions giving rise to environmental losses on the part of the indemnified party.

Buyers and sellers of real estate or businesses with known or suspected pollution conditions or other environmental loss contingencies often use indemnity agreements to contractually allocate environmental liabilities and risks. The indemnity agreements often obligate the seller to indemnify the buyer for environmental losses arising from known and unknown preexisting pollution conditions. Buyers are often required to indemnify sellers for pollution conditions arising after close of the sale.

Environmental indemnity agreements are also common in commercial leases and asset-based loan agreements. Sales agreements for products containing hazardous materials (e.g., asbestos-containing materials) may also contain environmental indemnity agreements protecting the buyer from potential future claims by the buyer's employees or customers.

In some circumstances, the parties will not agree to consummate a transaction involving significant environmental loss exposure without an environmental indemnity. In other cases, a significant reduction in the sales price, rental charge, or interest rate may be necessary.

Environmental loss contingencies covered by indemnity agreements may include:

- Third-party bodily injury or property damage claims relating to known historical pollution conditions.
- Cleanup cost overruns associated with known historical pollution conditions.
- Third-party bodily injury or property damage claims and cleanup costs associated with unknown preexisting pollution conditions.
- Diminution in value associated with the postsale discovery of unknown preexisting pollution conditions.
- Increased operating costs and business interruption losses incurred by the indemnified party as a result of undisclosed preexisting pollution conditions.

Frequently, environmental indemnity agreements are designed to cover all environmental losses of the indemnitee, without limit and without deductible. The agreements may be open-ended with no time limit, or may be limited to claims arising within a specified time period. Such indemnity agreements are sometimes assignable with consent, such that the indemnitor is obligated to indemnify the assigns of the indemnified party.

Environmental indemnity agreements are sometimes used as an alternative to comprehensive environmental investigation. Entities holding properties affected by known or suspected historical pollution conditions may prefer to alleviate the concerns of a prospective buyer, tenant, or lender by providing an indemnity rather than conducting a comprehensive environmental investigation to fully delineate the extent of the environmental impact, which could trigger environmental regulatory obligations. The parties may also prefer environmental indemnity agreements to environmental insurance. Environmental insurance may or may not be available for properties with known or suspected pollution conditions if a comprehensive environmental investigation has not been conducted. Indemnification agreements also have the advantage of not requiring an immediate payment of cash to an insurance company.

21.2 RECOGNITION

Prior to the issuance of FASB Interpretation No. 45, "Guarantor's Accounting and Disclosure Requirements for Guarantees, Including Indirect Guarantees of Indebtedness of Others" (FIN 45), there were differing interpretations about the disclosures required of guarantors under FAS 5 and about the need for a guarantor to recognize an initial liability for its obligation under a guarantee. FIN 45 both clarifies the disclosure requirements for guarantees and requires early recognition of a liability for certain aspects of guarantees.

(a) SCOPE

FIN 45 applies to a wide variety of guarantees, including irrevocable standby letters of credit, performance guarantees that require the guarantor to make payments to the guaranteed party based on another entity's failure to perform under an obligating agreement, and indirect guarantees of the indebtedness of others.

FIN 45 also applies to indemnification agreements (contracts) that contingently require the indemnifying party (or guarantor) to make payments to the indemnified party (or guaranteed party) based on changes in an *underlying* that is related to an asset, a liability, or an equity security of the indemnified party (e.g., an adverse judgment in an environmental lawsuit). An *underlying* is a specified interest rate, security price, commodity price, foreign exchange rate, index of prices or rates, or other variables, including the occurrence or nonoccurrence of a specified event (e.g., an environmental loss contingency).

As discussed in § 21.1, indemnification agreements are commonly used to allocate risks for environmental loss contingencies in commercial real estate and business transactions. Typically, such agreements contingently require the indemnifying party (guarantor) to make payments to the indemnified party (guaranteed party) based on changes in an underlying that is related to an asset, a liability, or an equity security of the indemnified party. These agreements thus fall within the scope of FIN 45.

FIN 45 does not encompass indemnifications or guarantees of an entity's own future performance (e.g., a buyer's agreement to indemnify a seller for claims arising from future pollution conditions caused by the buyer after the sale). FIN 45 does not apply to certain guarantee contracts, such as residual value guarantees provided by lessees in capital leases, vendor rebates, product warranties, and guarantees issued between either parents and their subsidiaries or corporations under common control. Warranties against product failure, which are excluded from FIN 45, are differentiated from indemnities covering potential bodily injury or property damage claims arising from use of a product, which *are* covered by FIN 45.

(b) CONTINGENT AND NONCONTINGENT OBLIGATIONS

FIN 45 clarifies that a guarantee represents two distinct obligations on the part of the guarantor. The first is the obligation to stand ready to perform over the term of the guarantee in case the specified triggering events or conditions occur. This obligation comes into existence upon execution of the guarantee. The obligation to stand ready is noncontingent in that it does not depend upon the occurrence of future events or conditions. The second obligation is the obligation to make payments in the event the specified triggering events or conditions occur. This obligation is contingent upon the occurrence of specified future events or conditions.

FIN 45 requires the guarantor to recognize a liability for the noncontingent component of the guarantee at its inception. Entering into a contract or agreement that imposes on the guarantor an ongoing obligation to stand ready to perform over the term of the guarantee warrants immediate recognition of a liability for the obligations under the guarantee, even if it is not probable that the specified triggering events or conditions (that would cause payments under the guarantor's related contingent obligation) will occur.

If a guarantor wants to be relieved of both its obligation to stand ready to perform over the remaining term and its contingent obligation to make future payments (before the triggering events or conditions have occurred and before the term of the guarantee has ended), the guarantor would likely be required to make a payment either to a third party (e.g., an insurance company) to assume the guarantor's obligations or to the original guaranteed party (e.g., a reduction in the sales price for an environmentally impaired asset). The need for the guarantor to make a future payment to be relieved of its obligations under the guarantee confirms the existence of the liability related to the guarantor's obligations under the guarantee. The guarantor's recognition of a liability at the inception of a guarantee for the obligations it has undertaken in issuing the guarantee is consistent with the definition of a liability in Statement of Financial Accounting Concept No. 6, "Elements of Financial Statements," which provides that responsibilities such as those to honor warranties and guarantees also create liabilities.

Paragraph 9 of FIN 45 provides that the manner of initial recognition of the noncontingent component of the guarantee depends on the nature of the transaction:

- When a guarantee is issued in a stand-alone, arm's-length transaction with an unrelated party, the liability recognized at the inception of the guarantee should be the premium received or receivable by the guarantor.
- When a guarantee is issued as part of a transaction with multiple elements with an unrelated party (such as in conjunction with selling an asset or entering into an operating lease), the liability recognized at the inception of the guarantee should be an estimate of the guarantee's fair value. In that circumstance, guarantors should consider what premium would be required by the guarantor to issue the same guarantee in a stand-alone, arm's-length transaction with an unrelated party.
- When a guarantee is issued as a contribution to an unrelated party, the liability recognized at the inception of the guarantee should be measured at its fair value, consistent with the requirement to measure the contribution made at fair value.

The contingent component of the guarantee is analyzed as a loss contingency pursuant to FAS 5. A liability for the contingent obligation thus will be accrued at the inception of the guarantee only in those relatively rare circumstances (e.g., environmental escrow agreements discussed below) in which future payments under the guarantee are deemed probable and the amount of such future payments can be reasonably estimated (see § 19.2).

Environmental indemnity agreements may be used in conjunction with escrow agreements that require the indemnitor to place cash or other assets in an escrow account as financial assurance of performance of the indemnified conditions or events (e.g., remediation of known pollution conditions). For example, the escrow amount may reflect a mutually acceptable estimate of the anticipated costs of addressing the indemnified conditions or events. If it turns out that the escrow funds are insufficient to cover the actual costs, however, the indemnitor is required to pay the difference. Amounts placed in escrow represent contingent components of the indemnity and are analyzed as a loss contingency pursuant to FAS 5. Because future payments from the escrow typically are considered probable and the amount of such future payments can be reasonably estimated (i.e., the amount of the escrow), it will in many cases be appropriate to recognize a contingent liability for some or all of the escrow amount at the inception of the agreement.

(c) EFFECTIVE DATE

The initial recognition and initial measurement provisions of FIN 45 are applicable on a prospective basis to guarantees issued or modified after December 31, 2002, irrespective of the guarantor's fiscal year-end. The disclosure requirements are effective for financial statements of interim or annual periods ending after December 15, 2002. Implementation of FIN 45 on a prospective basis eliminates the burden of gathering historical information about guarantees issued in the past and having to determine the fair value of the guarantee at the time it was issued.

21.3 MEASUREMENT

FIN 45 states that the objective of the initial measurement of the noncontingent component of the liability is the fair value of the guarantee at its inception. Environmental guarantees typically are issued as part of a transaction with an unrelated party involving multiple elements. Accordingly, the liability recognized at the inception of the guarantee should be an estimate of the guarantee's fair value. In that circumstance, the guarantor should consider what premium would be required by the guarantor to issue the same indemnity in a standalone, arm's-length transaction with an unrelated party.

The best evidence of the fair value of environmental indemnities will often be the estimated premium for one or more environmental insurance policies covering the same loss contingencies with comparable limits and deductibles. Because environmental insurance coverage typically is issued on a claims-made basis for a term not exceeding ten years, it may be appropriate to calculate the net present value of premiums for multiple policy renewals approximating the term of the indemnity. For indemnity agreements containing no maximum dollar limits, the quoted insurance policy should have limits approximating the high end of the estimated range of potential environmental loss covered by the indemnity.

As noted previously, environmental indemnity agreements are sometimes used as an alternative to comprehensive environmental investigation. However, environmental insurance premiums, which may be used as evidence of fair value, are generally inversely dependent on the amount of investigation that has been performed. The desire to reduce the fair value of an environmental liability by narrowing the range of values (i.e., reducing the value for the reasonable worst-case scenario) thus may drive the decision to conduct additional research and investigation.

In the absence of quoted market prices for environmental insurance, or observable transactions for identical or similar guarantees, expected present value measurement techniques as set forth in Statement of Financial Accounting Concepts No. 7, "Using Cash Flow Information and Present Value in Accounting Measurements," will likely provide the best estimate of fair value.

If the guarantor is required to recognize a liability under FAS 5 for the contingent component of the guarantee at its inception, the liability to be recognized should be the greater of the fair value of the obligation, or the amount required to be recognized under FAS 5 (see § 19.3).

21.4 DISPLAY AND DISCLOSURE

(a) BALANCE SHEET DISPLAY

FIN 45 requires creation of a liability for the fair value of the noncontingent component of the guarantee at its inception. FIN 45 does not prescribe a specific approach for subsequently measuring the guarantor's recognized liability over the term of the guarantee. The liability that the guarantor initially recognized for the noncontingent component of the guarantee would typically be reduced (by a credit to earnings) as the guarantor is released from risk under the guarantee. Depending on the nature of the guarantee, the guarantor's release from risk may be recognized over the term of the guarantee using a variety of methods, including: upon either expiration or settlement of the guarantee; by a systematic and rational amortization method; or as the fair value of the guarantee changes (e.g., as it might upon the completion of environmental remediation activities).

(b) INCOME STATEMENT DISPLAY

FIN 45 does not prescribe a specific account for the guarantor's offsetting entry when it recognizes the liability at the inception of a guarantee. That offsetting entry depends on the circumstances in which the guarantee was issued. Paragraph 11 of FIN 45 provides the following examples:

- If the guarantee is issued in a stand-alone transaction for a premium, the offsetting entry is the consideration received (such as cash or a receivable).
- If the guarantee is issued in conjunction with the sale of assets, a product, or a business, the overall proceeds (such as the cash received or receivable) are allocated between the consideration being remitted to the guarantor for issuing the guarantee and the proceeds from the sale. The allocation will affect the calculation of the gain or loss on the sale transaction.

- If the guarantee is issued in conjunction with the formation of a partially owned business or a venture accounted for under the equity method, recognition of the liability for the guarantee results in an increase to the carrying amount of the investment.
- If a guarantee is issued to an unrelated party for no consideration, on a stand-alone basis (that is, not in conjunction with any other transaction or ownership relationship), the offsetting entry is to expense.

(c) DISCLOSURE OF ACCOUNTING PRINCIPLES

APB Opinion 22, "Disclosure of Accounting Policies," provides guidance regarding accounting principles that should be described in the accounting policies note to the financial statements. APB Opinion 22, paragraph 12, indicates that entities should disclose those accounting principles that "materially affect the determination of financial position or results of operations." In particular, entities should disclose accounting principles and the methods of applying those principles when alternatives exist. For example, if an entity utilizes present value measurement techniques to determine fair value, additional disclosures are appropriate.

(d) DISCLOSURES FOR ENVIRONMENTAL GUARANTEES

Paragraph 13 of FIN 45 requires a guarantor to disclose the following information about each guarantee, or each group of similar guarantees, even if the likelihood of the guarantor's having to make any payments under the guarantee is remote:

- The nature of the guarantee, including the approximate term of the guarantee, how the guarantee arose, and the events or circumstances that would require the guarantor to perform under the guarantee.

  Note: Many environmental indemnity agreements are confidential, especially those executed in connection with settlement of litigation or preexisting exposure or claims. Reporting entities should consult with legal counsel to determine how to reconcile these conflicting requirements.
- The maximum potential amount of future payments (undiscounted) the guarantor could be required to make under the guarantee (without reduction for any amounts that may possibly be recovered under recourse or collateralization provisions in the guarantee).
  - If the terms of the guarantee provide for no limitation to the maximum potential future payments under the guarantee, that fact must be disclosed.
  - If the guarantor is unable to develop an estimate of the maximum potential amount of future payments under its guarantee, the guarantor must disclose the reasons why it cannot estimate the maximum potential amount.

- The current carrying amount of the liability, if any, for the guarantor's obligations under the guarantee (including the amount, if any, recognized as a contingent liability under FAS 5), regardless of whether the guarantee is freestanding or embedded in another contract.
- The nature of any recourse provisions that would enable the guarantor to recover from third parties any of the amounts paid under the guarantee and any assets held either as collateral or by third parties that, upon the occurrence of any triggering event or condition under the guarantee, the guarantor can obtain and liquidate to recover all or a portion of the amounts paid under the guarantee. The guarantor must indicate, if estimable, the approximate extent to which the proceeds from liquidation of those assets are expected to cover the maximum potential amount of future payments under the guarantee.

(e) ADDITIONAL CONSIDERATIONS FOR PUBLIC COMPANIES

Following issuance of FIN 45, the SEC modified its prior guidance in SAB 92 regarding disclosure with respect to environmental exit costs by expressly referring registrants to the disclosure requirements of FIN 45 for guarantees. The SEC's revised guidance states:

> Additionally, if the registrant may be liable for remediation of environmental damage relating to assets or businesses previously disposed, disclosure should be made in the financial statements unless the likelihood of a material unfavorable outcome of that contingency is remote. [*Footnote:* If the company has a guarantee as defined by Interpretation 45, the entity is required to provide the disclosures and recognize the fair value of the guarantee in the company's financial statements even if the "contingent" aspect of the guarantee is deemed to be remote.] The registrant's accounting policy with respect to such costs should be disclosed in accordance with Opinion 22.[1]

As discussed in §§ 11.3(a) and 11.3(b), material environmental guarantees may be subject to accelerated reporting requirements on Form 8-K. Public companies also are required to disclose additional information regarding critical accounting policies (§24.5(e)) in the MD&A section of their periodic SEC reports. These disclosures are in addition to the financial statement footnote disclosures described in § 21.4(d).

Section 404 of Sarbanes-Oxley imposes requirements on public companies to design, implement, and periodically assess the operational effectiveness of internal control over financial reporting (see Chapter 8). In addition, section 404 requires the reporting entity's independent financial auditor to examine the entity's internal control over financial reporting and annually attest to its design and operational effectiveness (see Chapter 27).

---

[1] Release No. SAB 103, 68 Fed. Reg. 26,840, 26,843 (May 16, 2003), codified at 17 C.F.R. pt. 211, Topic 5.Y, Question 4.

Exhibit 21.1 identifies certain process and control issues with regard to financial reporting of environmental guarantees that may warrant special attention for reporting entities and financial auditors.

EXHIBIT 21.1

Process and Control Considerations for Environmental Guarantees

PROCESS AREA	PROCESS AND CONTROL CONSIDERATIONS
Identification	• Identification of environmental guarantees and indemnities contained in acquisition and sale agreements, lease agreements, financing agreements, product sales agreements, settlement agreements, and so forth • Determination of retroactive date for application of FIN 45 • Monitoring of events that could result in increase or acceleration of the entity's obligations under the guarantees
Assessment	• Evaluation of the relative importance of the noncontingent components of guarantees to the overall transaction • Evaluation of probability of loss associated with contingent components of guarantees • Reliance on determinations of legal counsel
Measurement	• Process for determining fair value • Use of insurance quotes to estimate fair value • Use of actuaries and other specialists
Reporting	• Selection and application of criteria for assessment of materiality • Disclosures relating to guarantees (including confidentiality agreements) • Disclosures related to significant risks and uncertainties • Disclosures under accelerated reporting requirements

Notwithstanding an effective internal control system design, the operational effectiveness of the system will largely depend on the performance of employees and contractors in carrying out established policies and procedures. Employee and contractor performance in turn will depend largely on the company's control environment with respect to environmental financial reporting (see § 8.2(a)) and personnel qualifications, training, and incentives (or disincentives).

CHAPTER TWENTY-TWO

Asset Retirement Obligations

22.1 INTRODUCTION

Asset retirement obligations (AROs) are legal obligations associated with the retirement of a tangible long-lived asset that result from the acquisition, construction, development, and/or normal operation of a tangible long-lived asset. Property, plant, and equipment are examples of tangible long-lived assets.

FAS 143, "Accounting for Asset Retirement Obligations," establishes standards for recognizing and measuring the future costs to retire an asset and recognizing those costs in the financial statements both as a liability and as part of the depreciable cost of the asset. FAS 143 represents a fundamental change from FAS 5, "Accounting for Contingencies" (see Chapter 19), and SOP 96-1, "Environmental Remediation Liabilities" (Chapter 20), in the manner of accounting for certain types of environmental legal obligations. Most notable among the differences between FAS 143 and FAS 5 (as supplemented by SOP 96-1) are:

- FAS 143 applies to enforceable legal obligations without regard to whether future enforcement of the legal obligation is probable.
- Whereas uncertainty regarding uncertain future events is used to decide whether to recognize a liability under FAS 5, uncertainties in the amount and timing of settlement of an ARO are incorporated into the measurement of the liability.
- FAS 143 requires measurement of asset retirement obligations at their fair value. The measurement guidance in FAS 5 and FIN 14, "Reasonable Estimation of the Amount of a Loss," is not applicable to measurement of AROs.

Prior to the issuance of FAS 143, the FASB had found that many companies were either failing to recognize AROs entirely, or, if liabilities were being recognized as incurred, the recognized liabilities were not being measured or presented consistently. The FASB was concerned that diverse practices in accounting for AROs make it difficult for users of financial statements to compare the financial position and results of operations of companies with similar operations that have similar AROs.

FAS 143 was the culmination of an eight-year project by the FASB that initially focused on retirement obligations related to the costs of decommissioning nuclear power plants. The scope of the project was subsequently expanded to include similar closure or removal-type obligations in other industries. The final standard was expanded further and applies to all entities.

FAS 143 applies to all legal obligations associated with the retirement of long-lived assets that result from the acquisition, construction, development, and/or the normal operation of a long-lived asset, except for certain obligations of lessees. Capital lease assets of lessees and lessor assets leased under operating leases are subject to the standard. FAS 143 does not apply to:

- Obligations associated with the temporary idling of long-lived assets.
- Obligations arising solely from a plan to dispose of long-lived assets covered by FAS 144 (see Chapter 23).
- Obligations that result from the improper operation of an asset (e.g., environmental remediation liabilities covered by SOP 96-1; see Chapter 20).
- Obligations of a lessee constituting minimum lease payments or contingent rentals.

Legal obligations arising under environmental laws are a common source of AROs. Environmental laws frequently regulate the manner in which tangible long-lived assets, or components thereof, are disposed, recycled, remediated, or restored upon retirement of the asset.

Prior to FAS 143, unasserted claims for legal obligations arising under environmental laws generally were accounted for as loss contingencies under FAS 5, if at all. FAS 143 is now the prescribed manner to account for almost all environmental legal obligations associated with an entity's property, plant, and equipment. Because the recognition and measurement of environmental legal obligations under FAS 143 is so different from the recognition and measurement of environmental loss contingencies and environmental remediation obligations under FAS 5, entities must pay special attention to selecting and applying the appropriate accounting standards to a given situation.

22.2 RECOGNITION

(a) INITIAL RECOGNITION

FAS 143 requires recognition of a liability for an ARO in the period in which it is incurred if a reasonable estimate of its fair value can be made. If it is not possible to make a reasonable estimate of fair value in the period in which the ARO is incurred, the liability must be recognized when a reasonable estimate of fair value can be made. Guidance on determining when a reasonable estimate of fair value can be made is provided in § 12.4(a).

A liability for an asset retirement obligation may be incurred in a variety of ways. For example:

- *Upon acquisition of the asset.* If a tangible long-lived asset with an existing asset retirement obligation is acquired, a liability for that obligation is recognized at the acquisition date of the asset as if that obligation had been incurred on that date.
- *Upon construction of the asset.* Construction of the asset may involve the use of materials that will be subject to special legal requirements upon renovation or demolition of the asset.
- *Upon incremental use of the asset.* A liability for an ARO may be incurred incrementally over multiple reporting periods if the events that create the obligation occur over multiple reporting periods. Any incremental liability incurred in a subsequent reporting period should be treated as an additional layer of the original liability. Each additional layer should be initially measured at fair value. The liability for decommissioning a nuclear power plant, for example, is incurred over time as the plant is used and contamination occurs. In each period, as contamination increases, a separate layer of liability should be measured and recognized.
- *Upon a change in law or contractual obligations.* Passage of a new law or regulation or execution of a new contractual agreement can give rise to an asset retirement obligation.

(b) SUBSEQUENT RECOGNITION

Following initial recognition of an ARO, the amount of the liability will change as a result of either the passage of time or revisions to the original estimates of either the amounts of estimated cash flows or their timing, or both. Changes can arise due to the effects of inflation, changes in the assumptions relied upon in the original estimate, changes in interest rates, or changes in applicable laws and contracts.

Changes to the liability are recognized by first adjusting the carrying amount of the liability for changes due to the passage of time and then, if applicable, for changes due to revisions in either amounts or timing of estimated cash flows. Changes due to the passage of time increase the carrying amount of the liability. Because there are fewer periods remaining from the initial measurement date until the settlement date (the date at which the asset retirement costs must be paid), the present value of the discounted future amount of the liability for the ARO increases. The amount by which the liability for an ARO increases due to the passage of time is recorded as *accretion expense.* Accretion is computed using an interest method of allocation using the credit-adjusted risk-free rate used in the initial measurement of the liability for the ARO.

Accounting for changes in the ARO that result from changes in the estimates of the timing or amounts of future cash flows varies, depending on whether the changes result in an increase or decrease in the liability. If the expected present value increases, a new incremental liability is recognized following the same methodology used when the ARO was originally measured, but current market value assumptions and the current credit-adjusted risk-free rate are used. Thus, over time, a single long-lived asset may have multiple layers of AROs with each layer based on different assumptions measured at different dates during the asset's life. The incremental liability increases the recorded ARO and the capitalized asset retirement costs included in the carrying amount of the asset. The incremental increase in the carrying amount of the asset is then depreciated in the period of change and future periods, unless the increase affects only the current period, in which case the increase is fully depreciated in that period.

If the expected present value of a recorded liability for an ARO subsequently decreases, the previously recognized layers of liabilities are reduced pro rata and the difference between the new amount and the carrying amount of the liability (after adjustment for inception-to-date accretion) is recorded as a gain in the current period.

FAS 143 does not mandate detailed cash-flow estimates every reporting period. Rather, it allows the entity to exercise judgment as to when facts and circumstances indicate that the initial estimate should be updated.

(c) CONDITIONAL OBLIGATIONS

A *conditional asset retirement obligation* is a legal obligation to perform an asset retirement activity in which the timing and/or method of settlement are conditional on one or more future events that may or may not be within the control of the entity. Before and after the effective date of FAS 143 in June 2002, diverse accounting practices had developed with respect to the timing of liability recognition for conditional AROs. For example, some entities recognized the fair value of the obligation prior to retirement of the asset, regardless of the likelihood that the asset would be retired. Other entities recognized the fair value of the obligation only when it was probable that the asset would be retired or when the asset was in fact retired.

Paragraphs A17 and A18 of FAS 143 specifically address the issue of conditional obligations. These provisions state:

> A17. A conditional obligation to perform a retirement activity is within the scope of this Statement. For example, if a governmental unit retains the right (an option) to decide whether to require a retirement activity, there is some uncertainty about whether those retirement activities will be required or waived. Regardless of the uncertainty attributable to the option, a legal obligation to stand ready to perform retirement activities still exists, and the governmental unit might require them to be performed. Uncertainty about whether performance will be required does not defer the recognition of a retirement obligation; rather, that uncertainty is factored into the measurement of the fair value of the liability through assignment of probabilities to cash flows. Uncertainty about performance of conditional obligations shall not prevent the determination of a reasonable estimate of fair value.
>
> A18. A past history of nonenforcement of an unambiguous obligation does not defer recognition of a liability, but its measurement is affected by the uncertainty over the requirement to perform retirement activities. Uncertainty about the requirement to perform retirement activities shall not prevent the determination of a reasonable estimate of fair value. Guidance on how to estimate a liability in the presence of uncertainty about a requirement to perform retirement activities is provided in Appendix C.

Notwithstanding the statements regarding conditional obligations contained in FAS 143, many accounting firms and reporting entities concluded that FAS 143 did not apply to conditional AROs when the obligation to perform the retirement activity could be deferred indefinitely. To address the diversity in practice that continued after issuance of FAS 143, FASB issued FIN 47, "Accounting for Conditional Asset Retirement Obligations," in March 2005. FIN 47 clarifies that an entity must recognize a liability for a conditional ARO if the fair value of the liability can be reasonably estimated.

According to paragraph B11 of FIN 47, when an existing law, regulation, or contract obligates an entity to perform an asset retirement activity upon retirement of the asset, an unambiguous requirement to perform the retirement activity exists—even if that activity can be deferred indefinitely. At some point, deferral is no longer possible, as no tangible asset (except land) will last forever. The obligation to perform the asset retirement activity is unconditional even though uncertainty exists about the timing and/or method of settlement. Consequently, the fair value of conditional AROs should be recognized when the obligation is incurred—generally upon the acquisition, construction, or development of the asset, or through the normal operation of the asset. In sharp contrast to FAS 5, uncertainty regarding the timing and method of settlement of an ARO due to future contingencies (including management's intent to indefinitely defer settlement of the obligation) must be factored into the measurement of the liability rather than the recognition of the liability. If there is insufficient information to estimate the ARO, the liability should be recognized initially in the period in which sufficient information is available to estimate its fair value.

FIN 47 also clarifies when an entity would have sufficient information to reasonably estimate the fair value of an ARO, in light of existing uncertainties as to the timing or method of settlement of the obligation (see §§ 12.4(a) and (b)).

FIN 47 is effective for fiscal years ending after December 15, 2005 (December 31, 2005, for calendar-year enterprises). Paragraphs 9 and 10 of FIN 47 provide the following transition rules:

- For amounts recognized upon the initial application of FIN 47 the following items are recognized in the statement of financial position: (a) a liability for any existing asset retirement obligation(s) adjusted for cumulative accretion, (b) an asset retirement cost capitalized as an increase to the carrying amount of the associated long-lived asset(s), and (c) accumulated depreciation on that capitalized cost.
- Amounts resulting from initial application of FIN 47 are measured using current information, current assumptions, and current interest rates.
- The amount recognized as an asset retirement cost is measured as of the date the asset retirement obligation was incurred.
- Cumulative accretion and accumulated depreciation is recorded for the time period from the date the liability would have been recognized had the provisions of FIN 47 been in effect when the liability was incurred to the date of adoption of FIN 47 by the reporting entity.
- The cumulative effect of initially applying FIN 47 is recognized as a change in accounting principle.

(d) ENVIRONMENTAL LEGAL OBLIGATIONS

For purposes of FAS 143, a *legal obligation* is "an obligation that a party is required to settle as a result of existing or enacted law, statute, ordinance, written or oral contract or by legal construction under the doctrine of promissory estoppel." Promissory estoppel is an equitable legal doctrine used to enforce a promise in the absence of a valid contract if the promisor should have reasonably expected the promisee to rely on the promise and if the promisee did actually rely on the promise to his or her detriment.

Environmental legal obligations may arise under:

- Environmental laws, regulations, and permits.
- Enforcement and litigation.
- Contractual agreements, such as agreements between property buyers and sellers, landlords and tenants, and lenders and borrowers.
- Promissory estoppel.

(i) ENVIRONMENTAL LAWS, REGULATIONS, AND PERMITS

Legal obligations relating to the retirement of tangible long-lived assets can arise under many of the environmental laws described in Chapter 3, including CERCLA, RCRA, TSCA, and corresponding state and foreign laws.

(A) Enforced vs. Enforceable Legal Obligations

For purposes of FAS 143, the existence of a legal obligation arising under an environmental statute does not depend on a determination of the likelihood that the obligation will be enforced. A past history of nonenforcement of an unambiguous environmental legal obligation does not defer recognition of that liability. Rather, the uncertainty over the requirement to perform the retirement activities is considered in the measurement of the ARO.

When the only uncertainty is whether performance of a legal obligation will be enforced, and there is no information about which outcome is more probable, paragraph A23 of FAS 143 assumes a 50 percent likelihood for each outcome (obligation is enforced or obligation is not enforced) in determining the fair value of the obligation.

In contrast to recognition of environmental loss contingencies under FAS 5, uncertainty about the requirement to perform retirement activities cannot be used as a basis to avoid initial recognition of an ARO under FAS 143.

(B) Historical Pollution Conditions

A critical issue in determining the applicability of FAS 143 to historical pollution conditions is whether the owner of the property has a legal obligation to clean up the contamination in the absence of a government order to do so. This question must be resolved by the entity's legal advisors based on an analysis of the particular facts and relevant environmental law.

A key factor in this analysis is the determination of the obligating event (see § 18.2(b)). For purposes of assessing the probability criterion for an environmental remediation liability under FAS 5 and SOP 96-1, the *obligating event* is the event or circumstance that obligates the entity to settle the obligation by paying cash, transferring other assets, or providing services to one or more other entities. For purposes of determining whether a legal obligation for cleanup of historical pollution conditions exists under FAS 143, the obligating event is likely to be one of the following:

- Release of pollution to the environment.
- Discovery of the release.
- Enactment of laws making the owner of the property responsible for cleanup.
- Acquisition of property with preexisting contamination.

(C) Physical Controls

If buildings, structures, or other improvements are used as physical controls under risk-based corrective action programs, the entity may have a legal obligation to maintain these controls in perpetuity, even after the property is retired. Alternatively, if perpetual maintenance of such physical controls cannot be assured following retirement of the property, the entity may be legally obligated to conduct further cleanup so that such physical controls are no longer needed to satisfy the applicable risk-based cleanup objectives.

(D) Contaminated Components

Environmental laws require special handling and disposal of a wide range of spent materials used in the operation of long-lived assets. For example, environmental laws may require special handling and disposal of oil and gas exploration equipment contaminated with naturally occurring radioactive material, engine oil used in motorized vehicles and equipment, and transformers and batteries used to power buildings and equipment.

(E) Hazardous Building Materials

Environmental laws may require building owners to handle and dispose of asbestos-containing materials and other hazardous building materials and components in a special manner when buildings are renovated or demolished.

(ii) ENFORCEMENT AND LITIGATION

Recognition of an ARO under FAS 143 is not triggered by the threat (by governments or other parties) of litigation or of assertion of a claim or an assessment. Accordingly, FAS 143 does not apply to environmental loss contingencies (Chapter 19) or environmental remediation liabilities (Chapter 20) meeting the probability criterion under FAS 5 and SOP 96-1, respectively. By definition, such liabilities arise from pending or probable future legal proceedings to enforce existing legal obligations. Final judgments and settlement agreements, however, may give rise to environmental AROs. For example, a requirement in an EPA consent decree to perform closure and postclosure care at a facility owned or operated by the entity would constitute an environmental legal obligation under FAS 143.

(iii) CONTRACTUAL AGREEMENTS

Contracts between entities involving contaminated properties often contain an obligation for one party or the other to perform environmental remediation activities. In many cases, environmental law requires some level of remediation. The parties, however, may agree to perform a level of remediation beyond that required by law. For example, a lease agreement may require the property owner to clean up any environmental contamination resulting from historical activities to background conditions, even though the law would only require the owner to remediate the property to risk-based levels.

The other party may decide in the future to waive the obligation, or that party may have a history of waiving similar provisions in other contracts. Even if there is a reasonable expectation of a waiver or nonenforcement, the contract still imposes a legal obligation. The likelihood of waiver or nonenforcement is not considered with regard to recognition of an ARO, but is considered in the measurement of the liability.

(iv) EQUITABLE OBLIGATIONS

As discussed in § 18.1, liabilities can arise from equitable as well as legal obligations. Paragraph A4 of FAS 143 provides the following example of a situation in which the equitable doctrine of promissory estoppel can give rise to an asset retirement obligation:

> [A]ssume a company operates a manufacturing facility and has plans to retire it within five years. Members of the local press have begun to publicize the fact that when the company ceases operations at the plant, it plans to abandon the site without demolishing the building and restoring the underlying land. Due to the significant negative publicity and demands by the public that the company commit to dismantling the plant upon retirement, the company's chief executive officer holds a press conference at city hall to announce that the company will demolish the building and restore the underlying land when the company ceases operations at the plant. Although no law, statute, ordinance, or written contract exists requiring the company to perform any demolition or restoration activities, the promise made by the company's chief executive officer may have created a legal obligation under the doctrine of promissory estoppel. In that circumstance, the company's management (and legal counsel, if necessary) would have to evaluate the particular facts and circumstances to determine whether a legal obligation exists.

In this example, the company's chief executive officer promises to restore the underlying land after demolishing the building. This could be an ambiguous commitment under risk-based environmental cleanup programs, which often allow responsible persons to clean up contamination to any one of several levels, including preexisting background conditions, human health-based standards without use of institutional or physical controls, and human health-based standards with use of institutional or physical controls. If, in the preceding example, the company's chief executive officer had promised to restore the underlying land to its pristine condition prior to the company's operations, he may have legally obligated the company to undertake a much more expensive and time-consuming environmental cleanup than might otherwise have been minimally required under existing law.

(v) RESULTING FROM THE ACQUISITION, CONSTRUCTION, DEVELOPMENT, AND/OR NORMAL OPERATION

Environmental legal obligations may result from the acquisition, construction, development, and/or normal operation of a long-lived asset. Such obligations can arise from changes in environmental regulations and contractual obligations, acquisition of assets subject to existing environmental legal obligations, construction of an asset, or activities that result in actual or threatened releases of pollutants into the environment.

(A) Changes in Environmental Regulations and Contractual Obligations

If environmental regulations imposing new legal obligations become effective after the date of acquisition of the asset, the obligating event for purposes of FAS 143 is the enactment of the regulations. Similarly, if the entity enters into a contractual obligation, after the date of acquisition of the asset, to undertake environmental response actions that the entity is not otherwise legally obligated to perform, the obligating event is the execution of the contract.

(B) Asset Acquisition

If environmental laws are in place, at the date of acquisition of an asset, that impose environmental legal obligations, the obligating event is the acquisition of the asset. For example, an oil company may assume an ARO when it acquires an oil refinery with existing soil and groundwater contamination resulting from historical operations at the facility, if existing environmental laws or regulations require the company to dismantle and dispose of the refinery and clean up any existing environmental contamination upon discontinuation of refinery operations. Although performance of the asset retirement activity is conditional on removing the refinery from service, existing environmental law creates a duty or responsibility for the entity to dismantle the refinery in a special manner, and the obligating event occurs when the company acquires the refinery. When property subject to an existing environmental remediation obligation is acquired, a liability for that obligation must be recognized at the acquisition date of the asset as if that obligation had been incurred on that date.

(C) Construction

In certain cases, the construction of an asset may be subject to special environmental obligations upon the disposal of the asset. Hazardous materials still used in the construction of new buildings, such as light ballasts and switches containing mercury, may be subject to existing regulations that create a duty or responsibility for the entity to remove and dispose of these materials in a special manner. In such cases, the obligating event occurs when the entity constructs the building.

Under federal and state risk-based corrective action programs, governmental regulators may approve the construction of buildings or structures on top of contaminated soils to prevent human exposure to the contamination and leaching of contamination into groundwater. In such cases, it may be unlawful for the entity to remove the building or structure without cleanup of the soil contamination underneath. In such cases, the obligation to conduct future soil remediation occurs when the entity constructs the building or structure.

(D) Activities That Result in Actual or Threatened Releases of Pollutants to the Environment

Assets that are not subject to environmental legal obligations at the time of acquisition or construction may become subject to such obligations as a result of normal use when such use results in the actual or threatened releases of pollutants to the environment.

For example, nuclear fuel rods, which emit relatively little radioactivity when new, become contaminated after nuclear fission has taken place in the reactor. The nuclear power plant has a long useful life, but the fuel rods are replaced periodically. Environmental laws require that when the spent fuel rods are removed, they must be handled and disposed of in a special manner. If, as of the purchase date, the fuel rods have not yet been used in a nuclear reaction process, the rods would not yet have been contaminated. Therefore, at the date of purchase no obligation exists, because the fuel rods have not been contaminated and could be removed without the need for any special disposal activities.

However, the fair value of the cost to properly dispose of contaminated fuel rods must be recognized once the power plant has been placed into operation and the fuel rods have become contaminated.

Operation of the asset also may result in contamination of soil and groundwater, triggering legal requirements to perform environmental remediation. Here FAS 143 makes a distinction between "normal operation" and "improper (other than normal) operation" of the asset. FAS 143 applies to environmental cleanup obligations arising from the "normal operation" of a tangible long-lived asset. Environmental cleanup obligations that result from the improper (other than normal) operation of an asset (e.g., penalties and fines such as those described in SOP 96-1, "Environmental Remediation Liabilities"), however, are not accounted for as AROs.

The ability to delay environmental remediation until the related asset is retired is an indicator that the obligation arises from normal operation of the asset. For example, paragraph A13 of FAS 143 states that a certain amount of spillage may be inherent in the normal operations of a fuel storage facility, but a catastrophic accident caused by noncompliance with a company's safety procedures is not. Thus, FAS 143 applies to the environmental remediation of soils and groundwater contaminated by releases considered to be inherent in the normal operations of a facility and for which immediate response actions are not required. Conversely, FAS 143 does not apply to cleanup obligations arising from sudden and accidental pollution conditions for which emergency response action is required.

(vi) ASSOCIATION WITH ASSET RETIREMENT

Legal obligations arising under environmental laws may or may not be expressly tied to the retirement of the related asset. For example, the legal obligation to remediate historical pollution conditions under CERCLA is not triggered by the retirement of the contaminated property. Conversely, the legal obligation to abate asbestos-containing building materials is triggered by the renovation or demolition of the building.

Even though the legal obligation may not be directly triggered by the retirement of the asset, the obligation may nonetheless be "associated with" the retirement of the asset. In this regard, it is significant that FAS 143 broadly defines *retirement* to include the "sale" of the asset. Economically, the owner of an asset that is subject to existing environmental legal obligations, such as a property affected by confirmed historical pollution conditions, has five options available:

1. Sell the asset subject to the obligation to settle the legal obligation (e.g., remediated existing soil and groundwater contamination), in which case the owner must accept a lower price from a buyer in return for the buyer's assumption of the obligation.
2. Sell the asset at a higher price, but promise to reimburse the buyer for the costs to settle the legal obligation.
3. Settle the obligation before sale of the asset.

4. Maintain the asset until the end of its useful life and then settle the obligation.
5. Abandon the asset without settling the legal obligation, thereby sacrificing the residual value of the asset while incurring a perpetual obligation to pay for taxes, insurance, maintenance, and security on a nonproductive asset.

In each case, the existence of the legal obligation directly affects the owner's exit strategy for the asset. Only the timing and amount of the liability are in question (see § 18.2(b)(i)).

(e) EXAMPLES OF ENVIRONMENTAL AROs

Following are three examples of conditional AROs based on environmental legal obligations included in Appendix A ("Illustrative Examples") to FIN 47.

(i) CHEMICALLY TREATED UTILITY POLES

> A telecommunications entity owns and operates a communication network that utilizes wood poles that are treated with certain chemicals. There is no legal requirement to remove the poles from the ground. However, the owner may replace the poles periodically for a number of operational reasons. Once the poles are removed from the ground, they may be disposed of, sold, or reused as part of other activities. There is existing legislation that requires special disposal procedures for the poles in the particular state in which the entity operates.
>
> At the date of purchase of the treated poles, the entity has the information to estimate a range of potential settlement dates, the potential methods of settlement, and the probabilities associated with the potential settlement dates and methods based on established industry practice. Therefore, at the date of purchase, the entity is able to estimate the fair value of the liability for the required disposal procedures using an expected present value technique.
>
> Although the timing of the performance of the asset retirement activity is conditional on removing the poles from the ground and disposing of them, existing legislation creates a duty or responsibility for the entity to dispose of the poles in accordance with special procedures, and the obligating event occurs when the entity purchases the treated poles. Although the entity may decide not to remove the poles from the ground or may decide to reuse the poles and thereby defer settlement of the obligation, the ability to defer settlement does not relieve the entity of the obligation. The poles will eventually need to be disposed of using special procedures, because the poles will not last forever. Additionally, the ability of the entity to sell the poles prior to disposal does not relieve the entity of its present duty or responsibility to settle the obligation. The sale of the poles transfers the obligation to another entity. The assumption of the obligation by the buyer affects the exchange price. The bargaining of the exchange price reflects the buyer's and seller's individual estimates of the timing and (or) amount of the cost to extinguish the obligation.

The asset retirement obligation should be recognized when the entity purchases the poles because the entity has sufficient information to estimate the fair value of the asset retirement obligation. Because the legal requirement relates only to the disposal of the treated poles, the cost to remove the poles is not included in the asset retirement obligation. However, if there was a legal requirement to remove the treated poles, the cost of removal would be included.[1]

(ii) *CONTAMINATED ALUMINUM KILN BRICKS*

An entity recently purchased several kilns lined with a special type of brick. As of the date of purchase, the kilns had not yet been used in any smelting processes. The kilns have a long useful life, but the bricks are replaced periodically. Because the bricks become contaminated with hazardous chemicals while the kiln is operated, a state law requires that when the bricks are removed, they must be disposed of at a special hazardous waste site. The entity has the information to estimate a range of potential settlement dates, the method of settlement, and the probabilities associated with the potential settlement dates based on its past practice of replacing the bricks to maintain the efficient operation of the kiln. Therefore, at the date the bricks become contaminated because of the operation of the kiln, the entity is able to estimate the fair value of the liability for the required disposal procedures using an expected present value technique.

Although performance of the asset retirement activity is conditional on removing the bricks from the kiln, existing legislation creates a duty or responsibility for the entity to dispose of the bricks at a special hazardous waste site, and the obligating event occurs when the entity contaminates the bricks. As of the purchase date, the kilns have not yet been used in any smelting processes, and the bricks have not yet been contaminated. Therefore, at the date of purchase, no obligation exists because the bricks have not been contaminated and could be disposed of without performing any special disposal activities.

The fair value of the asset retirement obligation should be recognized once the kilns have been placed into operation and the bricks are contaminated. Although the entity may decide not to remove the bricks from the kiln and thereby defer settlement of the obligation, the ability to defer settlement does not relieve the entity of the obligation. The contaminated bricks will eventually need to be removed and disposed of at a special hazardous waste site, because a kiln will not last forever. Therefore, the obligation to perform the asset retirement activity is unconditional even though uncertainty exists about the timing of settlement. An asset retirement obligation should be recognized once the kilns have been placed into operation and the bricks are contaminated because the entity has sufficient information to estimate the fair value of the asset retirement obligation. The asset retirement obligation is the requirement to dispose of the contaminated bricks at a special hazardous waste site. The cost to remove the bricks is not part of the obligation and should be accounted for as a maintenance or replacement activity.[2]

---

1 FIN 47, ¶¶ A2–A5.
2 FIN 47, ¶¶ A6–A8.

(iii) *ASBESTOS-CONTAINING MATERIALS*

An entity acquires a factory that contains asbestos. At the acquisition date, regulations are in place that require the entity to handle and dispose of this type of asbestos in a special manner if the factory undergoes major renovations or is demolished. Otherwise, the entity is not required to remove the asbestos from the factory. The entity has several options to retire the factory in the future, including demolishing, selling, or abandoning it. At the acquisition date, it is not evident that the fair value of the obligation is embodied in the acquisition price of the factory because both the seller and the buyer of the factory believed the obligation had an indeterminate settlement date, an active market does not exist for the transfer of the obligation, and sufficient information does not exist to apply an expected present value technique. Ten years after the acquisition date, the entity obtains additional information based on changes in demand for the products manufactured at that factory. At that time, the entity has the information to estimate a range of potential settlement dates, the potential methods of settlement, and the probabilities associated with the potential settlement dates and potential methods of settlement. Therefore, at that time the entity is able to estimate the fair value of the liability for the special handling of the asbestos using an expected present value technique.

Although timing of the performance of the asset retirement activity is conditional on the factory undergoing major renovations or being demolished, existing regulations create a duty or responsibility for the entity to remove and dispose of asbestos in a special manner, and the obligating event occurs when the entity acquires the factory. [*Footnote: In this example, regulations are in place at the date of acquisition that require the entity to handle and dispose of the asbestos in a special manner. Therefore, the obligating event is the acquisition of the factory. If regulations were enacted after the date of acquisition, the obligating event would be the enactment of the regulations.*] Although the entity may decide to abandon the factory and thereby defer settlement of the obligation for the foreseeable future, the ability to defer settlement does not relieve the entity of the obligation. The asbestos will eventually need to be removed and disposed of in a special manner, because no building will last forever. Additionally, the ability of the entity to sell the factory does not relieve the entity of its present duty or responsibility to settle the obligation. The sale of the asset would transfer the obligation to another entity and that transfer would affect the selling price. Therefore, the obligation to perform the asset retirement activity is unconditional even though uncertainty exists about the timing and method of settlement.

In this example, an asset retirement obligation is not recognized when the entity acquires the factory because the entity does not have sufficient information to estimate the fair value of the obligation. The entity would disclose (a) a description of the obligation, (b) the fact that a liability has not been recognized because the fair value cannot be reasonably estimated, and (c) the reasons why fair value cannot be reasonably estimated. An asset retirement obligation would be recognized by this entity 10 years after the acquisition date because that is when the entity has sufficient information to estimate the fair value of the asset retirement obligation.[3]

(f) FINANCIAL ASSURANCE PROVISIONS

Environmental laws or other factors may require or cause an entity to provide third parties with assurance that the entity will be able to satisfy its environmental legal obligations in the future. Instruments such as surety bonds, insurance policies, letters of credit, guarantees, trust funds, and custodial arrangements may be used to provide such assurances. Providing such assurance does not satisfy the underlying obligation. The existence of funding and assurance provisions, however, may affect the determination of the credit-adjusted risk-free rate used in calculating the expected present value of the liability. Costs associated with funding and assurance provisions are accounted for separate from the asset retirement obligation.

(g) IMPAIRMENT

Assets with recognized environmental-related AROs may also be impaired (see Chapter 23). When testing an asset for impairment under FAS 144:

- Capitalized asset retirement costs should be included in the carrying amount of the asset.
- Estimated future cash flows related to the liability for the asset retirement obligation should be excluded from the undiscounted cash flows used to test the asset for recoverability and the discounted cash flows used to measure the fair value of the asset.

If the fair value of the asset is based on a quoted market price and that price considers the costs that will be incurred in retiring that asset, the quoted market price should be increased by the fair value of the ARO.

FAS 143 does not apply to obligations that arise solely from a plan to sell or otherwise dispose of a long-lived asset covered by FAS 144 (see § 23.2(b)). For example, brokerage commissions, legal fees, title transfer fees, and other closing costs that must be incurred prior to transfer of legal title do not constitute AROs.

22.3 MEASUREMENT

AROs are measured at fair value. The fair value of a liability for an ARO is the amount at which the liability could be settled in a current transaction between willing parties (e.g., other than in a forced or liquidation transaction). Whereas debt instruments such as promissory notes represent a liability to the debtor and a corresponding asset to the creditor, environmental cleanup obligations are one-sided—they do not represent assets of the government or other identifiable

[3] FIN 47, ¶¶ A11–A13.

individuals. Therefore, unlike debt instruments, environmental liabilities cannot be measured by reference to the market value of a corresponding asset. The fair value of AROs for environmental cleanup costs typically must be measured instead by observing (or, if direct observation is not possible, estimating) the price that the entity has paid (or would have to pay) a third party having a comparable credit rating to assume the liability.

FIN 47 specifies that the fair value of an ARO may be determined based upon:

- The amount of the obligation embedded in the acquisition price of the asset;
- A market quote in an active market for transfer of the obligation; or (if neither of these two situations applies)
- Application of an expected present value technique to estimate fair value.

The negotiated amount of an environmental ARO embedded in the acquisition price of the asset is determinative evidence of the fair value of the obligation. Evidence of the fair value of an ARO (or some portion thereof) may be reflected in several ways, including:

- A reduction in the purchase price of the asset to reflect the ARO.
- The existence of an indemnity agreement provided by the seller to protect the buyer from future losses arising from the ARO and the reduction in purchase price that would have been required to consummate the transaction in the absence of such indemnity. (The value of indemnity agreements must be valued in accordance with FIN 45, as discussed in Chapter 21.)
- An environmental insurance contract purchased in connection with the transaction to protect the buyer from future losses arising from the ARO.
- The existence and amount of financial assurance instruments (e.g., escrow, performance bonds, and so forth).

A market quote in an active market for transfer of the liability also provides determinative evidence of the fair value of the obligation. Active markets exist for the transfer of many types of environmental obligations, including obligations to address historical pollution conditions. The fair value of such obligations may be determined based on the quoted premium to transfer the obligation to an insurance company (or other third party) using various combinations of finite risk and environmental cost-cap insurance. Finite risk insurance involves the current payment of the expected net present value of future cleanup costs to the insurance carrier. Thereafter, the insurer bears the risks of investment return and timing of cash outflows. Cost-cap (stop-loss) insurance protects against unanticipated overruns in estimated cleanup costs.

Beyond a base amount of information necessary before an insurer will consider underwriting an environmental cleanup risk, quoted premiums for environmental insurance are generally inversely dependent on the amount of available data. The desire to reduce quoted premiums for transfer of environmental AROs by narrowing the range of values (i.e., reducing the value for the reasonable worst-case scenario) may thus drive the decision to conduct additional investigation.

Actual negotiated transactions and quoted market prices in active markets are the best evidence of fair value and should be used, if available. If such information is not available, fair value should be estimated by applying the expected present value techniques set forth in SFAC 7, using the best information available in the circumstances. When using present value techniques to estimate the fair value of a liability, the objective is to estimate the value of the assets required currently to settle the liability with the holder or to transfer the liability to an entity of comparable credit standing.

In estimating the fair value of a liability for an ARO using an expected present value technique, an entity begins by estimating cash flows that reflect, to the extent possible, a marketplace assessment of the cost and timing of performing the required retirement activities. The measurement objective is to determine the amount a third party would demand to assume the obligation. Considerations in estimating those cash flows include developing and incorporating explicit assumptions, to the extent possible, about all of the following:

- The costs that a third party would incur in performing the tasks necessary to retire the asset.
- Other amounts that a third party would include in determining the price of settlement (for example, inflation, overhead, equipment charges, profit margin, and advances in technology).
- The extent to which the amount of a third party's costs or the timing of its costs would vary under different future scenarios, and the relative probabilities of those scenarios.
- The price that a third party would demand and could expect to receive for bearing the uncertainties and unforeseeable circumstances inherent in the obligation, sometimes referred to as a *market-risk premium* (e.g., the premium charged for a cost-cap insurance policy to cover unanticipated cost overruns).

Uncertainties about the amount and timing of future cash flows can be accommodated using the expected cash-flow technique and therefore generally should not prevent the determination of a reasonable estimate of fair value. Guidance on determining when a reasonable estimate of fair value can be made is provided in § 12.4(a).

Aggregation techniques may be used to derive a collective asset retirement obligation when assets with AROs are components of a larger group of assets (e.g., a number of oil wells that make up an entire oil field operation). Estimates and computational shortcuts that are consistent with the fair value measurement objective may be used when computing an aggregate asset retirement obligation.

22.4 DISPLAY AND DISCLOSURE

(a) BALANCE SHEET DISPLAY

The initial accounting for an ARO involves both the recognition of a liability and the recapitalization of the related long-lived asset. First, the fair value of the legal obligation is recognized as a liability. Next, the carrying amount of the related asset is increased by the same amount as the liability. In this manner, the recognized cost of the asset increases, because the asset retirement costs are added to the carrying amount of the asset. Similarly, assets acquired with an existing retirement obligation are presented on a gross rather than a net basis.

The following simplified example demonstrates how FAS 143 captures the economic reality of cleanup obligations associated with contaminated properties.

> On January 1, 20XX, Company A buys a warehouse and five acres of land for $500,000. The property has known soil and groundwater contamination; however, there is no pending legal action to compel cleanup. In pristine condition, the property has a fair market value of $2,500,000. Cleanup costs are estimated to be $2,000,000.
>
> Prior to FAS 143, Company A would record the land and warehouse as an asset in the amount of $500,000 and would not recognize a liability for the estimated cleanup costs under FAS 5. Under FAS 143, Company A records an ARO in the amount of $2,000,000 and increases the carrying amount of the related asset by the same amount as the liability. Thus, the land and warehouse is shown with a gross carrying value of $2,500,000 along with an associated liability of $2,000,000. While the net amount of the asset minus the liability ($500,000) is the same as before, FAS 143 provides information about the estimated cleanup costs that would otherwise not be reported in the financial statements.

(b) INCOME STATEMENT DISPLAY

The capitalized asset retirement cost is subsequently allocated (depreciated) to expense over the remaining useful life of the asset using a systematic and rational method selected by the entity. This can be as simple as allocating an equal amount of asset retirement expense to each remaining year of the asset's useful life. For example, if the asset has an estimated life of ten years, the entity could choose to expense one-tenth of the asset retirement cost each year.

Capitalized asset retirement costs do not qualify as expenditures for purposes of paragraph 16 of FASB Statement No. 34, "Capitalization of Interest Cost."

(c) DISCLOSURE OF ACCOUNTING PRINCIPLES

APB Opinion 22, "Disclosure of Accounting Policies," provides guidance regarding accounting principles that should be described in the accounting policies note to the financial statements. APB Opinion 22, paragraph 12, indicates that entities should disclose those accounting principles that "materially affect the determination of financial position or results of operations." In particular, entities should disclose accounting principles and the methods of applying those principles when alternatives exist. With respect to environmental-related AROs, the financial statements should disclose the method or methods for determining fair value (whether based on a quoted market price, prices for similar assets, or another valuation technique).

(d) DISCLOSURES FOR AROs

The entity must disclose the following information about its asset retirement obligations:

- A general description of the ARO and the related asset(s).
- An explanation of how the fair value of the ARO was determined.
- The funding policy, if any, for the ARO and the fair value of assets dedicated to satisfy the liability, if any.
- A reconciliation of the beginning and ending aggregate carrying amount of the liability for the ARO, showing separately the changes attributable to:
    - The liability incurred in the current period;
    - The liability settled in the current period;
    - Accretion expense; and
    - Revisions in expected cash flows.

In circumstances in which the liability for an ARO cannot be reasonably estimated, the entity is required to disclose a description of the obligation, the fact that a liability has not been recognized because the fair value cannot be estimated reasonably, and the reasons why fair value cannot be estimated reasonably.

(e) ADDITIONAL CONSIDERATIONS FOR PUBLIC COMPANIES

Following the issuance of FAS 143, the SEC staff revised its prior guidance in SAB 92 on the appropriate accounting for site restoration costs, postclosure and monitoring costs, or other environmental costs incurred at the end of the useful life of an asset. SAB 92 reflected the SEC's pre-FAS 143 view that:

- Accrual of environmental exit costs over the useful life of the asset was an established accounting practice in some industries.
- In some circumstances, the use of the asset in operations gives rise to growing exit costs that represent a contingent liability under FAS 5. In such cases, the SEC would not object to recognition of the accrual of the liability as an expense in accordance with the consensus on EITF Issue 90-8.[4]

[4] Release No. SAB 92, 58 Fed. Reg. 32,843, 32,846 (June 14, 1993).

According to the SEC, its prior guidance on accounting for environmental exit costs is "no longer relevant due to the issuance of Statement 143, which establishes accounting standards for recognition and measurement of liabilities for asset retirement obligations and associated asset retirement costs."[5]

The SEC also modified its prior guidance regarding disclosure with respect to environmental exit costs by expressly referring registrants to the disclosure requirements of FAS 143 and to FIN 45 for guarantees. The SEC's revised guidance states:

> Registrants are reminded that Statement 143 provides guidance for accounting and reporting for costs associated with asset retirement obligations. The staff believes that material liabilities for site restoration, post-closure, and monitoring commitments, or other exit costs that may occur on the sale, disposal, or abandonment of a property as a result of unanticipated contamination of the asset should be disclosed in the notes to the financial statements. Appropriate disclosures generally would include the nature of the costs involved, the total anticipated cost, the total costs accrued to date, the balance sheet classification of accrued amounts, and the range or amount of reasonably possible additional losses. If an asset held for sale or development will require remediation to be performed by the registrant prior to development, sale, or as a condition of sale, a note to the financial statements should describe how the necessary expenditures are considered in the assessment of the asset's value and the possible need to reflect an impairment loss. Additionally, if the registrant may be liable for remediation of environmental damage relating to assets or businesses previously disposed, disclosure should be made in the financial statements unless the likelihood of a material unfavorable outcome of that contingency is remote. [*Footnote:* If the company has a guarantee as defined by Interpretation 45, the entity is required to provide the disclosures and recognize the fair value of the guarantee in the company's financial statements even if the "contingent" aspect of the guarantee is deemed to be remote.] The registrant's accounting policy with respect to such costs should be disclosed in accordance with Opinion 22.[6]

Public companies are required to disclose additional information regarding critical accounting policies (§ 24.5(e)) in the MD&A section of their periodic SEC reports. These disclosures are in addition to the financial statement footnote disclosures described in § 22.4(d).

Section 404 of Sarbanes-Oxley imposes requirements on public companies to design, implement, and periodically assess the operational effectiveness of internal control over financial reporting (see Chapter 8). In addition, section 404 requires the reporting entity's independent financial auditor to examine the entity's internal control over financial reporting and annually attest to its design and operational effectiveness (see Chapter 27).

Internal control over financial reporting of AROs presents a difficult set of challenges for several reasons, including:

---

5 Release No. SAB 103, 68 Fed. Reg. 26,840, 26,843 (May 16, 2003).

6 Release No. SAB 103, 68 Fed. Reg. 26,840, 26,843 (May 16, 2003), codified at 17 C.F.R. pt. 211, Topic 5.Y, Question 4.

- AROs are not triggered by notice of a claim. Identification of AROs therefore is not a passive exercise of waiting to be notified by the government or a private party of an alleged environmental cleanup obligation. Identification of AROs requires a proactive investigative process.
- Although many entities exercise extensive environmental due diligence to identify potentially material environmental liabilities and loss contingencies prior to closing acquisition transactions, internal application of such procedures to the entity's own assets and operations is less common.
- FAS 143 requires an ongoing periodic reassessment of recognized AROs.
- Discovery and assessment of environmental AROs may be a highly sensitive matter, because of the competing objectives discussed in Chapter 5. This raises increased concerns about the potential for management override of stated policies and procedures.
- Reporting entities may have acquired assets subject to agreements that the entity will not voluntarily investigate historical pollution conditions affecting the assets ("no-look" agreements). Section 404 and FAS 143 may conflict with these contractual restrictions.
- The prescribed measurement approach for AROs is significantly different from the approach used to measure environmental remediation liabilities. Application of the fair value measurement technique to environmental cleanup obligations will be unfamiliar and confusing to many reporting entities.
- Determining the fair value of AROs using expected value techniques involves a complex probabilistic analysis of uncertainties (e.g., timing and nature of conditions or events that may cause retirement of an asset, estimated costs of future retirement activities, discount rates, and so forth).
- Accounting for AROs is likely to require development of new information management systems.
- Reporting entities may be reluctant to disclose the assumptions used in estimating for the fair value of AROs.

Effective internal control over financial reporting of AROs requires appropriate processes to identify, assess, measure, and report environmental obligations associated with the entity's long-lived assets. Exhibit 22.1 identifies certain process and control issues with regard to financial reporting of environmental loss contingencies that may warrant special attention for reporting entities and financial auditors.

Notwithstanding an effective internal control system design, the operational effectiveness of the system will largely depend on the performance of employees and contractors in carrying out established policies and procedures. Employee and contractor performance in turn will depend largely on the company's control environment with respect to environmental financial reporting (see § 8.2(a)) and personnel qualifications, training, and incentives (or disincentives).

EXHIBIT 22.1

Process and Control Considerations for AROs

PROCESS AREA	PROCESS AND CONTROL CONSIDERATIONS
Identification	• Identification of long-lived assets subject to FAS 143 • Identification of surplus and nonproductive properties • Identification of transactions, conditions, or events giving rise to potential AROs
Assessment	• Evaluation of transactions, conditions, or events giving rise to potential AROs • Selection and application of criteria for distinguishing between AROs and environmental remediation liabilities (e.g., determination of improper use) • Policies and procedures for investigation and additional data gathering • Reliance on determinations of legal counsel
Measurement	• Selection and application of measurement techniques • Use of actuaries and other specialists • Determination of ability to reasonably estimate • Selection and application of criteria for determining useful life • Determination of the probability assigned to various settlement scenarios • Evaluation of potential for significant near-term changes in estimated amounts
Reporting	• Selection and application of criteria for assessment of materiality • Disclosures relating to AROs • Disclosures related to significant risks and uncertainties

CHAPTER TWENTY-THREE

Asset Impairments

23.1 INTRODUCTION

Impairment is the condition that exists when the carrying amount of a long-lived asset (or asset group) exceeds its fair value. Pollution conditions affecting land and buildings may result in the impairment of company-owned properties and facilities.

In 2001, FASB issued FAS 144, "Accounting for the Impairment or Disposal of Long-Lived Assets." FAS 144 carries forward the impairment provisions of an earlier standard, FAS 121, and clarifies the treatment of long-lived assets that are part of a segment of a business accounted for as a discontinued operation. FAS 144 applies to long-lived assets of all entities, whether such assets are to be held and used, or disposed of.

FAS 144 introduces the concept of the *asset group*, defined as the lowest level for which identifiable cash flows are largely independent of the cash flows of other assets and liabilities. An asset group could be:

- The whole company.
- An operating segment (as defined by FAS 131).
- A reporting unit (as defined by FAS 142).
- A business.
- A part of a business (such as a division or department).

If an asset, such as a corporate headquarters building, cannot be assigned to any asset group because it does not have identifiable cash flows largely independent of other assets (or asset groups), then that asset is evaluated for recoverability by reference to all assets and liabilities of the entity.

23.2 RECOGNITION

Accounting for impairments varies depending on whether the asset in question is to be held and used, and, if not, the manner in which it is to be disposed of.

(a) ASSETS TO BE HELD AND USED

Impairment losses for assets to be held and used are recognized when the carrying amount of the impaired asset exceeds the sum of the undiscounted cash flows expected to result from use and eventual disposition of the asset. An impairment is not recognized if the carrying value of the asset is recoverable from expected future cash flows from use and disposition of the asset, even though the asset's carrying value exceeds its fair value (and is thus technically impaired).

FAS 144 states that a long-lived asset should be tested for recoverability whenever events or changes in circumstances indicate that its carrying amount may not be recoverable. Following are examples of environmental-related transactions, conditions, and events indicating that the carrying amount of an asset may not be recoverable and thus is to be evaluated for recoverability to determine whether an impairment loss must be recognized:

- The occurrence of a sudden pollution condition having a significant adverse impact on the physical condition or liability exposure of company-owned properties and facilities.
- Initial discovery of historical pollution conditions representing a significant adverse impact on the physical condition or liability exposure of company-owned properties and facilities.
- Discovery of pollution conditions during preclosing environmental due diligence by a prospective buyer, lender, or tenant.
- A significant adverse impact on the marketability, mortgageability, or value of an asset due to known or suspected pollution conditions.
- A significant adverse change in environmental legal factors or in the business climate expected to have an adverse effect on the value of the asset, including a change in environmental laws or an adverse action or assessment by an environmental regulator.
- The assertion of legal claims for environmental losses allegedly arising from pollution conditions adversely affecting the asset, adjacent properties, or natural resources.
- A significant adverse change in the extent or manner in which the asset is used due to the occurrence or discovery of pollution conditions.

If the carrying amount of an asset (in use or under development) is found to be unrecoverable (carrying amount exceeds the gross, undiscounted cash flows from use and disposition), then an impairment loss must be recognized. Measurement of the impairment loss is discussed in § 23.3.

For the purposes of recoverability evaluation, *future cash flows* are defined as cash inflows less the associated cash outflows directly associated with, and that are expected to arise as a direct result of, the use and eventual disposition of the asset (or asset group), excluding interest that is recognized as a period expense when incurred. When testing the recoverability of an asset, the estimate of future cash flows:

- Is based on all available evidence.
- Incorporates assumptions regarding the use of the asset (or asset group).
- Must be consistent with assumptions used by the entity for comparable periods such as internal budgets and projections, accruals related to incentive compensation plans, or information communicated to others.
- Uses assumptions that marketplace participants would use in their estimates of fair value when that information is available without undue cost or effort.
- Is made for the remaining estimated useful life of the asset (or the primary asset of an asset group) to the entity.
- Takes into account future expenditures necessary to complete an asset under development.
- Includes future outflows necessary to maintain the existing service potential.
- Excludes cash flows for future capital expenditures that increase the service potential of the asset.
- Is required to take into account the likelihood of possible cash flow outcomes if alternative courses of action are being contemplated, or if ranges of cash flows are estimated to occur under different scenarios.

The degree to which auditors will rely on management's assertions of expected cash flows depends on management's prior track record. Auditors typically compare the most recent actual cash flows and near-term future forecasts with the cash-flow forecasts made by management in prior periods. This comparison determines the amount of credibility that the auditor should assign to management's current assertions about changes in the cash-flow model. If management's previous cash-flow predictions were highly inaccurate, then management's current assertions of estimated future cash flows will be given less weight in the impairment decision process.

FAS 144 recommends, but does not require, use of expected present value techniques in estimating expected future cash flows.

(b) ASSETS TO BE DISPOSED OF BY SALE

An asset may be disposed of individually or as part of a disposal group. A *disposal group* is a group of assets to be transferred in a single transaction along with the liabilities directly associated with those assets (e.g., environmental obligations, warranty obligations associated with a product line, etc.).

Impairment losses for assets to be disposed of by sale are recognized when the assets are classified as held-for-sale. According to paragraph 30 of FAS 144, assets (or disposal groups) are classified as held for sale in the period in which all of the following six criteria are met:

1. Management possessing the necessary authority commits to a plan to sell the asset (disposal group).
2. The asset (disposal group) is immediately available for sale on an "as is" basis (i.e., in its present condition subject only to usual and customary terms for the sale of such assets).
3. An active program to find a buyer and other actions required to execute the plan to sell the asset (disposal group) have commenced.
4. An assessment of remaining actions required to complete the plan indicates that it is unlikely that significant changes will be made to the plan or that the plan will be withdrawn.
5. Sale of the asset (disposal group) is probable, and transfer of the asset (disposal group) is expected to qualify for recognition as a completed sale within one year.
   Note: Certain exceptions to the one-year requirement are allowed for events and circumstances beyond the entity's control that extend the period required to complete the sale (e.g., buyer concerns regarding pollution conditions discovered during preacquisition due diligence).
6. The asset (disposal group) is being actively marketed for sale at a price that is reasonable in relation to its current fair value.

A newly acquired asset (disposal group) that is being held for sale is classified as held for sale on the date of acquisition if it meets criterion 5 above (subject to the same exceptions noted there), and any other of the required criteria that are not met at the date of acquisition are probable of being met within a short period (approximately three months or less) of acquisition.

Environmental impairments are frequently discovered by owners when preparing properties for sale or by prospective buyers (or their lenders) during preacquisition environmental due diligence. The discovery of environmental concerns may delay the sale of the asset beyond the maximum one-year holding period for a long-lived asset (disposal group) classified as held for sale. The delay may require reclassification of the asset. The following two examples illustrate situations in which reclassification of the asset would and would not be necessary.

First, assume that the entity commits to a plan to sell a manufacturing facility in its present condition and classifies the facility as held for sale at that date. After the entity enters into a contract for sale, the buyer's inspection of the property identifies pollution conditions not previously known to exist. The buyer insists that the entity perform environmental remediation, which will extend the period required to complete the sale beyond one year. The entity initiates corrective action immediately, and satisfactory remediation of the environmental damage is probable. In that situation, an exception to the one-year requirement in criterion 5 would be satisfied, and the asset should remain classified as held for sale.

Second, assume that the entity acquires through foreclosure a real estate property that it intends to sell after it completes renovations to increase the value of the asset. The delay in the timing of the transfer of the property imposed by the entity (seller) demonstrates that the property is not available for immediate sale and should not be classified as held for sale. After the renovations are completed and the property is classified as held for sale, but *before* a firm purchase commitment is obtained, the entity becomes aware of historical pollution conditions requiring remediation. The entity still intends to sell the property, but the property will be unmarketable until after the remediation is completed. The delay in the timing of the transfer of the property imposed by others *before* a firm purchase commitment is obtained demonstrates that the property is not available for immediate sale. The property should be reclassified as held and used.

(c) ASSETS TO BE DISPOSED OF OTHER THAN BY SALE

Long-lived assets may be disposed of by means other than sale. For example, they may be abandoned, exchanged, or distributed to owners in a spinoff. Until the actual disposal occurs, the assets continue to be classified on the balance sheet as held and used. During the period prior to disposal, they are subject to conventional impairment rules applicable to assets held and used (see § 23.2(a)).

When an asset is abandoned, its carrying amount should be adjusted to its salvage value, if any, but not less than zero. An entity abandons an asset when it discontinues use of the asset on an other-than-temporary basis. Temporary idling of an asset is not considered abandonment.

An entity may commit to a plan to abandon an asset prior to discontinuing use of that asset. If the entity commits to a plan to abandon an asset before the end of the asset's previously estimated useful life, the depreciable life of the asset is revised, and depreciation of the asset continues until the end of its shortened useful life.

If a long-lived asset is to be disposed of either by spinning it off to owners of the entity or in an exchange transaction for a similar productive asset, the disposal is recognized when the actual exchange or spinoff occurs. If the asset (or asset group) is evaluated for recoverability prior to disposal, estimates of future cash flows should assume that the disposal will not occur and that the asset will continue to be held and used for the remainder of its useful life.

(d) ENVIRONMENTAL EXIT COSTS

In June 2002, the FASB Emerging Issues Task Force addressed the issue of whether the cash flows associated with environmental exit costs (see § 13.2(b)) that may be incurred when a long-lived asset is sold, abandoned, or permanently idled should be included in the undiscounted expected future cash flows used to test a long-lived asset for recoverability under FAS 144. The outcome, described in EITF 95-23, "Treatment of Certain Site Restoration/Environmental Exit Costs When Testing a Long-Lived Asset for Impairment," depends on two factors: (1) whether the entity has previously recognized the environmental exit costs as a liability, and (2) management's intent regarding future use of the asset.

(i) PREVIOUSLY RECOGNIZED ENVIRONMENTAL LIABILITIES AND IMPAIRMENTS

To avoid double-counting, previously recognized environmental liabilities and impairments are *excluded* from the undiscounted expected future cash flows used to test the asset for recoverability under FAS 144. Similarly, previously recognized asset retirement obligations also are excluded (see § 22.2(g)).

(ii) PREVIOUSLY UNRECOGNIZED ENVIRONMENTAL LIABILITIES AND IMPAIRMENTS

When testing the recoverability of a contaminated property or facility, management's intent is considered in determining whether to include or exclude estimated future cash outflows for environmental costs for which the entity has not previously recognized a liability or impairment. Cash outflows for environmental exit costs may not occur until the end of the asset's life if the asset ceases to be used, or may be delayed indefinitely as long as management retains ownership of the asset and chooses not to sell or abandon it. Consequently, the EITF consensus is that management's intent regarding future actions with respect to the asset is to be taken into account in determining whether to include or exclude these cash outflows from computation of the expected future cash flows used to evaluate recoverability under FAS 144. In sharp contrast, management's intent regarding future use of a long-lived asset is not considered in determining whether an asset retirement obligation must be recognized under FAS 143. (See § 22.2(c) for a discussion of the impact of management intent with regard to conditional asset retirement obligations under FAS 143.)

In the following examples 1 through 4, environmental exit costs and loss contingencies not previously recognized as a liability should be *excluded* from the FAS 144 recoverability test, according to EITF 95-23:

1. Management intends to operate the asset for at least the remaining depreciable life of the asset; the sum of the undiscounted future cash flows expected from use of the asset during that period exceeds the carrying amount of the asset, including any associated goodwill; and management has no reason to believe that eventual disposition of the asset will result in a net cash outflow.

2. Management expects to operate the asset indefinitely and has the ability to do so; the asset is generating positive cash flows; management's best information indicates that the asset will continue to be profitable in the future; and there are no known constraints to the economic life of the asset. The FAS 144 recoverability test should include the future cash outflows for repairs, maintenance, and capital expenditures necessary to obtain the future cash inflows expected to be generated by the asset based on its existing service potential.

   Note: FAS 143 does not require recognition of a liability when insufficient information is available to estimate a range of potential settlement dates for the retirement obligation of an asset with an indeterminate useful life.

3. The asset has a finite economic life, but cleanup costs that have not yet been recognized as an environmental remediation liability pursuant to SOP 96-1 (Chapter 20) will be incurred only if the asset is sold or abandoned. At the end of the asset's life, management intends either to close the asset permanently, because the costs of remediating the asset exceed the proceeds that likely would be received if the asset were sold; or, alternatively, to idle the asset by reducing production to a minimal or nominal amount. Although the cleanup costs should be excluded from the FAS 144 recoverability test, the recoverability test should incorporate the entity's own assumptions about its use of the asset. That is, the recoverability test should consider the likelihood of the alternative courses of action (either closing or idling the asset) and the resulting cash flows associated with those alternative courses.

   Note: The ability to postpone environmental exit costs indefinitely does not avoid the requirement to recognize a liability for an asset retirement obligation. Thus, in this scenario, the entity typically would be required to recognize the fair value of the liability for such costs (see § 22.2(c)).

4. Management expects to sell the asset in the future, and sale of the asset will not require the environmental cleanup costs to be incurred.

   Note: Although the environmental cleanup costs are excluded from the FAS 144 recoverability test, the fair value of the asset is likely to be affected by the fair value of the liability for environmental cleanup costs. The diminished fair value should be considered in estimating the cash flows expected to arise from the eventual sale of the asset.

In the following examples 5 through 10, future environmental exit costs not previously recognized as a liability should be *included* in the FAS 144 recoverability test, according to EITF 95-23:

5. Management expects to take a future action related to the asset that may cause cleanup costs to be incurred. However, uncertainties or inconsistencies exist in how the related laws or regulatory requirements are applied. Management estimates, based on the weight of the available evidence, a

60 percent chance that the environmental cleanup costs will not be incurred and a 40 percent chance that those costs will be incurred.

6. The useful life of the asset is limited as a result of actual or expected technological advances, contractual provisions, or regulatory restrictions, and when the asset's service potential has ended, management will be required to dispose of the asset as in examples 8 or 9 below.

7. The asset has a current-period cash-flow loss from operations combined with a projection or forecast that anticipates continuing losses. Management expects the asset to achieve profitability in the future, but uncertainty exists about management's ability to fund the future cash outflows up to the time that net cash inflows are expected from use of the asset. In the event of a forced liquidation, management would likely dispose of the asset as in examples 8 or 9 below.

8. Management intends to abandon or close the asset in the future, and the event of abandonment or closure will cause the environmental cleanup costs to be incurred.

9. Management intends to sell the asset in the future, and environmental laws require that environmental remediation occur in connection with the sale.

10. Management expects to operate the asset for the remainder of its useful life. Related asset retirement costs are incurred over the life of the asset (for example, the operation of a landfill). Estimated cash flows associated with the asset retirement costs yet to be incurred and recognized should be included in the FAS 144 recoverability test.

23.3 MEASUREMENT

An impairment loss on assets classified as held and used is measured as the excess of the asset's carrying amount over the asset's fair value. Fair value is determined using quoted market prices in active markets, when available. When quoted market prices for comparable assets are not available, fair value is generally estimated using expected present value techniques.

An impairment loss on assets (disposal groups) classified as held for sale is measured at the excess of the asset's carrying amount over the asset's fair value less cost to sell. *Cost to sell* consists of costs that result directly from the sales transaction that would not have been incurred if no sale had been transacted, such as brokerage commissions, legal fees, title transfer fees, and other closing costs that must be incurred prior to transfer of legal title. Costs to sell contaminated properties are generally high relative to those of uncontaminated properties.

The carrying amount of an abandoned asset should be adjusted to its salvage value, if any, but not less than zero (i.e., a liability cannot be recorded upon abandonment). An abandoned asset may also be subject to an asset retirement obligation (see Chapter 22).

23.4 DISPLAY AND DISCLOSURE

(a) BALANCE SHEET DISPLAY

If an asset (or asset group) sustains an impairment loss, the loss reduces the carrying amount of the asset (or the assets in the group). In general, the loss is allocated to the assets in a group based on their relative carrying values. The adjustment to carrying values to reflect an impairment loss is permanent and cannot be reversed.

Assets that are held for sale are presented separately on the balance sheet and are not depreciated (amortized) while being presented under the held-for-sale classification.

(b) INCOME STATEMENT DISPLAY

An impairment loss recognized for a long-lived asset (asset group) to be held and used is included in income from continuing operations before income taxes in the income statement. If a subtotal such as "income from operations" is presented, it shall include the amount of that loss.

After recognition of an impairment loss on an asset classified as held and used, depreciation (amortization) of the adjusted carrying amount of the impaired asset is recognized prospectively over the remaining estimated useful life of that asset.

For assets classified as held for sale, a loss is recognized for any initial or subsequent writedown to fair value less cost to sell. A gain is recognized for any subsequent increase in fair value less cost to sell. Recognized gains may not exceed the cumulative losses previously recognized. Assets that are held for sale are not depreciated (amortized) while being presented under the held-for-sale classification. Interest and other expenses related to the liabilities of a held-for-sale disposal group are accrued as incurred.

(c) DISCLOSURE OF ACCOUNTING PRINCIPLES

APB Opinion 22, "Disclosure of Accounting Policies," provides guidance regarding accounting principles that should be described in the accounting policies note to the financial statements. APB Opinion 22, paragraph 12, indicates that entities should disclose those accounting principles that "materially affect the determination of financial position or results of operations." In particular, entities should disclose accounting principles and the methods of applying those principles when alternatives exist. With respect to environmental-related asset impairments, the financial statements should disclose the method or methods for determining fair value (whether based on a quoted market price, prices for similar assets, or another valuation technique).

(d) DISCLOSURES FOR ASSET IMPAIRMENTS

Paragraph 26 of FAS 144 requires the following information to be disclosed in the notes to the financial statements for the period in which an impairment loss is recognized:

- A description of the impaired long-lived asset (asset group) and the facts and circumstances leading to the impairment.
- If not separately presented on the face of the statement, the amount of the impairment loss and the caption in the income statement or the statement of activities that includes that loss.
- The method or methods for determining fair value (whether based on a quoted market price, prices for similar assets, or another valuation technique).
- If applicable, the segment in which the impaired long-lived asset (asset group) is reported under FASB Statement No. 131, "Disclosures about Segments of an Enterprise and Related Information."

Paragraph 47 of FAS 144 requires the following information to be disclosed in the notes to the financial statements that cover the period in which a long-lived asset (disposal group) either was sold or is classified as held for sale:

- A description of the facts and circumstances leading to the expected disposal; the expected manner and timing of that disposal; and, if not separately presented on the face of the statement, the carrying amount(s) of the major classes of assets and liabilities included as part of a disposal group.
- The gain or loss recognized for any initial or subsequent writedown to fair value less cost to sell; and, if not separately presented on the face of the income statement, the caption in the income statement or the statement of activities that includes that gain or loss.
- If applicable, amounts of revenue and pretax profit or loss reported in discontinued operations.
- If applicable, the segment in which the long-lived asset (disposal group) is reported under FAS 131.
- If applicable, a description of the facts and circumstances leading to the decision to change the plan to sell the long-lived asset (disposal group) and its effect on the results of operations for the period and any prior periods.

(e) ADDITIONAL CONSIDERATIONS FOR PUBLIC COMPANIES

As discussed in § 11.3(d), accelerated reporting requirements are applicable to environmental asset impairments, and certain extraordinary events (e.g., pollution conditions arising from a catastrophic accident) could give rise to the need for accelerated Form 8-K disclosure. However, accelerated reporting is not required if, as is typically the case, the impairment determination is made in connection with the preparation, review, or audit of financial statements at the end of a fiscal quarter or year and the plan is disclosed in the registrant's periodic report (e.g., Form 10-Q or Form 10-K) for that period.

Section 404 of Sarbanes-Oxley imposes requirements on public companies to design, implement, and periodically assess the operational effectiveness of internal control over financial reporting (see Chapter 8). In addition, section 404 requires the reporting entity's independent financial auditor to examine the entity's internal control over financial reporting and annually attest to its design and operational effectiveness (see Chapter 27).

Internal control over financial reporting of AROs will require appropriate processes to identify, assess, measure, and report environmental obligations associated with the entity's long-lived assets. Exhibit 23.1 identifies certain process and control issues with regard to financial reporting of asset impairments that may warrant special attention for reporting entities and financial auditors.

Notwithstanding an effective internal control system design, the operational effectiveness of the system will largely depend on the performance of employees and contractors in carrying out established policies and procedures. Employee and contractor performance in turn will depend largely on the company's control environment with respect to environmental financial reporting (see § 8.2(a)) and personnel qualifications, training, and incentives (or disincentives).

EXHIBIT 23.1

Process and Control Considerations for Asset Impairments

PROCESS AREA	PROCESS AND CONTROL CONSIDERATIONS
Identification	• Identification of long-lived assets susceptible to environmental-related impairments • Identification of conditions and events triggering the need for recoverability testing
Assessment	• Performance of recoverability testing • Policies and procedures for investigation and additional data gathering • Reliance on determinations of legal counsel • Procedures for determining and documenting management's intent with respect to the future use of long-lived assets with known or suspected pollution conditions
Measurement	• Selection and application of measurement techniques • Use of actuaries and other specialists
Reporting	• Selection and application of criteria for assessment of materiality • Disclosures relating to asset impairments • Selection and application of criteria for accelerated reporting

CHAPTER TWENTY-FOUR

Environmental Risks

24.1 INTRODUCTION

The preceding chapters in Part Three focused on the various types of environmental financial information to be quantified and presented in financial statements pursuant to generally accepted accounting principles. These include environmental costs (income statement), environmental assets (balance sheet), and environmental liabilities (balance sheet). Such information can be generally characterized as historical in nature, because it relates to past transactions, conditions, and events, as of the date of the financial statements. Although environmental estimates for contingent environmental liabilities and asset retirement obligations, for example, may incorporate expectations regarding anticipated future events, such estimates represent the probable future consequences of historical occurrences (see § 19.2(a)).

In contrast, descriptions of environmental risks are generally forward-looking. Environmental risks often cannot be reasonably estimated and are generally not presented in the financial statements. This is not to say, however, that environmental risks are irrelevant to a complete understanding of an entity's financial outlook. To the contrary, environmental risks can have a material effect on the future success of a business enterprise.

A meaningful discussion of environmental risks requires clear definitions of terms. As used in this book, *environmental risks* are exposures to potential environmental losses. The term *environmental loss exposures* is used interchangeably with environmental risks. *Environmental losses* represent the direct or indirect financial consequences to an organization associated with pollution conditions. For purposes of financial reporting, environmental risk concerns the potential for adverse financial impacts to the organization arising from environmental losses, as opposed to the degree of actual or potential risk to human health and the environment (although the latter may have an influence on the former).

Environmental losses can be subdivided into four categories:

1. Destruction or damage to the entity's tangible or intangible property (e.g., contamination of company-owned facilities and loss of goodwill).
2. Loss or impairment of entity personnel (e.g., resignation of experienced independent board directors due to concerns of potential personal liability for environmental matters).
3. Liability for obligations to third parties (e.g., claims for property damages, bodily injury, cleanup costs, and so forth).
4. Conditions that negatively affect net income by increasing company expenses or reducing revenues, or both (e.g., increased waste disposal costs, loss of sales due to damage of reputation with consumers, and so forth).

As used herein, environmental losses do not include environmental impacts (i.e., physical impacts on the environment, such as pollutants emitted into the air) wholly or partially resulting from an organization's activities, products, or services, unless such impacts otherwise fall into one of the four categories listed above. In other words, losses to the environment generally do not constitute losses to the reporting entity, unless these impacts affect, or are reasonably likely to affect *within a relevant time frame*, the financial position of the enterprise. The exclusion of environmental impacts as a category of environmental risks relates back to a point covered in Chapter 1 regarding external costs or externalities.

What exactly constitutes the relevant time frame for evaluating environmental risks is a matter of judgment. Although a serious problem associated with the environmental performance of a particular business model may not manifest itself in the short term, it may well show up in financial results and market valuation over time as consumers, regulators, voters, or plaintiffs lose confidence in the company and respond accordingly. U.S. securities laws do not prescribe a specific time frame for evaluating the probability of loss to the organization from environmental risks. The determination of what constitutes a relevant time frame is closely related to the determination of what information is considered material to investors in making current investment decisions (see § 12.2). Though investor attitudes regarding long-term social and environmental risks are changing, and will likely continue to evolve, attention to such nonfinancial factors within the wider investment community remains largely reactive and episodic.[1]

---

[1] *Mainstreaming Responsible Investment* 7, World Economic Forum (Jan. 2005).

EXHIBIT 24.1

Environmental Risk Matrix

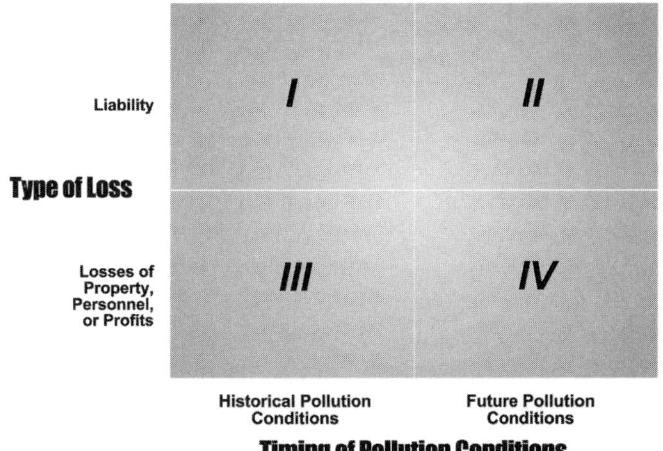

As shown in Exhibit 24.1, environmental loss exposures can be subdivided into two primary categories: (1) exposures related to historical pollution conditions and (2) exposures related to future pollution conditions. Environmental loss exposures related to historical pollution conditions in turn can be assigned to one of two subcategories: (1) contingent liabilities (e.g., environmental remediation liabilities) and (2) exposures to losses other than liabilities (e.g., losses to property, personnel, or profitability). Similarly, environmental loss exposures related to future pollution conditions can be classified into two subcategories: (1) exposures to future liabilities and (2) exposures to future losses other than liabilities.

The foregoing distinctions are important because they bear on whether and how information is to be reported under GAAP and the U.S. securities laws.

- *Quadrant I risks.* Environmental risks shown in quadrant I of Exhibit 24.1 (liability for historical pollution conditions) are evaluated as environmental loss contingencies under FAS 5 and SOP 96-1 (see Chapters 19 and 20). If the dual recognition criteria are satisfied (i.e., a loss is probable and can be reasonably estimated), these risks are to be quantified and presented on the balance sheet as a liability. Disclosure of quadrant I environmental risks may be required under Items 103 and 303 of Regulation S-K (discussed below), whether or not such risks are recognized in the financial statements. Examples of quadrant I environmental loss exposures include the incurrence of environmental liabilities through business acquisition, designation as a PRP at one or more Superfund sites, incurred but not reported product liability claims, and imposition of retroactive cleanup liability under new Superfund-type environmental laws adopted by foreign countries.

- *Quadrant II risks.* Environmental risks shown in quadrant II of Exhibit 24.1 (liability for future pollution conditions) are not subject to quantification and reporting under GAAP (see § 19.2(a)(i)). Disclosure of such risks under Item 303 of Regulation S-K may be necessary if management is aware of trends, events, or uncertainties that are reasonably likely to have a material adverse effect on the entity's financial condition. For example, if management is aware of an escalating trend in the rate of new pollution conditions associated with the entity's activities, products, or services, disclosure of such risks is required in the entity's SEC filings. Examples of quadrant II environmental loss exposures include potential future industrial and transportation accidents, failure of existing waste containment systems, and acts of terrorism targeted at nuclear power plants, chemical companies, or liquefied natural gas facilities.
- *Quadrant III risks.* Environmental risks shown in quadrant III of Exhibit 24.1 (nonliability losses related to historical pollution conditions) are not subject to quantification and presentation in the financial statements under GAAP. Whereas *actual* impairments to long-lived assets are reportable under GAAP (Chapter 23), exposures to possible future asset impairments (e.g., future changes in environmental laws that would have the effect of reducing the value of certain assets) are not. Similarly, whereas impacts to current profitability are reflected in the income statement (e.g., current expenditures for pollution control costs), exposures to future impairments of profitability are not. GAAP simply does not address losses to company personnel, whether actual or potential.
- *Quadrant IV risks.* Environmental risks shown in quadrant IV of Exhibit 24.1 (nonliability losses related to future pollution conditions) are not subject to quantification and presentation in the financial statements under GAAP. However, public companies may be required to disclose information regarding such risks under Items 101 and 303 of Regulation S-K. For example, if the entity is aware of known trends, events, or uncertainties that are reasonably likely to have a material adverse effect on the entity's liquidity, capital resources, or results of operations, disclosure of such information is required in the entity's SEC filings. Examples of quadrant IV environmental loss exposures include new government regulations that require changes in raw materials or installation of new pollution control equipment, and the impacts of climate change and associated carbon emission limits on an entity's operations, assets, and profitability.

With the exceptions noted above, environmental loss exposures are not subject to quantification and presentation in the financial statements under GAAP. Public companies, however, are required to file periodic reports with the SEC that include disclosures outside of the financial statements of financial and nonfinancial information about various types of risks facing the enterprise. SEC rules include general disclosure requirements as well as certain specific disclosure requirements for environmental risks.

SEC Regulation S-K describes the narrative and quantitative information to be included in the nonfinancial statement portions of SEC reports. Item 101 ("Description of Business"), Item 103 ("Legal Proceedings"), Item 303 ("Management's Discussion and Analysis of Financial Condition and Results of Operations," known as the MD&A), and Item 503(c) ("Risk Factors") bear the greatest relevance to environmental financial reporting. In addition, the antifraud provisions of the federal securities laws may require issuers to include environmental information in SEC filings (beyond that specifically required by Regulation S-K) to ensure that the reports are not otherwise misleading.

24.2 ANTIFRAUD PROVISIONS

The antifraud provisions of the federal securities laws—sections 11 and 12(a)(2) of the Securities Act and section 10(b) of the Exchange Act and SEC Rule 10b-5—prohibit the making of false or misleading statements or omissions in connection with the purchase or sale of securities. In some situations, it may be necessary or appropriate for public companies to disclose environmental-related information in a registration statement or periodic report beyond those matters specifically addressed by Regulation S-K. For example, an issuer engaged in the acquisition of other businesses in an industry subject to significant environmental regulations and risks might need to explain to current and prospective investors how the issuer uses preacquisition environmental due diligence to protect itself from unwittingly assuming unidentified environmental liabilities. If the issuer overstates its competency in conducting environmental due diligence and environmental losses ensue, injured shareholders may bring private actions against registrants and issuers under the antifraud provisions of the federal securities laws.[2]

24.3 ITEM 101 DESCRIPTION OF BUSINESS

Under Item 101, of Regulation S-K issuers must disclose, among other things, the material effects of compliance with federal, state, and local environmental provisions on their capital expenditures, earnings, and competitive position. Section (c)(1)(xi) of Item 101 requires registrants to disclose

> the material effects that compliance with Federal, state and local provisions which have been enacted or adopted regulating the discharge of materials into the environment, or otherwise relating to the protection of the environment, may have upon the capital expenditures, earnings and competitive position of the registrant and its subsidiaries. The registrant shall disclose any material estimated capital expenditures for environmental control facilities for the remainder of its current fiscal year and its succeeding fiscal year and for such further periods as the registrant may deem material.[3]

[2] *See, e.g.*, Collmer v. U.S. Liquids, Inc., 268 F. Supp. 2d 718 (S.D. Tex. 2003).
[3] 17 C.F.R. § 229.101(c)(1)(xi).

According to SEC guidance in SAB 92,[4] a registrant's discussion of historical and anticipated environmental expenditures should, to the extent material, describe separately:

- Recurring costs associated with managing hazardous substances and pollution in ongoing operations.
- Capital expenditures to limit or monitor hazardous substances or pollutants.
- Mandated expenditures to remediate previously contaminated sites.
- Other infrequent or nonrecurring cleanup expenditures that can be anticipated but that are not required in the present circumstances.

SAB 92 further advises that disaggregated disclosure describing accrued and reasonably likely losses with respect to particular pollution conditions that are individually material may be necessary. If management's investigation of potential liability and cleanup costs is at different stages with respect to individual sites, the consequences of this with respect to amounts accrued and disclosed should be discussed.

24.4 ITEM 103 LEGAL PROCEEDINGS

Under Item 103, of Regulation S-K registrants must describe certain administrative or judicial legal proceedings arising from federal, state, or local environmental provisions. Item 103 directs registrants to briefly describe:

> [A]ny material pending legal proceedings, other than ordinary routine litigation incidental to the business, to which the registrant or any of its subsidiaries is a party or of which any of their property is the subject. Include the name of the court or agency in which the proceedings are pending, the date instituted, the principal parties thereto, a description of the factual basis alleged to underlie the proceeding and the relief sought.[5]

Registrants must also disclose similar information as to any such proceedings known to be contemplated by governmental authorities.

Instruction 5 to Item 103 specifically addresses environmental legal proceedings, providing that proceedings arising under any environmental laws shall not be deemed "ordinary routine litigation incidental to the business." Environmental legal proceedings must be described if the proceeding:

> (A) Is material to the business or financial condition of the registrant;
>
> (B) Involves primarily a claim for damages, or involves potential monetary sanctions, capital expenditures, deferred charges, or charges to income and the amount involved, exclusive of interest and costs, exceeds 10 percent of the current assets of the registrant and its subsidiaries on a consolidated basis; or

---

4 Release No. SAB 92, 38 Fed-Reg. 32, 843 (June 14, 1993).

5 17 C.F.R. § 229.103.

> (C) Involves potential monetary sanctions by a governmental authority, unless the registrant reasonably believes that such proceeding will result in no monetary sanctions, or in monetary sanctions, exclusive of interest and costs, of less than $100,000, regardless of materiality.[6]

For purposes of determining the monetary threshold criteria identified in Instruction 5, the SEC has indicated that cleanup costs incurred pursuant to a remediation agreement do not have to be included in the calculation.

In a 1989 interpretive release, the SEC noted that the availability of insurance, indemnification, or contribution may be relevant in determining whether the criteria for disclosure have been met with respect to a contingency under Instruction 5(A) or (B).[7] The registrant's assessment in this regard should include consideration of facts such as the periods in which claims for recovery may be realized, the likelihood that the claims may be contested, and the financial condition of third parties from which recovery is expected.

Cleanup costs anticipated to be incurred under Superfund, pursuant to a remedial agreement entered into in the normal course of negotiation with the EPA, generally are not *sanctions* as that term is used in either Instruction 5(B) or (C) to Item 103. Cleanup costs normally constitute charges to income, or in some cases capital expenditures.[8] Because Instruction 5(C) concerns proceedings involving potential monetary sanctions, permit proceedings and requests for waivers or variances are not subject to this disclosure requirement.

The SEC indicated in a 1979 release that a *proceeding* includes any administrative or judicial proceeding pending or contemplated by a governmental authority with respect to environmental matters; or any administrative order relating to the environment, whether or not the order follows a literal proceeding (e.g., consent order or negotiated settlement arrived at prior to the initiation of a formal proceeding).[9] For example, the receipt of a Notice of Violation may constitute a sufficiently concrete indication of governmental action that it may require disclosure. However, being named a potentially responsible party with respect to environmental cleanup costs does not automatically trigger disclosure, as such a designation does not necessarily indicate that the government is contemplating a proceeding against the registrant. A registrant's particular circumstances will indicate whether the government is contemplating a proceeding. The SEC has construed *administrative proceeding* to include actions commenced by the registrant, as well as those commenced by the government.

According to SEC guidance in SAB 92, examples of specific disclosures typically relevant to an understanding of historical and anticipated environmental claims include the nature of personal injury or property damages alleged by claimants, aggregate settlement costs by type of claim, and related costs of administering and litigating claims. Generally, environmental legal proceedings that are similar in nature may be grouped and described generically. Disaggregated disclosure that describes accrued and reasonably likely losses with respect

---

6 17 C.F.R. § 229.103, Instruction 5.

7 Securities Act Release No. 33-6835, 54 Fed. Reg. 22427 (May 24, 1989).

8 *Id.* n.309.

9 Securities Act Release No. 33-6130, 1979 WL 169925 (Sept. 27, 1979).

to particular claims may be necessary, however, if they are individually material. If a loss contingency involves a large number of relatively small individual claims of a similar type, such as personal injury from exposure to asbestos, it may be necessary to disclose the number of claims pending at each balance sheet date; the number of claims filed for each period presented; the number of claims dismissed, settled, or otherwise resolved for each period; and the average settlement amount per claim. Disclosures should address historical and expected trends in these amounts and their reasonably likely effects on operating results and liquidity.

24.5 ITEM 303 MANAGEMENT DISCUSSION AND ANALYSIS

The purpose of the Management Discussion and Analysis (MD&A) is to provide investors and other users information relevant to an assessment of the financial condition and results of operations of the registrant as determined by evaluating the amounts and certainty of cash flow from operations and from outside sources. At its best, the MD&A provides investors with an inside view of the state of the business through the eyes of management. Although Item 303 contains no specific environmental requirements, environmental financial information may be necessary to understand the registrant's financial condition, changes in financial condition, and results of operations.

Item 303 of Regulation S-K generally requires the registrant to disclose known trends, events, or uncertainties that have affected, will affect, or are reasonably likely to affect the registrant's liquidity, capital resources, or results of operations. Disclosures should focus specifically on material events and uncertainties known to management that would cause reported financial information not to be indicative of future operating results or of future financial condition. The registrant should describe both matters that are expected to have an impact on future operations, but that have not had an impact in the past, and matters that have had an impact on reported operations and are expected to have a continuing impact on future operations.

(a) LIQUIDITY

Item 303(a)(1) requires registrants to identify any known trends or any known demands, commitments, events, or uncertainties that will result in or that are reasonably likely to result in the registrant's liquidity increasing or decreasing in any material way. If a material deficiency is identified, indicate the course of action that the registrant has taken or proposes to take to remedy the deficiency. Registrants must also identify and separately describe internal and external sources of liquidity, and briefly discuss any material unused sources of liquid assets.

The term *liquidity* as used in Item 303 refers to the ability of an enterprise to generate adequate amounts of cash to meet its needs for cash. Among other things, environmental claims and demands under environmental indemnities that are reasonably likely to have a material effect on the registrant's liquidity should be disclosed under this subsection.

(b) CAPITAL RESOURCES

Item 303(a)(2) requires registrants to describe:

- The registrant's material commitments for capital expenditures as of the end of the latest fiscal period (indicating the general purpose of such commitments and the anticipated source of funds needed to fulfill such commitments); and
- Any known material trends, favorable or unfavorable, in the registrant's capital resources (indicating any expected material changes in the mix and relative cost of such resources).

Material commitments for pollution control costs or cleanup costs should be disclosed under this subsection of Item 303. Such costs should also be addressed under Item 101 of Regulation S-K (discussed in § 24.3).

(c) RESULTS OF OPERATIONS

Item 303(a)(2) requires registrants to describe:

- Any unusual or infrequent events or transactions or any significant economic changes that materially affected the amount of reported income from continuing operations (in each case indicating the extent to which income was so affected) and any other significant components of revenues or expenses that, in the registrant's judgment, should be described in order to understand the registrant's results of operations.
- Any known trends or uncertainties that have had, or that the registrant reasonably expects will have, a material favorable or unfavorable impact on net sales or revenues or income from continuing operations (indicating any material change anticipated in the relationship between costs and revenues).
- A narrative discussion of the extent to which material increases in net sales or revenues are attributable to increases in prices or to increases in the volume or amount of goods or services being sold or to the introduction of new products or services.
- The impact of inflation and changing prices on the registrant's net sales and revenues and on income from continuing operations.

A wide range of environmental matters may be subject to disclosure under this subsection, if they are material to the registrant. Examples include:

- Impacts on the enterprise associated with continuing compliance with environmental laws.
- Estimated future pollution control costs associated with a final or proposed environmental law.

- Potential cleanup costs and other environmental losses associated with Superfund sites and corrective action under RCRA, TSCA, or other environmental laws (see Chapter 3).
- Estimated future liabilities associated with hazardous products or workplace exposures.
- Environmental business risks arising from known trends or uncertainties, such as water shortages, global warming, and environmental terrorism.

SEC guidance regarding environmental disclosures under Regulation S-K is discussed in § 24.7.

(d) PROSPECTIVE INFORMATION

Several specific provisions in Item 303 require disclosure of forward-looking information. For example, Item 303 requires discussions of "known trends or any known demands, commitments, events or uncertainties that will result in or that are reasonably likely to result in the registrant's liquidity increasing or decreasing in any material way." Further, descriptions of known material trends in the registrant's capital resources and expected changes in the mix and cost of such resources are required. Disclosure of known trends or uncertainties that the registrant reasonably expects will have a material impact on net sales, revenues, or income from continuing operations is also required. Finally, the Instructions to Item 303 state that the MD&A "shall focus specifically on material events and uncertainties known to management that would cause reported financial information not to be necessarily indicative of future operating results or of future financial condition."

Required disclosure of environmental loss exposures arising from the future impact of presently known trends, events, or uncertainties and optional forward-looking information about environmental risks (or opportunities) both may involve some prediction or projection. In a 1989 Release,[10] the SEC clarified that the distinction rests with the nature of the prediction required. Required disclosure is based on currently known trends, events, and uncertainties that are reasonably expected to have material effects. In contrast, optional forward-looking disclosure involves anticipating a future trend or event or anticipating a less predictable impact of a known event, trend, or uncertainty.

Entities must disclose environmental loss exposures when a trend, demand, commitment, event, or uncertainty is both presently known to management and reasonably likely to have material effects on the issuer's financial condition or results of operation. When a trend, demand, commitment, event, or uncertainty is known, management must make two assessments:

1. Is the known trend, demand, commitment, event, or uncertainty reasonably likely to come to fruition? If management determines that it is not reasonably likely to occur, no disclosure is required. For example, if man-

---

10 Securities Act Release No. 33-6835, 54 Fed. Reg. 22427 (May 24, 1989).

agement determines that new U.S. laws to regulate global warming are not reasonably likely to be enacted, no disclosure is required regarding the effect such laws might have on the company.

2. If the known trend, demand, commitment, event, or uncertainty is reasonably likely to come to fruition, management must evaluate objectively the consequences of the known trend, demand, commitment, event, or uncertainty, on the assumption that it will come to fruition. Disclosure is then required unless management determines that a material effect on the registrant's financial condition or results of operations is not reasonably likely to occur. For example, if management determines that new U.S. laws to regulate global warming are reasonably likely to be enacted, management must objectively evaluate and disclose the consequences of the new laws, unless management determines that such laws are not reasonably likely to have a material effect on the company's financial condition or results of operations.

Each final determination resulting from the assessments made by management must be objectively reasonable, viewed as of the time the determination is made.

(e) CRITICAL ACCOUNTING ESTIMATES

In a December 2003 Release, the SEC addressed the topic of *critical accounting estimates*. These are accounting estimates and assumptions that may be material due to the levels of subjectivity and judgment necessary to account for highly uncertain matters or the susceptibility of such matters to change, and that have a material impact on financial condition or operating performance.[11] Estimates of environmental loss contingencies and environmental asset retirement obligations are examples of critical accounting estimates.

The SEC advises registrants that are preparing disclosure under Item 303 to consider whether they have made accounting estimates or assumptions when:

- The nature of the estimates or assumptions is material due to the levels of subjectivity and judgment necessary to account for highly uncertain matters or the susceptibility of such matters to change; and
- The impact of the estimates and assumptions on financial condition or operating performance is material.

If so, registrants should disclose the following information regarding such critical accounting estimates or assumptions:

- Why the accounting estimates or assumptions bear the risk of change (e.g., inherent uncertainty attached to the estimate or assumption, difficulty in measurement, etc.).
- How the estimate was determined.

---

11 Securities Act Release No. 33-8350, 68 Fed. Reg. 75,056 (Dec. 29, 2003).

- How accurate the estimate/assumption has been in the past.
- How much the estimate/assumption has changed in the past.
- Whether the estimate/assumption is reasonably likely to change in the future.
- Sensitivity to change based on other outcomes that are reasonably likely to occur and would have a material effect.
- Quantitative as well as qualitative disclosure when quantitative information is reasonably available and will provide material information for investors.

Disclosures regarding critical accounting estimates should supplement, not duplicate, the description of accounting policies provided in the notes to the financial statements. Whereas accounting policy notes in the financial statements generally describe the method used to apply an accounting principle, the MD&A disclosure should present a registrant's analysis of the uncertainties involved in applying a principle at a given time or the variability that is reasonably likely to result from its application over time.

(f) OFF-BALANCE-SHEET ARRANGEMENTS

Regulations adopted by the SEC pursuant to section 409 of Sarbanes-Oxley amend Item 303 to require disclosure regarding off-balance-sheet arrangements. These amendments are discussed in Chapter 10.

24.6 ITEM 503(C) RISK FACTORS

When appropriate, registrants must include in the prospectus, under the caption "Risk Factors," a discussion of the most significant factors that make the offering speculative or risky. Risk factors may include, among other things:

- Lack of an operating history.
- Lack of profitable operations in recent periods.
- Financial position.
- Business or proposed business.
- Lack of a market for the entity's common equity securities or securities convertible into or exercisable for common equity securities.

Risk factors fall into three categories: (1) industry risk, (2) company risk, and (3) investment risk. Examples of environmental-related industry risks include:

- An entity's plans to acquire properties or businesses with significant environmental remediation or compliance issues.
- Seasonal demand and uncertain supply of natural resources used as raw materials.
- Restrictions on the sale or use of certain products and raw materials.

Examples of environmental-related company risks include:

- Specific company-owned properties that require environmental cleanup.
- Pending environmental litigation.
- The fact that the registrant does not have and will not obtain environmental insurance.

Examples of possible environmental-related investment risks include:

- The lack of appeal of the registrant's securities to socially responsible investment funds, because of the nature of environmental impacts associated with the registrant's operations.
- Environmental-related loan covenants.

24.7 ENVIRONMENTAL DISCLOSURES

The SEC and various court cases have provided guidance regarding disclosure of environmental risks in the following areas:

- Designation as a PRP.
- Historical and anticipated environmental expenditures.
- Historical and anticipated product liability costs.
- Anticipated regulatory changes.

(a) PRP DESIGNATION

In a 1989 Release, the SEC used a common environmental scenario to explain the criteria for disclosing prospective information under Item 303.

> Facts: A registrant has been correctly designated a PRP by the EPA with respect to cleanup of hazardous waste at three sites. No statutory defenses are available. The registrant is in the process of preliminary investigations of the sites to determine the nature of its potential liability and the amount of remedial costs necessary to clean up the sites. Other PRPs also have been designated, but the ability to obtain contribution is unclear, as is the extent of insurance coverage, if any. Management is unable to determine that a material effect on future financial condition or results of operations is not reasonably likely to occur.

Based on the facts of this hypothetical case, MD&A disclosure of the effects of the PRP status, quantified to the extent reasonably practicable, would be required. In conducting its analysis, the registrant must consider the aggregate potential cleanup costs in light of the joint and several liability to which a PRP is subject. The registrant may also consider, however, potential rights of recovery that would reduce its liability. For example, the availability of insurance coverage and whether and to what extent potential sources of contribution or indemnification constitute reliable sources of recovery may be factored into the determination of whether a material future effect is reasonably likely to occur.

(b) HISTORICAL AND ANTICIPATED ENVIRONMENTAL EXPENDITURES

In SAB 92, the SEC staff provided the following guidance as to the contents of environmental disclosures regarding historical and anticipated environmental expenditures under Regulation S-K:

> Disclosures . . . should be sufficiently specific to enable a reader to understand the scope of the contingencies affecting the registrant. For example, a registrant's discussion of historical and anticipated environmental expenditures should, to the extent material, describe separately (a) recurring costs associated with managing hazardous substances and pollution in on-going operations, (b) capital expenditures to limit or monitor hazardous substances or pollutants, (c) mandated expenditures to remediate previously contaminated sites, and (d) other infrequent or non-recurring clean-up expenditures that can be anticipated but which are not required in the present circumstances. Disaggregated disclosure that describes accrued and reasonably likely losses with respect to particular environmental sites that are individually material may be necessary for a full understanding of these contingencies. Also, if management's investigation of potential liability and remediation cost is at different stages with respect to individual sites, the consequences of this with respect to amounts accrued and disclosed should be discussed.

(c) HISTORICAL AND ANTICIPATED PRODUCT LIABILITY COSTS

In SAB 92, the SEC staff provided the following guidance as to the contents of environmental disclosures regarding historical and anticipated product liability costs under Regulation S-K:

> Examples of specific disclosures typically relevant to an understanding of historical and anticipated product liability costs include the nature of personal injury or property damages alleged by claimants, aggregate settlement costs by type of claim, and related costs of administering and litigating claims. Disaggregated disclosure that describes accrued and reasonably likely losses with respect to particular claims may be necessary if they are individually material. If the contingency involves a large number of relatively small individual claims of a similar type, such as personal injury from exposure to asbestos[,] disclosure of the number of claims pending at each balance sheet date, the number of claims filed for each period presented, the number of claims dismissed, settled, or otherwise resolved for each period, and the average settlement amount per claim may be necessary. Disclosures should address historical and expected trends in these amounts and their reasonably likely effects on operating results and liquidity.

24.8 TIMING OF DISCLOSURES

Disclosure under Regulation S-K is generally required on a periodic basis in the registrant's Form 10-Q and Form 10-K. Accelerated reporting is required on Form 8-K in certain circumstances. Accelerated reporting is discussed in Chapter 11.

24.9 ADDITIONAL CONSIDERATIONS FOR PUBLIC COMPANIES

As explained previously in this chapter, the financial reporting requirements applicable to environmental risks under GAAP are limited. With the exception of environmental loss contingencies (Chapter 19) and environmental remediation liabilities (Chapter 20), environmental risks are not subject to GAAP. Nonpublic companies are therefore subject to limited financial reporting requirements for environmental risks.

Public companies must disclose environmental risks encompassed by Regulation S-K. In addition, public companies are subject to the certification requirements for disclosure controls and procedures contained in section 302 of Sarbanes-Oxley (see § 8.4). Although not subject to audit by the entity's independent financial auditor, disclosure controls and procedures for financial reporting of environmental risks are subject to legal standards for design and operational effectiveness.

Disclosure controls and procedures for financial reporting of environmental risks warrants special attention for several reasons, including:

- Public companies are facing escalating pressure from institutional investors and environmental groups to provide greater disclosure of environmental risks.
- Effectiveness in managing environmental risks is emerging as a barometer of the quality of corporate governance and long-term financial performance.
- The nature of estimates and assumptions about environmental risks involve high levels of subjectivity and judgment.
- Environmental risks generally can be expected to have an increasingly material impact on corporate financial condition and operating performance.

Effective disclosure controls and procedures for environmental risks require appropriate processes to identify, assess, measure, and report trends, events, and uncertainties that are reasonably likely to affect the entity's liquidity, capital resources, or results of operations. Exhibit 24.2 identifies certain process and control issues with regard to financial reporting of environmental risks that may warrant special attention for reporting entities and financial auditors.

Exhibit 24.2

Process and Control Considerations for Environmental Risks

Process Area	Process and Control Considerations
Identification	• Identification of significant internal and external risks facing the enterprise • Identification of significant actions required to achieve and maintain compliance with existing and anticipated environmental laws • Identification of significant environmental trends, events, and uncertainties
Assessment	• Evaluation of the effects of compliance with existing and anticipated environmental laws on capital expenditures, earnings, and competitive position • Selection and application of criteria for determining the probability that known trends, events, or uncertainties will affect the entity's liquidity, capital resources, or results of operations • Policies and procedures for investigation and additional data gathering • Reliance on determinations of legal counsel and other specialists
Measurement	• Selection and application of measurement techniques • Use of actuaries and other specialists • Determination of ability to reasonably estimate • Evaluation of potential for significant near-term changes in estimated amounts
Reporting	• Selection and application of criteria for assessment of materiality • Procedures for drafting and reviewing disclosures • Policies and procedures regarding voluntary disclosure of environmental performance, environmental impacts, and environmental business opportunities

CHAPTER TWENTY-FIVE

Supplemental Reporting Standards

25.1 INTRODUCTION

In 2001, ASTM International issued two standards pertaining to the measurement and disclosure of environmental liabilities:

- E 2137, "Standard Guide for Estimating Monetary Costs and Liabilities for Environmental Matters"
- E 2173, "Standard Guide for Disclosure of Environmental Liabilities"

ASTM International (formerly known as the American Society for Testing and Materials) is one of the largest voluntary standards development organizations in the world. ASTM is not an authoritative body for the development of generally accepted accounting principles, and it lacks authority to impose mandatory financial reporting standards. The standards are intended, however, to supplement and be consistent with GAAP and SEC disclosure rules.

ASTM E 2137 and E 2173 do not represent authoritative pronouncements of GAAP, and compliance with the standards is not expressly required under the federal securities laws. Since their adoption, however, several developments have added to the authoritative stature of the standards, including:

- In 2002, The Rose Foundation for Communities and the Environment petitioned the Securities and Exchange Commission to promulgate rules based on the ASTM standards to clarify the intent of the SEC's disclosure requirements with respect to material environmental liabilities and to help ensure compliance with existing disclosure requirements. To date, the SEC has not taken action on the petition.
- In 2003, a coalition of state, municipal, and labor pension funds known as the Investor Network on Climate Risk publicly called for the SEC to strengthen current environmental disclosure requirements as requested by The Rose Foundation petition.
- The ASTM standards have been introduced in various legal proceedings as evidence of good commercial and customary practice in the United States for estimation and disclosure of environmental costs and liabilities.

Although not mandated by law, some companies may be contractually obligated to comply with the standards. ASTM International has long been a leading source of technical standards for materials, products, systems, and services. Standard commercial agreements in some industries obligate the contracting parties to comply with all applicable ASTM standards. Although intended primarily to require compliance with material and product standards, these contracts may incidentally impose a contractual obligation to comply with ASTM E 2137 and E 2173 as well.

The ASTM standards represent a significant attempt to improve the quality of environmental financial reporting by addressing certain perceived gaps in GAAP. The most significant of these gaps addressed by the ASTM standards are:

- Use of the known minimum value or most likely value to estimate environmental loss contingencies and environmental remediation liabilities under FIN 14 when sufficient information exists to enable a more robust cost estimate.
- Assessment of materiality on an incremental (as opposed to aggregate) basis.

The rising prominence of the ASTM standards may have significant ramifications for public companies. In the future, the SEC, investors, and the courts may turn to the ASTM standards—and demonstrate the difference that application of the standards would have made for an entity's reported environmental financial information—as evidence that a company failed to fairly present its financial condition (without limitation to GAAP) for purposes of sections 302 and 906 of Sarbanes-Oxley (see § 7.2).

25.2 ASTM E 2137

ASTM E 2137, "Standard Guide for Estimating Monetary Costs and Liabilities for Environmental Matters," is a voluntary guide for estimating costs and liabilities for environmental matters. ASTM E 2137 is not intended to supersede accounting standards under GAAP, and the standard does not expressly address the establishment of accounting reserves for environmental liabilities (although it could be used for such purposes) or disclosure requirements. The companion standard, ASTM E 2173, however, directs a reporting entity to disclose the approach used to estimate its environmental liabilities and cross-references ASTM E 2137.

ASTM E 2137 is intended to serve many possible uses for estimates of environmental costs and liabilities, including but not limited to:

- Business decision making.
- Communications and negotiations involving change of property ownership.
- Regulatory requirements.
- Third-party lawsuits.
- Insurance premium calculation and claim settlement.
- Change of property use.
- Revitalization.
- Compliance planning.
- Construction.
- Analysis of remedial alternatives.
- Budgeting.
- Strategic planning.
- Financing.
- Investment analysis by shareholders.

Although it is not intended to supersede applicable financial reporting standards, ASTM E 2137 may be used to facilitate the implementation of GAAP (i.e., measurement of environmental loss contingencies and environmental remediation liabilities under FAS 5 and FIN 14; see Chapters 19 and 20).

(a) PRINCIPLES

ASTM E 2137 identifies several principles underlying the estimation of environmental costs and liabilities. These principles, which are summarized and cross-referenced with related principles under GAAP and generally accepted auditing standards (GAAS) below, are generally relevant to the estimation of environmental costs and liabilities for financial reporting purposes:

- *Estimation does not eliminate uncertainty.* The future resolution of contractual, technological, regulatory, legislative, and judicial issues can affect estimated costs and liabilities (see § 12.3). The corollary to this principle is that uncertainty does not preclude the need or the ability to estimate environmental costs and liabilities, unless the degree of uncertainty is so great that a reasonable estimate cannot be made (see § 12.4).

- *The assumptions underlying environmental estimates should be reviewed periodically.* Environmental estimates should be reviewed periodically for the purpose of incorporating new information (e.g. changes in regulatory requirements, technology, property use, and inflation) (see §§ 12.6 and 26.3(b)).
- *Subsequent estimates based on additional information should not discredit earlier estimates.* The reasonableness of estimates should be evaluated on the analyses and judgments made at the time given the information then available. This principle is consistent with GAAP and GAAS. Subsequent estimates based on information that was known, or should have been known, by the company during a prior period, however, may discredit an earlier estimate (see §§ 12.6 and 26.3(b)).
- *Estimation of environmental costs and liabilities does not necessarily require an exhaustive evaluation of all possible outcomes.* A point exists at which the cost of obtaining information or the time required to gather it outweighs improvement in the quality of the estimate (see also § 12.4(b)).
- *Estimates of environmental costs and liabilities should consider environmental risk.* The degree of actual or potential risk to human health and the environment should be a factor in developing environmental cost and liability estimates. This analysis is relevant to the quantitative and qualitative assessment of materiality (see § 12.2).
- *Estimators of environmental costs and liabilities must be appropriately qualified.* It is the responsibility of the entity sponsoring the cost and liability estimates to select an estimator with the appropriate level of knowledge, training, and experience. This principle corresponds to the use of specialists under GAAS (see § 26.3(g)).

(b) PROCEDURES

(i) INFORMATION TYPES AND SOURCES

After identifying the conditions giving rise to potential environmental costs and liabilities, the process of estimation begins with a review of existing relevant information. ASTM E 2137 provides a laundry list of possible types and sources of information, including:

- Number and location of affected operations and facilities.
- Use of surrounding property.
- Past, current, and potential future site uses.
- Environmental studies.
- Environmental risks (in the sense of risk to human health and the environment).
- Litigation activities related to the event.
- Bodily injury or other claims.

- Relevant state or other regulatory requirements and alternatives.
- State or federal agency involvement.
- Public involvement.
- Planned or completed remedial activities.
- Resources, tasks, and deadlines.
- Available technologies and designs.
- Type and extent of contamination.
- Information on prior experience with similar events.

In the absence or insufficiency of such information, ASTM E 2137 advises that an assessment should be made of applicable regulatory and industry standards and requirements to determine whether further data creation and analysis are warranted.

(ii) *ESTIMATION APPROACHES*

The central component of ASTM E 2137 is a decision framework that guides an entity in choosing among four different various estimating methods. These methods are:

- *Expected value. Expected value* is defined as an estimate of the weighted mean value of an unknown quantity that represents a probability-weighted average over the range of all possible values.
- *Most likely value.* The *most likely value* is the estimated cost of the scenario believed to be most likely to occur (e.g., a stated preferred remedy). This approach may be used when cost or other considerations preclude development of a full range of possible outcomes to support an expected value estimate. This measurement technique is not useful if no scenario, grouping, or cluster of outcomes has a probability of occurrence that is significantly greater than others.
- *Range of values.* The range-of-values approach provides a low cost estimate and a high cost estimate, comparable to a reasonable best-case and reasonable worst-case scenario. The range-of-values technique can be used in place of the expected value or most likely value approaches when probabilities or rankings for various outcomes cannot be determined based on existing information and circumstances.
- *Known minimum value.* The *known minimum value* represents an estimate of costs that are reasonably certain to be incurred. Use of this technique is appropriate in those rare situations when uncertainties are so great that it is not practicable to estimate a range of values.

The methods described above are listed in the order of their robustness and comprehensiveness and degree of effort required. An expected value estimate provides the highest degree of robustness and comprehensiveness, whereas a known minimum value estimate provides the least. Likewise, the level of effort required to prepare an expected value estimate is generally greater than the level of effort needed to prepare an estimate of the most likely value, and so forth. The standard also recognizes that in some circumstances in which the level of uncertainty is sufficiently high, it may not be possible to make a reasonable cost estimate.

Although the expected value approach provides the highest degree of robustness and comprehensiveness, it generally requires the greatest amount of information and effort. ASTM E 2137 recognizes that, based on the principles cited in § 25.2(a), an expected value estimate is not always the most appropriate or *best* estimate for a given set of circumstances.

(c) COMPARISON TO GAAP

The underlying principles and decision framework set forth in ASTM E 2137 are generally consistent with the measurement principles applicable to environmental loss contingencies (Chapter 19) and environmental remediation liabilities (Chapter 20) under GAAP. However, for the reasons described below, application of the decision framework in ASTM E 2137 can be expected to result in cost estimates materially different from (and generally higher than) those developed under GAAP:

- *Decreased use of the known minimum value.* FAS 5 does not provide a specific measurement methodology or decision framework for estimating loss contingencies. FIN 14 was developed to provide a simplistic decision framework for selecting among alternative measurement approaches. According to FIN 14, when some amount within a range of values appears at the time to be a better estimate than any other amount within the range (most likely value), that *best estimate* amount should be accrued. FIN 14 does not describe the measurement techniques that may be used to determine the best estimate. Under FIN 14, when no amount within the range is a better estimate than any other amount, the minimum amount in the range (i.e., the minimum known value) should be accrued. In practice, reporting entities sometimes use the known minimum value to estimate environmental loss contingencies, even though reasonably available information would support a more robust measurement approach. Application of ASTM E 2137 would be expected to result in a reduction in the use of known minimum value estimates.
- *Increased use of expected value estimates.* FIN 14 does not discuss the expected value methodology and does not encourage its use as a means of developing the best estimate. Historically, reporting entities have used expected value estimates infrequently, even though circumstances would permit use of this measurement approach. Application of ASTM E 2137 should result in an increase in the use of expected value estimates, which tend to be significantly higher than most likely value estimates

- *Increased disclosure of the range of values.* ASTM E 2137 encourages entities to determine and disclose the range of values for environmental loss contingencies. Disclosure of the range of values informs users of financial statements of the degree of uncertainty surrounding the cost estimate and the reasonable worst-case amount of the loss. FIN 14 neither requires nor encourages disclosure of the range of values.

ASTM E 2137 does not address the fair value measurement approach required by GAAP for measurement of environmental guarantees under FIN 45 (Chapter 21), asset retirement obligations under FAS 143 (Chapter 22), and asset impairments under FAS 144 (Chapter 23). Quoted market prices in active markets are the best evidence of fair value and should be used, if available. Expected value measurement techniques are used to develop fair value estimates when quoted market prices in active markets are not available.

25.3 ASTM E 2173

ASTM E 2173, "Standard Guide for Disclosure of Environmental Liabilities," is intended to provide a series of options or instructions for determining the conditions warranting disclosure for environmental liabilities and the content of appropriate disclosure to accompany audited and unaudited financial statements in the United States. ASTM E 2173 expressly references E 2137 regarding estimation of environmental costs and liabilities. The standard is intended to supplement and be consistent with disclosure requirements and guidelines under GAAP.

(a) PRINCIPLES

ASTM E 2173 identifies several principles for disclosure of environmental costs and liabilities. These principles are summarized and cross-referenced with related principles under GAAP and SEC disclosure requirements below:

- *Disclosure does not eliminate uncertainty.* The future resolution of contractual, technological, regulatory, legislative, and judicial issues can affect the entity's position with regard to the existence and extent of its environmental liabilities. This principle is consistent with GAAP and SEC disclosure guidance (see, e.g., §§ 19.4, 20.4, and 24.5).
- *Disclosure is case-specific.* The nature and degree of disclosure for environmental liabilities depends on the materiality of the environmental liability and the level of information available. Not every environmental liability warrants the same level of detail in its disclosure. This principle is consistent with GAAP and SEC disclosure regulations (see § 12.2).
- *Subsequent estimates based on additional information should not discredit earlier estimates.* The reasonableness of disclosures should be evaluated on the analyses and judgments made at the time given the information then available. This principle is consistent with GAAP and SEC disclosure

regulations. Subsequent disclosures based on information that was known, or should have been known, by the company during a prior period, however, may discredit an earlier disclosure (see §§ 12.6 and 26.3(b)).

- *Appropriate disclosure need not be exhaustive.* Though all relevant and reasonably ascertainable information should be used to determine the content of appropriate disclosure for environmental liabilities, appropriate disclosure does not necessarily mean an exhaustive disclosure of the reporting entity's environmental liabilities. The appropriate degree of disclosure is based on usability and cost-benefit considerations. This principle is consistent with GAAP and SEC disclosure regulations (see, e.g., § 12.4(b)).
- *Disclosures of environmental liabilities should consider environmental risk.* As the entity becomes aware of an environmental liability, it should assess the actual or potential risk to human health and the environment associated with the underlying environmental condition or event. The degree of actual or potential risk to human health and the environment should be a factor in developing disclosures of environmental liabilities. This analysis is relevant to the quantitative and qualitative assessment of materiality (see § 12.2).

(b) PROCEDURES

(i) CONDITIONS GIVING RISE TO ENVIRONMENTAL LIABILITIES

ASTM E 2173 lists several circumstances that may give rise to environmental liabilities. These include:

- Commencement of environmental regulatory enforcement actions.
- Contractual assumptions of risk or risk-transfer agreements (e.g., environmental insurance, guarantees, and indemnification agreements).
- Commencement of litigation or assertion of an environmental claim or assessment by a party alleging legal liability on the part of the reporting entity.
- Information known by the reporting entity that indicates an environmental liability has been incurred.

(ii) SOURCES OF INFORMATION

ASTM E 2173 identifies standard sources that should be reviewed by a reporting entity to identify and evaluate environmental liabilities. These sources include, but are not limited to:

- Published list of Superfund PRPs.
- Federal National Priorities List site list.
- Comprehensive Environmental Response, Compensation and Liability Information System (CERCLIS).

- Published lists of sites and identified responsible parties under state environmental laws.
- Environmental suits involving the reporting entity.
- Lists of leaking underground storage tanks (LUSTs).
- 50-year title searches on currently or previously owned or operated sites.
- Known payments by the reporting entity for environmental claims and costs.
- Environmental claims or demands involving the reporting entity other than filed suits.
- Environmental records of the reporting entity (e.g., the results of site assessment or investigation reports, environmental audits, monitoring results).

(iii) DETERMINATION OF MATERIALITY

ASTM E 2173 provides that disclosure should be made when an entity believes its liability for environmental costs relating to an individual circumstance *or its environmental liability in the aggregate* is material (*materiality* is defined in terms that are consistent with GAAP and the federal securities laws). In other words, some environmental matters are material, while others are not. However, a reporting entity should not determine that its environmental costs and liabilities are immaterial simply because it has determined that each individual environmental matter, standing alone, is immaterial. Rather, the entity should consider the materiality of its environmental costs and liabilities both individually and in the aggregate. Amounts to be aggregated include, but are not limited to, damages attributed to the entity's products or processes, environmental cleanups, reclamation costs, fines, and litigation costs.

The assessment of materiality on an individual and aggregate basis is required under GAAP and GAAS (see § 12.2(b)(v)).[1] However, in practice, reporting entities may be motivated to subdivide environmental matters until a sufficiently immaterial component level is reached to avoid disclosure. For example, a company might break down its environmental remediation liabilities into component parts (e.g., remediation liabilities for solid waste management unit A at facility X, and so forth), so that no single component of the company's aggregate environmental liabilities exceeds a threshold amount considered to be material (e.g., 5 percent of current assets). Such practices can have the effect of significantly underdisclosing a company's aggregate environmental costs and liabilities.

(iv) CONTENT OF DISCLOSURES

ASTM E 2173 provides guidance on the recommended content of disclosures for material environmental liabilities. The recommended disclosures are intended to supplement and not to replace the disclosure requirements prescribed by GAAP and SEC rules. Disclosures should address the following matters:

---

1 *See*, e.g., minutes of March 9, 2005 FASB board meeting (Section 12.2(b)(v)).

- Judgments or assumptions about the likelihood and potential materiality of liability.
- Number of instances giving rise to environmental liabilities.
- Quantitative estimates of environmental liabilities (before offset for potential rights of recovery), measurement techniques used, reasons why reasonable estimates cannot be made, and amounts recognized in the financial statements.
- Potential rights of recovery and related uncertainties as to collectibility.
- Key factors regarding the timing or amount of the liabilities and related recoveries.

(c) COMPARISON TO GAAP AND SEC DISCLOSURE REQUIREMENTS

The guidance set forth in ASTM E 2173 is generally consistent with disclosure requirements and guidelines under GAAP, GAAS, and SEC regulations and interpretations, as discussed in Chapters 12 through 24. Strict application of the standard, however, can be expected to significantly increase the amount of environmental disclosure by explicitly recognizing the need to assess the materiality of environmental liabilities on both individual and aggregate bases.

PART FOUR

Audit Standards and Practices

CHAPTER TWENTY-SIX

Financial Statement Auditing

26.1 INTRODUCTION

The accounting and disclosure issues relating to environmental financial information are complex and require the application of knowledge and experience across many disciplines. Exposure to environmental liabilities and impairments and the controls implemented to identify and evaluate these exposures vary from industry to industry and from entity to entity within the same industry.

The lack of consistent environmental accounting practices, combined with the following general characteristics of environmental financial reporting, greatly increase audit risk in an audit of financial statements in accordance with generally accepted auditing standards:

- Environmental matters typically involve significant risks and uncertainties (see § 12.5).
- Environmental financial information is usually predicated on accounting estimates and assumptions involving high levels of subjectivity and judgment (see § 24.5(e)).
- Environmental matters typically involve a high degree of inherent risk (see § 26.2(c)(i)).
- Standards for internal control over financial reporting of environmental matters are not well developed, thus adding to the level of control risk (see § 26.2(c)(ii)).
- Environmental financial reporting is susceptible to risk factors for fraud (see § 26.2(d)).

The significant potential for audit risk with regard to environmental financial reporting is a concern for both auditors and reporting entities. Management—of both public and nonpublic companies—is responsible for establishing and maintaining controls that will enable it to identify, assess, measure, and report environmental financial information in a manner that conforms with GAAP and (for public companies) fairly presents the financial condition of the entity. The same factors that give rise to audit risk in the planning of a financial statement audit should be of concern to management when seeking to design and implement effective internal control over environmental financial reporting.

This chapter discusses the application of GAAS to the audit of an entity's financial statements as it relates to environmental financial information. In 1996, the AICPA addressed the issues associated with auditing environmental remediation liabilities in SOP 96-1, "Environmental Remediation Liabilities." The auditing guidance in SOP 96-1 focuses on environmental remediation liabilities arising under CERCLA, the corrective action provisions in RCRA, and other analogous state and foreign environmental laws. It does not address, for example, pollution control costs, environmental exit costs, and asset retirement obligations. SOP 96-1 also expressly does not apply to voluntary environmental cleanup activities that are undertaken at the sole discretion of management and that are not induced by threat of litigation or assertion of a claim or assessment.

This chapter describes the audit guidance in SOP 96-1 and suggests supplemental audit guidance to address key areas not addressed in that pronouncement. In particular, this chapter seeks to identify audit issues associated with FAS 143, which did not exist when SOP 96-1 was developed.

26.2 AUDIT PLANNING AND OBJECTIVES

(a) UNDERSTANDING THE BUSINESS

The nature, timing, and extent of audit planning will vary with the size and complexity of the entity and with the auditor's familiarity with the entity's business. Planning for an audit of environmental financial information requires the auditor to obtain an understanding of the accounting and disclosure requirements for environmental costs, assets, liabilities, impairments, and risks set forth in Part Three of this book. The auditor should also understand the nature of the entity's business, its organization, and its operating characteristics. Examples of such matters that pertain to environmental financial information include:

- The industry or industries in which the entity operates.
- The types of products or services provided and used by the entity.
- The number and characteristics of the entity's operating locations.
- The number and characteristics of the entity's nonoperating locations.
- The entity's history of acquisitions and divestitures.
- Applicable environmental laws.
- The entity's current and former production and distribution processes.
- The entity's current and former waste management practices.
- The entity's overall approach to environmental risk management.

An understanding of such matters generally is obtained through prior experience with the entity or its industry and inquiries addressed to entity personnel. Accounting, finance, operations, real estate, environmental, health and safety, compliance, risk management, public affairs, and legal personnel are all likely to have relevant information about environmental matters. Appropriate questions of such personnel may include:

- Has the entity documented its environmental financial reporting policies and procedures?
- What controls are in place to identify potential environmental loss contingencies, remediation liabilities, environmental guarantees, asset impairments, or asset retirement obligations affecting the entity?
- Does the entity have a formal environmental management system, such as ISO 14001?
- What environmental due diligence procedures does the entity follow when acquiring real estate properties or other businesses?
- Is the entity required to have environmental permits, such as hazardous waste transporter permits or hazardous waste treatment, storage, and disposal permits?

- Are landfills or underground storage tanks used to store or dispose of environmentally hazardous substances?
- Has the entity been designated as a PRP by the EPA under CERCLA or by state regulatory agencies under analogous state laws?
- Have governmental authorities or private citizens previously alleged violations of environmental laws?
- Is the entity subject to any pending or threatened administrative, civil, or criminal environmental investigations or legal actions?
- Have regulatory authorities or environmental consultants issued any reports about the entity, such as site assessments or environmental impact studies?
- Does the entity own or operate any locations that are known or reasonably suspected to have environmental contamination but which are not the subject of any pending government investigations or legal actions?
- Does the entity own surplus, nonproductive real estate or facilities with only nominal operations? If so, why is the entity continuing to hold these properties?
- Are the entity's properties subject to land use restrictions?
- For property sold, abandoned, purchased, or closed, are there any requirements for site cleanup or for future removal and site restoration?
- Has the entity previously agreed to indemnify or to be indemnified by other parties for environmental costs or loss contingencies?
- Does the entity regularly purchase and maintain pollution legal liability insurance?
- What is the status of the relationship between the entity and its historical insurance carriers of pollution liability coverage?

In addition to company personnel, the auditor should research other sources of information about environmental financial information, which may include:

- The entity's prior financial statements and SEC reports.
- Minutes of meetings of the board of directors (or committees, especially the audit committee and environmental affairs committee).
- Reports prepared by the entity's internal auditors, compliance officers, risk manager, environmental manager, or other individuals responsible for environmental matters.
- Information available through the Internet or subscription-based online information services.
- Publicly available information about entities in the same industry (including financial statements and SEC reports).
- Industry publications.

- Information available from regulatory agencies.
- Other sources of information identified in ASTM E 2137 and E 2173 (see §§ 25.2(b)(i) and 25.3(b)(ii)).

Depending on the extent of the entity's environmental exposures and level of audit risk, the auditor may decide to involve a specialist in the audit planning process. For public companies, the financial statement auditors should coordinate closely with internal control auditors when planning for an audit of environmental financial information.

(b) AUDIT OBJECTIVES

It is management's responsibility to develop appropriate estimates and disclosures of environmental financial information for use in preparation of the financial statements. It is the auditor's responsibility to evaluate the reasonableness of those estimates and disclosures in forming an opinion on the financial statements taken as a whole. Most of the auditor's work in forming an opinion consists of obtaining and evaluating evidence concerning management's assertions in the financial statements. *Assertions* are representations by management that are embodied in the financial statements and notes.

With respect to environmental financial information, the relevant financial statement assertions and the related objectives of the auditor are shown in Exhibit 26.1.

With respect to completeness and valuation, historically, auditors have focused principally on valuation rather than completeness. As discussed in various points throughout this chapter, recent changes in applicable financial accounting standards—most notably, FAS 143—pose significant challenges for the auditor in evaluating the extent to which management has comprehensively identified the wide range of underlying environmental conditions, events, and transactions that could give rise to environmental financial reporting obligations under GAAP. In the future, it will be necessary for auditors to dedicate greater attention to the evaluation of completeness when planning the financial statement audit.

EXHIBIT 26.1

Audit Assertions and Objectives

ASSERTIONS	OBJECTIVES
Completeness and valuation	To determine whether all environmental financial information that should be presented in the financial statements is identified and reflected in the financial statements in conformity with GAAP
Presentation and disclosure	To determine whether environmental financial information is classified, described, and disclosed in the financial statements in conformity with GAAP

(c) ASSESSING AUDIT RISK

When planning the audit, the auditor assesses *inherent risk, control risk,* and *detection risk* to determine the nature, timing, and extent of the substantive procedures that will be performed to achieve the audit objectives. Once the auditor has obtained an understanding of the entity's potential environmental loss exposures, he or she should make preliminary judgments about materiality (§ 12.2) and should assess audit risk. The application of the concept of materiality in the context of determining audit risk is further addressed in the following sections. *Audit risk* is the risk that the auditor may unknowingly fail to appropriately modify his or her opinion on financial statements that are materially misstated. Audit risk is comprised of inherent risk, control risk, and detection risk.

(i) INHERENT RISK

AICPA Statement of Auditing Standards No. 47, "Audit Risk and Materiality in Conducting an Audit" (SAS 47), defines *inherent risk* as the susceptibility of an assertion to a material misstatement, assuming there are no related internal controls. In other words, assuming that the entity has absolutely no procedures and controls for identifying, assessing, estimating, and reporting environmental financial information in accordance with GAAP, how great is the risk that the entity's financial statements, taken as a whole, may contain material misstatements or omissions?

In assessing inherent risk for assertions about environmental financial information, the auditor should consider the following:

- *Knowledge about the industry in which the entity operates.* Certain industries, by nature, tend to have a significant risk of exposure to environmental liabilities, loss contingencies, impairments, and asset retirement obligations. Examples of such industries include hazardous materials transportation, waste management, chemicals, petrochemicals, oil and gas, pharmaceuticals, mining, utilities, wood products, and manufacturing. Environmental exposures are not limited, however, to these industries. Examples of other industries with potentially material environmental loss exposures are real estate, banking, insurance, hospitality, and health care. Certain research and development activities (including those engaged in by some not-for-profit entities) also may be subject to significant exposures.
- *Knowledge about the entity's prior operations.* The entity's current operations may be environmentally benign. Nonetheless, the entity's former operations (including offsite waste disposal) may be a source of significant environmental loss exposure. Because of the nature of liability under CERCLA and analogous state and foreign environmental laws, an entity's environmental remediation liability exposure, for example, may extend long after it has divested itself of environmentally hazardous operations.
- *Knowledge about prior transactions.* Certain transactions, such as past acquisitions involving real property (including foreclosures on contaminated properties), may expose an entity to environmental liabilities. Under

EXHIBIT 26.2

Examples of Transactions (and Nontransactions) Indicative of Environmental Risk

- Past or current operation or ownership of property on which hazardous substances are being or were released or disposed of
- Sales of real estate or businesses under arrangements whereby the seller retained responsibility for environmental cleanup costs and liabilities pursuant to indemnification clauses
- Sales of operating facilities under arrangements whereby the buyer was prohibited from performing preacquisition or postacquisition subsurface environmental testing to identify and evaluate historical pollution conditions
- Aborted real estate sales transactions
- Recent purchases of property at prices that appear to be significantly below market value
- Sales of businesses involving the retention of real property by the seller
- Retention of nonproductive, surplus real estate
- Maintenance of nominal operations at outdated or unprofitable facilities to avoid permanent retirement or abandonment

Superfund, current and former owners and operators of contaminated facilities may be responsible for cleanup costs and natural resource damages. Situations such as those listed in Exhibit 26.2 may indicate the existence of environmental risk:

- *Trends in environmental standards, enforcement, and litigation.* Conditions that may have constituted significant environmental loss exposures in the past may not constitute significant loss exposures in the future, and vice versa. For example, factors such as the regulatory trend toward risk-based corrective action and state voluntary cleanup programs, and the expanded use of innovative remediation technologies, have reduced the severity of liability exposures associated with many contaminated sites. Conversely, the increase in governmental claims for natural resource damages poses significant future loss exposures for companies responsible for widespread historical pollution conditions that have impacted rivers, lakes, wetlands, and sensitive ecological systems.

- *Magnitude of environmental loss exposures.* Environmental loss exposures are typically characterized as low frequency and high magnitude. In other words, environmental losses, such as claims for Superfund liability, tend to occur infrequently, but when they occur, they can have a significant adverse financial impact. For entities subject to environmental loss exposures based on prior or current operations, it is inherently difficult to conclude that such exposures are not material, in the absence of effective controls to identify and evaluate these exposures.

- *Existence of environmental insurance.* Generally, environmental liabilities and loss contingencies are not covered by the entity's current general liability and property/casualty insurance policies. With the exception of potential coverage under historical occurrence-based policies, separate pollution legal liability and stop-loss policies must be in place before the entity will be protected against environmental losses. The absence of insurance coverage for environmental liabilities and loss contingencies increases the inherent risk that undisclosed environmental matters will result in a significant adverse financial effect on the entity.

When assessing inherent risk of environmental loss contingencies associated with known or suspected historical pollution conditions, in particular, the auditor should recognize that the entity's potential loss exposure is affected by factors that management cannot control, such as changing public opinions, the actions of regulators and adjacent property owners, the recommendations and opinions of technical and engineering experts, the demands of investors and creditors, and natural phenomena (e.g., fires, floods, wind damage, migration of contaminants in surface water and groundwater, etc.). For this reason, the evaluation of environmental loss contingencies usually involves considerable analysis and subjective estimation by management and requires the assistance of third parties such as attorneys, environmental scientists and engineers, and risk-management specialists.

(ii) *CONTROL RISK*

SAS 47 defines *control risk* as the risk that a material misstatement that could occur in an assertion will not be prevented or detected on a timely basis by the entity's internal control. Control risk is a function of the effectiveness of the design and operation of internal control in achieving the entity's environmental financial reporting objectives (see Chapter 5). Some control risk will always exist because of the inherent limitations of internal control (see § 8.3(c)).

Statement of Auditing Standards No. 55, "Consideration of Internal Control in a Financial Statement Audit" (SAS 55), as amended by SAS 78, identifies the components of internal control and explains how an independent auditor should consider internal control in planning and performing an audit. PCAOB Auditing Standard No. 2, "An Audit of Internal Control over Financial Reporting Conducted in Conjunction with an Audit of Financial Statements," sets forth the standards for conducting an audit of internal control for public companies subject to section 404 of Sarbanes-Oxley. The components of internal control are described in Chapter 8. Auditing of public company internal control systems is covered in Chapter 27.

There is no "one size fits all" standard for environmental internal control. The appropriate level of internal control will vary from entity to entity. Some entities have specially designed processes and supporting information management systems for data collection and quantification, and expert personnel involved in the evaluation and oversight of environmental compliance, operational, and financial reporting activities. Other entities have less formal means of gathering information and may rely on outside parties to assist management in its evaluation and oversight of environmental activities. Some entities have extensive documentation of their environmental internal control systems, whereas others have only limited documentation.

When considering the appropriate level of documentation and sophistication of an entity's environmental internal control system, the auditor should consider such factors as:

- The extent of environmental exposure to which the entity is subject.
- The number of operating divisions and locations.
- The geographical diversity of the entity's facilities.
- The entity's history of mergers, acquisitions, and divestitures.
- Remediation activities undertaken or expected to be required.
- Commercial standards and practices for environmental due diligence in the context of mergers, acquisitions, and real estate transactions in the entity's industry.
- The entity's historical policies and practices regarding environmental financial reporting.

The standards set forth by the PCAOB for auditing internal control systems (Chapter 27) describe additional factors that auditors may wish to consider when evaluating the control risk of nonpublic entities.

(iii) DETECTION RISK

SAS 47 defines *detection risk* as the risk that the auditor will not detect a material misstatement that exists in an assertion. Detection risk is a function of the effectiveness of an auditing procedure and of its application by the auditor. It arises partly from uncertainties that exist when the auditor examines less than 100 percent of an entity's environmental account balances and environmental transactions and partly because of other uncertainties that exist even if he or she were to examine 100 percent of such account balances and transactions. For example, an auditor might select an inappropriate auditing procedure, misapply an appropriate procedure, or misinterpret the audit results.

Detection risk differs from inherent risk and control risk in that it does not exist independent of the audit itself. Detection risk should bear an inverse relationship to inherent and control risk. The less the inherent risk and control risk the auditor believes exists, the greater the detection risk that can be accepted. Conversely, the greater the perceived inherent risk and control risk, the less the detection risk that can be accepted. The auditor's assessment of inherent risk and control risk thus forms the basis for his or her decisions about the nature, timing, and extent of substantive audit procedures to be performed.

(d) CONSIDERATIONS OF FRAUD

Statement of Auditing Standards No. 99, "Consideration of Fraud in a Financial Statement Audit" (SAS 99), establishes standards and provides guidance to auditors in fulfilling their responsibility to meet those standards, as they relate to fraud, in a financial statement audit. SAS 99 addresses the following topics:

- Description and characteristics of fraud.
- The importance of exercising professional skepticism.
- Discussion among engagement personnel regarding the risks of material misstatement due to fraud.

- Obtaining the information needed to identify risks of material misstatement due to fraud.
- Identifying risks that may result in a material misstatement due to fraud.
- Assessing the identified risks after taking into account an evaluation of the entity's programs and controls.
- Responding to the results of the assessment.
- Evaluating audit evidence.
- Communicating about fraud to management, the audit committee, and others.
- Documenting the auditor's consideration of fraud.

SAS 99 defines *fraud* is an intentional act that results in a material misstatement in financial statements that are the subject of an audit. Fraudulent financial reporting is not always associated with grand conspiracies. SAS 99 reminds auditors that fraudulent financial reporting can occur in more subtle situations; for example, when management representatives rationalize the appropriateness of a material misstatement as an aggressive (but not indefensible) interpretation of complex accounting rules, or a temporary misstatement of financial statements, expected to be corrected later when operational results improve.

Fraudulent financial reporting may be accomplished by:

- Manipulation, falsification, or alteration of accounting records or supporting documents (e.g., environmental audit and assessment reports).
- Misrepresentation or intentional omission of environmental conditions, events, transactions, or other significant environmental financial information.
- Intentional misapplication of accounting principles relating to amounts, classification, manner of presentation, or disclosure (e.g., intentionally biasing assumptions and judgments used to estimate environmental liabilities).

When obtaining information about the entity and its environment, SAS 99 instructs the auditor to consider whether the information indicates that one or more of the following three *fraud risk factors* are present:

- Management or other employees have an incentive or are under pressure, which provides a reason to commit fraud.
- Circumstances exist—for example, the absence of controls, ineffective controls, or the ability of management to override controls—that provide an opportunity for a fraud to be perpetrated.
- Those involved are able to rationalize committing a fraudulent act.

Identification and assessment of environmental matters that may be subject to financial reporting and development of environmental estimates and disclosures are two areas where one or more fraud risk factors are likely to be present. First, as discussed in § 5.4, management faces numerous competing objectives with regard to environmental financial reporting. These competing objectives may create an incentive to delay or avoid identification, assessment, and measurement of pollution conditions for financial reporting purposes. Fraudulent financial reporting can result when senior management intentionally or unintentionally projects a "don't ask, don't tell" control environment. Second, environmental financial reporting is typically characterized by weak internal control and susceptibility to management override. This condition has been fostered in part by financial reporting standards that explicitly rest upon management's intent regarding the future use of contaminated assets (see § 23.2(d)(ii)). Moreover, environmental estimates and assessments of materiality are inherently susceptible to intentional bias of assumptions and judgments and management override of existing controls. Finally, and perhaps most significantly, the complexity and ambiguity of the financial reporting standards applicable to environmental matters leave ample opportunity for management to rationalize an aggressive position favoring minimal reporting of environmental financial information.

26.3 SUBSTANTIVE AUDIT PROCEDURES

Substantive audit procedures are designed to reduce detection risk to an acceptable level. Traditionally, as described in SOP 96-1, the auditor's substantive tests of environmental financial information generally have focused primarily on evaluating the reasonableness of management's estimates of identified environmental conditions, and consisted of the following three principal types of activities:

1. Obtaining representations from management.
2. Making inquiries of legal counsel or identified specialists.
3. Testing the accounting estimates recorded by management.

Following the adoption of new accounting standards applicable to environmental financial reporting (primarily FAS 143, "Accounting for Asset Retirement Obligations"; FIN 47, "Conditional Asset Retirement Obligations"; and FIN 45, "Guarantor's Accounting and Disclosure Requirements for Guarantees, Including Indirect Guarantees of Indebtedness of Others"), auditors can be expected to dedicate greater attention to substantive tests designed to ensure completeness (see Exhibit 26.1); that is, to ensure that the entity has identified and adequately assessed all environmental-related conditions, transactions, and events that should be reflected in the financial statements and related disclosures.

(a) EVALUATING COMPLETENESS

The audit guidance in SOP 96-1 focuses exclusively on environmental remediation liabilities subject to accrual or disclosure under FAS 5. As discussed in § 19.2(c)(ii), prior to the initiation of formal legal action, FAS 5 provides that accrual of a liability is not required unless assertion of a claim or assessment is probable, an unfavorable outcome is probable, and the amount of the loss can be reasonably estimated. If assertion of a claim or assessment is not probable, neither accrual nor disclosure is required. FAS 5 thus generally does not require accrual or disclosure of unasserted environmental claims, even though an enforceable legal obligation may exist.

To gain reasonable assurance that the entity has reported all environmental loss contingencies subject to reporting under FAS 5, the auditor generally must do no more than ask management to provide a list of all identified pending or threatened environmental legal proceedings, and confirm the completeness of management's list by inquiring of the entity's internal and external legal counsel. However, for reasons discussed in § 26.3(i), *to the extent GAAP applies to unasserted legal obligations, the audit inquiry letter is essentially useless as a substantive audit procedure.*

FAS 143, as interpreted by FIN 47, and FIN 45 specifically apply to unasserted claims relating to enforceable environmental legal obligations. Audit inquiry letters simply cannot be used to validate management's assertions regarding the identification of the entity's environmental asset retirement obligations and environmental indemnities. An evaluation of the entity's internal control procedures for identification of environmental asset retirement obligations and environmental indemnities may satisfy the auditor that the degree of control risk is very low. If, however, effective controls do not exist, the auditor must determine whether exclusive reliance on management's representations presents an unacceptable level of detection risk. If so, alternative substantive audit procedures must be applied. Such procedures may include:

- Comparison of the entity's reported balances with those of other companies in the same industry or with similar environmental profiles.
- Research of information about the entity's environmental exposures available through the Internet or subscription-based online information services.
- Use of environmental specialists to identify and evaluate the entity's environmental asset retirement obligations and environmental indemnities in a manner comparable to environmental due diligence in a merger and acquisition (M&A) context.
- Evaluation of the entity's insurance coverage with respect to unidentified environmental asset retirement obligations and environmental indemnities.

(b) EVALUATING THE REASONABLENESS OF ENVIRONMENTAL ESTIMATES

When evaluating the reasonableness of management's environmental estimates, the auditor should understand how management developed the estimates. Based on that understanding, the auditor should use one or a combination of the following three approaches set forth in Statement of Auditing Standards No. 57, "Auditing Accounting Estimates" (SAS 57), to audit the estimate:

1. Review and test the process used by management to develop the estimate.
2. Develop an independent expectation of the estimate to corroborate the reasonableness of management's estimate.
3. Review subsequent events or transactions occurring prior to the completion of fieldwork.

Typically, methods 1 and 2, or a combination thereof, will be most effective for evaluating environmental estimates, as pollution control costs and cleanup costs generally are expended over a long period of time, usually extending well beyond the completion of fieldwork. Due to the complexity involved in developing independent environmental estimates, including the possible need to use the work of a specialist, method 1 normally will be most efficient.

(c) AUDITING FAIR VALUE MEASUREMENTS AND DISCLOSURES

SAS 57 (see § 26.3(b)) provides guidance on auditing accounting estimates in general. Statement of Auditing Standards No. 101, "Auditing Fair Value Measurements and Disclosures" (SAS 101), addresses issues similar to those in SAS 57, as well as other considerations of specific relevance to fair value measurements and disclosures.

SAS 101 instructs the auditor to obtain sufficient competent audit evidence to provide reasonable assurance that fair value measurements and disclosures are in conformity with GAAP. GAAP requires that certain types of environmental assets and liabilities (e.g., emission credits, asset retirement obligations, asset impairments, and the noncontingent component of environmental guarantees) be measured at fair value. FASB Statement of Financial Accounting Concepts No. 7, "Using Cash Flow Information and Present Value in Accounting Measurements" (SFAC 7), defines the *fair value* of an asset (or liability) as the amount at which that asset (or liability) could be bought (or incurred) or sold (or settled) in a current transaction between willing parties; that is, other than in a forced or liquidation sale.

Observable market prices are the best evidence of fair value. In the absence of observable market prices, GAAP requires that valuation methods incorporate assumptions that marketplace participants would use in their estimates of fair value whenever that information is available without undue cost and effort. If information about market assumptions is unavailable, an entity may use its own assumptions as long as there are no contrary data indicating that marketplace participants would use different assumptions. These concepts generally are not relevant for accounting estimates made on measurement bases other than fair value (e.g., estimates of environmental loss contingencies made under FAS 5 and FIN 14).

To fulfill its responsibility for making the fair value measurements and disclosures for environmental assets and liabilities, management must first establish a process to identify and assess the conditions, events, and transactions that require fair value measurement and disclosure (see Chapter 1). Thereafter, management must:

- Establish an accounting and financial reporting process for determining the fair value measurements and disclosures.
- Select appropriate valuation methods.
- Identify and adequately support any significant assumptions used.
- Prepare the valuation.
- Ensure that the presentation and disclosure of the fair value measurements are in accordance with GAAP.

The auditor should obtain an understanding of the entity's process for determining fair value measurements and disclosures, and of the relevant controls, sufficient to develop an effective audit approach. In some cases, the measurement of fair value and therefore the process set up by management to determine fair value may be simple and reliable. For example, management may be able to refer to published price quotations in an active market to determine fair value for emission credits held by the entity. Fair value measurements of environmental obligations, however, are inherently more complex. They generally involve uncertainty about the occurrence of future events or their outcome, and typically involve significant assumptions and the use of judgment.

When obtaining an understanding of the entity's process for determining fair value measurements and disclosures, the auditor considers, for example:

- Controls over the process used to determine fair value measurements (e.g., controls over data and the segregation of duties between those committing the entity to the underlying transactions and those responsible for undertaking the valuations).
- The expertise and experience of those persons determining the fair value measurements.
- The role that information technology has in the process.
- The types of accounts or transactions requiring fair value measurements or disclosures (e.g., whether the accounts arise from the recording of routine and recurring transactions or whether they arise from nonroutine or unusual transactions, as is generally the case with environmental liabilities).

- The extent to which the entity's process relies on a service organization to provide fair value measurements or the data that supports the measurement. When an entity uses a service organization, the auditor considers the requirements of Statement of Auditing Standards No. 70, "Service Organizations" (SAS 70), as amended.
- The extent to which the entity engages or employs specialists in determining fair value measurements and disclosures (see § 26.3(g)).
- The significant management assumptions used in determining fair value.
- The documentation supporting management's assumptions.
- The process used to develop and apply management assumptions, including whether management used available market information (e.g., active insurance markets for transfer of environmental remediation liabilities) to develop the assumptions.
- The process used to monitor changes in management's assumptions.
- The integrity of change controls and security procedures for valuation models and relevant information systems, including approval processes.
- The controls over the consistency, timeliness, and reliability of the data used in valuation models.

The auditor should evaluate whether the entity's method for determining fair value measurements is applied consistently and, if so, whether the consistency is appropriate considering possible changes in the environment or circumstances affecting the entity, or changes in accounting principles. For example, the introduction of an active insurance market for transfer of a previously nontransferable environmental liability may indicate that use of the expected present value method to estimate the fair value of the liability is no longer appropriate.

When management's intent to carry out specific courses of action is relevant to a fair value measurement (e.g., management's intent to indefinitely avoid settlement of an asset retirement obligation), the auditor should evaluate management's intent and management's ability to carry out those courses of action. The auditor should not simply rely on management's representations, but should instead corroborate management's representations by examining management's relevant performance history and challenging management's ability to carry out its stated intentions. This can be done, for example, by:

- Considering management's past history of carrying out its stated intentions with respect to assets or liabilities.
- Reviewing written plans and other documentation, including, as applicable, budgets, minutes, and other such items.
- Considering management's stated reasons for choosing a particular course of action.

- Considering management's ability to carry out a particular course of action given the entity's economic circumstances, including the implications of its contractual commitments.

SAS 55 discusses the inherent limitations of internal control. As fair value determinations often involve subjective judgments by management, this may affect the nature of controls that are capable of being implemented, including the possibility of management override of controls (see § 26.2(d)). If observable market prices are not available to support fair value, the auditor faces an increased risk of material misstatement, due to both fraud and error, and must accordingly devise an adequate audit response. For example, the auditor should consider engaging a specialist and using the work of that specialist as evidential matter in performing substantive tests to evaluate management's fair value assertions. Alternatively, the auditor might consider making an independent estimate of fair value (e.g., by using an auditor-developed model) based on his or her own assumptions instead of management's assumptions.

Disclosure of fair value information in the notes to the financial statements is required under GAAP. Important considerations in auditing disclosures regarding fair value measurements of environmental liabilities include:

- Are valuation principles appropriately and consistently applied?
- Are the methods of estimation and significant assumptions adequately disclosed in accordance with GAAP?
- For items involving a high degree of measurement uncertainty, are the disclosures sufficient to inform users of such uncertainty?
- When fair value information is omitted from the financial statements because it is not practicable to reasonably estimate fair value, are the disclosures required in these circumstances adequate?
- If the entity has not appropriately disclosed fair value information required by GAAP, are the financial statements materially misstated?

(d) EVALUATING CHANGES IN ESTIMATES

A change in an estimate is generally the result of new information or new circumstances that cause a change in the assumptions underlying the estimate. Pending or probable claims for Superfund liability, for example, are generally reported as an estimate of expected future remediation costs. The sudden bankruptcy of a significant participating PRP, or other new circumstances causing management to increase its estimated share of the remediation costs, would be considered a change in estimate. Changes in estimates are treated as accounting adjustments in the year in which new information causes the estimate to be changed.

A change in estimate, particularly if it is material, may call into question the use of the estimate in a prior reporting period. SAS 57 states that accounting estimates are appropriate when either the measurement of some amounts or the valuation of some accounts is uncertain, pending the outcome of *future* events, or relevant data concerning events that have already occurred cannot be accumulated on a timely, cost-effective basis. If the change in estimate is based on information that was known, or reasonably should have been known, by the company during the prior period, a restatement of the prior-period financial statements may be required. For example, if management failed to implement appropriate procedures to identify, assess, measure, and report environmental-related asset retirement obligations in the prior period, and then later reports preexisting but previously unidentified obligations, the prior omissions may be considered erroneous. If further investigation shows that management intentionally used erroneous estimates or failed to develop estimates for known environmental obligations in order to manipulate the financial statements, this would constitute fraud.

(e) REVIEWING AND TESTING PROCESSES USED BY MANAGEMENT

The auditor may evaluate the reasonableness of environmental estimates by reviewing the process used by management to develop the estimate and by performing procedures to test it. This approach often is the most appropriate when the estimates are developed by or based on the work of an environmental specialist. As discussed in § 26.3(g), environmental specialists may be employees of the entity, employees of the auditor's firm, or independent experts. Estimates prepared by a specialist give higher assurance of reasonableness. An estimate prepared by a specialist who is independent of the reporting entity provides an even greater assurance of reasonableness.

SAS 57 identifies the following procedures auditors may consider performing when using this approach:

- Identify whether there are controls over the preparation of accounting estimates and supporting data that may be useful in the evaluation. Some of the more common controls over the preparation of environmental estimates that might be considered by the auditor include:
    - The nature and extent of monitoring by senior management or the board of directors of the entity's consideration of environmental financial information.
    - The nature and extent of procedures in place for assessing compliance with applicable environmental laws and for evaluating possible violations.
    - The nature and extent of procedures in place for involving appropriate operating, financial, legal, and compliance personnel in monitoring the entity's environmental legal obligations, and in developing the estimates in accordance with GAAP.
    - The information systems used by the entity to compile and access data about the entity's waste generation, emissions, and other environmental impacts.

  - The entity's use of environmental specialists, including its procedures for determining whether the specialists have the requisite skill or knowledge regarding environmental matters, knowledge of the entity's business, and understanding of the available methodologies for calculating environmental estimates.
  - The procedures in place for verifying that data about the nature, destinations, and volumes of hazardous substances or wastes are appropriately collected, classified, and summarized in accordance with regulatory requirements.
  - The procedures in place for assessing the appropriateness of industry or other external sources of data used in developing assumptions (e.g., information provided by other PRPs, regulatory authorities, and industry associations) and, when applicable, for substantiating such information.
- Identify the sources of data and factors that management used in forming the assumptions, and consider whether such data and factors are relevant, reliable, and sufficient for the purpose, based on information gathered in other audit tests. Sources of data and factors used may include:
  - Internal company records, such as payroll records for employees who devote significant time directly to environmental efforts.
  - Information from published sources about socioeconomic trends or other factors that might affect environmental liabilities, loss contingencies, and asset retirement obligations, such as inflation rates, judicial decisions, and enacted changes in legislation.
- Consider whether there are additional key factors or alternative assumptions about the factors. Key factors that might be considered include:
  - Information about environmental loss contingencies included in the response to the inquiry of the entity's lawyer.
  - Studies or reports by environmental consultants.
  - Reports, notices, or correspondence issued by regulatory authorities.
  - Notices of environmental claims and related cost estimates submitted by the company to its insurance carriers.
- Evaluate whether the assumptions are consistent with each other, the supporting data, relevant historical data, and industry data. For example, assumptions that might be evaluated with respect to environmental remediation liabilities include:
  - Allocations of remediation responsibilities (and consequently the attendant liabilities) among PRPs.
  - Remediation technologies and expected time frames.
  - Postclosure monitoring requirements.
  - Estimates of the remaining useful life of long-lived assets.
  - Discount rates used in calculating net present value.

- Analyze historical data used in developing the assumptions to assess whether the data are comparable and consistent with data of the period under audit, and consider whether the data are sufficiently reliable for this purpose. Factors to consider include:
  - Whether the entity's current process for developing environmental estimates has resulted in reasonably accurate, appropriate estimates in prior periods, and the extent to which current data indicate changes from prior experience.
  - Whether changes in the entity's business have been factored into the estimate.
  - Relationships between estimates of environmental liabilities for one location and estimates or actual costs incurred for similar locations.
- Consider whether changes in the business or industry may cause other factors to become significant to the assumptions.
- Review available documentation of the assumptions used in developing the accounting estimates and inquire about any other plans, goals, and objectives of the entity, as well as their relationship to the assumptions. Consider the following, for example:
  - Practices concerning the resolution of environmental contingencies that may have a significant effect on the entity's ultimate environmental liability (e.g., a practice of vigorously contesting remediation plans proposed by regulators as opposed to a practice of tacitly accepting those plans).
  - Plans to sell, dispose of, or abandon specific facilities.
  - Financial statements or other information used by management to assess the financial viability of potential sources of recovery.
- Consider using the work of a specialist regarding certain assumptions.
- Test the calculations used by management to translate the assumptions and key factors into the accounting estimate.

(f) DEVELOPING AN INDEPENDENT EXPECTATION OF ESTIMATES

The auditor may decide to develop an independent expectation of environmental estimates by using the work of an environmental specialist. This approach is appropriate, for example, when management has not engaged or employed an environmental specialist, or when the auditor must assess the reasonableness of, or the effects of alternative key factors and assumptions on, an estimate prepared by a specialist engaged or employed by management.

(g) USING THE WORK OF A SPECIALIST

Because of the complexity and highly specialized knowledge and experience involved in identifying, assessing, and measuring environmental financial information, it will often be necessary for management or the financial auditor to engage or employ a specialist to perform this work. Examples of such specialists are environmental engineers, consultants, remediation technologies specialists, responsibility allocation specialists, claims specialists, actuaries, appraisers, and environmental attorneys. Specialists might be involved in one or more stages of the process of developing environmental estimates, including:

- Identifying and evaluating environmental legal obligations.
- Evaluating potential rights of recovery.
- Identifying situations in which discovery of historical pollution conditions should be reported to the environmental regulatory agencies or third parties under applicable environmental laws.
- Identifying situations for which environmental remediation is required.
- Designing or recommending remedial action plans.
- Gathering and analyzing data on which to base the estimates of cleanup costs (e.g., performing a baseline risk assessment).
- Providing information to management that will enable management to estimate the entity's environmental liabilities and develop the related financial statement disclosures.

Statement of Auditing Standard No. 73, "Using the Work of a Specialist" (SAS 73), provides guidance to the auditor who uses the work of a specialist in performing an audit.

(i) QUALIFICATIONS AND WORK OF A SPECIALIST

SAS 73 provides guidance on evaluating the professional qualifications of a specialist to determine whether the specialist possesses the necessary skill or knowledge in a particular field. The specialist's level of skill or knowledge should be commensurate with the nature and complexity of the environmental matters that the specialist has been asked to address. Matters that might be relevant in evaluating the professional qualifications of a specialist include:

- Knowledge of various pollution control and remediation technologies, including their acceptability, strengths, weaknesses, and applicability.
- Knowledge of environmental issues that are likely to affect the entity, including legal, regulatory, industry, financial, investment, and sociopolitical developments.
- Specialized knowledge in the field of environmental management systems, including internal control with regard to environmental financial reporting.
- Technical or educational background related to environmental matters.
- Environmental work experience.

The auditor should obtain an understanding of the nature of the work performed or to be performed by the specialist. That understanding should include:

- The objectives and scope of the specialist's work.
- The specialist's relationship to the entity, if any.
- The methods and assumptions used by the specialist, including, for example, a comparison of the methods and assumptions used by the specialist with those used by management or other specialists, or with those used in the preceding period.
- The appropriateness of using the specialist's work for the intended purpose. In most cases, it will be appropriate, if not necessary, to contact the specialist to determine whether the specialist is aware that his or her work will be used for evaluating assertions in the financial statements.
- The form and content of the specialist's findings (for example, the extent of detail included or to be included in the report).

Reports issued by environmental specialists generally are not standard in either form or content, and do not always clearly express the underlying assumptions or methods used by the specialist. Communication with the specialist in these circumstances may assist the auditor in obtaining the necessary understanding.

(ii) SPECIALIST'S RELATIONSHIP TO THE ENTITY

If a specialist is employed by the entity being audited, or otherwise has a relationship that might directly or indirectly influence the findings and conclusions of the specialist, the auditor should assess the risk that the specialist's objectivity might be impaired. Factors that the auditor might consider when determining whether the specialist's objectivity might be impaired include the auditor's prior experience with the specialist, discussions with the specialist and management, and additional information about the specific nature and significance of the relationship. If the auditor concludes that the specialist's objectivity might be impaired, the auditor should perform additional procedures with respect to the specialist's work (for example, engaging another specialist to review some or all of the related specialist's work).

(iii) USING THE SPECIALIST'S FINDINGS

The specialist is responsible for the appropriateness and reasonableness of the methods and assumptions used and for applying them properly. However, the auditor should obtain an understanding of the methods and assumptions used by the specialist; make appropriate tests of data provided to the specialist, taking into account the auditor's assessment of control risk; and evaluate whether the specialist's findings support the related financial statement assertions. If the auditor concludes that the specialist's findings are unreasonable, the auditor should apply additional procedures that may include obtaining the opinion of another specialist.

(h) AUDITING POTENTIAL RIGHTS OF RECOVERY

As discussed in Chapter 16, potential claims for recovery from insurers, participating PRPs, nonparticipating PRPs, prior property owners, current and former tenants, and governmental or third-party funds should be evaluated separate from the related environmental liability. To evaluate whether recovery where there is a potential right of recovery is probable, correspondence or communication with the potential sources of recovery or their legal counsel generally is necessary. Requests for confirmation of amounts recoverable from such parties should be carefully designed to ensure that the parties fully understand what is being requested. Also, because confirmations do not necessarily provide sufficient evidence regarding the recoverability of such amounts, the auditor may need to obtain other evidence to evaluate the recoverability of recorded amounts. If a claim is the subject of litigation, a rebuttable presumption exists that realization of the claim is not probable. Statement of Auditing Standards No. 67, "The Confirmation Process," provides guidance to the auditor about the confirmation process in audits performed in accordance with GAAS.

(i) INQUIRIES OF A CLIENT'S LAWYERS

Environmental loss contingencies subject to reporting under GAAP by definition involve pending or probable legal proceedings. The auditor therefore should consider requesting information about environmental loss contingencies in the letter of inquiry sent to the entity's counsel. The letter of inquiry to a client's lawyer should include a list of asserted environmental claims prepared by management (or a request by management that the lawyer prepare such a list) that describes each of the matters the lawyer is currently handling and the expected outcomes of those matters. The auditor may include in the audit inquiry letter a request for the lawyer to discuss unasserted environmental claims (e.g., outstanding environmental indemnities, environmental asset retirement obligations, and obligations relating to formerly owned and operated facilities). The auditor should be aware, however, that a 1975 treaty jointly developed by the AICPA and the American Bar Association, "Statement of Policy Regarding Lawyer's Responses to Auditor's Request for Information," instructs lawyers not to provide the auditor with information about unasserted claims unless, and only to the extent that, the client has requested the attorney to comment on specific unasserted claims.[1] To do otherwise could risk waiver of the attorney-client privilege.

Statement of Auditing Standards No. 12, "Inquiry of a Client's Lawyer Concerning Litigation, Claims, and Assessments," provides guidance on the procedures an auditor should consider performing to identify litigation, claims, and assessments and to satisfy himself or herself as to the financial reporting and disclosure of such matters.

[1] American Bar Association Statement of Policy Regarding Lawyers' Responses to Auditors' Requests for Information, 31 Bus. Law. § 5 (no. 3, Apr. 1976).

(j) CLIENT REPRESENTATIONS

The auditor should consider obtaining written representations from management about environmental estimates and disclosures, including specific representations as to the adequacy of such disclosures and the expected outcomes of uncertainties. Statement of Auditing Standards No. 19, "Client Representations," provides guidance to the auditor about representations to be obtained from management as part of an audit.

(k) ASSESSING DISCLOSURES

Guidelines for disclosures related to environmental matters are presented in Part Three of this book. Statement of Auditing Standards No. 32, "Adequacy of Disclosure in Financial Statements," requires the auditor to assess the adequacy of disclosures of material matters in the financial statements in connection with rendering an opinion on the presentation of financial statements in conformity with GAAP.

When disclosure is required, the auditor should assess the adequacy of the disclosures, including any conclusions expressed by management regarding the expected outcome of future events and contingencies, based on evidence obtained, as applicable, from the following:

- Operations, environmental, legal, and financial management personnel.
- Specialists.
- Other audit tests.

(l) EVALUATING AUDIT TEST RESULTS

The auditor should evaluate the results of tests of environmental estimates and related disclosures in the context of the entity's financial statements taken as a whole. Auditors should also consider the guidance in SAS 99, "Consideration of Fraud in a Financial Statement Audit," which provides guidance on the evaluation of audit test results, and paragraph 29 of SAS 47, which provides additional guidance on the auditor's responsibility for evaluating the reasonableness of estimates in relationship to the financial statements taken as a whole.

26.4 REPORTING

Departures from GAAP or scope limitations related to environmental financial information may require modification of the auditor's standard report on an entity's financial statements. Statement of Auditing Standards No. 58, "Reports on Audited Financial Statements," provides guidance to the auditor on reporting when there is a GAAP departure or a scope limitation.

(a) DEPARTURES FROM GAAP

Departures from GAAP involving environmental financial information generally involve inadequate disclosures, the application of inappropriate accounting principles, or unreasonable accounting estimates. The auditor should determine whether the presentation and disclosure of environmental liabilities, loss contingencies, asset impairments, and asset retirement obligations, and related disclosures, comply with the guidance in Part Three of this book. The auditor should also assess the appropriateness of the accounting policies used and the reasonableness of the estimates. SOP 96-1 states that if the auditor concludes that the financial statements are not fairly presented in all material respects because the accounting principles followed are inappropriate or misapplied, the disclosures are inadequate, or management's estimates are unreasonable, the auditor should express a qualified or adverse opinion.

(b) SCOPE LIMITATIONS

The auditor should consider whether he or she has obtained sufficient evidence to support management's assertions about environmental financial information and its presentation and disclosure in the financial statements. The auditor should distinguish between situations involving uncertainties and those involving scope limitations. An uncertainty exists if resolution of a loss contingency or other condition is expected to occur at a future date at which time conclusive evidence concerning the outcome of the uncertainty is expected to become available. Depending on the applicable financial reporting standard, the degree of uncertainty regarding future conditions or events may affect whether a liability is recognized or the measurement of the liability.

Conversely, an uncertainty is not involved if sufficient information currently exists, did exist, or could be obtained, but is not available to the auditor because of restrictions imposed by management, inadequate recordkeeping, or other conditions that prevent the auditor from gaining access to the information. For example, management's intentional or inadvertent failure to estimate cleanup costs for known or reasonably suspected historical pollution conditions is not an uncertainty. Such situations may constitute a limitation on the scope of the auditor's work sufficient to cause the auditor to qualify or disclaim an opinion because of a scope limitation.

(c) MAKING REFERENCE TO A SPECIALIST

Use of specialists is common in the determination and development of environmental estimates and environmental disclosures. SAS 73 precludes the auditor from referring to the work of a specialist in the auditor's report, because such reference might be interpreted as a qualification of the auditor's opinion or a division of responsibility, neither of which is intended. The auditor may, however, refer to the specialist in the auditor's report if the auditor believes such reference will facilitate an understanding of the reason for a departure from an unqualified opinion.

(d) COMMUNICATIONS WITH AUDIT COMMITTEES

Statement of Auditing Standards No. 61, "Communication with Audit Committees" (as modified by SAS No. 89 and SAS No. 90; codified at AU section 380), provides the auditor with guidance on the types of audit matters that should be reported to the audit committee or those of equivalent authority and responsibility. Such matters include management judgments and accounting estimates. The auditor should determine whether the audit committee is informed about critical accounting policies; the processes used by management in formulating estimates that are particularly sensitive because of their significance to the financial statements and because of the possibility that future events affecting them may differ markedly from management's current judgments (see discussion of critical accounting estimates in § 24.5(e)); and the basis for the auditor's conclusions regarding the reasonableness of those estimates.

CHAPTER TWENTY-SEVEN

Internal Control Auditing

27.1 INTRODUCTION

Section 404(a) of Sarbanes-Oxley requires the management of a public company to assess the effectiveness of the company's internal control over financial reporting as of the end of the company's most recent fiscal year, and to include in the company's annual report to shareholders management's conclusion, as a result of that assessment, about whether the company's internal control is effective. Section 404(a) became effective on June 5, 2003.[1]

Section 404(b) of the Act requires the company's auditor to attest to and report on the assessment made by the company's management. Sections 103(a)(2)(A) and 404(b) of the Act direct the PCAOB to establish professional standards governing the independent auditor's attestation.

PCAOB Auditing Standard No. 2, "An Audit of Internal Control over Financial Reporting Performed in Conjunction with an Audit of Financial Statements" (PAS 2), establishes requirements and provides directions that apply when an auditor is engaged to audit both a company's financial statements and management's assessment of the effectiveness of internal control over financial reporting. Key provisions of PAS 2 include:

- Evaluating management's assessment.
- Obtaining an understanding of internal control over financial reporting, including performing walkthroughs.

[1] Securities Act Release No. 33-8238, 68 Fed. Reg. 36,636, 36,640 (June 18, 2002).

- Identifying significant accounts and relevant assertions.
- Testing and evaluating the effectiveness of the design of controls.
- Testing operating effectiveness.
- Timing of testing.
- Using the work of others.
- Evaluating the results of testing.
- Identifying control deficiencies.
- Forming an opinion and reporting significant deficiencies and material weaknesses.
- Testing controls intended to prevent or detect fraud.

This chapter contains an overview of the provisions of PAS 2 that are of particular relevance to internal control over environmental financial reporting.

27.2 AUDIT PLANNING AND OBJECTIVES

(a) AUDIT OBJECTIVES

The auditor's objective in an audit of internal control over financial reporting is to express an opinion on management's assessment of the effectiveness of the issuer's internal control over financial reporting. To form a basis for expressing such an opinion, the auditor must obtain reasonable assurance about whether the issuer maintained, in all material respects, effective internal control over financial reporting as of the date specified in management's assessment.

Effective internal control over financial reporting is defined by the absence of *material weaknesses* (defined in § 27.2(b) below). The objective of the audit of internal control over financial reporting is therefore to obtain reasonable assurance that no material weaknesses exist as of the date specified in management's assessment.

(b) CONTROL DEFICIENCIES

A *control deficiency* exists when the design or operation of a control does not allow management or employees, in the normal course of performing their assigned functions, to prevent or detect misstatements on a timely basis.

- A deficiency in design exists when a control necessary to meet the control objective is missing or an existing control is not properly designed so that, even if the control operates as designed, the control objective is not always met.
- A deficiency in operation exists when a properly designed control does not operate as designed, or when the person performing the control does not possess the necessary authority or qualifications to perform the control effectively.[2]

[2] Exchange Act Release No. 34-49544, 69 Fed. Reg. 20,672, 20,674 (Apr. 16, 2004).

In evaluating the significance of a control deficiency, the auditor must initially determine:

- The likelihood that a deficiency, or a combination of deficiencies, could result in a misstatement of an account balance or disclosure (see § 26.2(c)(ii) on control risk).
- The magnitude of the potential misstatement resulting from the deficiency or deficiencies (see § 26.2(c)(i) on inherent risk).

Using the gradations of probability set forth in FAS 5 (§ 19.2(a)(iii)), which are incorporated by reference in PAS 2, the likelihood that a misstatement will occur (*control risk*) can range from remote, to reasonably likely, to probable. For purposes of an internal control audit, the likelihood of a control deficiency to result in a misstatement is classified as either remote or more than remote. A *remote likelihood* means that the chance of the future event occurring is slight.

The magnitude of a potential misstatement (*inherent risk*) is measured in terms of materiality, assessed at both the financial-statement level and at the individual account-balance level. For purposes of an internal control audit, the magnitude of a potential misstatement arising from a control deficiency is measured on a scale that ranges from inconsequential, to more than inconsequential, to material. A misstatement is *inconsequential* if a reasonable person would conclude, after considering the possibility of further undetected misstatements, that the misstatement, either individually or when aggregated with other misstatements, would be clearly immaterial to the financial statements. If a reasonable person could not reach such a conclusion regarding a particular misstatement, that misstatement is *more than inconsequential*.

Exhibit 27.1 shows the various categories of control deficiencies.

Exhibit 27.2 shows how the dual assessment of the likelihood and the magnitude of a potential misstatement underlies the various categories of control deficiencies.

EXHIBIT 27.1

Control Deficiencies

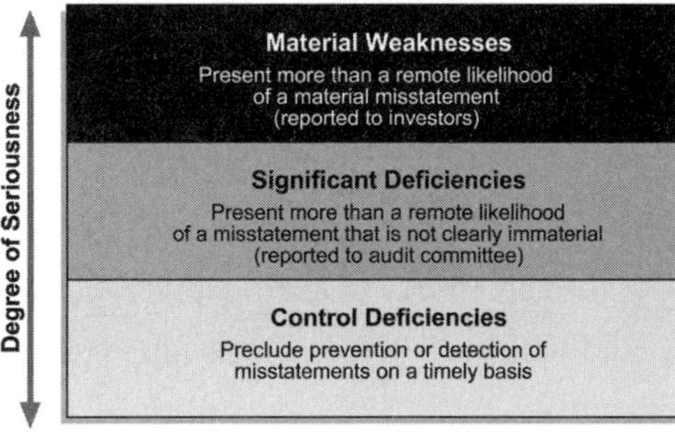

EXHIBIT 27.2

Control Deficiencies Matrix

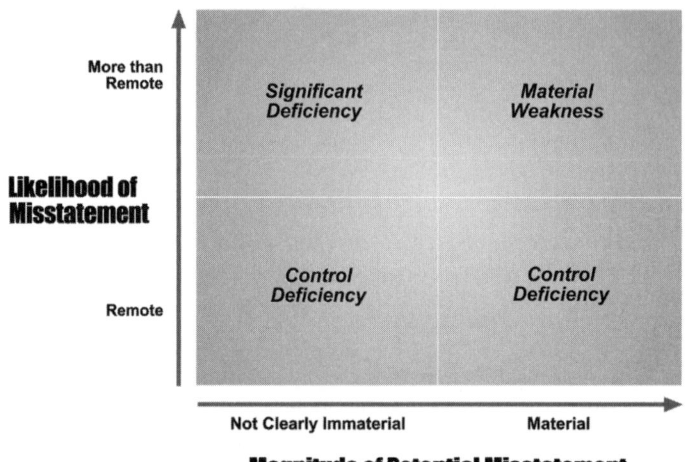

A *significant deficiency* is a control deficiency, or combination of control deficiencies, that adversely affects the entity's ability to initiate, authorize, record, process, or report external financial data reliably in accordance with GAAP such that there is more than a remote likelihood that a misstatement of the entity's annual or interim financial statements that is more than inconsequential will not be prevented or detected.

A *material weakness* is a significant deficiency, or combination of significant deficiencies, that results in more than a remote likelihood that a material misstatement of the annual or interim financial statements will not be prevented or detected.

(c) FRAMEWORK USED BY MANAGEMENT TO CONDUCT ITS ASSESSMENT

Management is required to base its assessment of the effectiveness of the company's internal control over financial reporting on a suitable, recognized control framework established by a body of experts that followed due-process procedures, including the broad distribution of the framework for public comment. In addition to being available to users of management's reports, a framework is suitable only when it:

- Is free from bias;
- Permits reasonably consistent qualitative and quantitative measurements of a company's internal control over financial reporting;
- Is sufficiently complete so that those relevant factors that would alter a conclusion about the effectiveness of a company's internal control over financial reporting are not omitted; and
- Is relevant to an evaluation of internal control over financial reporting.

According to the SEC and the PCAOB, the COSO Internal Control—Integrated Framework (COSO Framework) published by the Committee of Sponsoring Organizations (COSO) of the Treadway Commission provides a suitable and available framework for purposes of management's assessment. The performance and reporting directions in PAS 2 are largely based on the COSO Framework. Other suitable frameworks have been published in other countries and may be developed in the future. Such other suitable frameworks may be used in an audit of internal control over financial reporting.

The COSO Framework identifies three primary objectives of internal control: (1) efficiency and effectiveness of operations, (2) financial reporting, and (3) compliance with laws and regulations. Internal control *over financial reporting* ordinarily does not include the other two objectives of internal control. Thus, in general, internal control over financial reporting does not encompass environmental operations and environmental compliance management to the extent these activities are unrelated to financial reporting.

The controls that management designs and implements, however, often may achieve more than one objective, and not all controls relevant to financial reporting are accounting controls. According to the PCAOB, all controls that could materially affect financial reporting—including controls that focus primarily on environmental operations and compliance with environmental laws directly related to the presentation of and required disclosures in financial statements and that also have a material effect on the reliability of financial reporting (e.g., reporting of material environmental loss contingencies, guarantees, asset retirement obligations, and impairments)—are encompassed in internal control over financial reporting (see § 8.3(a)).

(d) MANAGEMENT'S RESPONSIBILITIES

For the auditor to satisfactorily complete an audit of internal control over financial reporting, management must do the following:

- Accept responsibility for the effectiveness of the company's internal control over financial reporting.
- Evaluate the effectiveness of the company's internal control over financial reporting using suitable control criteria.
- Support its evaluation with sufficient evidence, including documentation.
- Present a written assessment of the effectiveness of the company's internal control over financial reporting as of the end of the company's most recent fiscal year.

If the auditor concludes that management has not fulfilled these responsibilities, the auditor must communicate in writing to management and the audit committee that the audit of internal control over financial reporting cannot be satisfactorily completed and that he or she is required to disclaim an opinion.

(e) MATERIALITY CONSIDERATIONS

Paragraph 22 of PAS 2 states that the auditor should apply the concept of materiality in an audit of internal control over financial reporting at both the financial-statement level and at the individual account-balance level (see also § 12.2(d)). The auditor uses materiality at the financial-statement level in evaluating whether a deficiency, or combination of deficiencies, in controls is a significant deficiency or a material weakness. Materiality at both the financial-statement level and the individual account-balance level is relevant to planning the audit and designing procedures. Materiality at the account-balance level is necessarily lower than materiality at the financial-statement level.

The same conceptual definition of *materiality* that applies to financial reporting applies to information on internal control over financial reporting, including the relevance of both quantitative and qualitative considerations (see § 12.2). The quantitative considerations are essentially the same as in an audit of financial statements. They relate to whether misstatements that would not be prevented or detected by internal control over financial reporting, *individually or collectively*, have a quantitatively material effect on the financial statements. The qualitative considerations apply to evaluating materiality with respect to the financial statements and to additional factors that relate to the perceived needs of reasonable persons (see § 12.2(e)) who will rely on the information.

For example, the auditor should be aware that persons who rely on the information concerning internal control over financial reporting include investors, creditors, the board of directors and audit committee, and regulators in specialized industries, such as banking or insurance. The auditor should be aware that external users of financial statements are interested in information on internal control over financial reporting because it enhances the quality of financial reporting and increases their confidence in financial information, including financial information issued between annual reports, such as quarterly information. Information on internal control over financial reporting is also intended to provide an early warning to those inside and outside the company who are in a position to insist on improvements in these controls, such as the audit committee and regulators in specialized industries.

(f) FRAUD CONSIDERATIONS

Paragraph 24 of PAS 2 instructs the auditor to evaluate all controls specifically intended to address the risks of fraud that have at least a reasonably possible likelihood of having a material effect on the company's financial statements (see § 26.2(d)). These controls may be a part of any of the five components of internal control over financial reporting (see § 8.2).

PAS 2 reminds auditors that it is part of management's responsibility, when designing a company's internal control over financial reporting, to design and implement programs and controls to prevent, deter, and detect fraud. Management, along with those who have responsibility for oversight of the financial reporting process (such as the audit committee), should set the proper tone, create and maintain a culture of honesty and high ethical standards, and establish appropriate controls to prevent and detect fraud.

Controls relevant to the prevention and detection of fraud regarding environmental financial reporting include, but are not limited to:

- Environmental risk assessment processes.
- Code of ethics/conduct provisions, especially those related to environmental responsibility and environmental financial reporting and the monitoring of the code by management and the audit committee or board.
- Adequacy of the internal audit activity with regard to environmental financial reporting and whether the internal audit function reports directly to the audit committee, as well as the extent of the audit committee's involvement and interaction with internal audit.
- Adequacy of the company's procedures for handling complaints and for accepting confidential submissions of concerns about questionable environmental, accounting, or auditing matters.

In an audit of internal control over financial reporting, the auditor's evaluation of controls is interrelated with the auditor's evaluation of controls in a financial statement audit (see § 26.2). Often, controls identified and evaluated by the auditor during the audit of internal control over financial reporting also address or mitigate fraud risks, which the auditor is required to consider in a financial statement audit. If the auditor identifies deficiencies in controls designed to prevent and detect fraud during the audit of internal control over financial reporting (see § 26.2(d)), the auditor should alter the nature, timing, or extent of procedures to be performed during the financial statement audit to be responsive to such deficiencies.

27.3 SUBSTANTIVE AUDIT PROCEDURES

(a) EVALUATING DESIGN EFFECTIVENESS

The auditor must obtain an understanding of the design of controls related to each component of internal control over financial reporting, as discussed below:

- *Control environment.* Because of the pervasive effect of the control environment on the reliability of financial reporting, the auditor's preliminary judgment about its effectiveness often influences the nature, timing, and extent of the tests of operating effectiveness considered necessary. Weaknesses in the control environment should cause the auditor to alter the nature, timing, or extent of tests of operating effectiveness that otherwise should have been performed in the absence of the weaknesses. An evaluation of the control environment with respect to environmental financial reporting should consider in particular the environmental financial reporting objectives established by the audit committee and management (see Chapter 5).

- *Risk assessment.* When obtaining an understanding of the company's risk assessment process, the auditor should evaluate whether management has identified the risks of material misstatement in the significant accounts and disclosures and related assertions of the financial statements and has implemented controls to prevent or detect errors or fraud that could result in material misstatements. For example, the risk assessment process should address how management considers the possibility of unrecorded transactions, conditions, or events giving rise to environmental loss contingencies or identifies and analyzes significant environmental estimates recorded in the financial statements.
- *Control activities.* The auditor's understanding of control activities relates to the controls that management has implemented to prevent or detect errors or fraud that could result in material misstatement in the accounts and disclosures and related assertions of the financial statements. For the purposes of evaluating the effectiveness of internal control over environmental financial reporting, the auditor's understanding of control activities encompasses a broader range of activities than normally addressed for the financial statement audit. For example, it may be necessary for the auditor to consider controls regarding the identification and assessment of environmental conditions, events, and transactions (as opposed to only the measurement of identified environmental liabilities; see § 8.3(a)).
- *Information and communication.* The auditor's understanding of internal control over environmental financial reporting involves understanding the systems and processes used by management to identify, collect, process, and maintain environmental data, information, and communications. In addition, this understanding requires an emphasis on comprehending the safeguarding controls and the processes for authorization of transactions and the maintenance of records, as well as the period-end financial reporting process.
- *Monitoring.* The auditor's understanding of management's monitoring of controls over environmental financial reporting extends to and includes its monitoring of all controls, including control activities, that management has identified and designed to prevent or detect material misstatement of environmental costs, liabilities, impairments, and risks and related disclosures and assertions in the financial statements.

(b) EVALUATING OPERATING EFFECTIVENESS

Pursuant to paragraph 92 of PAS 2, the auditor should evaluate the operating effectiveness of a control by determining whether the control is operating as designed and whether the person performing the control possesses the necessary authority and qualifications to perform the control effectively. Tests of controls over operating effectiveness include a mix of inquiries of appropriate personnel, inspection of relevant documentation, observation of the company's operations, and performance of the application of the control. For example, the auditor might observe the procedures for reviewing purchase and sale agreements to test the operating effectiveness of controls over identification of environmental guarantees. Because an observation is pertinent only at the time at which it is made, the auditor should supplement the observation with inquiries of company personnel and inspection of documentation about the operation of such controls at other times.

The nature of the control influences the nature of the tests the auditor can perform. For example, the auditor might examine documents regarding controls for which documentary evidence exists (e.g., estimates of environmental liabilities). However, documentary evidence regarding some aspects of the control environment, such as management's objectives with regard to environmental financial reporting, might not exist. In circumstances in which documentary evidence of controls or the performance of controls does not exist and is not expected to exist, the auditor's tests of controls would consist of inquiries of appropriate personnel and observation of company activities.

The auditor must perform tests of controls over a period of time that is adequate to determine whether, as of the date specified in management's report, the controls necessary for achieving the objectives of the control criteria are operating effectively. The period of time over which the auditor performs tests of controls varies with the nature of the controls being tested and with the frequency with which specific controls operate and specific policies are applied. Some controls operate continuously (e.g., controls over sales), whereas others operate only at certain times (e.g., controls over the identification, assessment, measurement, and reporting of environmental asset impairments).

The auditor's testing of the operating effectiveness of such controls should occur at the time the controls are operating. Controls "as of" a specific date encompass controls that are relevant to the company's internal control over financial reporting "as of" that specific date, even though such controls might not operate until after that specific date.

For controls over significant nonroutine transactions, or controls over accounts or processes with a high degree of subjectivity or judgment in measurement (e.g., estimates of environmental liabilities), the auditor should perform tests of controls closer to or at the "as of" date rather than at an interim date. The auditor must, however, balance the performance of tests of controls closer to the "as of" date with the need to obtain sufficient evidence of operating effectiveness.

In an audit of internal control over financial reporting, the auditor should evaluate the effect of the findings of all substantive auditing procedures performed in the audit of financial statements on the effectiveness of internal control over financial reporting. With respect to internal control over environmental financial reporting, this evaluation should include, but not be limited to:

- The auditor's risk evaluations in connection with the selection and application of substantive procedures, especially those related to fraud.
- Findings with respect to illegal acts.
- Indications of management bias in making accounting estimates and in selecting accounting principles.
- Misstatements of environmental costs, liabilities, and impairments detected by substantive procedures.

(c) USING THE WORK OF OTHERS

PAS 2 provides several factors the auditor should consider when evaluating the nature of the controls that are subject to the work of others. Several of these factors are of particular relevance to environmental financial information, including:

- The materiality of the accounts and disclosures that the control addresses and the risk of material misstatement (see § 26.2(c)).
- The degree of judgment required to evaluate the operating effectiveness of the control (i.e., the degree to which the evaluation of the effectiveness of the control requires evaluation of subjective factors rather than objective testing) (see § 26.3).
- The level of judgment or estimation required in the account or disclosure (see §§ 12.5, 24.5(e), and 26.3(b)).
- The potential for management override of the control (see § 26.2(d)).

Generally, as these factors increase in significance, the need for the auditor to perform his or her own work on those controls increases. With regard to evaluation of controls for the identification, assessment, measurement, and reporting of environmental financial information, the auditor often will need to rely on the work of one or more specialists (see § 26.3(g)).

APPENDIX A

Authoritative Documents Pertaining to Environmental Financial Reporting

Issue Date	Document
1972	Securities and Exchange Commission, Regulation S-X, "Form and Content of and Requirements for Financial Statements, Securities Act of 1933, Securities Exchange Act of 1934, Public Utility Holding Company Act of 1935, Investment Company Act of 1940, Investment Advisers Act of 1940 and Energy Policy and Conservation Act of 1975," 37 *Fed. Reg.* 14,592, *codified at* 17 C.F.R. Part 210.b
1975	Financial Accounting Standards Board, Statement of Financial Accounting Standards No. 5, "Accounting for Contingencies"
1976	Financial Accounting Standards Board, Interpretation No. 14, "Reasonable Estimation of the Amount of a Loss: An Interpretation of FASB Statement No. 5"
1982	Securities and Exchange Commission, Regulation S-K, "Standard Instructions for Filing Forms under Securities Act of 1933, Securities Exchange Act of 1934 and Energy Policy and Conservation Act of 1975," 47 *Fed. Reg.* 11401, *codified at* 17 C.F.R. Part 229.c
1989	Securities and Exchange Commission, SEC Interpretation, "Management's Discussion and Analysis of Financial Condition and Results of Operations; Certain Investment Company Disclosures [Release Nos. 33-6835; 34-26831; IC-16961; FR-36]," 54 *Fed. Reg.* 22,427
1990	Financial Accounting Standards Board, Emerging Issues Task Force 90-8, "Capitalization of Costs to Treat Environmental Contamination"
1992	Financial Accounting Standards Board, Interpretation No. 39, "Offsetting of Amounts Related to Certain Contracts: An Interpretation of Accounting Principles Board (APB) Opinion No. 10 and Financial Accounting Standards Board Statement No. 105"

1993	Financial Accounting Standards Board, Emerging Issues Task Force 93-5, "Accounting for Environmental Liabilities" Securities and Exchange Commission, Staff Accounting Bulletin No. 92, Topic 5.Y, "Accounting Disclosures Relating to Loss Contingencies," 58 *Fed. Reg.* 32,843. (Staff Accounting Bulletin No. 103, listed below, amended SAB 92)
1994	American Institute of Certified Public Accountants, Statement of Position 94-6, "Disclosure of Certain Significant Risks and Uncertainties"
1996	American Institute of Certified Public Accountants, Statement of Position 96-1, "Environmental Remediation Liabilities"
1999	Securities and Exchange Commission, Staff Accounting Bulletin No. 99, "Materiality," 64 *Fed. Reg.* 45,150
2001	Financial Accounting Standards Board, Statement of Financial Accounting Standards No. 143, "Accounting for Asset Retirement Obligations" Financial Accounting Standards Board, Statement of Financial Accounting Standards No. 144, "Accounting for the Impairment or Disposal of Long-Lived Assets" Securities and Exchange Commission, Action, "Cautionary Advice Regarding Disclosure about Critical Accounting Policies [Release Nos. 33-8040; 34-45149; FR-60]," 66 *Fed. Reg.* 65,013
2002	Securities and Exchange Commission, "Commission Statement about Management's Discussion and Analysis of Financial Condition and Results of Operations [Release Nos. 33-8056; 34-45321; FR-61]," 67 *Fed. Reg.* 3746
2003	Securities and Exchange Commission, "Commission Guidance Regarding Management's Discussion and Analysis of Financial Condition and Results of Operations [Release Nos. 33-8350; 34-48960; FR-72]," 68 *Fed. Reg.* 75,056 Securities and Exchange Commission, Staff Accounting Bulletin No. 103, "Update of Codification of Staff Accounting Bulletins," 68 *Fed. Reg.* 26,840
2005	Financial Accounting Standards Board, Interpretation No. 47, "Accounting for Conditional Asset Retirement Obligations: An Interpretation of FASB Statement No. 143"

APPENDIX B

Selected Bibliography

GLOBAL REPORTING INITIATIVE (GRI)

A "Watershed" Moment for GRI, Int'l Envtl. Sys. Update (CEEM), Dec. 2000, at 3

Mallen Baker, *Analysis: The Global Reporting Initiative: Raising the Bar Too High?,* Ethical Corp., Oct. 16, 2002, *available* at http://www.ethicalcorp.com/content_print.asp?ContentID=235

Mark Brownlie, The Business Case for Sustainability Reporting, Presentation at Corporate Environmental and Sustainability Reporting: A New Look for the Information Age, Vanderbilt Center for Environmental Management Studies (May 2001), *available* at http://www.vanderbilt.edu/vcems/cesr2/markbrownliepresentation.pdf

Disclosure Guideline Calls for Patience and an Open Mind, Bus. & The Env't (Aspen), May 2002, at 2

John Elkington, The Global Reporters, Presentation at GEMI 2001: An Odyssey to Environmental Excellence, Baltimore, Md. (Mar. 19-20, 2001), *available* at http://www.steeleweb.com/graphics/gemi_files/workshop_07/tranparency_elkington.ppt

Sean Gilbert, *The Transparency Revolution,* The Envtl. F., Nov./Dec. 2002, at 19

Grades Vary for Users of Global Reporting Initiative, Bus. & The Env't (Cutter), Jan. 2001, at 5

Martin Holysh, Corporate Manager, Sustainable Development, Suncor Energy, Inc., Using the GRI Guidelines to Produce a Sustainability Report: The Opportunities and the Challenges, Remarks at Globe 2002, Vancouver, Canada (Mar. 13-15, 2002)

Dennis M. Hussey et al., *Global Reporting Initiative Guidelines: An Evaluation of Sustainable Development Metrics for Industry,* Envtl. Quality Mgmt., Autumn 2001, at 1

Players React to Revised Guideline for Sustainability Reporting, Bus. & The Env't (Cutter), Sept. 2000, at 6

Janet Ranganathan & Alan Willis, The Global Reporting Initiative: An Emerging Tool for Corporate Accountability (WRI July 1999), *available* at http://wri.igc.org/meb/pdf/janetgri.pdf

Donald Sutherland & Graham Cooper, *GRI Moves Up a Gear,* Envtl. Fin., Apr. 2000, at 18

Allen White, The 2002 GRI Guidelines: Clearing Up the Misunderstandings, Ethical Corp., May 21, 2003, *available* at http://www.ethicalcorp.com/content_print.asp?ContentID=595

Allen L. White, The Power of Full Disclosure: The Global Reporting Initiative, Presentation at Conference on Finance, Environment, and Development, Paris, France (Jan. 10, 2003), *available* at http://unepfi.net/SocGen/Presentations/unep%20fi%20paris%20final%20Allen%20white250403.pdf

Allen L. White, GRI and the Transparency Initiative, Presentation at GEMI 2001: An Odyssey to Environmental Excellence, Baltimore, Md. (Mar. 19-20, 2001, *available* at http://www.steeleweb.com/graphics/gemi_files/workshop_07/transparency_white.ppt (last visited Mar. 6, 2002)

John Wilson, Toward a Kinder, Gentler GRI?, Bus. & The Env't (Cutter), June 1999, at 6

Maef Woods, *The Global Reporting Initiative*, The CPA J., June 2003, *available* at http://www.nysscpa.org/cpajournal/2003/0603/dept/d066003a.htm

SHAREHOLDER AND STAKEHOLDER ADVOCACY

Duncan Austin, Emerging Environmental Risks and Disclosure in the Oil and Gas Sector, Presentation at Commission for Environmental Cooperation Conference on Environmental Disclosure in Financial Statements: New Developments and Emerging Issues (Feb. 26, 2003), *available* at http://www.cec.org/files/pdf/ECONOMY/austin_en.pdf

Duncan Austin, Changing Oil: Emerging Environmental Risks and Shareholder Value in the Oil and Gas Industry (WRI 2002), *available* at http://pubs.wri.org/pubs_description.cfm?PubID=3719

F. Azzone et al., *A Stakeholder's View of Environmental Reporting*, 30 Long Range Plan. 799 (1997)

Ricardo Bayon, *Is the SEC Raising the Disclosure Stakes?*, Envtl. Fin., July/Aug. 2001, at 16

Susannah Blake et al., The Environmental Fiduciary: The Case for Incorporating Environmental Factors into Investment Management Policies (Rose Foundation for Communities and the Environment, Aug. 21, 2002), *available at* http://www.rosefdn.org/images/EFreport.pdf

Michele Chan-Fichel, After Enron: How Accounting and SEC Reform Can Promote Corporate Accountability While Restoring Public Confidence, 32 ELR 10965 (Aug. 2002), *available* at http://www.corporatesunshine.org/afterenron.pdf

Michelle Chan-Fishel, New Economy, Old Accounting: Expanding SEC Disclosure Rules for Investor Protection & Corporate Responsibility, Reporting to the Environmental Regulators: Environmental and Financial Consequences, American Bar Association Section of Environment, Energy, and Resources, 30th Annual Conference on Environmental Law, Keystone, Colo. (Mar. 2001)

Crackdown Sought on Companies That Fail to Disclose Risks, Bus. & the Env't, Mar. 2001, at 8

R. Gray et al., *Standards, Stakeholders, and Sustainability (Environmental Reporting)*, Certified Acct., Mar. 1995, at 20

Innovest Strategic Value Advisors, Carbon Finance and the Global Equity Markets (Carbon Disclosure Project, Feb. 2003), *available* at http://www.cdproject.net/

Institute of Social and Ethical Accountability, Redefining Materiality: Practice and Public Policy for Effective Corporate Reporting (2003)

Investor Responsibility Research Center, Environmental Reporting and Third Party Statements (Global Environmental Management Initiative 1996)

Sanford Lewis & Tim Little, Fooling Investors & Fooling Themselves, The Rose Foundation for Communites and the Environment (July 2004)

Mark Mansley, Open Disclosure: Sustainability and the Listing Regime (Claros Consulting, February 2003), *available* at http://www.foe.co.uk/resource/reports/open_disclosure.pdf

Richard MacLean, *Opacity or Transparency?*, Envtl. Solutions, Mar. 2001, at 93, *available* at http://www.enviroreporting.com/others/opacity.pdf

Richard MacLean, *Making the Move: From Spin to Strategy*, 3 Corp. Strategy Today 14 (2001), *available* at http://www.enviroreporting.com/others/MacLean_CST3.pdf

Richard MacLean & Romi Gottfrid, *Corporate Environmental Reports: Stuck Management Processes Hold Back Real Progress*, 7 Corp. Envtl. Strategy 244 (2000), *available* at http://www.enviroreporting.com/others/CES_Environmental_Reporting.pdf

New Economic Foundation, Corporate Spin: The Troubled Teenager Years of Social Reporting (Aug. 2000), *available* at http://www.neweconomics.org/uploadstore/pubs/doc_2811200045047_New%20Eco%20Text.pdf

Mark Nicholls, *Never Mind the Ballots*, Envtl. Fin., June 2001, at 12

Presentations by Kerrie Laughlin, Penny Bonda, Paul Reynolds, and others, Transparency: Corporate Communications in a Globalized Economy: Greenwashing or Genuine Storytelling, at CERES 2001 Conference, What Is Global Citizenship?: Society in an Era of Rapid Change, Atlanta, Ga. (Apr. 5, 2001)

Robert Repetto & Duncan Austin, *Market Failure*, Envtl. F., July/Aug., 2001, at 30

Robert Repetto & Duncan Austin, Coming Clean: Corporate Disclosure of Financially Significant Environmental Risks (World Resources Institute 2000)

Robert Repetto & Duncan Austin, Pure Profit: The Financial Implications of Environmental Performance (World Resources Institute 2000)

Rio + 10 and the Corporate Greenwash of Globalisation, Eur. Corp. Observer Newsl. (Corp. Eur. Observatory), June 2001, *available* at http://www.xs4all.nl/~ceo/observer9/greenwash.html

United Nations Development Programme et al., 2002 – 2004: Decisions for the Earth – Balance, Voice, and Power (World Resources Institute, 2003), *available* at http://pubs.wri.org/pubs_pdf.cfm?PubID=3764

W.D. Walden & B.N. Schwartz, *Environmental Disclosures and Public Policy Pressure*, 16 J. Acct. & Pub. Pol'y 125 (1997)

Claire Windsor, *Analysis: Communicating Corporate Social and Environmental Reporting*, Ethical Corp., June 20, 2003, *available* at http://www.ethicalcorp.com/content.asp?ContentID=755

Mainstreaming Responsible Investment, World Economic Forum (January 2005),

VOLUNTARY CORPORATE DISCLOSURE

Mark D. Abkowitz et al., *Environmental Information Disclosure and Stakeholder Involvement: Searching for Common Ground*, 6 Corp. Envtl. Strategy 415 (1999)

Owen Andrews, *Getting Started on Sustainability Reporting*, Envtl. Quality Mgmt., Spring 2002, at 3

Robert A. Axelrod, *Ten Years Later: The State of Environmental Performance Reports Today*, Envtl. Quality Mgmt., Winter 1998, at 1

Amanda Ball et al., *External Transparency or Internal Capture?: The Role of Third-Party Statements in Adding Value to Corporate Environmental Reports*, 9 Bus. Strategy & the Env't 1 (2000)

S.D. Beets & C.C. Souther, *Corporate Environmental Reports: The Need for Standards and an Environmental Assurance Service*, Acct. Horizons, June 1999, at 129

Martin Bennett & Peter James, "Key Themes in Environmental, Social and Sustainability Performance Evaluation and Reporting," in Sustainable Measures: Evaluation and Reporting of Environmental and Social Performance 29 (Martin Bennett et al. eds., Greenleaf 1999)

Bill Birchard, *Making Environmental Reports Relevant*, CFO, June 1996, at 79

David W. Case, *Legal Considerations in Voluntary Corporate Environmental Reporting*, 30 ELR 10375 (May 2000), *available* at http://www.vanderbilt.edu/VCEMS/CERartic.pdf

Paige Davis-Walling & Stuart A. Batterman, *Environmental Reporting by the Fortune 50 Firms*, 21 Envtl. Mgmt. 865 (1997)

John Elkington, *Triple Bottom-Line Reporting: Looking for Balance*, Australian CPA, Mar. 1999, at 18

EU Accounting Guidelines—A Damp Squib?, Envtl. Fin., July-Aug. 2001, at 12

European Federation of Accountants, Towards a Generally Accepted Framework for Environmental Reporting (2000)

European Federation of Accountants, Review of International Accounting Standards for Environmental Issues (1999)

European Federation of Accountants, Analysis of Responses to FEE Discussion Paper Providing Assurance on Environmental Reports (Oct. 1999)

C. Fayers, *Environmental Reporting and Changing Corporate Environmental Performance*, Acct. F., June 1998, at 74

Carol J. Forrest & Robert A. Axelrod, *Business Finds Value in Environmental Report Cards*, Envtl. Solutions, Jan. 1, 1995, at 34

Rob Gray, *Forbidden Fruit*, Tomorrow Mag., June 2001, at 50

Global Environmental Management Initiative, Environment: Value to Business 46-7 (1999)

Adam B. Greene, Director, Environmental Affairs and Corporate Responsibility, U.S. Council for International Business, Transparency in Reporting: The International Context, Presentation at GEMI 2001: An Odyssey to Environmental Excellence, Baltimore, Md. (Mar. 19-20, 2001), *available* at http://www.steeleweb.com/graphics/gemi_files/workshop_07/transparency%20_greene.ppt

Timothy Herbst, *Environmental Disclosure: Corporate Use of the World Wide Web*, Corp. Envtl. Strategy, Winter 1998, at 81

Ralf Isenmann & Christian Lenz, *Internet Use for Corporate Environmental Reporting: Current Challenges—Technical Benefits—Practical Guidance*, 11 Bus. Strategy & the Env't 181 (2002)

Marcel Jeucken, Sustainable Finance & Banking: The Financial Sector and the Future of the Planet 45-48 (Greenleaf 2001)

M. Jones, *Going Green in the USA*, Certified Acct., Nov. 1993, at 33

Ans Kolk et al., *Environmental Reporting by the "Fortune" Global 500: Exploring the Influence of Nationality and Sector*, 10 Bus. Strategy & the Env't 15 (2001)

Ans Kolk, The Internet as a Green Management Tool, 6 Corp. Envtl. Strategy 307 (1999)

Erin Kreis, Reporting on the Internet, Presentation at Corporate Environmental and Sustainability Reporting: A New Look for the Information Age, Vanderbilt Center for Environmental Management Studies (May 2001), *available* at http://www.vanderbilt.edu/vcems/cesr2/erinkreispresentation.pdf

J.G. Kreuze et al., *Environmental Disclosures: What Companies Are Reporting*, Mgmt. Acct., July 1996, at 37

Riva Krut, *Verification of Environmental Reports: Balancing Innovation and Standardization*, Bus. Strategy & the Env't (Cutter), Jan. 2000, at 4

Riva Krut & Ashley Moretz, *Environmental Reporting: The State of Global Reporting: Lessons from the Global 100*, 7 Corp. Envtl. Strategy 85 (2000)

Riva Krut & Ken Munis, *Sustainable Industrial Development: Benchmarking Environmental Policies and Reports*, Greener Mgmt. Int'l, Spring 1998, at 87

Level of Environmental Reporting Slips Due to Corporate Refocus, Int'l Envtl. Sys. Update (CEEM), Feb. 2003, at 6

Mark Line et al., *The Development of Global Environmental and Social Reporting*, 9 Corp. Envtl. Strategy 69 (2002)

Mark Line, Benchmarking Performance Measures, Presentation at Corporate Environmental and Sustainability Reporting: A New Look for the Information Age, Vanderbilt Center for Environmental Management Studies (May 2001), *available* at http://www.vanderbilt.edu/vcems/cesr2/marklinepresentation.pdf

Douglas J. Lober, *What Makes Environmental Reports Effective?: Current Trends in Corporate Reporting*, Corp. Envtl. Strategy, Winter 1997, at 15

Richard MacLean et al., Organizations in Transition: Preliminary Report of Existing Literature and Model Development 25-31 (2002)

Dick MacLean, *Making the Move From Spin to Strategy*, Corp. Strategy Today, Oct. 2001, at 14

A. Mastrandonas & P.T. Strife, *Corporate Environmental Communications*, 27 Colum. J. World Bus. 234 (1992)

J. Emil Morehardt, *Scoring Corporate Environmental Reports for Comprehensiveness: A Comparison of Three Systems*, 27 Envtl. Mgmt. 881 (2001)

Janet Ranganathan & Heidi Sundin, *The GHG Protocol Initiative: A New Breed of Standard Evolves*, Int'l Envtl. Sys. Update (CEEM), June 2002, at 8

David F. Sand & Ariane van Buren, *Environmental Disclosure and Performance: The Benefits of Standardization*, 12 Cardozo L. Rev. 1347 (1991)

Andrew Savitz, *Sustainability Reporting: Daring to Hold Yourself Accountable*, Compliance Wk. (Apr. 17, 2003)

Bernd Schanzenbaecher, Credit Suisse Group, Sustainability—A Growing Challenge for Corporate Communication, Symposium on Sustainability, Fairleigh Dickinson University Corporate Communications Institute (Apr. 2001)

C. Russell H. Shearer, *Costs and Benefits of Audit Disclosure*, 11 Nat. Resources & Env't 48 (1996)

Kristen Shepherd et al., *On-line Corporate Environmental Reporting: Improvements and Innovation to Enhance Stakeholder Value*, 8 Corp. Envtl. Strategy 307 (2001)

Social and Environmental Disclosure by Giant Corporations Is Deepening, Int'l Envtl. Sys. Update (CEEM), June 2003, at 4

Andrea Spencer-Cooke, "A Dinosaur's Survival Kit—Tools and Strategies for Sustainability," in Sustainability Strategies for Industry: The Future of Corporate Practice 99, 105 (Nigel J. Roome ed., Greenleaf 1998)

Sustainable Enterprise Academy, Report on the Summit on Corporate Environmental and Sustainability Reporting (2001)

William L. Thomas, "Rio's Unfinished Business: American Enterprise and the Journey toward Environmentally Sustainable Globalization," in Stumbling Toward Sustainability (John Dernbach ed., Environmental Law Institute 2002), and 32 ELR 10873 (August 2002)

Hendrik A. Verfaillie & Robin Bidwell, Measuring Eco-Efficiency: A Guide to Reporting Company Performance (WBCSD 2000)

Mark Wade, Sustainable Development Reporting on the Internet: A Shell Perspective, Presentation at Corporate Environmental and Sustainability Reporting: A New Look for the Information Age, Vanderbilt Center for Environmental Management Studies (May 2001), *available* at http://www.vanderbilt.edu/vcems/cesr2/markwadepresentation.pdf

J.R. Wambsganss & Brent Sanford, *The Problem with Reporting Pollution Allowances*, 7 Critical Persp. on Acct. 643 (1996)

D. Wheeler & J. Elkington, *The End of the Corporate Environmental Report? Or the Advent of Cybernetic Sustainability Reporting and Communication*, 10 Bus. Strategy & the Env't 1 (2001)

Allen L. White & Diana M. Zinkl, *Raising Standardization*, Envtl. F., Jan./Feb. 1998, at 28

T.D. Wilmshurst & G.R. Frost, *Corporate Environmental Reporting: A Test of Legitimacy Theory*, 13 Acct., Auditing & Accountability J. 10 (2000)

Simon Zadek, Comment: The Business Case for Non-financial Reporting, Ethical Corp., Nov. 5, 2002, *available* at http://www.ethicalcorp.com/content_print.asp?ContentID=253

Glossary

Note: Italicized terms within a definition refer to other entries in this glossary.

AICPA. American Institute of Certified Public Accountants.

all appropriate inquiry. The level of preacquisition environmental due diligence on contaminated property required to qualify for various liability exemptions under CERCLA.

APB. Accounting Policy Board.

ARB. Accounting Research Bulletin.

ARO. *See* Asset retirement obligation.

asset. Probable future economic benefits obtained or controlled by a particular entity as a result of past transactions or events.

asset group. The lowest level for which identifiable cash flows are largely independent of the cash flows of other assets and liabilities.

asset impairment. The condition that exists when the carrying amount of a *long-lived asset* (or *asset group*) exceeds its fair value.

asset retirement obligations (AROs). *Legal obligations* associated with the retirement of a *tangible long-lived asset* that result from the acquisition, construction, development, or normal operation of a tangible long-lived asset.

bodily injury. Physical injury, including death, or sickness, disease, mental anguish or emotional distress, sustained by any person, arising from *pollution conditions.*

book value. The cost of a *long-lived asset* less the related accumulated depreciation or amortization to the date of measurement (also called *carrying value*).

brownfields. Abandoned, idled, or underused industrial and commercial sites where expansion or redevelopment is complicated by real or perceived *historical pollution conditions* that can add cost, time, or uncertainty to a redevelopment project. The U.S. Environmental Protection Agency estimates that there are more than 400,000 brownfields sites in the United States.

carrying value. The cost of a *long-lived asset* less the related accumulated depreciation or amortization to the date of measurement (also called *book value*).

certifying officers. A public company's principal executive officer or officers and the principal financial officer or officers, or persons performing similar functions.

claim. An oral or written demand received by the reporting entity seeking a remedy or alleging liability or responsibility for *environmental loss.*

cleanup costs. Expenses, including legal expenses, consulting expenses, and administrative oversight costs, incurred for the investigation, removal, remediation (including associated monitoring), or disposal of soil, surface water, groundwater, or other contamination as required by *environmental laws*, contract, or company policy, plus costs incurred to repair, replace, or restore real or personal property damaged in the course of such activities. Cleanup costs include emergency response costs and *environmental exit* *costs*. Specific elements of cleanup costs for Superfund and RCRA remediation efforts are described in § 20.3(a).

conditional asset retirement obligation. A legal obligation to perform an asset retirement activity in which the timing and/or method of settlement are conditional on a future event that may or may not be within the control of the entity.

contingency. An existing condition, situation, or set of circumstances involving uncertainty as to possible gain (gain contingency) or loss (loss contingency) to an enterprise that will ultimately be resolved when one or more future events occur or fail to occur.

contingent liability. A loss contingency giving rise to the *probable* incurrence of a liability.

control deficiency. A deficiency in the design or operation of a control that results in the inability of management or employees, in the normal course of performing their assigned functions, to prevent or detect misstatements on a timely basis.

disclosure controls and procedures. Controls and other procedures of an *issuer* that are designed to ensure that information required to be disclosed by the issuer in the reports it files or submits under the Exchange Act is recorded, processed, summarized, and reported within the time periods specified in the SEC's rules and forms. Disclosure controls and procedures include, without limitation, controls and procedures designed to ensure that information required to be disclosed by an issuer in the reports it files or submits under the Exchange Act is accumulated and communicated to the issuer's management, including its *certifying officers*, as appropriate, to allow timely decisions regarding required disclosure.

EITF. Emerging Issues Task Force (a division of the FASB).

environmental asset impairment. The condition that exists when the carrying amount of a *long-lived asset* (or *asset group*) exceeds its fair value due to the adverse impact of *pollution conditions*.

environmental assets. *Environmental costs* that are capitalized because they satisfy the criteria for recognition as an *asset*, environmental rights of recovery and credits emissions.

environmental costs. Expenditures for steps taken to manage an enterprise in an environmentally responsible manner, including compliance with *environmental laws*, as well as other costs driven by the environmental objectives and requirements of the enterprise. Environmental costs include *cleanup costs*, *pollution control costs*, and *environmental damages*.

environmental damages. Costs associated with noncompliance with *environmental laws* or breach of a duty owed to others under principles of common law, including: monetary awards or settlements of compensatory damages; punitive, exemplary, or multiple damages; civil fines, penalties, or assessments for *bodily injury* or *property damage*; and costs, charges, and expenses incurred in the defense, investigation, or adjustment of *claims*.

environmental exit costs. Site restoration costs, postclosure and monitoring costs, or other *environmental costs* incurred when a property or facility is sold, abandoned, or ceases operations. Environmental exit costs are an element of *cleanup costs* and are differentiated from other cleanup costs that are not incurred in connection with retirement of a *long-lived asset*.

environmental financial information. Information subject to environmental financial reporting requirements under GAAP or SEC regulations.

environmental financial reporting. Activities associated with the presentation of financial and nonfinancial environmental information in financial statements and SEC filings.

environmental guarantees. Contracts, including indemnification agreements, that contingently require the guarantor to make payments (either in cash, financial instruments, other assets, shares of its stock, or provision of services) to the guaranteed party upon the future occurrence of specified events or conditions giving rise to *environmental losses* on the part of the guaranteed party.

environmental laws. Broadly defined, any federal, state, provincial, or local laws (including, but not limited to, statutes, rules, regulations, ordinances, guidance documents, and governmental, judicial, or administrative orders and directives) of the United States or a foreign country, the primary purpose of which is the protection of the environment, or the prevention of a danger to human life or health, through: (1) the prevention, abatement, or control of the release, discharge, or emission of pollutants or environmental contaminants; (2) the control of environmentally hazardous or toxic chemicals, substances, materials, and wastes, and the dissemination of information related thereto; (3) the protection of wild flora or fauna, including endangered species, their habitat, and specially protected natural areas; or (4) the protection, conservation, or management of natural resources.

environmental liabilities. Obligations to pay *environmental costs* at some point in the future. Environmental liabilities may be recognized in connection with *environmental loss contingencies, environmental remediation liabilities, environmental guarantees,* or environmental *asset retirement obligations.*

environmental loss. *Losses* associated with actual, threatened, or suspected *pollution conditions.* Such losses include, but are not limited to, first-party losses for *cleanup costs, property damages,* and *bodily injury,* and liability for third-party *claims.*

environmental loss contingency. An existing condition, situation, or set of circumstances involving uncertainty as to possible *environmental loss* to an enterprise that will ultimately be resolved when one or more future events occur or fail to occur. Resolution of the uncertainty may confirm the loss or impairment of an asset (an *environmental asset impairment*) or the incurrence of a liability (an *environmental liability*). Environmental loss contingencies include *environmental remediation liabilities.*

environmental loss exposure. *See* environmental risks.

environmental media. Air, soil, groundwater, surface water, sediment, and biota (plants and animals).

environmental remediation liabilities. A subset of *environmental loss contingencies* that relates to asserted or probable legal claims, generally arising under the provisions of the Comprehensive Environmental Response, Compensation, and Liability Act of 1980 (CERCLA or Superfund); the corrective action provisions of the Resource Conservation and Recovery Act (RCRA); or analogous state and foreign laws and regulations, for *cleanup costs* associated with *historical pollution conditions.*

environmental risks. Exposures to potential *environmental losses* (environmental loss exposures). Environmental risks can be subdivided into two primary categories: (1) exposures related to *historical pollution conditions,* and (2) exposures related to *future pollution conditions.* Environmental loss exposures related to historical pollution conditions can be subclassified into two categories: (1) *contingent liabilities,* and (2) exposures to losses other than liabilities (e.g., losses to property, personnel, or profitability).

Similarly, environmental loss exposures related to future pollution conditions can be subclassified into two categories: (1) exposures to future liabilities, and (2) exposures to losses other than liabilities. As used in this book, *environmental risk* concerns the potential for adverse financial impacts to the organization arising from environmental losses, as opposed to the degree of actual or potential risk to human health and the environment (although the latter may have an influence on the former).

EPA. U.S. Environmental Protection Agency.

fair value. The amount at which a liability could be settled in a current transaction between willing parties; that is, other than in a forced or liquidation transaction. Quoted market prices in active markets are the best evidence of fair value and must be used as the basis for the measurement if available. If quoted market prices are not available, the estimate of fair value must be based on the best information available in the circumstances, including prices for similar liabilities and the results of expected present value (or other valuation) techniques.

FAS. Financial Accounting Standard.

FASB. Financial Accounting Standards Board.

FIN. FASB Interpretation Number.

fixed assets. Those assets that are used in a productive capacity, have physical substance, are relatively long-lived, and provide future benefit that is readily measurable. Fixed assets typically are classified as property, plant, or equipment.

future pollution conditions. *Pollution conditions* that have not yet occurred, but may possibly occur in the future.

GAAP. *See* generally accepted accounting principles.

GAO. U.S. Government Accountability Office.

generally accepted accounting principles (GAAP). A set of rules and practices that are recognized as authoritative guidance for financial reporting purposes. In the United States, GAAP is developed by the Financial Accounting Standards Board (*FASB*), the American Institute of Certified Public Accountants (*AICPA*), and the Securities and Exchange Commission (*SEC*).

GHG. Greenhouse gases.

gradual pollution conditions. *Pollution conditions* that do not take place at a clearly identifiable point in time (e.g., the occasional spillage inherent in the normal operations of a fuel storage facility and the migration of contamination in groundwater over long periods of time).

guarantees. Contracts that contingently require the guarantor to make payments (either in cash, financial instruments, other assets, shares of its stock, or provision of services) to the guaranteed party upon the future occurrence of specified events or conditions.

historical pollution conditions. *Pollution conditions* that occurred at one or more specified or unspecified points in the past. Historical pollution conditions often are associated with *environmental remediation liabilities*, but can also give rise to "toxic tort" claims for *property damages* and *bodily injury*.

impairment. The condition that exists when the carrying amount (*book value*) of a *long-lived asset* is not expected to be recoverable over the remainder of the expected life of the asset.

Fixed assets and intangibles with a finite useful life are evaluated for impairment under FAS 144 (see Chapter 23).

intangible assets. Assets that provide future economic benefit but have no physical substance. Examples include goodwill, patents, and copyrights.

internal control over financial reporting. A process designed by, or under the supervision of, the entity's certifying officers, or persons performing similar functions, and effected by the entity's board of directors, management, and other personnel, to provide reasonable assurance regarding the reliability of financial reporting and the preparation of financial statements for external purposes in accordance with *GAAP*; includes those policies and procedures that pertain to the maintenance of records that in reasonable detail accurately and fairly reflect the transactions and dispositions of the assets of the entity; provide reasonable assurance that transactions are recorded as necessary to permit preparation of financial statements in accordance with *GAAP*, prove that receipts and expenditures of the entity are being made only in accordance with authorizations of management and directors of the entity; and provide reasonable assurance regarding prevention or timely detection of unauthorized acquisition, use, or disposition of the entity's assets that could have a material effect on the financial statements.

issuer. An entity that has a class of securities registered under section 12 of the Exchange Act of 1934, or that is required to file reports under section 15(d) of the Exchange Act, or that files or has filed a registration statement that has not yet become effective under the Securities Act of 1933. Generally, issuers are public companies under the oversight of the Securities and Exchange Commission.

legal obligation. An obligation that a party is required to settle as a result of an existing or enacted law, statute, ordinance, or written or oral contract, or by legal construction of a contract under the doctrine of promissory estoppel.

liabilities. Probable future sacrifices of economic benefits arising from present obligations of a particular entity to transfer assets or provide services to other entities in the future as a result of past transactions or events. In this definition, *probable* is used with its usual general meaning, rather than in a specific accounting or technical sense (such as that in FAS 5), and refers to that which can reasonably be expected or believed on the basis of available evidence or logic but is neither certain nor proved. Its inclusion in this definition is intended to acknowledge that business and other economic activities occur in an environment characterized by uncertainty in which few outcomes are certain. The term "obligations" is used with its usual general meaning to refer to duties imposed legally or socially; to that which one is bound to do by contract, promise, moral responsibility, and so on. It includes equitable and constructive obligations as well as *legal obligations.*

long-lived assets. Assets that provide an economic benefit to the enterprise for a number of future accounting periods. Long-lived assets are divided into two categories, tangible and intangible. Tangible assets have physical substance and are categorized as depreciable, depletable, and other tangible assets.

loss contingency. An existing condition, situation, or set of circumstances involving uncertainty as to possible loss to an enterprise that will ultimately be resolved when one or more future events occur or fail to occur.

loss. The direct or indirect financial consequences to an organization resulting from natural, human, or economic perils. Losses can be subdivided into four categories: (1) destruction or damage to the entity's property; (2) loss or impairment of entity personnel;

(3) liability for obligations to third parties (e.g., claims for *property damage, bodily injury, cleanup costs,* and so forth); and (4) conditions that negatively affect profitability by increasing expenses or reducing revenues (e.g., increased operating and maintenance expenses, damage of reputation with consumers resulting in lost revenues, and so forth).

material weakness. A *significant deficiency*, or combination of significant deficiencies, that results in more than a remote likelihood that a material misstatement of the annual or interim financial statements will not be prevented or detected.

materiality. Generally, the degree to which *environmental financial information* is relevant for purposes of financial reporting. The concept of materiality is a primary consideration in every aspect of financial reporting. The specific application of the concept varies slightly depending on the circumstances and the particular application. Materiality is examined in § 12.2.

natural resource damage. Physical injury to land, fish, wildlife, biota, air, water, groundwater, drinking water supplies, and other public resources.

PCAOB. *See* Public Company Accounting Oversight Board.

pollution condition. The discharge, dispersal, release, or escape of any solid, liquid, gaseous, or thermal irritant or contaminant, including, but not limited to, smoke, vapors, soot, fumes, acids, alkalis, toxic chemicals, medical waste, and waste materials into or upon land, or any structure on land, the atmosphere, or any watercourse or body of water, including groundwater, provided such conditions are not naturally present in the environment in the amounts or concentrations discovered. Pollution conditions can be classified as either *historical pollution conditions* or *future pollution conditions.* Preexisting pollution conditions may be known or unknown. Pollution conditions may also be classified as *sudden and accidental* or *gradual.*

pollution control costs. Expenditures other than *cleanup costs* incurred to achieve or maintain compliance with *environmental laws.*

pollution risk oversight. The process by which the entity's directors and officers attain reasonable assurance that the entity's environmental-related objectives will be met. It comprises oversight of the corporation's compliance with environmental laws, financial reporting of environmental liabilities, and management of environmental risk.

probability. Generally, the likelihood that a given future event or events will occur. Probability is examined in § 12.3.

probable. (1) Generally, that which can reasonably be expected or believed on the basis of available evidence or logic but is neither certain nor proven; (2) For purposes of *environmental financial reporting, probable* means that one or more specified future events are likely to occur.

property damage. Physical injury to or destruction of tangible property arising from *pollution conditions,* including the resulting loss of use and diminution in value thereof, and *natural resource damage.*

Public Company Accounting Oversight Board (PCAOB). A federal board established by Sarbanes-Oxley with responsibility for registering, monitoring, investigating, and disciplining the activities of public accounting firms, including establishing the guidelines for the conduct of certain auditing procedures.

reasonably likely. The probability threshold for mandatory disclosure of specified forward-looking information under Item 303 of Regulation S-K ("Management

Discussion and Analysis"). *Reasonably likely* is a lower disclosure threshold than "more likely than not."

reasonably possible. The *probability* of one or more specified future events occurring is more than *remote* but less than likely.

registrant. An *issuer* for whom a registration statement is filed under the Securities Act of 1933.

remote. The *probability* of one or more specified future events occurring is slight.

retirement. The other-than-temporary removal of a *long-lived asset* from service by sale, abandonment, recycling, or disposal in some other manner. Retirement does not encompass the temporary idling of a long-lived asset.

SAB. SEC Staff Accounting Bulletin.

SEC. U.S. Securities and Exchange Commission.

SFAC. Statement of Financial Accounting Concept.

significant deficiency. A *control deficiency*, or combination of control deficiencies, that adversely affects the entity's ability to initiate, authorize, record, process, or report external financial data reliably in accordance with GAAP such that there is more than a *remote* likelihood that a misstatement of the company's annual or interim financial statements that is more than inconsequential will not be prevented or detected.

sudden and accidental pollution conditions. *Pollution conditions* that take place at a clearly identifiable point in time (e.g., a spill caused by sudden rupture or explosion of a storage vessel).

Superfund. The Comprehensive Environmental Response, Compensation, and Liability Act of 1980.

Superfund sites. Sites listed on the National Priorities List (NPL) under CERCLA. Superfund sites are generally former hazardous waste treatment and disposal sites. Of the hundreds of thousands of sites in the United States affected by *historical pollution conditions*, these sites represent the greatest threat to human health and the environment.

tangible long-lived assets. *Long-lived assets* having physical substance. *Fixed assets*, such as property, plant, and equipment, are examples of tangible long-lived assets.

Index

D

E

F

T

U

V

W

Z